5

DATE DUE

DEC 16 2005			
GAYLORD			PRINTED IN U.S.A.

The Arms of the Family

The Arms
OF THE
Family

THE SIGNIFICANCE OF JOHN MILTON'S
RELATIVES AND ASSOCIATES

JOHN T. SHAWCROSS

THE UNIVERSITY PRESS OF KENTUCKY

Publication of this volume was made possible in part
by a grant from the National Endowment for the Humanities.

Scholarly publisher for the Commonwealth,
serving Bellarmine University, Berea College, Centre
College of Kentucky, Eastern Kentucky University,
The Filson Historical Society, Georgetown College,
Kentucky Historical Society, Kentucky State University,
Morehead State University, Murray State University,
Northern Kentucky University, Transylvania University,
University of Kentucky, University of Louisville,
and Western Kentucky University.

Editorial and Sales Offices: The University Press of Kentucky
663 South Limestone Street, Lexington, Kentucky 40508-4008
http://www.kentuckypress.com

08 07 06 05 04   5 4 3 2 1

Genogram by Dick Gilbreath.

Library of Congress Cataloging-in-Publication Data
Shawcross, John T.
    The arms of the family : the significance of John Milton's relatives
and associates / John T. Shawcross.
        p.   cm.
    Includes bibliographical references and index.
    ISBN 0-8131-2291-0 (hardcover : alk. paper)
    1. Milton, John, 1608–1674—Family. 2. Milton, John, 1608–1674—
Friends and associates. 3. Poets, English—Early modern, 1500–1700—Biography.
4. Poets, English—Early modern, 1500–1700—Family relationships.
5. Great Britain—History—Stuarts, 1603–1714—Biography. 6. Royalists—
Great Britain—History—17th century. 7. Milton, Christopher, Sir, 1615–1693.
8. Phillips, Edward, 1630–1696? 9. Phillips, John, 1631–1706. I. Title.
PR3583.S53   2003
821'.4—dc21   2003011387

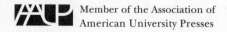

Member of the Association of
American University Presses

Contents

Preface

I thank most sincerely Edward Jones, who has shared his very important archival investigations with me, as noted in different chapters of this study. He has also offered significant suggestions that I have followed, and assistance by way of information has also been given by Carol Barton, Philip Birger, Ilana Flinker, Anne Barbeau Gardiner, and Michael Lieb. All have been so very gracious in sharing their knowledge and own studies. I owe special thanks to Mary Fenton, Blair Hoxby, Edward Jones, Kristin Pruitt, John Rumrich, Elizabeth Sauer, and Hugh Wilson for allowing me to cite their respective important forthcoming essays and books.

A difficult problem for me in pursuing this book has been the disagreement so very often with William Riley Parker in his indispensable *Milton: A Biography*. He was my mentor and a good friend. But aside from my discovering certain pieces of information in investigating sources that I would have thought he and so many before him would have uncovered, I frequently find a narrowness of traditional reading and interpretation (despite Professor Parker's even more frequent cogent dispelling of traditional readings and interpretations), which led him to reassert attitudes—for example, about Christopher Milton or about John Milton's relationship with his nephew John Phillips, and indeed about Phillips himself—that have no or little basis in actuality. My hope is that the current study will alter the way in which scholars view Milton and his family and relationships with some of his associates, while encouraging further archival study and its rewarding results. For family matters do matter in how we understand John Milton and read his works and place him within the milieus in which he moved.

My title comes from Milton's last lifetime published work *A Declaration, or Letters Patents of the Election of this present King of Poland John the Third* (1674). This translation of *Diploma Electionis S.R.M. Poloniæ* records that the "Commonwealth" of Poland "recalled the grateful, and never to be forgotten memory of [the late King Michael's] Renowned Father, . . . who by his Golden

Eloquence in the publick Counsels, and by his Hand in the Scene of War, had so often amplified the State of the Commonwealth, and defended it with the Arms of his Family" (9). Milton's "arms" were his golden eloquence and his own public wars, forged from many and sometimes opposed familial relationships. Their amplification and defense of the English Commonwealth arise from varied familial sources, but especially from "his Renowned Father," and not "without Divine Providence." It is perhaps significant, in view of chapter 4 here, that the copy of *Declaration* in the Houghton Library, Harvard University, has an anonymous title page inscription, "John Phillips J.M. 1674."

Introduction

Biography can be a detailed and fact-filled account of a person's life that does not engage a world outside the person's immediate activities and family. It can also be an expansive account placing that person in social, political, religious, and cultural worlds that may encounter fewer immediate family and associates, even those not directly involved in the subject's life though important to it, depending upon that person's significance in such worlds. When that person has produced creative work and nonfictional tracts as John Milton did, a "literary" biography is in order, stressing readings of that creative work and nonfictional expositions. The subject of this book, Milton, has been honored with numerous "lives" and biographies from the seventeenth century onward, notably the six-volume "Life" by David Masson that takes the reader through the various worlds of contemporary politics, religion, and culture in addition to presenting the facts of his life and synopses of the written work; the two-volume biography by William Riley Parker (updated by Gordon Campbell) that builds upon and informatively extends Masson, including synopses of both poetry and prose, while eschewing the expansive account of Milton's worlds; and Barbara K. Lewalski's "literary life" that offers interpretations of the work, particularly in terms of recent developments in the areas of criticism that have exploded in recent years and have led us to revised understanding of those works and of their author.[1]

Since Masson's still major and most useful biography, much has been discovered about Milton and his family, associates, and worlds, and much has been speculated. Parker (and Campbell's added notes) supplies many additional facts and some speculations derived therefrom; and Lewalski offers interpretations of the works that often bypass the author as a person as well as his specific worlds. Our reinterpretations of Milton's personal and political worlds arising from more contemporary interests and methodologies—such as psychological study, political and "new historical" investigations, along with gender considerations—have been the foci of various studies and some "biographical" accounts, like William Kerrigan's *The Sacred Com-*

plex and my own *The Self and the World*.[2] The many articles and books touching Milton have corrected or revised errors and suppositions, prejudiced and short-sighted readings, superficial meaning or perhaps unrecognized substance, evolving a different Milton and different creative worlds. A notable example is certainly the political Milton of *Paradise Lost* or *Samson Agonistes* that is far from congruent with Samuel Johnson's or William Blake's or Mark Pattison's icon. The revisionism of seventeenth-century British history that has been rampant in the last quarter of a century has brought forth a very different political animal from the simplistic "Parliamentarian" that criticism used to be satisfied with. Yet one wonders just what is the nature of Milton's republicanism that has been urged upon us in recent years. Similar questions arise about his theology and its expression in his works, particularly in the two epics and the treatise *De doctrina christiana*. Unfortunately, there has been a persistence of past readings and supposed "facts" in many of these studies and in both Parker's and Lewalski's work, even though Milton's critical past, like others', has been rewritten often.

His life has been told many times, yet how much have those accounts depended upon received notions passed down from one commentator to another without adequate reexamination of his activities and his personal attitudes about himself and his relationships with others? Perhaps no Miltonist today gives any credence to the idea that his daughters acted as amanuenses for *Paradise Lost*, but many other people seem to—not knowing or else forgetting the mental and physical condition of the eldest, Anne, not realizing that the youngest, Deborah, was only nine when, around 1661, he moved most steadily forward to complete his epic by 1665, when she was but thirteen. How many Miltonists and non-Miltonists continue to believe that he was mean to those daughters, forgetting psychology at least of a middle child, in this case Mary who was apparently the only "accuser" of his tyranny. People also forget antagonisms toward stepparents—in this case his third wife Elizabeth Minshull Milton—regardless of truth, and ignorant of what little evidence—primarily attestations concerned with adjudication of the nuncupative will in 1674—there is. Christopher in his deposition concerning Milton's nuncupative will did, however, attest that John referred to his "unkind children." Commentators very often ignore the person, ignore what life is and what life presents to anyone, ignore the logical conclusions that circumstance presents even though absolute "fact" has not been discovered. The "circumstance" of the will is an obvious case that a competent lawyer today would rip to pieces.

The subject of this book is the significance of Milton's family, his extended family. My paronomastic title is important: here are matters that involve Milton's family in his worlds and here is the argument that family makes a difference in one's life. Family *is* significant in one's life, but it also establishes "signifiers" that tell us about the person, that may lead us to awarenesses that we otherwise may miss (in Milton's case, *have* missed). And again, if we would only acknowledge that much that is familial today for most people has its parallel in the lives of those of the past, "family" would be looked at as not only the nuclear family of husband, wife, and children, but would extend well beyond, through siblings, through in-laws, through relatives even two- and three-times removed, through non-family close associates known to the child as "Aunt Ethel" or one's sister's friend "Bill." These all impinge on an individual and may be significant in creating who that person is. The arms of the family encompass and conjoin many relatives and friends within their reach; the arms of the family, as Milton has used the term, provide one with means to determine one's thoughtful being, whether in agreement or in disagreement with "family," and to employ whatever is necessary to express that being. There is not only significance, but also signification.

A preponderance of the material presented in this book is derived from archival reports that supply not only significant biographical information for our knowledge and understanding of Milton the person, but also a number of signifiers that lead to logical conclusions not previously admitted and to some speculations concerning Milton's political and religious attitudes that infiltrate the writings, not only the psychological person. The significance of archival work (and further archival work that should be undertaken) can be seen in two general matters that I here cite. First, the documents laying forth Milton's loan of £500 to Thomas Maundy, a goldsmith (his wife was Mary), and Milton's assumption of property in Kensington as collateral, dated 14 January 1657/8,[3] have pointed us in a direction to add knowledge of his financial condition, his financial dealings, and a network of acquaintances. That is and especially was a large sum. But heretofore Parker could say only "we know nothing about Thomas Maundy" (1063–64) although various potentially specious conclusions have been drawn about *De doctrina christiana* since the second part of that document was penned by Jeremy Picard, who was Milton's amanuensis in these negotiations and others from 1658 to 1660. The surname "Maundy," which appears several times in these documents, is not frequently found (but there are various people named "Maund" or "Maunder"). Thomas Maundy signed the second and third indentures "Maundye" but he signed Milton's receipt to him without the "e." Definite references, not previously noted, occur in the *Calendar of State Papers, Domestic* (hereafter, *CSPD*) and the Historical Manuscripts Commission reports (hereafter, HMC). HMC, Eighth Report, Part I (1881), 437, records in the Hall Papers, Vol. 12, owned by the Corporation of the Borough of Leicester, dated 6 June 1649: "Copy of order of the parliament respecting

Maces. Ordered by the Commons assembled in Parliament that the Mace made by Thomas Maundey of London, goldsmith, bee deliuered into the charge of the Sergeant at Armes, attending the Parliament, and that the said Mace be carried before the speaker, and that all other great Maces to bee vsed in this Common Wealth bee made according to the same forme and patterne, and that the said Thomas Maundy haue the making thereof and none other.—Henry Scobell, Clerc. Parl." This is followed up on 29 July 1650 with a "Letter from the above mentioned Thomas Maundy to John Turvil. Announcing that the writer has made a good mace for the borough of Leicester; and giving particulars as to its weight, price, &c. &c." Under Warrants by the Council of State for Payment of Money, dated 12 March 1651, is the entry, "From John Jackson to Thos. Maundy, goldsmith. Making a mace and altering a sword and scabbard for the Lord Deputy of Ireland. £133/8/9" (*CSPD,* 1649–50, I, 551). Jackson was Cromwell's Treasurer of Excise. Such work for the government may easily have brought Maundy into contact with Milton, and so we have the probable connection for the indentures. On 1 March 1654/5, *CSPD,* VIII, 61 records "A mace provided by Thos. Maundy for the serjeant-at-arms attending the Treasury Commissioners being presented to Council, with a bill for 161/3/4 for it;—Clerks of Council are to see what weight of silver there is in it, and how much it is worth an ounce, and to report."

This is followed (VIII, 122) on 12 April 1655: "Order on Scobell and Jessop's report that the value of the mace provided for the Treasury Commissioners, with a case to put it in, is 145/17/6, to advise a warrant to the Treasury Commissioners to pay Thos. Maundy the same." Again (VIII, 400), "Mr. Maundy having prepared a mace for Scotland, now presented;—that Mr. Secretary take order for sending it and the Seal to Scotland" on 26 October 1655. A warrant of £119/8/0 from Gualter Frost to Thomas Maundy "For a mare [mace] provided by him for Scotland" is accordingly recorded on 26 October 1655 (VIII, 608). This mace for Scotland was ordered on 29 August 1655 (VIII, 303) but in error to "Hen. Maundy to make a mace for the Scotch Council of £100 value." It is thus clear how Maundy and Milton would have known each other, leading to the loan, rather than the previous total unawareness and the questioning of commentators on Milton about their connection.

These archival reports take us through 1655, a significant date in the political world because of Cromwell's creation of a provincial rule by ten (later eleven) Major-Generals in August, put into operation in October. We will revisit this important—and strongly denounced— "hierarchy" and establishment of "blue laws" in chapters 4 and 5. Whatever Maundy's further connections with the government may have been, his need for a loan, in spite of his landownership of property in Kensington and what that implies about his former financial state, suggests the financial problems that Cromwell's oppressive and unpopular action caused. We cannot be certain of Milton's fortunes during these difficult years, but Edward Phillips tells us of his loss of money from the failure of the Excise (and through his trust in officials involved) as well as some bad financial advice. (See chapter 1.) This loan strongly suggests that Milton's financial difficulties reared up after the Restoration, as has been assumed. John Jackson is cited by Masson (II, 519, and index) as a preacher at Gray's Inn and as a member of the Westminster Assembly, but Parker ignores him entirely, even though his position in the Cromwellian government and Phillips's report concerning the Excise might prove meaningful. *A Catalogue of the Names of the Dukes, Marquesses, Earles and Lords* [etc.] published in 1642 lists him as one of the "Orthodox Divines" who is a fit person "to be consulted with by the parliament, touching the Reformation of Church-government and Liturgie, Aprill, 25, 1642," called "Master John Jackson of Grayes Inne" (see Peacock, 62). He was Milton's neighbor in Petty France, where he is listed in the St. Margaret's Overseer Rate Book, E166 (1652) through E170 (1656). Maundy's Kensington property, "conteining by estimacin three Acres," was "on the South East side," a location not very far from Milton's residence in Petty France, Westminster, at that time. It abutted property owned by William Hobson, who had bought the Ludgate property owned by Christopher Milton in February 1654. (See also chapter 1.) These facts set up suspicions of a closed interconnected world of finance that transcends "political" allegiances. In all of the financial dealings of Milton, commentators generally seem to forget that the only "earned remuneration" he received was payment for tutoring and for secretarial duties. Monies, starting early on, came from properties and rents, loans and bonds, investments—the primary source as well by all accounts for his father, his brother, and his brother-in-law Edward Phillips's family and thus from the 1650s onward probably for his nephews Edward and John.

A William Maundy, apparently a provider of shipping services, received payment from Gualter Frost, secretary of the Council of State, for watermen's badges on 31 December 1649 (I, 461) and for wharfage and storehouse room of provisions for Ireland on 24 September 1649 (I, 589). Perhaps Thomas and William were relatives. A Thomas Mawndy from County Kent is listed in the Chancery Series II, Vol. 746, No. 111, "Inquisitions Post Mortem," in the PRO Lists and Indexes, No. XXXIII (Vol. IV, Charles I and Later), dated 2 Charles I, that is, 1626–27. In the PRO Lists and Indexes, Supplementary Series, No. IV, of the Proceedings in the Court of Requests of the Star Chamber under Elizabeth I, is listed Thomas Maunde (B.64/6). The following, however, have bearing upon the recipient of Milton's financial aid and probably upon the financial problems at the end of the Interregnum. In the *CSPD* (Charles II), II, 46 and 68, there are notices of a "Petition of Thomas Moore, Thos. Maundy, and others, to the King, for a patent for 31 years for the sole exercise of their inventions of improving ground for corn, and better making of salt-petre, salt, and pans, helping smoking chimneys, and draining lands, mines, and coal pits. With reference thereon to the Attorney General," dated 29 July 1661 from Whitehall, and again, "a patent for the sole exercise, for 31 years, of sundry inventions of their own with reference thereon to Solicitor General Finch, and his report, August 27, that the patent should be granted for 14 years only," dated 21 August 1661 from Whitehall. (For Finch and Milton's brother-in-law Thomas Agar's connection, see chapter 2 here.)

These latter items give us no direct information about Milton, but with the indentures noted before from 1658 they suggest Maundy as a person who became involved in various schemes and who needed money in the difficult years ending the Protectorate. The notices recorded for August and October 1655 are, as remarked above, noteworthy because of the institution of Cromwell's scheme for the oversight of the nation and its people by the Major-Generals, which had cultural, political, and financial effect (various taxes had also been imposed since the Protectorate of 1653). (Parker has only one passing reference to this momentous action by Cromwell on p. 503.) Between Maundy's work for the Council of State that extended through 1655 and the documents of 1661, not only had Oliver Cromwell died and his son Richard become Lord Protector, but a sallying back and forth of Parliament and its adherents set in motion repression, increased financial problems for the people, the Spanish War and a continuing Dutch menace, and led to the Restoration. At the Restoration, from statements in Cyriack Skinner's manuscript life of Milton and Phillips's "Life," Milton lost £2000 with the collapse of the Excise Office, not being fast enough to act and trusting of "the Great ones of those Times." Maundy's financial troubles began prior to the Restoration and one attempt to get back on his feet was apparently to get involved in various inventions. But he did not pay off the loan to Milton, and on 7 June 1665 Milton assigned Maundy's statute staple to Baldwin and Jeremy Hamey, receiving back his original investment of £500.[4] A possible speculation from the above is that Milton quite foolhardily loaned Maundy money at a time when he should have realized the impending collapse of the government and, with it, the Excise Office as it had been operating. But with some false allegiance to and hope in the governmental leaders, he did not rein in his financial dealings. Just how politically savvy was Milton?

A second example of the importance of archival work, musty and removed as it may be from the "literary" Milton: further documents that were, apparently, not known to French or Parker concerning the Powell family, Milton's in-laws, and their home in Forest Hill, Oxford, and the forests of Shotover (where, it will be remembered, Milton's grandfather had been a ranger, or keeper of the forest) proffer more interconnections. In November 1657 Sir Bulstrode Whitelocke was offered to buy Anne Powell's interest in Shotover Woods, "butt he held it not convenient"; this refers to a case in the Court of Exchequer concerning Anne as widow of Richard Powell, "and her interest in a lease of coppices on Shotover and in Stowood, granted by the late King, 30 March 1636 [1637]."[5] Later, British Library MS Stowe 498, p. 154, records from Treasurer Southampton's Crown Lease book for 1661 a warrant "to Sir Thomas Fanshaw, the King's Remembrancer [that is, collector of debts due to the Crown], and to John Osborne, esq., the Lord Treasurer's Remembrancer, to supersede, till further order, all process on the bond or debt of £1050 arrears of a rent of £100 per an. reserved to the Crown out of the forests of Shotover and Stowood, co. Oxford, upon a lease dated 1637, Mar. 30, thereof to Richard Powell, now deceased, proceed having lately issued out of the Treasurer's Remembrancer's Office. Thereon, whereby the manor of Forest Hill, co. Oxford, being the lands late of the said Powell, is seized upon; but it appearing upon the plea of Ann Powell, his relict, which is yet depending in the Exchequer Court [that] in discharge of the said debt and rent a bond has been given by Richard and John Powell, sons of the said Richard Powell, to stand to the judgment of the said Court upon the said Ann Powell's bill in equity and the said Ann having petitioned the King and obtained a reference thereon." Appended is a statement of opinion by the Surveyor General of Crown Lands that the abovesaid order is just, as Powell made no benefit of his lease since 1642, and but little before "and the said forest being now under an improvement and a new rent to be raised for his Majesty's service."[6] The son John Powell was still alive in 1661 but apparently dead before 1678, the date of his mother's will. We will look further at the son Richard in chapter 1.

Suggested by the documents are these points: Richard Powell continued in poor financial condition after 1637, Milton's father having lent him £300 on 11 June 1627 with a staple bond for £500 as security, made out to John, which caused much litigation between Milton and Ann Powell in succeeding years; the audit of Powell's debts to Sir Robert and Sir John Pye, on 4 July 1651, confirms his indebtedness despite some payments. Not previously noted, as far as I can find, these lands came by lease through Charles I a week before Milton's mother died in relatively nearby Horton. Powell's making "no benefit of his lease since 1642" is questionable in view of payment of £110 to Pye on 28 May 1642 and of interest to Milton from 12 December 1642 through June 1644. He certainly was able to acquire monies from some of his investments, confused as they are. (See Parker, 866–70.) To be remarked concerning the Wheatley property are the following items: (A) payments made after 11 June 1627 through 12 June 1644, (B) Milton's assumption of the Wheatley property on 20 November 1647 (paying Ann Powell a third of the income from it, as then required by law), (C) recorded payments of thirds on 19 April 1648,[7] 13 November 1648, 23 April 1649, 20 October 1649, 10 April 1650, and 12 October 1650, (D) the confirmation that Milton had received £180 in interest by 28 February 1651, (E) the governmental order of 24 March 1651 that Milton no longer had to pay Ann Powell thirds, (F) on the next day he received increased rents from Wheatley (£47/12/4) and two days later (27 March) he received clearance of the property by payment of a fine, (G) receipt of rents on 25 March 1652, 29 September 1652, 25 March 1653, 29 September 1653, (H) receipt of £65 from John Robinson on 25 March 1656, bringing the total paid to £345 (see Campbell, *Chronology*, 164, for four probable payments in 1655), (I) another payment of £4/17/4 on 29 September 1656, and (J) the 5 June 1657 record (PRO, C33/207, ff. 1250–51v) that (as French words it, V, 154) "he has by now received from the property at Wheatley the full amount of the Powell debt plus £4/17/04."

Significantly, to repeat, the Powells received the lease on the Shotover property from Charles I shortly before Milton's mother's death in 1637. The Powells lived in Forest Hill prior to that date, and the fathers Richard Powell and John Milton had known each other since at least 1627. The proximity to Horton, where the Miltons resided from around middle 1635, is particularly noteworthy since Milton's future wife Mary would have been ten when his parents moved to Horton. (She was baptized on 24 January 1625 at Forest Hill; French, I, 90.) Thus, during the period of 1632 through June 1644, payments to Milton by Powell and the acquisition of the lease on property in Shotover and Stowood in 1637 suggest that Powell was not particularly financially strapped, although his receiving "no benefit of his lease since 1642" raises a question and speculation. Was his ability to pay Pye £110 on 28 May 1642 and the lack of record of payment to Milton in June 1642 related to Milton's marriage around that time? Indeed, had some arrangement been made prior to that time? This will be taken up later. But when we jump to 1657 and Whitelocke's entry into Anne Powell's affairs, further speculations arise. As chapter 2 records, the Bulstrode family resided at the Manor House in Horton after 1595; Elizabeth, eldest daughter of Edward Bulstrode, married Sir James Whitelocke (a justice of King's Bench) in 1602, and their son was Sir Bulstrode Whitelocke who became President of the Council of State under Cromwell. Is Milton the link between Anne Powell and Whitelocke at this late date? Whitelocke's employment of *The Tenure of Kings and Magistrates* in his *Parliamenti Angliæ Declaratio* and the various references in his *Diary* and *Journal of the Swedish Embassy* suggest that the reference in *Memoirs of English Affairs* (1682), 633, to the Swedish treaty, reflect only the attitude of the Swedish ambassador in reporting that particular matter, not some slight by Whitelocke as some commentators have seemed to interpret it.[8]

The archival material reported in this book and the discussions of Milton's extended family and the various associates of that family lead to a number of sharp disagreements with what is presented in Parker's biography, particularly in reference to John Phillips and his relationship with his uncle, and to awareness of the limited biography of Milton presented by Lewalski, who, for one instance, only once references Thomas Agar, as the second husband of Milton's sister Anne, despite the significances revealed in chapter 2 here that Agar (and his family) played in Milton's life and the lives of those around him.[9]

This book attempts to correct the definitely wrong and the questionable statements about and evaluations of people around Milton and to lead us to a rethought description of Milton's political beliefs and political relationships. This is a kind of biography, a study with a thesis, one that points up much of a biographical nature but one that is not simply a repetition of a "Life." I find John Milton to be a different political being, a different republican with acknowledged "royal" relationships (and a "protestant" who has only sometimes been validly described), from what the past has offered and from what some in the present have only sometimes recognized. Reinterpretation of his works will emerge, and I hope there will be the removal of sentimental and unexamined "information" or readings from the past both for Milton himself and for those of his "family," who do "matter."

Part 1

Expanding the Biography

The need for further investigation into John Milton's biography is shown by the many hiatuses and puzzles that remain in his life despite the efforts of numerous scholars of the past to collect every fragment of information and restore it to its proper place in the full picture.[1] Some of these obscurities are minor, mere matters of fact; some bulk large. One is the explanation of the fascinating fact of Milton's immunity from Royalist reprisal during the tangled period of the civil conflict.[2] That these hiatuses and puzzles do remain is, in one sense, not surprising. Indeed, the reconstruction of the simplest life is no easy task, and a mere glance at the complexities of Milton's life and of the history of the seventeenth century is enough to give the most ambitious second thoughts. One of the complications of Milton biography is his being so eminent a "Puritan" and Parliamentarian. That he looms so large as a Puritan tends to obscure what is recognized as an obvious truth about men of lesser stature and commitment, that there was what might be called a Royalist side to his life. The cleavage between Puritan and Royalist was in actuality not so emphatic and wide as abstractions lead one to believe. Families, friends, and parties cut across the political and religious lines irregularly drawn. If one were to assume, therefore, that the Puritan side of Milton's life has been overstressed, despite his Parliamentarianism and what today has been particularly advanced as his republicanism, to the neglect of the Royalist, then one is led inevitably to examine the possibility that the Royalist side of his life may cast some light on the remaining hiatuses and puzzles.[3] Connections earlier in the 1630s with Henry Lawes, the Egertons, and Sir Henry Wotton are well known, and his meeting in Paris with John Scudamore, Viscount Sligo and Charles I's ambassador to France, who later was a neighbor when Milton moved to rather exclusive Petty France, is suggestive. Scudamore is said to have been a "zealous royalist" and "enthusiastically attached to the English church" of Archbishop Laud. (See the DNB entry.) Milton's residence in the Barbican from 1645 was next to the Ellesmere (Bridgewater) mansion and is thus even more suggestive. Just where does Milton fit in this Royalist/non-Royalist world? This aristocratic world?

In the following chapters, I look at aspects of Milton's extended family and family relationships to encounter his many Royalist connections, and one implication of such connections involves his Protestantism—a broad term that includes the prelatical contingent and the antiprelatical contingent (like SMECTYMNUUS), all of whom were calvinist, if not adherents of strict Calvinism. First, I draw together what we know of his brother Christopher and his family; second, what has been discoverable concerning his generally ignored brother-in-law Thomas Agar and his relatives; and then, in two chapters, what will present a more balanced and accurate picture of his nephews Edward Phillips, who has been integral in studies of Milton, and John Phillips, who has generally been cast as estranged from and in conflict with his uncle.[4] While much in these discussions will involve the dull dust of archival materials, little known and long ignored, it furnishes a different portrayal of Milton, whom too many (most?) people in the present see only as the past's skewed and prejudicially scarred king-killer. One's family in many broad and many subtle ways defines the individual: these chapters will add insight into the life and character of the subject of this book.

1

Christopher Milton
Royalist and Brother

1

Not a great deal has been added to our knowledge of Christopher Milton since Masson first published his *Life of Milton*,[5] most material relating to his legal activities. Yet besides the immediate familial importance of Christopher and his children to John Milton, there is the unresolved question of the bearing of Royalist relations and friends upon Milton to warrant research into the life of the younger brother. I here attempt to draw together all known information of significance concerning Christopher, and to examine such published source material as parish registers, governmental records, and so forth, in an effort to achieve a fuller understanding of the relationship between the Parliamentarian and "Puritan" and the Royalist and Roman Catholic.

We know that Christopher, baptized at All Hallows, Bread Street, 3 December 1615,[6] attended, as had his brother, St. Paul's public school under Alexander Gill and Christ's College, Cambridge, under Nathaniel Tovey (I, 29, 227). Admitted 15 February 1631, Christopher soon left Christ's to enter the Inner Temple on 22 September 1632, a mere boy of sixteen.[7] Of his life at Cambridge we can only infer routine activity, including attendance at a performance of the Latin comedy *Senile Odium* at Queen's.[8] Just before his mother's death in April 1637, Christopher filed an affidavit of his father's infirmity in answer to Thomas Cotton's bill (I, 320); this is the first example we have of his legalistic work. He seems to have left the Inner Temple around early 1638,[9] and apparently soon after married Thomasin Webber, daughter of John Webber, a tailor of St. Clement Danes,[10] perhaps just before Milton sailed for the continent in April or May. However, Parker suggests that they married early in 1637 and their son Christopher may have been born in London around October 1637 (before May 1638).[11] As an unnamed son was buried at Horton on 26 March 1639 (I, 409), Christopher and his bride clearly had settled at Horton with his widowed father. They were still there on 11 August 1640, for a baptismal of a daughter Sarah is recorded in the parish register under that date (II, 25).[12] In the meanwhile, Christopher had been called to the bar on 26 January 1640 (II, 12). Our only other scrap of information about Christopher up to 1641 is that he seems to have been attacked while on a trip to London on 14 April 1640 (II, 13).

In the past, the family group, including the father, had been recorded as residing in St. Laurence, Reading, a Royalist stronghold, by 27 August 1641, for his daughter Anne's baptismal occurred then (II, 43). We now know through the research of Edward Jones (personal communication) that Christopher lived in Reading in April 1641, for the 1641 subsidy roll values the goods of "Christopher Milton Esq" at £5 and assesses a tax of —/26/4 (PRO document E179/75/355). In 1642, father and son took the Protestation Oath of 1641/42 (Berkshire Records Office record, discovered by Jones); this oath was intended to indicate loyalty to the Parliament (or rather government, instead of rebellious belief against it), but it was also widely interpreted as an oath of allegiance to the King. Christopher was bound to furnish arms or supplies, but not personal services, to the royal army, according to a Muster Roll of 21 October 1642 (II, 81). The Reading Corporation manuscript XXXIX cites issuance in June 1642.[13] Probably before the siege of Reading and capitulation on 27 April 1643, John Milton, Sr., joined his elder son at Aldersgate Street. The political action may be the reason that Thomasin and her children moved back to her mother's in the parish of St. Clement Danes before 29 June 1643 when a son John was baptized. (See Parker, 234, 877 n28.) Before or after 22 November 1643, when goods of his were seized for delinquency in unstated claims in Reading (II, 92), and note Jones's recent discovery, Christopher was forced by the Parliamentarian army to move to Wells, where he was Royal Commissioner of Excise, and then to Exeter.[14] The evidence thus tells us that the household was altered in 1642 or early 1643 (before 27 April) with the father moving to London and the wife and children joining her family there, and Christopher going to Wells, with perhaps a stay in London.

Thus, Milton, Sr., was in Horton until after August 1640 and in Reading before April 1641, remaining there until 1642 to early 1643. Where did Milton, Jr., go immediately upon his return from the continent? It is possible that he returned to Horton—at least he did visit—or had there been some stay in London prior to his leaving for Italy, to which he returned for a few days at least before he found a place with Mr. Russell, though no evidence exists? He took lodgings in London apparently in 1639 and then proceeded to Aldersgate Street, according to Phillips's account. (See chapter 3.) But Jones, on the basis of records from Aldersgate Street (see later), suggests that that move may have been later in 1640; this implies, in turn, either a longer stay in St. Bride's than Phillips's statement records, or the existence of an unspecified period after his return from the continent before going to Mr. Russell's in St. Bride's. When the father joined John is uncertain, but perhaps it occurred because Milton married in mid-1642, and the father may have come to London then or just after Mary returned to her parents in Forest Hill.

The delinquency warrant suggests that Christopher was a Roman Catholic as well as a Royalist during this time, and one wonders thus what were the relationships with his father. Perhaps matters had reached the point that the father resolved to sever the domestic situation and to join his elder son even though, at this particular time (1642–43), John was either just married or then alone with his two nephews Edward and John Phillips, Mary Powell Milton having returned to Forest Hill, Oxford. Or had he, indeed, joined the household immediately after the marriage when Mary was still in London? A frequent reason offered for the father's moving in with his elder son has been the father's health and infirmity, and impending hostilities; however, that John, perhaps without wife and with his two nephews as charges, would have supplied better care seems questionable, although London offered a safer venue. A likely cause, it seems to me, may have been frequent wrangling over Christopher's adamant Roman Catholicism and Royalism. John Milton, Sr., after all, had permanently severed connections with his Catholic father over religion. We do not really know his political beliefs but his taking the Protestation Oath does imply a backing of Parliament. Remaining with Christopher, in any case, would have kept him in dangerous Royalist locations.

Christopher paid a fine of £10 on 28 March 1644 as a holder of Royalist property (II, 99), but exactly where he resided is unknown. He was soon taxed for a house in Ludgate Hill, London, 21 June 1644, and then fined as a delinquent 9 October 1644 (II, 108). This is the house in St. Martin's Parish, Ludgate, called "The Cross Keys," that he declared during compounding in 1646.[15] Apparently, it came into John Milton, Sr.'s possession, and thence into Christopher's (Parker suggests around 1636 when Christopher became 21), after its owner Sir John Suckling (father of the poet) died, 27 March 1627; the annual rent for the property was set at £40.[16] He may have been further fined as a delinquent in November 1644 (II, 109).

He was in Wells, at any rate, before 7 November 1644 (I, 110–11) and in Exeter from around seven months before 10 April 1646 (the capitulation of Exeter), that is, around September 1645.[17] A citation for delinquency of taxes in Reading before 22 November 1643 (probably the 1642 assessment for goods rather than land) was made on 16 January 1652 (III, 148), but a certificate is recorded that he had not been living in Berkshire for about eight years (III, 177). This would seem to indicate no ownership of land in Berkshire (the subsidy roll noted before does not indicate assessment for land) and removal from Reading before January 1644. To restate these movements, then, Christopher Milton was probably in Reading until at least early 1643, and he arrived in Wells before November 1644. He may have gone directly from Reading to Wells, or there may have been some intervening residence, including London with his family.

It seems that Christopher Milton did not have his children with him all the time he was in Wells and Exeter, if at all. In addition to the birth of John in London in June 1643, Christopher paid a Mrs. Elijah Webster in London £2/14/—, for the keeping of his children on 1 July 1644, 16 December 1644, and 17 October 1645 (II, 104, 115, 130).[18] As far as we know, these children were Sarah, four years old in 1644; Anne, three years old in 1644; and John, one year old in 1644, and, if Parker's guess is valid, Christopher, seven years old or two years old in 1644.[19] He may have boarded them in London all the while he was in Wells and Exeter because of the military activity that was imminent there—and in that case we do not have records of all the payments to Mrs. Webster.

While in Reading, Christopher, as an active Royalist, was a Commissioner for the King under the great seal of Oxford, for sequestering the Parliament's friends of three counties (II, 157). Which three counties Christopher was in charge of has not been determined, but it is logical that they may have been Berkshire, Buckinghamshire, and Oxfordshire. Perhaps it was this new position that brought about the change in residence from insignificant Horton, in Bucks, after August 1640, to garrisoned Reading, in Berks, by April 1641. Significant in all of this is the fact that civil war was declared in August 1642. Having held this important commissionership caused Christopher much harassment after the capitulation at Exeter in April 1646. First he took the Covenant before William Barton, minister of St. John Zachary in Aldersgate Ward, on 25 April 1646.[20] His petition for compounding was sent to the Goldsmiths' Hall Committee on 7 August 1646 (II, 155–56). In it, he states himself as of Reading, but at Exeter at the time of its surrender. Accompanying this petition, apparently, was a schedule of possessions in which Christopher declared a messuage in St. Martin's, Ludgate, "at the Signe of the Crosse Keys," but no personal estate (II, 156). He took the Oath on the following day, 8 August (II, 156). On 25 August 1646—the rapidity with which Christopher was handled being due perhaps to his high positions in the Royalist cause—the committee acted on his petition and fixed his fine for his London property at a third of its value calculated at twenty years' purchase, £200 (II, 156–57). But on 24 September, after further action on 7 September (II, 158), he paid half his fine, which had been reduced to £80 at a tenth, and arranged to have William Keech, Fleetstreet, London, a goldbeater, stand co-surety for the remainder (II, 158–59). The second payment of £40, due on 24 December 1646, was probably paid.[21] The fine had perhaps been lowered through the elder brother's intervention.[22] Masson (III, 486) suggests that Christopher lived at the home of his mother-in-law in St. Clement Danes during this period, that is, during and after 1646, but the date for the family should probably be revised to 1643. In proof of Masson's suggestion is the baptism of Thomas Milton there on 2 February 1647 (II, 177).

As Masson remarks (III, 633), the Committee for Compounding seemed unsatisfied that Christopher had given a full accounting of his estate, since at least through 1652 and perhaps through February 1658 he was considered a delinquent. There is an unpaid fine from the Committee at Westminster, 24 December 1649 (II, 277–78), and the citation of delinquency of taxes in Reading on 16 January 1652, recorded before. On 15 February 1658, T. Bayly examined the records concerning Christopher's estate taken on 7 September 1646, noted before, perhaps indicating his continued delinquency. The only reason for the Committee's writing to Reading may have been that Christopher himself called it his residence during the litigation of 1646. It was probably his last established home before the early 1650s; even his children seem not to have been with him between 1644 and 1645, as we have seen. All of these delinquencies must give one pause about Christopher as a person.

It would have been the authorities at Reading who informed the Committee for Compounding that Milton had a residence in Suffolk, for a letter presumably from the Committee was sent to Suffolk, requesting information concerning Christopher's property there, probably around 18 February 1652 (III, 190). Another letter of this date from the Committee, at any rate, expresses thanks to the authorities in Berkshire for the certificate of 16 January (III, 190). How the Reading people were aware that Milton was connected with Suffolk we do not know, for, as noted before, he is supposed to have gone to Wells, Exeter, and London, in that order, from Reading. Obviously though, Milton was in Suffolk before 1652. In 1644, the time between Reading and Wells would hardly have been spent in Suffolk, for Milton would surely not proceed northeast from Reading, going to Parliamentarian areas, and then retrace his steps, going farther into the southwest, within a year. Besides, Edward Phillips tells us "he steer'd his course according to the Motion of the King's Army." (Phillips described his uncle as "being a great favourer and assertor of the King's Cause, and Obnoxious to the Parliament's side, by acting to his utmost power against them, so long as he kept his Station at Reading; and after that Town was taken by the Parliament Forces, being forced to quit his House there" [vi], followed the King, v-vi.) Further, the statement of the Reading authorities seems to deny his return there after 1646, before going to Suffolk. All that we can logically conclude is that he resided in Suffolk after having returned to London, some time after 1646 and before 1652, and that somehow the Reading authorities obtained knowledge of this change.

Christopher Milton returned to the practice of law after the first Civil War in 1646. He apparently resided both in London and in Ipswich during the time he maintained quarters in the Inner Temple. The earliest record that places the Miltons in Suffolk is the baptism of "Mary Dawghter of Christopher Milton" on 29 March 1656 at St. Nicholas, Ipswich.[23] "It was Christopher Milton's custom," Masson tells us (VI, 727), "before going to Ipswich, which he generally did for each vacation after the midsummer term, to call on his brother for a special leave-taking. . . ." Although Masson was referring to a time from around 1670, this double residence must have been in force before 1652, as we have seen. In London, did he reside only at the Inner Temple or was there also a town residence? Property has been reported in St. Martin's, Ludgate, and his mother-in-law probably lived in St. Clement Danes beyond 1645, the latest date we have for her activities being April 1652. We do not know when she died. But where his town residence was after 1646, if there was one, has not been ascertained. He sold the land in Ludgate to William Hobson on 3 February 1654 (French, III, 356–57), and Thomas, we remember, was baptized at St. Clement Danes in 1647. It is just as likely that the family lived, at least a bit later, in St. Dunstan's in the West, for Anne is said to be of that parish in 1683, and Thomas was buried there in 1694. Although Christopher seems to have been in Suffolk during this time more than in London, his children may have used the town residence.

Of his legal activities in or around London after 1646, we have many references connected with the Inner Temple and eight documents from 1653 to 1655.[24] He acted as counsel for Anne Powell (John Milton's mother-in-law) in her petition for relief against the Committee for Compounding, 26 May 1653 (III, 329),[25] and on 16 June of the next year, he acted in the same capacity on a bill suing Lady Elizabeth and Sir Anthony Cope for failure to repay his brother for a loan of long standing (III, 397). The suit continued and Christopher is named in items dated 6 February and 14 July 1655 (IV, 17, 41). References also occur in Elizabeth Ashworth's legal action (as a holder of mortgage on the property) in relation to John Milton's suit against his in-laws, the Powells, on 22 February 1654, 13 May and 2 December 1656, and 26 May 1657 (III, 357–66; IV, 90, 127, 143). In addition there is the will of his cousin John Jeffrey of Essex, dated July 1657 and proved 21 September 1657, which includes bequests to John and to him,[26] and a deposition on 25 May 1658 (IV, 226).

We hear nothing more of him until after the Restoration.[27] In a property settlement of 18 June 1660 "between Wm. Brewse, son and heir of Sir John Brewse, Knt., deceased, and Dorothy his wife, and John Brewse, 2nd son of the said Sir John Brewse, of the first part; Christopher Milton, of Ipswich, and Edward Sheppard, of Ipswich, of the second part; Benjamin Culler and Robert Sparrow, of Ipswich, of the third part," Little Wenham Hall and about fifteen acres of land were transferred to him and Sheppard.[28] Culler and Sparrow, who had been bailiff with Nicholas Phillips in 1658–59, 1665–66, 1670–71,[29] must have been the counsellors who drew up the contract. On 25 November 1660, he was called to the bench, probably such action arising from the change in government.[30] He testified to drawing up a will in July 1662 on 17 February 1663 (IV, 384–86), and he was named attendant to readers in the Inner Temple in 1664[31] and reader himself on 23 April 1665 and afterward.[32] In 1666, Christopher paid for the supply of water to his house, the earliest record Redstone seems to be aware of for Christopher's being in Ipswich.[33] When he was taxed in 1674, he is listed from St. Margaret's parish in Ipswich, as reported before, which is a relatively short distance north from St. Nicholas's,[34] yet the entries before this date, the burial of his daughter Thomasin in 1675, and his own burial in 1693 all show that he maintained connections with St. Nicholas to the south. Other legal documents exist for 22 May 1667, 24 May 1668, 20 June 1668 (IV, 432, and V, 465), and on 9 January 1669 he presided as Justice of the Peace over a murder investigation in Ipswich (IV, 448). (See *CSPD*, IX, 149–50, for the latter case.)[35]

"For he was a person of a modest quiet temper," writes Christopher's nephew Edward Phillips (vi-vii), "preferring Justice and Vertue before all Worldly Pleasure or Grandeur: but in the beginning of the Reign of K. James the II. for his known Integrity and Ability in the Law, he was by some Persons of Quality recommended to the King, and at a Call of Serjeants received the Coif, and the same day was Sworn one of the Barons of the Exchequer, and soon after made one of the Judges of the Common Pleas. . . ." Again called to the bench, as noted before, Christopher was elected counsel for Ipswich "at great Courts" in 1670,[36] and Deputy Recorder in 1674 according to Peile (I, 406). Whether that is so or not, he was appointed to this office on 8 July 1685 in the charter for Ipswich, supposedly from Charles II, although the king had died on 6 February 1685. Christopher's presence as part of the gentry in Suffolk is noted in 1671;[37] his sitting on the Parliament of the Inner Temple is recorded often;[38] he deposed his writing of a will for Sir Robert Clench on 13 May 1672 (V, 41–43); and apparently acted in a revival of Richard Brome's "Britannica" in 1673 (V, 48). Further activities recorded in the Inner Temple books are summarized by French, V, 232–34, from 16

July 1675 through 19 November 1687. Other legal documents are extant for 10 February 1675, 15 April and 12 July 1680, 7 March 1682, 26 February 1684, and 8 July 1685 (and citing July 1675). The February 1684 item, prepared and signed by Christopher, provides reasons for a royal warrant against Ipswich, for which he has been labelled a hireling of James II.[39] HMC, Eighth Report, Part II, p. 531, includes an affidavit, dated 11 May 1680, from Henry Guy to Sir Charles Littleton on a riot committed by some of the latter's soldiers, "The information and examination of William Parsons, of Felixstow, husbandman, taken before Chr Milton, a justice of Peace, co. Suffolk." On 12 July 1680 (p. 620), Guy wrote to the governor of Landguard Fort (where the riot occurred) concerning the examination of George Gosnell, collector of Ipswich, again before Christopher. In a previously uncited letter from William Douglas, Third Duke of Hamilton, to William Douglas, Earl, first Marquis, and first Duke of Queensbury, dated 14 June [1683?], from Glasgow, Christopher's Catholic reputation underlies an erroneous report: "But, sure, euery body sees that I haue not been well used even since I tooke the test, but les trusted then befor; . . . and iff I had been trusted to oversee Halyeards and Miltons carrage in giueing informations, as you know I desired, the circuite had been to better purpose and les charge to King or countrey, and as good service done. . . ."[40] He later indicates that John Graham of Claverhouse, Viscount of Dundee, had been the informer.

Following upon the royal warrant against Ipswich, a new and short-lived charter came into existence on 28 July 1685, according to G.R. Clarke,[41] Wodderspoon (92), and Mrs. Redstone (137–38), who states that by the charter Charles II had "sought to control the borough in the interests of the Roman Church and royal autocracy, tenets with which Christopher . . . was in full sympathy." A further statement of support for James II's dispensing powers as king and as head of the church (April 1686; French, V, 269–71) has brought charges of Christopher's motives as being both self-serving and religiously oriented. His rewards were advancement to Serjeant-at-Law on 21(?) April and Baron of the Exchequer on 24 April, apparently being knighted on the next day.[42] A money warrant dormant for the salary of £1000 per annum was approved on 15 May 1686 to "Christopher Milton, Serjeant at Law and one of the Barons of the Exchequer: and to Richard Heath, Serjeant at law and one of the Barons of the Exchequer" (Treasury Books, VIII, Part II, 741). A similar warrant dormant for the same amount, noting him as Sir Christopher Milton, a Justice of Common Pleas, is dated 10 May 1687 (ibid., 1353); "Royal Letters Patent," on 14 April 1687, constituted him to be one of the "Justices of Common Pleas: during pleasure" (ibid., 1304). He was assigned as Judge for the Midland Circuit in June, for the Norfolk Circuit in January 1687, and for others successively. (See French, V, 279,

281, 285–87.) He was ordered with Justice Wright of the Home Circuit to obtain reports from Clerks of Assize, as "Baron Milton for the Norfolk Circuit" (Treasury Books, VIII, Part III, 1199) on 15 February 1686/7.

He was one of eleven judges who allowed "the Printing and Publishing of the REPORTS in the Court of King's-bench at Westminster, in the Reign of our late Sovereign Lord King CHARLES the IId. Taken by Joseph Keble of Gray's-Inn, Esq;"; the imprimatur for the first part is dated 2 June 1686, but the volume title page gives "MDCLXXXV." The same dates are given for the separate publication of the second and third parts. He is one of twelve judges (two of the former are not listed and three are added) who allowed "the Reprinting of the Three Parts of the Reports of Edward Bulstrode Esq;" on 1 July 1687 (published in 1688). Bulstrode of the Inner Temple died in 1659; these reports deal with matters "In the time of the Reign of KING JAMES I. And KING CHARLES I." He and two of the judges referred to above, Edward Atkyns and Richard Heath, signed an order relating to the Fleet Prison on 28 October 2 James II (that is, 1687).[43] (Heath, giving opinions favorable to the King, nonetheless did not approve of royal policy; he was superseded in December 1688, having succeeded Sir Edward Atkyns to the Court of Exchequer on 21 April 1686. He died in 1702.) Christopher was again an approver "of the Printing of Serjeant Benloe's Reports and Pleadings" on 25 January 1687/8 (after first approval by Robert Wright on 12 January 1687/8), which appeared as "Les Reports de Gulielme Benloes Serjeant del Ley; et Gulielme Dalison Un des Justices del Banke le Roy." In "A Diary of Events in Ireland From 1685 to 1690" he is cited as being involved in a Bishops' case on 5 July 1688.[44]

As cited above, Christopher received the coif at a call of sergeants, according to Masson (VI, 762), on 21 April 1686. He was then sworn in as a Baron of the Exchequer on 24 April and knighted at Whitehall on 25 April. John Evelyn, in his diary under 9 June 1686, remarks, "New-Judges also here, among which Milton a papist, & bro: to the Milton who wrot for the Regicides, who presum'd to take his place, without passing the Test."[45] It will be noted that Evelyn was aware of Christopher's pro-Catholic beliefs. That negative note of his legal career is sounded also by Inderwick, "As a lawyer he had little, if any success" (lvi), and he received some negatives epitomes because of seeming arrears in payment of duties in the Inner Temple. Inderwick cites arrears in November 1679 as suggesting that he was then "in some financial difficulties" (lvii). The records of 12 November report an order "that the head butler attend Milton, of the bench, for his duties, otherwise that he be proceeded against by the laws of the House, and that the said butler demand 4li from Milton, the son, for caution money" (III, 151). (Curiously, Inderwick cites Richard, Jr., in his introduction but does not include this reference for him in the index.) The above is followed on 13 November with "Orders that application be again made to Milton, and if his duties be not paid by Saturday, the table will proceed to padlock his chambers; that none of his changes be allowed for repairing his chamber, unless he show better cause; and that the chief butler give an account daily what duties he has received." The next day both Milton and Richard Powell are ordered to make payment. Further orders appear on 2 February and 6 February 1679/80 (III, 152). But as French remarks (IV, 245), "There are numerous records of about this date concerning the unpaid dues of members of the society; apparently there was a financial crisis which called for quick money, which was hard to raise." Inderwick seems to be jumping to an unfounded conclusion, and besides, Christopher is frequently in Suffolk engaged in legal activities at this time, although he did also sit in Parliament during 1679 and 1680.

Masson (VI, 762) is again our informative source for the knowledge that on 18 April 1687 Christopher was transferred from the Exchequer to the Chief Justiceship of the Common Pleas. But French (V, 280), citing the Calendar of Treasury Books, 1685–1689, Part III, 1304, indicates that the date should be 14 April, that it was not a transfer, and that there is no mention of any ranking. This kind of extrapolation of "fact" has frequently occurred, it seems, and has become accepted. Other items connected with his judgeship have been discovered for 15 February and 10 May 1687 (V, 279–80). A letter apparently to Archbishop of Canterbury William Sancroft, dated 11 May 1687, requests a dispensation for Samuel Reynolds of Ipswich to receive Orders (V, 281).[46] He was removed from the bench of the Inner Temple on 19 November 1687,[47] and dismissed as Justice on 3 July 1688.[48]

A news item in the *London Gazette* for 5–9 June 1688 specifically says that the King is "pleased, in consideration of the great Age and Infirmities of Sir Christopher Milton, one of the Justices of the Common Pleas, to permit him to have his Writ of Ease." However, "A Diary of Events in Ireland," 5 July 1688, implies that it was a dismissal, along with others, because of opinions contrary to those of the Crown.[49] According to Parker, who gives no source for his comments, Narcissus Luttrell placed the appointment as Justice of Common Pleas on 15 April 1687 and "retirement" on 4 July 1688; see II, 1170 n104, and 1171 n105. His reference, however, is to the publication of Luttrell's manuscript in the papers owned by All Souls College Library, Oxford, of "A Brief Historicall Relation of State Affairs from September 1678 to April 1714," in six volumes. French nowhere cites Luttrell. Luttrell's entry of 15 April 1687 (which may reflect only his date of entry, not the date of occurrence) reads: "His majestie hath been pleased to constitute . . . Mr. baron Milton from the exchequer to the common pleas" (I, 400); and that of 4 July 1688 makes either word "dismissal" or "retirement" possible: "his majestie hath dismist Mr. justice Milton on his desire, and continues his salary to him" (I, 449).

Under 23 April 1686 Luttrell also records that Christopher (and others) "being called to the state of a serjeant at Law, performed this day the ceremonies and duty required at the Inner Temple and at Westminster" (compare French V, 271–72, under 21 April) and that "His majestie hath constituted sir Christopher Milton one of the barons of the exchequer." (Compare French 3V, 272–74, under 24 April.) Unmentioned by French or Parker is an important entry under 8 June 1686: "The same day, all the judges, except Mr. baron Milton, took the oathes in the court of chancery for their places; but he (tis said) owns himself a Roman catholick" (I, 379). One further reference occurs dated 28 May 1687: "The same day, Sir Richard Allibon was sworn before the Lord Chancellor one of the kings bench, in the room of Sir Francis Withens; and Mr. Serjeant Powel was sworn one of the barons of the exchequer, in the room of Milton" (I, 402). (The Lord Chancellor was George Jeffreys [1648–89], first Baron Jeffreys and a judge in the Inner Temple, who presided at the trials of Titus Oates, Algernon Sidney, and Richard Baxter, and often ran afoul of both political sides.) The lapse in the latter appointment between Milton and Sir John Powell was, thus, a little more than a month. Luttrell's family members were Jacobites, but he himself espoused the cause of King William; he died in 1732. The amount of legal work in which Sir Christopher was engaged and some attendant travelling outlined above, plus his recent leaving the bench of the Inner Temple, may explain his continuance there until 7–19 November 1687, when an order is given to "inquire of Justice Milton when he intends to remove out of his bench chambers" (*Inner Temple Records*, III, 249). The tone is peremptory and the removal may have been less than amicable, but due to his residence and work in Suffolk one can suppose that he was seldom in London and in residence. Wodderspoon (122) states that he retired to Ipswich "and resided in a house in Tacket Street, where it is believed he died" because he had become infirm, his dismissal being due to his advanced age and to nothing unworthy, we may note, as Masson and others imply. We know, however, that he left Ipswich proper and made his home in his last years in a mansion called The White House in the village of Rushmere, just outside Ipswich, a relatively short distance northeast (V, 281–86). Sir Christopher Milton of Rushmere was buried at St. Nicholas, Ipswich, on 22 March 1693 (V, 293).[50]

The picture of Christopher Milton in all of this is: Royalist, Roman Catholic, not very reliable member of the Inner Temple, not very competent lawyer and justice of the peace, and not a person of integrity. His nephew's epitome of him suggests overtones of negative criticism: "he was a person of

a modest quiet temper, preferring Justice and Vertue before all Worldly Pleasure or Grandeur: <u>but</u> in the beginning of the Reign of K. James the II. for
his known Integrity and Ability in the Law, he was by some Persons of Quality recommended to the King" (vi-vii). My underscoring of the word "but"
points to possible opposed readings of Christopher. His "known Integrity
and Ability in the Law" may be saying more about the "Persons of Quality"
who recommended him to James and their political (and religious?) position than about Christopher's character. As a Royalist from around 1641
onward and particularly his apparent adherence to Charles I, his relationships with his brother must have been strained, in the 1640s and 1650s especially. There were, nonetheless, seven legal links between 1654 and 1657, as
noted before. Even more alarming, in view of both the father's and John's
abhorrence of the Papacy and Catholicism, is Christopher's seeming involvement reported from various sources; the total lack of any connections to
emerge between Christopher and his father after the father had moved to
London adds to a disturbing disassociation of the brothers.

2

I have noted above some information about Christopher's children, including the baptism of Mary in 1656 at St. Nicholas, Ipswich. The family group at
St. Nicholas, Ipswich, at this time included Christopher, his wife Thomasin,
perhaps his daughter Anne, his sons Christopher, John, and Thomas, and
any other children whose birth records have not been discovered. Apparently by 1674 the father Christopher had connections in the parish of St.
Margaret, Ipswich; see n34 here. Masson (IV, 763), without detail or even
general explanation, wrote that in 1674 the three youngest children (apparently meaning the unnamed child, Sara, and Anne) were dead. Edward Jones
has discovered the date of Sarah's death in the St. Clement Danes records as
26 May 1645, and the only other item significant here may be the Ann Milton
buried on 10 May 1647 at St. Margaret's, Westminster.[51] However, Anne must
have been dead before the same name was given to another child around
1661 (see later) or else she is the same person born in 1641. We cannot
conclude that Anne died young simply because nothing further has been
discovered about her. Parker's speculation (1173) that Sarah married John
Younger, who is called her late brother by Thomas Milton's widow Martha in
1696 (French, V, 470), has proved to be inaccurate. Thomas apparently lent
£100 to Younger; see later. No reliable explanation of Martha's reference
has been forthcoming.

    Thomas, who was the third of four sons, is called the "eldest son of Mr.
Milton of the bench" and was given special admission, at the request of his

father, into the Inner Temple on 27 November 1670.[52] He was called to the bar on 29 November 1677 and was "appointed to standing committee to regulate expenses of the buttery and kitchen."[53] Having worked under his uncle Thomas Agar in chancery and having succeeded to the Deputy Clerkship in the Crown Office upon Agar's death (1673), Thomas still held the position in 1694 when he died.[54] A bill against John Arden of London on 22 May 1693 says that Thomas is now of the Middle Temple, according to French, who probably is inaccurate as he is concerning the Hoskins document discussed later (I do not find him in their records) and Deputy Clerk of the Crown. Orders for payment of salary and for other government work exist for 15 December 1679 and 16 December 1679, 28 April 1680, 15 June 1683, and 1694 (V, 249–50, 252, 262, 295). He and his brother Richard, both of the Inner Temple, signed an indenture for property in Suffolk with John Peed on 10 December 1677 (V, 240–41); his wife Martha is referred to in the document. The delinquency of dues to the Inner Temple recorded on 12 November 1679 for "Mr. Milton his sonne" perhaps more likely means Richard (V, 245). Thomas was buried in St. Dunstan's in the West, 17 October 1694, according to the Parish Register (V, 296). (See below for remarks concerning property at Rushmere.) He had married Martha, daughter of William Fleetwood of Aldwinkle on 22 July 1672 at St. Mary le Bone;[55] as his widow, she was granted administration of his estate on 3 November 1694,[56] according to the Administration Act Book of the Prerogative Court of Canterbury (f. 229). A marginal note has been read to say that he died on 6 November; probably the abbreviated notation ("——t'") does not mean "died" ("[Mor]t'") but "jurat'" (sworn [on 6 November]), which is the immediately preceding word in the notice of administration.

I should here also note a clearly manufactured report involving Thomas. A lock of hair at one time in the nineteenth century was supposed to be at the Chalfont St. Giles Cottage (in addition to the alleged lock of hair taken at the disinterment of Milton's grave in 1790), and was said to be the lock of hair that Joseph Addison owned and later passed down to Dr. Samuel Johnson, to John Hoole (translator of Tasso's *Jerusalem Delivered* in 1763), to Dr. Batty, to Leigh Hunt in part, and thence from Hunt in part to Robert Browning (although John Keats has also gotten into the picture because of his poem, "Chief of organic numbers!"). This is the same story of a (different) lock of hair that was reunited in the Keats Memorial House in Hampstead and is now in the Keats-Shelley House in Rome. Addison, of course, died in 1719, when Johnson was ten years old, although no one offers a scenario of the hair's progress from one to the other. French (V, 135) says it "probably came to Addison from the poet's daughter Deborah," whom he talked with shortly before his death, and Parker (unbelievably to me) accepts this preposterous account (1158 n11). Why Deborah would have a lock of her father's hair and why she would have kept it for almost fifty years in various venues is not pursued by Masson, French, or Parker. She left his home around 1669, going to Ireland as a companion to a Mrs. Merian around 1672, and marrying Abraham Clarke there on 1 June 1674. Two reports, which may be true enough, have apparently spawned this legend: Addison met Deborah and had asked her to bring proof that she indeed was Milton's daughter (according to John Ward as communicated by Thomas Birch in his "Life," lxi-lxii, *Complete Collection of the . . . Works* [1738]), although no "proof" brought by her is recorded, and second, George Vertue reports her rejection of a picture as that of her father because "of a Brown Complexion & black hair & Curled-locks. on the contrary he was of a fair complexion a little red in his cheeks & light brown lanck hair" (British Library, MS Harleian 7003, ff. 175v-176, in a letter to Charles Christian, dated 12 August 1721). And then Thomas Hollis and Francis Blackburne, reproducing this letter and referring to a different picture shown Deborah, extrapolated from Vertue's report to say: "when she perceived the drawing she cried out, 'O Lord! that is the picture of my father—how came you by it?' And, stroaking the hair of her forehead, added 'Just so my father wore his hair.' This daughter resembled Milton greatly" (*Memoirs of Thomas Hollis,* 619–20). It should be obvious that the legend of Deborah's having a lock of her father's hair, which she gave to Addison (and its future passage), is spurious.

But back to Thomas Milton: In 1927 Hunter Charles Rogers presented a lock of hair (among other relics) to the Cottage and gave this same parade of owners, except that instead of from Deborah, it was acquired by Addison from "a Mr. Thomas Milton of Bury St. Edmunds, a descendant of John Milton." That is, of course, even more far-fetched, and the "a Mr. Thomas Milton" indicates he knew little about the genealogy involved, but the "Bury St. Edmunds," which is not very far from Ipswich and Rushmere, shows he had some kind of real information for his substitution of source. Addison, of course, was twenty-two when Thomas died, and any connection between them is highly improbable. Rogers's statement to the Cottage alleged, "They [the locks] were given to Samuel Rogers the Banker Poet and on his death they came into the possession of my Father William Rogers. He gave them to his sister Ann Rogers, and she gave them to me. I sold part of John Milton's Lock to a Mr. George Smith, Book sellers of New York, and was then sold to a Mr. Rogers of Lowell Massechutis, and before he died he gave it back to me, and I still have it." Hunter Charles Rogers also sold forged Shakespearean documents, but his account here is strange in its language (he doesn't call "Ann Rogers" his aunt and he brings in another Mr. Rogers whose relationship to him is ignored) and in its attempt to relate himself with Samuel

Rogers. Samuel Rogers once owned the contract for *Paradise Lost* that Milton made with Samuel Simmons, with Milton's signature affixed by an amanuensis, dated 27 April 1667. It had been owned by William Pickering, the publisher (for example, of John Mitford's eight-volume edition of *The Works* in 1851, where it is reproduced facing clxxxviii), and then by Samuel Rogers, who gave it to the British Museum. It is now British Library MS Additional 18861. Among the items given to the Cottage (but refused and given back to him) was "a receipt for £5 by John Milton for the second edition of 'Paradise Lost'," which makes him an even more amazing forger.[57]

In addition to the unnamed infant son of 1639, who was buried 26 March in Horton, Christopher had three other sons besides Thomas, as noted above, Christopher, John, and Richard—all of whom, it appears, entered or may have entered the Inner Temple before Thomas. Christopher (born ca. 1637–38) was given special admission to the Inner Temple as "son of Mr. Milton of the bench, at the request of his father," on 30 June 1661.[58] Special admission may have been necessary because he had not gone to college or he was young (if born in mid-1642). He may, therefore, have entered Kings, Cambridge, as a pensioner in the Easter term, 1663.[59] He was called to the bar on 9 February 1668,[60] and died a month later on 12 March 1668 in Ipswich.[61] John Milton, baptised on 29 June 1643, although this record may be in error, has been identified as having been called to the bar on 22 November 1663,[62] and entered Pembroke, Cambridge, as a pensioner on 29 January 1667/8, matriculating 1668, as the "son of Christ. of Ipswich."[63] These pieces of evidence are in conflict, and the John Milton called to the bar has not been accepted as Christopher's son, logic says correctly, by French or Parker. The identification is clearly an error; see n62. The son, John, was buried on 29 December 1669 at St. Nicholas, Ipswich.[64] It is certainly possible that some of the year dates just cited are in error; the chronology implied above follows a possible and usual order of naming for the father first, for the grandfathers second. Undoubtedly, "Thomas" was named after Thomasin Milton. (Significant would be the name of the son who died in 1639.) Yet a problem has not been dealt with. When Thomas, upon being admitted to the Inner Temple in 1670, was labelled the "eldest son" of Sir Christopher, it was simply wrong. There had been three sons born before him, although all three were then dead; and he was in 1670 only the "elder son," Richard being younger. Likewise, at least two sons—Christopher and Richard—entered the Inner Temple before Thomas. The answer is, I suggest, a scribe's commonplace bad diction, using the superlative when the comparative was correct. (Note that Edward Phillips calls his uncle John Milton the father's "Eldest Son" with the same illogical diction, xxi.)

Richard, named for a great-grandfather, is the only child noted by John Aubrey in a genealogy found with his notes and overlooked by Masson and Perceval Lucas.[65] The family tree is given on the verso of Sheet A, f. 2, and is a kind of addendum to the notes; the minutes are dated 1681. Parker infers that it was Sir Christopher who gave this information to Aubrey (1175). If so, he may have purposely omitted Thomas, with whom he may have been estranged over religious views, and he patriarchally ignored his daughters— an unfortunately common practice. Richard was also given special admission to the Inner Temple as "son of Mr. Milton of the bench, at the request of his father," on 24 November 1667.[66] Aubrey places him in "Paper buildings, Inner Temple." Richard was called to the bar on 26 November 1676.[67] He and his father signed an indenture to Joseph Horenby on 13 February 1674 (V, 469), and again with his father, he signed a postnuptial marriage settlement, dated 10 May 1674, between Nicholas Haly and Frances Dixon, widow and relict of Fenner Dixon in connection with the marriage of their children Francis Haly, eldest son of Nicholas, and Elizabeth his wife.[68] "Christopher Milton of Ipswich aforesaid Esq' and Richard Milton his Sonne" are recorded as of the third part, meaning that they had drawn up the document. All parties were from Suffolk. Father and son witnessed an indenture on 13 May 1674, the document being in Richard's hand (V, 79). On 2 December 1674 there was a purchase of land in Oxfordshire by father and son (V, 209–10). He was a witness to the release for £100, dated 22 February 1674/5, relating to the nuncupative will of John Milton, on behalf of the latter's daughter Anne, as well as signer for Anne (V, 226–27). As noted before, Richard and his brother Thomas signed an indenture concerning property in Suffolk on 10 December 1677 (V, 240–41) and either of them (although Richard would seem to be the more likely candidate) was cited for nonpayment of dues at the Inner Temple on 12 November 1679. A Chancery action involving his father included interrogatories signed by him on 26 October 1687 (V, 469). His last recorded activity in England before he moved to Ireland occurred on 8 and 15 March 1688, when he was appointed with others to a study of fines on "any Recusant or other Dissenter" in the Midlands.[69]

The close workings together of Christopher and his son Richard, rather than many close connections with Thomas, it can be speculated, may have had religious reasons behind them. Thomas was Church of England, not Roman Catholic, the religion that Richard, like his father, followed. Richard's appointment, just noted, to study Recusant fines epitomizes the strange and questionable political/religious actions of these times. He left England for Ireland after 1688, the Glorious Revolution of that date undoubtedly contributing to that decision. He died there some time before August 1713, intestate and unmarried.[70] On 12 August 1713, a commission was "issued to John Taylor, of Highgate, gardener, to administer goods and credits of Richard Milton, late of Ipswich, *bachelor, deceased who died in the Kingdom of Ireland,* as regards the manor of Norwoods in Sproughton, Suffolk, of which the deceased held the remainder of a lease for 500 years acquired under indenture 2 October 1686, between William and Charles Burrough, of the first part, and Richard Milton, of the second part."[71] These various transactions and this document indicate that he engaged in real estate transactions as had his father, his uncle, and his grandfather. It is surely significant that the Taylor cited was "of Highgate," for Richard's two unmarried sisters, Mary and Catherine, lived at Highgate for many years until the former's death in 1742. (Mary was buried on 26 April 1742 in Farningham, Kent, and Catherine, next to her in April 1746.) Perhaps this Taylor was gardener for the sisters and acted as executor in their behalf.

If Thomas were the eldest son (which is incorrect under any definition of "eldest"), then the other three—Christopher, John, Richard—were born after 1647 and, figuring back from Richard's admission date to the Temple, before at least 1653 (based on possible admission at age 14 or 15). Other evidence that has been cited clearly negates this allegation. Thomas's long delay in entering the Inner Temple at age 23 is confusing for these reconstructions, but certainly possible. While Christopher's two sons Christopher and Richard followed their father's profession (we cannot be sure about John), Thomas—psychology concerned with fathers and sons has taught us—may have rebelled against following his father's profession and way of life, and we do see a split in their religious views. The delay in preparing to become a lawyer is not, in such a situation, unusual. Again a lack of evidence of communication between this father and this son seems to parallel that in the former two generations; compare inferences that a genogram, as in the Afterword here, posits.

There were at least two additional children born to Christopher and Thomasin Milton, both girls, Mary and Catherine (sometimes spelled "Katherine"). Two others, Anne and Thomasin, raise questions. The burial of "thomsing Duater of Mr Melton" occurred on 6 July 1675 at St. Nicholas, Ipswich.[72] This is surely their daughter, although nothing further is known of her. Anne, baptized in Reading on 27 August 1641, as noted before, may be the same daughter who married John Pendlebury of Enfield, bachelor, on 19 February 1683 at St. Sepulchre's.[73] She is listed as from St. Dunstan's in the West, aged 22, and her parents deceased. Parker takes them to be the same person, although nothing is known of her between her baptism and her marriage. The problem of age is most curious, for Anne would have been 41 at this marriage and that age discrepancy hardly seems unnoticeable! Another possibility, one might suggest, is that the first Anne died and another child was later given the same name. Why she is said to be from St. Dunstan's except that a family residence may have been there (Thomas was buried there later) is uncertain. Why her parents are said to be deceased is unexplainable, for Christopher was residing near Ipswich at this time. We do not know when his wife Thomasin died. Parker speculates that these falsifications may have been because of Pendlebury's religious position and rejection of Christopher's Catholicism. If the age given is not in error, then she was born around 1661. Anne Pendlebury, however, is definitely the daughter of Christopher and the sister of Mary and Catherine. She was buried at Farningham on 24 February 1721. Her will[74] bequeaths £5 be given each to a servant, Elizabeth Collins, and the poor of Farningham, the residue going to her sisters Mary and Catherine Milton, jointly. On the marriage allegation Pendlebury is said to be 24, but his gravestone indicates he was 66 when he died meaning that he was actually 30 when he married. An M.A. from Magdalen College, Cambridge, 1679, he was Vicar of Farningham, Kent, 1684–1719. He was buried there 14 December 1719. In his will he left £100 each to Mary and Catherine.

Mary, whose baptism in 1656 has already been cited, died unmarried, having lived for many years with her sister Catherine at Highgate.[75] She was buried at Farningham, Kent, where her sister Anne had settled.[76] Administration of her goods was granted to Catherine, her sister and "only next-of-kin," on 5 May 1742. When her sister Mary died, Catherine went to Lower Holloway to live with her second cousin Elizabeth Foster, Deborah Milton Clarke's daughter, and her husband Thomas, a chandler. We do not know when she was born, although Parker gives "1656?" which would require her birth near the beginning of 1657 at earliest, unless Mary and she were twins, which is unlikely since only Mary's birth is recorded. She died at the Fosters' home. The entries in the parish register reverse the deaths of Mary and Catherine. Her will dated 19 July 1744, with a codicil 8 April 1745, was proved 23 April 1746.[77] In it she expressed the wish to be buried at Farningham, leaving small legacies to her "cousin Ann Lambourne" and "her brother Mr. Thomas Lambourne," as well as other bequests. "Cousin" must mean merely close friend, and Thomas, that close friend's brother.

Of all of Christopher and Thomasin Milton's children, only Thomas married and had children, but whether any survived him is uncertain. The Hoskins document (dated 4 December 1695) specifically says, "Thomas Milton ab^t ye month of [blank] Last past departed this Life without issue Leaving one Martha Milton his Widow & Relict" (PRO C6/27/42; as indicated before, Thomas died on 17 October 1694). In the answer from Martha and Catherine (PRO C33/287/12), referring to 1 October 1688, they are said to attest "to be true that the said Thomas Milton departed this life about Michaelmas last was a twelvemonth and as they have heard & doe believe without issue and Intestate as by the said Bill." Later we read: "And these Defend's doe also take it to be true that they with their Sister Anne who is in full life as they believe are the Sisters and Coheires of him the said Thomas Milton their Brother." Masson (VI, 763), without giving his source says that Thomas left a daughter, "who is heard of in 1749 as 'Mrs. Milton of Grosvenor Street,' a maiden lady, housekeeper to Dr. Secker, and who died 26 July 1769. She seems to have been the last living descendant of Sir Christopher Milton." The first part of that statement comes from Richard Baron's revision of Thomas Birch's biography of John Milton, included in *The Works of John Milton* (London, 1753), ed. Baron, I, lxxvii. But, strangely, *Lloyd's Evening Post, and Chronicle,* No. 1097, Vol. XV, 20–23 July 1764, pp. 78–79, gives notice of Mrs. Martha Milton's death on 14 July 1764; only Perceval Lucas makes reference to this periodical, but his account places the death on 24 July 1769. *Lloyd's* reports that she "was a descendant of the great English Poet John Milton," the daughter of Thomas Milton, son of Sir Christopher "a professed Papist." Even more strangely, the notice (with various changes) appears in *Lloyd's,* No. 1881, Vol. XXV, 24–26 July 1769, p. 86: "Mrs. Milton, in King-street, Covent-garden, many years Housekeeper to the late Dr. Secker, Archbishop of Canterbury, and descended from Christopher Milton, a Judge in the reign of K. James II and brother of John Milton, the great Poet." On the other hand, *The Annual Register, or a View of the History, Politics, and Literature,* for the year 1769 (London, 1770) records the death of "Mrs. Milton, a descendant from the brother of Milton the great poet. She was housekeeper to Dr. Secker" (120, first pagination). This was undoubtedly taken from the obituaries in the *Gentleman's Magazine* 39 (1769): 367, which has the same statement and has been cited by French and Parker.[78] Birch or Baron reports from Thomas Newton (editor in 1749 of an important life and edition of *Paradise Lost*) that Elizabeth Clarke Foster, Deborah Milton Clarke's daughter, believed that there were no living descendants of Christopher, Thomas's spinster sisters Mary and Catharine having died. Newton wrote that "she knows nothing of her aunt Philips or Agar's descendents, but believes that they are all extinct: as is likewise Sir Christopher Milton's family, . . . but unknown to her, there is a Mrs. Milton living in Grosvenor street, the granddaughter of Sir Christopher, and the daughter of Mr. Thomas Milton before mentioned."[79] It seems strange that Mrs. Foster was unaware of this second cousin, though her other cousins did visit her home often, it seems, and Catharine lived with the Fosters before she died. Perhaps, of course, Thomas was estranged from the whole family; perhaps the report is wrong, for Newton does not cite his source of information. Some question should also probably be raised because while there is a King Street in Covent Garden, there is also a different King Street in St. James, Westminster, where Secker was bishop until he removed to become Dean of St. Paul's in 1750. Have they been confused? Had she moved to Covent Garden after Secker's death or has some kind of confounding in reportage occurred? It is also possible that she moved to Grosvenor Street after Secker went to St. Paul's. Or perhaps she left his employ before that move? One assumes that "housekeeper" means that she lived at the prelate's home at St. James.

If this Mrs. Martha Milton were a descendant of Christopher, she would have to be descended through Thomas since the other sons died unmarried. Perceval Lucas is both informative and confusing in his article on Christopher and his family. He wrote that the first name of "Mrs. Milton" was Elizabeth, without any evidence, and that she died in King Street, Covent Garden, 24 July 1769, aged seventy-nine. This would mean that she was born in 1690, eighteen years after Thomas's marriage and when he was forty-three. Parker accepts this information, unaware of the first statement in *Lloyd's*. Lucas remarks, however, that this "Mrs. Milton" may be another case of questionable assignment, like the *DNB's* calling John Milton, the painter who flourished in 1770 in London, a descendant of Christopher. And he may be right, for the stories sound more like suppositions and the dates have discrepancies. There is no evidence that the Mrs. Milton, whether Martha or Elizabeth, who lived on Grosvenor Street or on King Street, Covent Garden, and who died in 1764 or 1769, was related to Thomas Milton, Christopher's son. If Mary Milton's "only next-of-kin" statement concerning her sister Catherine is accurate, then there is added reason to believe Lucas's contention that Mrs. Elizabeth (as well as Martha) Milton of Grosvenor (or King) Street was not Thomas's daughter; "Mrs. Milton" would have been Mary's niece. Her second cousin Elizabeth Foster would not have been designated "next-of-kin," though a niece might have been.[80]

Of other possible children of Thomas and Martha Milton, records are scarce and assignment to their family of all of these is uncertain. One item is a note on a manuscript pedigree of John Milton in the New York Public Library that says, "a grand daughter of Ch. Milton. marr^d. Iohn Lookup advocate Edinb." (V, 352–53). Jonathan Richardson mentioned "a relation of Milton's, Mr. Walker of the Temple"; perhaps as Parker points out, this was William Walker, admitted to the Inner Temple on 1 March 1669, and the same William Walker who married a Sarah Milton, of St. Mary Whitechapel, on 5 September 1700.[81] A son, Thomas was baptized on 26 June 1679 and was buried on either 1 July 1680 or 30 December 1683. (There are two burial entries of a Thomas Milton.) A daughter Margaret was baptized on 7 March 1681 at St. Dunstan's in the West and was buried on 25 June 1685. Another child, Charles, son of Thomas and Martha, was baptized on 20 January 1684, but nothing further is known of him. Parker speculates that "he may have lived on to perpetuate the family name," and perhaps this is what French is thinking of when he so enigmatically writes, "the families of his [Milton's] sister Anne and his brother Christopher have continued into the twentieth century" (V, 352), although he does not record anything about a Charles Milton. (For the reference to Anne he meant Thomas Agar's daughter Ann, whose descendants do continue; see chapter 2.) In the twentieth century, Lowther Bridger is called "a descendant of Milton's brother Christopher."[82] The question of relationship is not pursued by either French or Parker, even though they both repeat the allegation. If it is correct, possibly this Charles Milton provides the line of descent. Bridger (through his father William Milton Bridger of Halvaker, Sussex) had been in possession of a snuff box and a writing case supposedly owned by John Milton, acquired ultimately through Richard Lovekin, the nephew of Milton's widow Elizabeth.[83] Bridger's affidavit makes no such familial claim, and Parker's skepticism about the writing case itself should have extended to the alleged relationship. A William Milton was buried on 3 September 1684, but whether he has any connection is not known. Parker comments that he may have been the husband of Phoebe Milton, who was buried on 16 September 1685, her daughter Mary being baptized the same day (1176–77 n138). Needless to say, I trust, the surname "Milton" was very common and probably most, if not all, of these excavations are irrelevant. As pointed out in n56, there are no children indicated in William Coward's will.

3

Other puzzles remain that must be addressed: Christopher's religion which has been referred to often, the matter of the Rushmere property, and John Milton's death and will as well as his financial condition in 1674. Apparently Christopher had become a Roman Catholic well before 1685, as my former remarks suggest.[84] Parker, trying to dissociate him from this unacceptable religion, calls it a "conversion," that "may have occurred as late as 1682" (658). Campbell (*Chronology*) simply iterates Parker's position. Masson (VI, 761), Peile (I, 406), and Clarke (226) report his later religion as Catholic, Clarke remarking that "Adjoining to the Tankard, is the Theatre: on which spot was a Catholic chapel, for Judge Milton . . . in the time of James II." Mrs. Redstone (138) adds some information to this remark, "[He] is reputed to have had a chapel, where he heard mass, in Tacket Street, on the site later occupied by the Theatre, before he removed his home to the village of Rushmere," and Wodderspoon (122) tells us that this private chapel was annexed to his residence. (Tackett Street is in midtown Ipswich in the parish of St. Nicholas.) Yet papers supposedly having belonged to Judge Milton were examined on 11 February 1690 by the Earl of Shrewsbury, a Secretary of State to King William, apparently for subversive material; "nothing of Moment" was found. French prints some of the items calling attention to his religion (V, 119–22). Uncertain of this religious classification, Parker is skeptical (1172–73 n116). "Although it is mentioned confidently by many writers, I do not find conclusive evidence of Christopher's Roman Catholicism. Some of his actions . . . and his rapid promotion by James II could easily have brought him the unearned reputation of being a papist, in an age which even brought this charge absurdly against his brother. . . ." This religious designation is given by John Evelyn, John Oldmixon, John Lord Campbell, William Binckes (all noted by Parker) and, aside from references already cited, by such writers as Laurence Echard, *The History of England* (London, 1718), 1077; Samuel Boyse, II, 178; and Sir William Scott, First Baron Stowell (letter to Thomas Warton, 29 June/1 July 1789), discussing the nuncupative will, Milton's widow and daughters, his servants, and Christopher Milton (Bodleian MS Dep.c.638, ff. 15–16). Probably, one writer simply copied another, as one suspects in the case of the entry for Christopher in *Großes Vollständiges Universal-Lexicon aller Wissenschaften und Künste*, XXI, column 258. John Le Neve's pedigree describes him as "a lawyer in Suff. not a considerable one but being a Papist was p'moted at this time," referring to his being knighted.[85]

Unknown to French or to Parker is a brief, undated discussion by Sir John Percival in his "Adversaria, Vol. II," a manuscript once owned by the Earl of Egmont: "Milton, the poet, died a Papist. Dr. Charlette, Master of University College, Oxford, told me lately at Bath that he remembers to have heard from Dr. Binks that he was at an entertainment in King James' reign, when Sir Milton, one of the Judges and elder brother to the famous Mr. Milton, the poet, was present; that the Judge did then say publickly his brother was a Papist some years before he died, and that he died so. . . . I am still more persuaded of it from what Dr. English told me that he had often heard Mr. Prior, the poet, say that the late Earl of Dorset told him the same thing."[86] Clearly this rumor of John Milton's religious persuasion was frequently repeated, even here with the obvious ignorance of which brother was the elder, but implication suggests that Sir Christopher's religion was being transferred to his brother by those in opposition to the undercurrent of papal influence during the late seventeenth and eighteenth centuries.

The apparent misquotation of Bincks evidences antagonists' confusion over the issue of Catholicism.

However, suits involving the Rushmere property are confusing and suggest some wheeling and dealing by the participants. The suits refer to various pieces of property owned at one time or another by Christopher and his heirs. A piece of property in Rushmere, Clopton, and Debach was transferred to John Wallace, a medical doctor, from "Christopher Milton, Knight, one of the justices of the Bench of our lord the King" (French's translation, V, 282) and John and Elizabeth Allen on 12 November 1687 before four justices, one of whom is listed as "Christopher Milton."[87] Such conflict of interest seems hardly legal or likely; rather, as French suggests, the scribe has perhaps made an error of line-skip. Yet it is a strange error that should give us pause about Christopher's activities. Further complication exists in relation to Rushmere, for "Sr Christofer Milton of Rushmer Knight" bought this property on 29 December 1687 from John and Elizabeth Allen, John Wallace, and Elizabeth Cutteris.[88] This action, a little more than a month after the prior transfer, is suspiciously curious. Other property purchased from Robert Rednall of Ipswich, occupied by a tenant, George Groome, was transferred to Sir Henry Felton on 12 February 1688 (Ref. No. XI/5/4.3). A suit brought by William Hoskins on 4 December 1695 argues that Thomas and Martha Milton mortgaged this home to Martha Hoskins for £600, but it remained unpaid (Thomas having died in 1694). The property is cited as being in the parish of St. Andrew. An inventory of Thomas Milton's estate (goods and such) accompanies the suit (PRO C6/427/42) on p. 3, both sides. In answer, Mary and Catherine Milton, knowing nothing about the Hoskinses, allege that on 1 October 1688 their father Christopher had mortgaged the property to Sir Henry Felton to provide for them, and thus that they still owned it. Missing from French's account (V, 470–71) is the superscripted insertion referring to the mortgage and title that Mary and Catherine Milton claimed they still owned: "and unto John Pendlebery Clerke and Anne the wife which said Anne is another of the sisters of the sayd Thomas Milton." A similar insertion occurs three more times in the document. Martha Milton's answer to the Hoskins suit on 20 May 1696 (a week before her marriage to William Coward) is strange: she denies knowledge of the arrangement with Hoskins; she cites other mortgages and borrowings, remarking Thomas' recognizance of a Statute Staple (bond) for £2000 (to Miles Fleetwood, as later stated) and that Thomas borrowed £200 from Henry Cooke in 1693 but this was repaid. French's version of the section in Martha's deposition relating to her father Miles Fleetwood, Thomas, and herself, is misleading. Apparently before Thomas married Martha he made provision for her but "after which Statute or recognizance was agreed to be defezeeanced for that purpose" (that is, it would be null and void if fulfilled). She reports that, to her grief, she had heard that Thomas had "been prevailed upon to marry with one Martha Spencer notwithstanding this def's being alive."[89] Her friends urged a payment of £100 per annum to her "during the joynt lives of her this def[t] & the sd Thomas Milton in case she this Def[t] should think fitt to live apart from the sd Thomas Milton for her this Def's maintanance as well for the paym[t] of one Hundred pounds per Annum during her life in case she should survive & out live him the sd Thomas." It does not say that Thomas married Martha Spencer, nor does it say that he and his wife (whom he married in 1672) lived apart, and later "this Def[t] further saith that shee did not separate herselfe from the sd Thomas Milton during his life but continued to live with him to the time of his death." The Statute Staple "was by Indenture bearing date" 23 May 1691 made with Fleetwood to have the £100 per annum paid to him, his executors, administrators, or assignees for her use or maintenance even should she survive him. There is no evidence that Thomas and Martha divorced or even separated, but the inclusion of a clause that would make this "maintanance in satisfacion of alimony during the life of Thomas Milton" and the repeated emphasis on their living separately surely implies that the marriage was not a fully happy or untroubled one. Thus Martha in her deposition argues that since no maintenance had been paid, it should now come out of Thomas's estate, although "rents & profits of the Freehold will hardly amount to seaventy pounds per Annum." Accordingly she "humbly hopes & insists upon it . . . that she ought to have a Satisfaccion for the residue of the sd Thomas Miltons personall estate." Raised as financial problems are all the charges concerned with the many legal actions and with unpaid bills listed in the attached inventory. Either she should receive the money due her by the agreement and defeasance or "she is intitled to her dower & thirds in the whole of her said late husbands Estate." The property continued in litigation between Mary and Catherine Milton and a Mr. Aston (18 July 1701) and between Catherine and a Thomas Thurston (14 April 1714), with other land and bonds also being entailed in the confusing documents. See French, V, 470–72, for some discussion. Mary and Catherine Milton, we can infer from comments in these writs, were estranged from their sister-in-law Martha and her new husband William Coward to the point of animosity.

The matter of Christopher's part in his brother's last days, and his reported testimony on 23 November 1674 at the Prerogative Court of Canterbury and examination before Dr. Richard Lloyd on 5 December in connection with John's nuncupative will has been told at length by Masson (VI, 727–43) and Parker (639–40, 647–49; 1120, 1157–58, especially). Nonetheless, there are difficulties that are hard to dismiss. As Parker notes, Thomas Warton, in this 1791 edition of the shorter poems, pointed out that "for the oral will to be valid, Milton should have been in his last sickness, should have informed his auditors that he was going to deliver his will, and should have had three witnesses to anything he then said" (1157–58 n7). However, rejection of the probate by the Court that Warton concludes must have occurred, but that Masson in turn rejects for lack of evidence, is legally beside the point. "A Nuncupative Will is not pleadable in any Court before Probate" according to "De Term. Sanct. Hill. Anno Regis 22 & 23 Car. II. In Cancellaria" with Judge Moreton presiding in the case of "Verhorn *against* Brewine *and others.* Jun. 18 [1671]."[90] For, as the account reads: "On debate it was ruled, that before probate of the nuncupative Will (which is to be proved only in the Ecclesiastical Court) it is not pleadable in any Court against an Administrator; and so the Plea was over ruled." According to this recent legal precedent, no probate was possible at the Prerogative Court of Canterbury, where, according to Warton, Sir Leoline Jenkins was judge and Secretary of State: it had to pass through the Ecclesiastical Court, which seems not to have entered the picture at all. The more one looks at this episode in Milton's life and death, the more one suspects both collusion and fabrication.

The question of the validity of the will *seems* now to be settled, but the inheritance of Christopher's children (i.e., apparently Thomas, Richard, Anne, Mary, and Catherine) over John's own children or Edward and John Phillips is nonetheless suspect. We do not know which of Christopher's children Elizabeth and then Christopher were referring to as heirs in his court testimony. While specific inheritances for the three daughters are given, it is difficult to understand the lack of any reference to Edward Phillips. (See the court testimonies given in French, V, 206–09, 211–24, and the releases and inheritances in French, V, 225–32.) Parker—perhaps extrapolating from Christopher's testimony—writes "there is evidence that then [1660] or later he paid regular visits to his brother" (I, 578) and adds with no evidence whatsoever, "He may also have sent his sons to serve as amanuenses." Did Christopher, indeed, visit his brother regularly? Are, indeed, his sons among the unidentified amanuenses? Parker's rather sentimental account of John's last months (639–40), drawn from the court testimony, dismisses the curious point that "As a lawyer, Christopher should have done one of two things if he had thought his brother in any real danger of dying soon": had the will put on paper, and had it witnessed. "He did neither." Can we impugn Christopher's testimony? On this count, the opinion of John Toland in his *Life of John Milton* (1699) is provocative: "CHRISTOPHER bred to the Common

Law, who, more resembling his Grandfather than his Father or Brother, was of a very superstitious nature, and a man of no Parts or Ability" (10). For Toland, that word "superstitious" referred to belief in Catholic "miracles" and the like, but is "man of no Parts or Ability" indicative of more than antagonism toward Christopher's religion and politics? In conflict with Christopher's testimony is that of Elizabeth Fisher, Milton's servant, and her sister Mary (PRO Prob 24/13/311–313) on 15 December 1674. Mary reported that Milton said to his wife, "thou knowest J have given thee all when I dye at thy disposall," and Elizabeth, "when J dye thou knowest that J have left thee all." Circumstances under which these statements are alleged to have been said may modify them, but they are in direct opposition to Christopher's deposition. Parker's questioning of the nuncupative will affair (1158–59 n13) remains and casts a most questionable light on Christopher's honesty and veracity, although Parker does not pursue that rather obvious problem.

The court records of the nuncupative will indicate that Milton, some months later than his discussion with Christopher, told his wife Elizabeth, who informed Christopher, that any estate above £1000 should go to Christopher's children; there is nothing in the testimonies that records Elizabeth's agreement or disagreement with this deposition of Christopher's. That is, there is no document recording her testimony in the inquiry into the nuncupative will, another strange legal lapse, surely, and this is given only in Christopher's deposition. As Parker reports: "The interrogatories, therefore, strongly suggested collusion" (548). Further, the children are not named. As pondered above, it is surely strange that Milton makes no reference to Edward Phillips, who supposedly often saw and did scribal work for his uncle during the 1660s and apparently the 1670s, and who allegedly needed financial help around this time (note Thomas Agar's will cited in chapter 2). It is assumed that Edward aided in the production of the second edition of *Paradise Lost* in 1674, and according to Aubrey, citing Milton's widow, "she gave all his papers . . . to his Nephew" Edward (Sheet A, f2v), although the assignment to Edward may be in error. (See chapter 3.) That John Phillips was not referred to will be explained by their alleged estrangement, but see chapter 4 here. Did Elizabeth get things confused or simply forget certain details? Did Christopher? Edward's affiliations were primarily Royalist, although he seems not to have taken political stands; John's affiliations were non-Royalist, and he did take political stands. Here is a question that has not been previously raised even though questions about this oral will have been.

Skeptics would also wonder about Christopher and his son Richard's purchase of property in Oxfordshire on 2 December 1674, less than a month after John's death and a few days before depositions concerning the nuncupative will began. The timing is certainly suspicious. While some of the puzzles of Milton's life may have some solution in the above discussion of relatives' and friends' political and religious philosophies, the "life records" that we have nonetheless raise questions of their full validity and the assumptions therefrom. It certainly appears to the scrupulous observer that Christopher's attestation was fraudulent and self-serving.

A further question is the state of Milton's financial condition at his death. During the eighteenth century, it was generally lamented that this great author received only £10 for his masterpiece (see, for one instance, Richardson's "the Price for which *Milton* sold his Copy is Astonishing. . . . the Price this Great Man Condescended to take for such a Work; Such a Work! was Ten Pounds, and if a Certain Number went off, then it was to be made up Fifteen," cxv) and that he died in what was almost tantamount to poverty. (See the uncited section in the previous quotation from Richardson, "and Here we were in Another Danger of Losing This Poem. Happy was it for the World that Milton was Poor and Depress'd, Certainly he must be so at This time".) Aside from remembering the alteration in the value of money between 1674 and 1734 and today, we should register Edward Phillips's statement: "He is said to have dyed worth 1500 l. in Money (a considerable Estate, all things considered) besides Houshold Goods; for he sustained such losses as might well have broke any person less frugal and temperate then himself; no less then 2000 l. which he had put for Security and improvement into the Excise Office, but neglecting to recall it in time, could never after get it out, with all the Power and Interest he had in the Great ones of those Times; besides another great Sum, by mismanagement and for want of good advice" (xliii).[91] Taking Phillips at his word, we can understand that Milton had had a larger estate, reduced by financial collapses and poor investment, and we would have expected such a larger estate because of the various assets from land, rent, and loans that he (following his father and inheriting from him) should have realized. In his statement, taking Christopher at his word, Milton may have thought his estate larger than it was, consisting of "Money" (not the debt from the Powells from the Wheatley property, however; see the Introduction here) and whatever realty or investments, though none is cited, that still might have existed. Parker concludes "that the estate left by Milton would not come to more than a pitiful £900" (I, 648) and appends a note, "Phillips may be right, and Masson wrong, but I have accepted Masson's reasoning in my text" (1157 n5). (See Masson, VI, 743–44.) The fact of the matter that we can come closest to is that the report in the nuncupative will may be accurate or faulty in terms of money, that Phillips may have erred or been correct in terms of money, and that Milton did not die well off but less impoverished than "a pitiful £900" has suggested.[92] But added to this is the unexplained bond given to Richard Hayley (or Haley) of Elstree, Hertford, on 27 July 1674 for £40 (French, V, 92–94), the original of which was among documents of the daughters' releases (all now in the New York Public Library). This certainly does not back up Parker's contention that Milton did the translation of *Declaration* for a small sum of money, and does not suggest that he was scrimping to remain solvent. In all, puzzles and hiatuses remain in our knowledge of Milton's financial condition at his death, in the nuncupative will as presented, and in Christopher's veracity and/or his competence as a lawyer.

A further crux, however, exists in connection with Milton's financial position and the nuncupative will. Christopher deposed that Milton said, "the porcon due to me from mr Powell, my former wives father, J leave to the unkind children J had by her but J have receaved noe part of it" (French, V, 213). It is assumed that Milton's visit to Forest Hill "about Whitsuntide [29 May] . . . or a little after," 1642, was made ostensibly to collect payment on the 1627 loan (noted in the Introduction). Phillips wrote that Milton returned from this trip a married man "after a Month's stay." Since Milton seems to have been in London on 2 June, Parker (870n11, 871n15; Campbell, *Chronology,* 74–75) infers payment of interest to Milton of the 1627 staple bond on 12 June, when it was due although there is no documentary evidence of such payment at that time, and suggests (230) that the marriage took place actually in July. Parker's (and others') sentimental account has Milton falling in love at first sight during this trip which was ostensibly only to pick up money owed, a scenario that hardly conforms to the Milton that otherwise emerges. (Aside from the "whirlwind romance" improbability, the Milton/Powell associations of the past and proximities of residence make that scenario highly incomplete.) The argument that, having fallen in love, he remained for a month with (or nearby) people who only then became potential relatives stretches credulity much too far. Rather, I wonder whether the fact of the matter is that this was one of the commonplace arranged marriages of the period? Milton at thirty-three and Mary at seventeen fit that pattern and particularly raise questions that a whirlwind romance occurred. Parker (870 n7) derides Henry John Todd's suggestion of an arranged marriage (1826 edition of Milton's poems, I, 80) on the basis of *The Doctrine and Discipline of Divorce,* which reads: "As for the custom that some parents and guardians have of forcing mariages, it will be better to say nothing of such a savage inhumanity, but only this, that the Law which gives not all freedome of divorce to any creature endu'd with reason so assasinated, is next in crueltie" (1643 edition, 19). We cannot be sure, but this statement, of which it is "better to say nothing," appears in August(?) 1643, about a year after the possibly "forced" bride had left her husband of almost double her age, and it may just possibly be mentioned in this tract because he has come to realize the inhumanity of such a marriage. Possibly he cannot psychologically get himself to say something about such an act in which he has been a major participant. (Commentators also seem to forget that she, seventeen, now was foster-mother to Edward Phillips, aged thirteen—whose remembrance fifty-two years later is the major source of information—and to John Phillips, aged twelve![93] And the fact that Milton, Sr. joined the household before April 1643 is consistently ignored as a factor in Mary's untenable circumstances.)

What we should wonder about is where the funds came from that Richard Powell had on 28 May 1642 to make a payment to Pye? Was the payment of £12 to Milton actually paid? Was it actually paid on 12 June? Were such payments usually made by Milton's travelling to Forest Hill to pick up the money? There is certainly no evidence that this was the case before or after June 1642—and that seems unlikely in any case. Why just then? What possibilities did the relative proximity of Forest Hill in Oxfordshire and Horton in Buckinghamshire from 1635 on have for two fathers that the 1627 loan evidences had connections? And we cannot ignore the requirement—although it has been ignored—that banns should be published "three several Sundays or holydays in the time of service," suggesting, first, that the marriage was less precipitous than Phillips's comment makes it seem;[94] second, that the month that Phillips reports that Milton was away may have further corroboration; and third, that, indeed the marriage may have been in July and now less likely in May. Phillips's comment about "a Journey into the Country" and "no body about him certainly knowing the Reason, or that it was any more than a Journey of Recreation" in no way hints at a business trip: not only should it not be read as Milton's clandestine action (the public statement of banns would have at least filtered back to the adults in the family), it also says without substance that his father (although now in Reading and perhaps intending soon to remove to London) was not aware he would be going to Forest Hill to collect the interest on the loan originally made between the two fathers. But did father and brother know of the trip, though the young nephews did not? May the seeming precipitousness of the action have been created by something that I have alluded to before: the father's possibly unhappy situation of living with Christopher (Catholic? and Royalist) in the Royalist stronghold of Reading? (Ostensibly the first Civil War began on 22 August and passage between Oxford and London was prohibited by Parliament in December 1642 and again in January 1643.) Perhaps it was recognized that John Milton needed someone, more than just a servant, in his home to aid in raising two young boys and the impending addition of an elderly father. Phillips's further remark that the Powells "began to repent them of having Matched the Eldest Daughter of the Family to a Person so contrary to them in Opinion" may simply mean "allow matching the eldest daughter" to Milton; but it more literally makes the matching a considered action of the Powells'—which raises questions about Richard Powell's motives. Were financial pipedreams in effect?

Ann Powell's deposition on 4 June 1656 that she had known Milton for about fourteen years fits 1642, but of course Milton was not in Horton so far as we know from early 1638 on, and perhaps not much after the death of his mother in April 1637, when Mary was twelve. (Mary was ten to twelve years of age when Milton probably was in Horton during the years 1635–1637. As I have wondered, he may have returned to Horton briefly in 1639 when Mary would have been fourteen.) Who, indeed, picked up earlier installments from Powell and where? In any case, a dowry from a bride's father to the groom was standard, and in his will of 30 December 1646 Powell subscribes that "my desire is that my daughter Milton be had a reguarde to in the satisfieing of her portion and adding thereto in Case my estate will beare it." Christopher's answer to the eighth interrogatory (French, V, 215) cites "the portion which he was promised with his former wife in marriage, being a 1000/. which is still unpaid besids the interest thereof for about twenty yeares." That such rancor on Milton's part maintained itself in 1674 since 1652 when Mary died and since 1647 when Powell died, and, worse, since 1642 allows no approbation of anyone involved in this curious marriage happening. (The "about twenty yeares" above refers to 1652 when Mary died, of course.)

4

The foregoing indicates one circumstance through which John Milton was closely connected with those who espoused the Royalist cause, his brother and his brother's family, indeed his brother's extended family. It also offers corroboration to Jane Lane's contention that prominent families of the seventeenth century included members on both sides of the ideational and actual conflict—her inference that some members may have even deliberately been urged to join opposed sides is not refuted. The assumption that John and Christopher Milton maintained happy filial relationships has perhaps been too easily accepted, and John Milton, Sr.'s associations with his younger son have been passed over, although his move to Aldersgate Street as the Civil War began and the lack of evidence of rapport with his younger son thereafter suggest a disruption. Indeed, might there have been sibling rivalry at work here? Christopher seems to follow his brother's educational experiences at first; with his entry into a legal career and his marriage, and John's Grand Tour and lack of employment for remuneration (although his teaching brought in some money), we may be observing a rearing up of cause for disjuncture. With the addition to that of political and apparently religious differences, the assumed happy relationship becomes less certain. Christopher's Royalism must have created contentions. Christopher's relationship with his son Thomas, particularly as contrasted with his relationship with his younger son Richard, implies possible political divergence as well, but more surely divergent religious practices, leading one to wonder about Christopher's acceptance by his father and his brother. (Thomas became a Clerk in Chancery well after the Restoration and through his uncle Thomas Agar, a Royalist; the position does not necessarily say anything about his political position. He did, however, continue to hold his office under William III.) The closeted Catholicism of Charles I and of Charles II may not be very different from Christopher's religious conduct, and the open avowal of James II seems to have allowed for Richard's, if not his father's, exercise of belief. Christopher's fortunes certainly seem to have taken a turn downward with the ascendency of William III. Parker's word "conversion" may be misleading: perhaps Christopher accepted some degree of Catholicism by around 1641–1643.

A further important relationship that smacks of a kind of opposition to John Milton is Christhopher's frequent legal connections with Richard Powell, the brother of Mary Powell Milton, who figures often in Milton's biography. We should note the citation of Richard's services to the Royalist cause and government, dated 1667, in British Library MS Egerton 2539, f. 101. He is also listed (as "Esquire") on a broadside, *A Declaration of the Nobility, Knights & Gentry of the County of Oxon Which have adhered to the late King* (28 April 1660).[95] On the other hand, "The examination of Wm. Griggs and Thos. Bradford [is] referred to Rich. Powell, a justice of peace for co. Middlesex, to deal with them; and Mr. Berners to acquaint Mr. Powell with this business" is one piece of late Commonwealth activity involving him on 15 September 1659 (*CSPD*, Commonwealth, 1659–60, XIII, 200). Josias Berners was a member of the Council of State.

Powell was a major member of the Inner Temple, often being cited along with Christopher. He was frequently a member of various committees of the Society, usually dealing with financial matters and building projects; see III, 20, 35, 36, 40, 42, 51, 60, 61 (2), 64, 69, 74–75, 77, 80 (two committees), 83. 84, 87–88 (2), 91, 93–94, 97, 100, 101, 103 (two items), 104, 113. These entries are dated from 10 January 1662/3 through 7 May 1677. He served as auditor and as Treasurer for the Society as well; see III, 47, 52 (three items), 71, 79, 112, 115–16, 118 (2), 119, 120 (2), 122 (2), 123, 124, 126, 127, 133, 141, 142 (he is indicated as the "last treasurer" to the House), 151 (two items). These activities are recorded from 3 November 1667 through 30 June 1679. He was also a member of Parliament of the Inner Temple as recorded on III, 85, 96, 105 (2), 106, 121 (2), 131, 241, 259, 272, 288, ranging from 10 June 1672 through the year 1691–92. Other evidence of his significance to the Inner Temple will be found on III, 20 (5 January 1662/3, the suspension of Ralph Hare for affronting Powell), 70 and 71 (his attendance on readers Richard Crooke and William Lister in 1670), 75 (when on 24 May 1671 he was chosen reader), 81 (regarding his reading), 86 (his request for special admission on 10 June 1672 for Richard Cooke, son of William Cooke), 89 (reference to work done for him), 144 (on the pulling down of his building, in accounts of 3 November 1678–4 November 1679). He is further referred to as Baron Powell on p. 306, 7 and 8 February 1693/4 and 26 April 1694. His political position toward impending governmental troubles may be suggested by payment of four shillings for a coach to take him to the Duke of Monmouth's, 3 November 1678–4 November 1679, III, 145.

Neither French nor Parker, it would seem, was aware of three letters from Milton's brother-in-law to Sir Joseph Williamson. Powell was involved in the division of land in Wildmore Fen to commoners and others but especially to the King; see *CSPD*, IV, 102–03 (5 December 1664) and 126 (31 December 1664). Both letters were sent from the Inner Temple. The third letter, dated 30 December 1678, from Hare Court, Inner Temple, reads: "I send herewith the book concerning the Dutch affair and a state of the case in writing with the objections answered. In the index some particulars of principal note are marked with a hand. My occasions hasten me to the country, where my stay will not be long. At my return I shall wait on you" (SP Dom, Car. II, 408, No. 110). Another letter from Sir William Coventry from the St. James Palace to Williamson, dated 14 June 1667 (*CSPD*, VII, 187), includes a note from Powell, "desiring the enclosure of a letter in Lord Arlington's packet to Lord Ambassador Coventry." Two references from 1670(?) appear in *CSPD*, X: for a lease in reversion of the Ashton manor as part jointure of the Queen (625), and a warrant concerning the survey of Windsor Forest includes a note for "Sir Rich. Powell to be added to the Commissioners" (635). (Thomas Agar, the son of Milton's brother-in-law's brother John, was appointed Surveyor of His Majesty's Woods and Forests in November 1664, continuing in this position until his death in August 1687; see chapter 2. The interconnections of the extended family should be constantly remembered.) Sir Robert Southwell refers to Powell in a letter to James, first Duke of Ormond, on 17 August 1678.[96]

Numerous citations in HMC, Thirteenth Report, Appendix, Part V, of the House of Lords MSS for 1690–1693, include Baron Powell from 22 October 1691 through 17 February 1692/3 (196, 197 [2], 198, 216, 262, 263, 293, 336, 447 [2], 490), and the Fourteenth Report, Appendix, Part VI (65), notes his work in connection with the Clandestine Mortgage Bill on 20 February 1691/2. Further citations occur in Part VI for 1692–93 (80, 90, 103, 104, 110, 255, 310, 352, from 17 February 1691/2 through 15 February 1692/ 3) and in Vol. I of the New Series, Part VI continued, for 1693–95 (41, 304, 318, 395, 411, 417, 452, 456, from 20 December 1693 through 25 January 1694/5). On 24 October 1695, p. 348, we learn that "Mr. Justice Rokeby is to be advanced to the court of King's Bench in place of Mr. Justice Eyres, deceased, and will be succeeded in the Common Pleas by Mr. Baron Powell; and Mr. Sergeant Powis, now a puisne judge of Chester, will be made a Baron in room of Baron Powell."[97] He had made his will in 1693 and it was proved in 1696. While John Milton was not involved in these affairs of Richard before his death, Richard did have much to do with other matters, and of course was important in the resolution of inheritances upon Milton's death. The Royalist adherence, as with Christopher, suggests little true friendship with John.

I might add a comment about Richard Powell's son, Richard, who was a member of the Inner Temple, noted in both French and Parker, but neither gives further information about him, and Parker in his index gives his death date as 1682, on what grounds I do not know. He was given special admission "at the request of his father, Powell of the bench," on 28 April 1667 (*Inner Temple Records*, III, 45), and was called to the bar on 26 November 1676 (III, 109–10). He is mentioned in his grandmother's will (Milton's mother-in-law) made on 24 October 1678 and proved on 6 November 1682. A warrant for a grant to Richard Powell of the Inner Temple, who is thus apparently Milton's nephew, from the Office of the King's attorney of Glamorganshire in the room of Richard Seys of Lincoln's Inn during pleasure was given from Hampton Court on 27 July 1682 (*CSPD*, Charles II, 1682), 315. Another warrant for a grant during pleasure to Robert Price of Lincoln's Inn of the Office of Attorney of Glamorganshire in the place of Richard Powell, deceased, was made from Whitehall on 15 February 1684 (*CSPD*, Charles II, October 1683-April 1684), p. 275.[98] (Glamorganshire is a county in southern Wales and numerous Powells appear in its records.)

Comment on John Milton's association with the Fleetwood family, a family evidencing the polar political camp of the times,[99] has paid some attention to Charles, as member of the Council of State and as general of the army, largely because of Milton's encomium in *Pro Populo Anglicano Defensio Secunda*, 157–58, but has generally ignored Colonel George Fleetwood, who was a regicide, a member of the Council of State, and knighted by Cromwell on 15 September 1656. This is a different branch of the family, located at Chalfont St. Giles. This George was son of Charles, who was son of Sir George of the Vache. He was baptised at Chalfont St. Giles on 15 February 1621/2. (Parker's index does not make distinctions amongst the Fleetwoods.) Interestingly, the cottage at Chalfont St. Giles was owned by Anne Fleetwood, George's daughter, and Thomas Ellwood, through whom Milton moved there during the visitation of the plague in London, was associated with the Fleetwoods. Ellwood, of course, had connections with nearby Old Jordans, a center of the Friends, and he and his family are buried there. According to Masson (VI, 98n) George, the regicide, was condemned in October 1660 but not executed. Instead he was ultimately released from prison and died in America. Yet despite General Charles and Colonel George, Sir Miles and Sir William, Martha Fleetwood Milton's grandfather and father, as well as other descendants of Sir Miles, were Royalist, as were many of those descended from Sir George of the Vache. Religiously, all seem to have been Protestant. One wonders, thus, about grandson George's treatment, which was ameliorated from that of others in similar position at the Restoration. Were Royalist factors involved in saving him just as they seem to be in the case of Charles, the former Major-General, and brother to Martha Fleetwood Milton? Do Christopher and his uncle Thomas Agar, avowed Royalists and officials, have something to do with such treatment of those, including Milton, who should have had every expectation of drastic sentences put upon them in 1660?

For John Milton, the upshot of all of this is an awareness of important Royalist connections, a possible significance for his escaping condemnation in the Act of Indemnity in 1660 and later release from prison (rather than only the action of Sir William Davenant and Andrew Marvell), and a questioning of his relationship with his brother Christopher and Christopher's family, particularly during the 1650s and 1660s. We have seen as well the significance for a rethinking of Milton's marriage to Mary Powell, of this alleged will, and his financial state. Our lack of evidence of John's connections with Christopher and his family during those periods may not be just the happenstance of nonreportage.

2

Thomas Agar

Royalist and Brother-in-Law

1

One of the complications of John Milton's biography, to repeat, is his being so eminent a "Puritan."[1] The first blatant problem is that "Puritan" is basically a religious term, even if it does define some social and political position as against "Cavalier" and "Royalist." These terms, too, the latter especially, do often bring in added meanings of a religious category, what comes to be called Anglicanism, in their wake, even if unjustifiably. "Puritan" does not equate with "Parliamentarian," although the terms have been used interchangeably by some. Chapter 1 detailed Milton's brother Christopher and his family's life with comments concerning the issue of "Royalist" and Roman Catholicism, and chapter 4 will explore the political tendencies of his nephew John Phillips (with necessary examination of the life of the older brother Edward Phillips in chapter 3). The matter of "Puritan" or "Anglican" raises other concerns, of course.

Milton had many Royalist connections, familial and otherwise; the records indicate more than have previously been noted and examined. One area of such Royalist relationships, which predicates many others not previously investigated, is the forebears, connection, and activities of his brother-in-law Thomas Agar. Agar's monument in Temple Church, London, is testimony to his loyalty to the Royalist cause. The inscription praises his fidelity to his office of Deputy Clerk of the Crown, to the Church of England, and to his king. "Thomas Agar, Viri verè Generosi, à suis, ab amicis, & ab egenis desideratissimi. Qui cum in Cancellaria Officium Clerici Coronæ multos annos suma cum Industria & probitate exercuisset, Ecclesiæ Anglicanæ & causis Regiis, semper addictissimus, mortalitatem exuit firma fide, & spe beatæ Resurrectionis, primo die Nov. An. Sal. humanæ MDCLXXIII. Ætat. suæ LXXVI. Arms; Argent a chevron ingrailed Gules, bet[n] 3 Boars Heads couped sable."[2] Certainly his political and governmental

connections had bearing upon Milton's fortunes in governmental and financial arenas, and probably specifically in 1660, when the monarchy returned. Yet the term Royalist, however convenient, does not convey fully the
significance of the role Thomas Agar played in Milton's life. There is also
the more subtle impact arising not so much from Agar's Royalist leanings,
although connected with them, as from money, family, occupation, and class.
It will be shown that Agar was no mere average citizen with respect to property. His family was distinguished, if not eminent. Descended from the landed
gentry, he was always designated as a gentleman, and he was entitled to bear
arms, as his monument shows. His immediate family and descendants maintained and perhaps even improved this social position. He participated in
the community of lawyers, from which were drawn many powerful men. Yet,
for all his importance, Agar's role in Milton's life has been neglected, no
doubt because he was a Royalist. The intention of this chapter is to present
evidence of the maze of social, political, and governmental connections that
the relationship with Agar brought to Milton. Further investigation of the
Royalist world in which Milton was enmeshed is charted by the numerous
roads suggested herein.

Little has been added to what we know about Thomas Agar since Masson's
account, which offers these bare facts and suppositions. He was said to have
been educated at St. Paul's School, somewhat before the time Milton was
there.[3] He became the "intimate friend" and co-worker of Edward Phillips,
Anne Milton's husband, in the Crown Office in Chancery. When Phillips
died in August 1631, Agar succeeded him as Deputy Clerk of the Crown.
Masson infers that at this time he was married to Mary, daughter of Dr. Thomas Rugeley, a highly esteemed London physician, for she seems to have
been alive in 1633, by which time she had borne a daughter named Ann(e).
Mary then having died at a later uncertain date, Agar married Anne Milton
Phillips before 1637, when we find Thomas and his brother John Agar witnessing John Milton, Sr.'s affidavit, sworn to at Horton on 13 April 1637,
that he is too infirm to attend Court in Westminster on Sir Thomas Cotton's
bill. Anne and Thomas Agar's first child, Mary, had been born by this time;
another daughter Ann followed at some uncertain date. Masson supposes
that since Agar as Deputy Clerk of the Crown had to be in frequent attendance on the Lord Keeper of the Seal and Lord High Chancellor, the family
probably lived in the area of the Crown Office in London. The High Court
of Chancery was in Westminster Hall, next to the King's Bench, in
Westminster. The Phillipses lived in this area, on the Strand near Charing
Cross in the parish of St. Martin's in the Fields, and possibly the home was
maintained after Anne's marriage to Agar. Despite his first wife's death, Agar

continued his association with the Rugeleys, as is indicated by his will, and Milton will have come to know the Rugeleys through Agar. From 1639 onward, let it be noted, Agar's holograph appears in numerous entries of administration of oaths by the Clerk and the Deputy Clerk of the Crown. Receipts signed by him in 1640 and 1641 are found in British Library MS Additional 5756, ff. 128 and 131.

Although Edward and John Phillips, Agar's stepsons, were assigned to Milton's care as the civil conflict neared, there is no reason to suppose that there was any break between the Agars and the Miltons. (See chapter 3 for discussion of Milton's "foster" parenthood.) True, Agar was a Royalist, as is evident by his losing his office during the ascendency of the Cromwellian government and his recovering that office upon the Restoration. There may have been a coolness between Agar and John Milton because of political thinking, but not necessarily more than that between Milton and his brother Christopher, another Royalist and in Royalist employ, as recorded in the previous chapter. When the Restoration did come, Agar may have been one of those who were most anxious about Milton's fate and most relieved by his escape. Perhaps through his governmental position and contacts, he contributed to assure that Milton's treatment did not endanger his brother-in-law. It is clear that Agar's contact with the Milton family continued until his death. Thomas Milton, son of Christopher, as remarked also in the previous chapter, was taken into the Crown Office under his uncle and succeeded him on the latter's death in 1673. Agar's will, dated 10 June 1671, in which he styled himself "Thomas Agar, of London, gentleman," bequeathed £200 to Edward Phillips, for purchasing an annuity or bettering his employment, Phillips to be guided in this attempt by Agar's nephew Thomas Agar (son of John Agar), who, the will tells us, bore much love for his stepcousin. Notably Agar left nothing to John Phillips. The will gives further indications of the fates of the various members of the family. Anne Milton Phillips Agar was then dead, Masson supposing the date of her death to be nearer 1671 than 1637. Mary, her daughter, had died very young, and Mary Rugeley Agar's children, Mary and Anne, must also have died long before. Agar's only natural heir was his and Milton's sister's daughter Anne Agar Moore, wife of David Moore, of Chertsey, Surrey, and mother of an infant son Thomas. Agar pointedly excluded his son-in-law from any control over his wife's inheritance. Leaving £1000 and the income from two houses to his daughter, he appointed his nephew Thomas Agar as residuary legatee and executor. To his dear brother Dr. [Luke] Rugeley, whose love and kindness to himself and his relations he could not repay, he left twenty "broad gold pieces." Agar's will was proved 5 November 1673 by his nephew.[4]

2

Little can be discovered in published records about Thomas Agar's immediate antecedents or early history. He first emerges into history in London. His father was Thomas Agar, member of the Inner Temple in November 1613, from London, who died before 1636, according to the Middle Temple records. However, in view of the fact that the Miltons owned property in Bread Street at this time, and in view of the fact that no other Agars are recorded in the parish of All Hallows, Bread Street, the following burial entry, dated 23 November 1637, is of great interest: "in the Chancell, Thomas Agar of this p[ar]ish."[5] If the Middle Temple records inaccurately report Thomas Agar, Sr.'s death date, then it appears that this burial record refers to him, an important possibility since his son Thomas was by then a member of the Milton family by marriage, but even more significant, as Edward Jones has pointed out to me, is the fact that on this burial date of 23 November 1637 Milton was in London (rather than in Horton) and wrote a letter to his friend Charles Diodati. The coincidence of his brother-in-law's father's burial and his having travelled to London to be there on that same day provides almost certain proof of the date of the father's death. The letter is No. 7 in the 1674 *Epistolarum Familiarium,* 17–20, and in it Milton reports, "seriously," that he is thinking of migrating into one of the Inns of Court. While the senior Agar is listed in the Middle Temple records and said to be of the Inner Temple, there is no published record of his admission to any of the four Inns of Court. Yet through such connection as the father had, Milton may have expected to be able to find this "more convenient habitation among a number of companions." No record of Thomas, Jr.'s birth has been located in published documents. As his monument in Temple Church gives his age as seventy-six on 1 November 1673, he was born in or around 1597. He had a younger brother, John, an attorney, who will be discussed later.

Upon first examination of the published records, the task of determining the antecedents of those three London Agars seems insuperable, since Agars turn up in the records, either as residents or property holders at some time, in at least nineteen counties. However, one happy fact narrows the area of possibility; that is, Agar's monument bears his coat of arms as given before. These arms also appear on the monument in St. Anne's, Westminster, of his nephew Thomas Agar.[6] Records of visitations reveal two major Agard family lines of some prominence, the Agars or Agards of Yorkshire and the Agards of Derbyshire. The difference in the spelling of the name seems to be inconsequential since the records ignore the difference and since the subject of this chapter himself is once styled "Thos. Agard."[7]

The Yorkshire line can, in all probability, be eliminated from consideration. During the visitation of 1665 these Agards showed no arms; they were granted a respite.[8] When an eighteenth-century descendant of the line, a Benjamin Preston, assumed the name of Agar, his arms were: "Arg., a chev. gu. between three boars' heads, erased, sa."[9] That this coat of arms and that of Thomas Agar differ in two respects suggests that he was not directly connected with the Yorkshire line. The arms and crest of the Yorkshire line connect it with Lancashire Agards.[10] Moreover, no connection of any kind can be made between Thomas and the Yorkshire Agards, either according to genealogical charts[11] or according to the listing of the six Yorkshire Agars as members of Gray's Inn during the seventeenth century.[12] In fact, since the Yorkshire line began with John of Stockton, who died about 1636, it offers no place for Thomas Agar except for the possibility that his father may have been an unrecorded brother of John of Stockton.

The story of the Derbyshire line is provocative, although slightly inconclusive. Dugdale reported the arms of this line, both the Foston and the Sudbury branches, to be, in 1662, exactly those of Thomas Agar, except that the chevron was not engrailed.[13] However, there is disagreement about the arms of the Derbyshire Agards. Burke reports that the Foston branch, the main line, bore arms exactly like those of Thomas Agar, and that the Sudbury branch had arms as reported by Dugdale with a fleur-de-lis, or for a difference, designating a sixth son. Joseph Tilley agrees with Burke.[14] The error in Dugdale's report can be accounted for: as will be shown later, the Agard who supplied Dugdale with the Agard lineage was a member of the Sudbury branch, who had inherited Foston through a failure of the main line, and so recorded the arms of his branch of the family. Despite the almost sure connection between Thomas Agar of London and the Derbyshire Agards seated at Foston, genealogical reconstructions do not provide the specific point of contact. The search, nevertheless, does not end here. Some of the Derbyshire Agards settled in neighboring Staffordshire; in fact, some of those listed in the charts given by Dugdale as decendants of the Derbyshire line were indeed resident in Staffordshire. A record of a visitation to Staffordshire in 1583 lists three Agards—George of Barton, William of Dunstall, and Humphrey of Newborough—to be summoned, and gives the Agard arms as reported by Dugdale; that is, actually the arms of the Sudbury line.[15] Unfortunately, no report of these families appears in the records of any visitation. That these were originally Sudbury Agards does not preclude the probability that Foston Agards had contacts and even at a later date lived in the county. The significance of this branching of the family into Staffordshire is that this is the same county in which the Rugeleys, the family into which Thomas Agar first married, figured prominently, and the parish of Tatenhill, where Barton and Dunstall were located, was the same parish in which the Rugeleys owned a manor, Callingwood.[16]

The records of Staffordshire are rife with the activities of the Agards, both of Derbyshire and of Staffordshire. The following is a highly selective record of their possible and actual contacts with the Rugeleys, with whom Dr. Thomas Rugeley, the London physician and Thomas Agar's first father-in-law, was directly and closely connected. The Agards first appear in available records involved in Staffordshire when Walter Agard of Foston was sued by William de Ridware in a land dispute in 1272.[17] A Nicholas Agard was owner of holdings in Newborough and Annesley in 20 Edward IV[18] (1480–81) and probably was the same Nicholas who owned land in Tatenhill in 1494.[19] Another Nicholas Agard was apparently established at Dunstall from 1496 to 1508, when he served as justice of the peace.[20] From about 1504 to 1515, Ralph Agard laid claim to holdings in King's Bromley.[21] Agard lands in King's Bromley passed from Francis to William Agard near the end of the sixteenth century. A Rydgeley was then one of William's free tenants.[22] Both William "Agerr" and Thomas Rugeley acted as the Queen's bailiffs and collectors of rents for Staffordshire manors that had come into Elizabeth I's hands on the attainder of Thomas, Lord Paget, for high treason.[23] The Rugeleys and the Agards came into more direct contact than mere propinquity when both Humphrey Agard of Newborough, gentleman, and William Rydgeley of Smallwood, esquire, sat as jurors for the Liberty of the Duchy of Lancaster, the name of Agard immediately preceding that of Rydgeley on the jury list.[24] Before this time, the two families had become involved in land transactions. In 4 and 5 Philip and Mary (1557–58) Clement Agard, armiger, seated at Foston, and Eleanor his wife remitted all rights in lands in Rolston and Barton, Staffordshire, for £130 to Roland Ruggeley, armiger, and his heirs.[25] This Roland was the grandfather of the Richard Rugeley who later settled the claims on his inheritance of Thomas Rugeley, the London physician and Agar's father-in-law. The same Clement Agard brought a suit in chancery against the same Roland over property in Rolston and Tatenhill in 1561.[26] Finally, the Richard Rugeley, armiger, involved in property settlements with Dr. Thomas Rugeley, was a participant in a land transaction with George Agard, gentleman, and Henry Agard, gentleman, among others, in 43 Elizabeth I (1600–01).[27] George Agard was no doubt George of Newborough, the third son of Clement above, and brother of William, seated at Foston. Henry Agard was the son and heir of William, and the Henry Agard appointed high sheriff of Derbyshire in 1615[28] and created knight on 28 August 1617.[29] The conjunction of the London Rugeleys and Agars and the Staffordshire-Derbyshire Agards and Staffordshire Rugeleys cannot be merely fortuitous. Logic dictates that the former grew out of the latter. Hence, it is certain that Thomas Agar was a descendant of the Staffordshire-Derbyshire Agards. Furthermore, although it is possible that the record of his birth may be hidden in yet unpublished London parish registers, it is also possible that it may be hidden in the yet unpublished parish register of Derbyshire or Staffordshire, especially in those of the parish of Tatenhill, Staffordshire.

The Agards of Derbyshire-Staffordshire were an old and rather distinguished family of the landed gentry. The pedigree recorded by Dugdale in 1662 begins with Thomas Agard, living 1310, and his sons, John de Sudbury and Thomas de Foston, the family seat. Yet unpublished records in the Egerton and Harleian manuscripts indicate that the family began much earlier. The pedigrees give five generations before Walter Agard, living during the years 1275–1294, commencing with Richard Agard de Foston.[30] The Agards were early holders of extensive lands in Derbyshire and Staffordshire. Foston and Scropton nearby were held by Henry de Ferrers at the time of the Domesday Survey (1086), but soon passed into the hands of the Agards, almost immediately after the compilation of the Domesday Book.[31] These lands were held by the family until they were sold by John Agard of Sapperton, the last of his line, to Richard Bate in 1665[32] or 1675.[33] It is not clear when Sudbury came into the family's hands. There is a record, dated 17 July 12 Edward IV (1472), of a quarrel between the Montgomeries and Nicholas Agard of Sudbury over title to various lands, including the manor of Sudbury.[34] That the quarrel was settled in favor of the Agards is suggested by the fact that the John Agard who endowed a chantry for souls at the church of Scropton in 1515 is spoken of as John Agard of Foston and Sudbury.[35] No available records indicate when this holding left the family's possession. It is not included in a list of the Agard lands in 1634.[36] Other major holdings were at Boylestone, acquired during the reign of Elizabeth I[37] and still held in 1634,[38] and at Sapperton, finally sold by John Agard to Richard Bate in 1665.[39] These by no means exhaust the list of Agard properties, which are too extensive for citation.

The status of the family is also indicated by its intermarriages and the offices held by some of its members. For example, the family was connected by marriage with the Vernons of Haddon, the Ferrers of Walton and Tamworth,[40] with the Irelands of Yeldresley,[41] and with the Stanhopes of Elvaston.[42] A Thomas Acard is listed as a member of Parliament for the borough of Derby in the twenty-ninth Parliament, reign of Henry VI.[43] The family also produced Arthur Agard, born 1540, died 22 August 1615, of Foston and Sapperton, one of the first and most active members of the Society of Antiquaries and one of the Deputy Chamberlains of the Exchequer, where he served for about forty-five years. He was a younger son of Clement of

Foston, by Eleanor, daughter of Thomas Middleborough of Egbaston, Warwickshire. He matriculated as a sizar in 1553 at Queen's College, Cambridge, but there is no record of his having received a degree. He was educated to the law[44] and apparently entered the Exchequer Office about 1570. He enjoyed a long friendship with Sir Robert Cotton and at least association with such antiquarians as Sir Francis Leigh, Francis Thynne, Sir John Savile, Sir James Whitelocke, James Ley, Michael Heneage, Sir Walter Cope, William Camden, and John Selden. His historical researches in manuscript are housed in the Bodleian Library and the British Library. He was buried under the cloisters, just by the Chapter House, Westminster Abbey.[45]

Another eminent member of the family was Francis (d. 1577) of King's Bromley, Staffordshire; Foston, Derbyshire; and Grange Gorman, Dublin, Ireland. He was a privy councillor in Ireland, an Irish member of Parliament, Treasurer of the Irish Mint in 1548, and secretary to Sir Henry Sydney, Lord Deputy of Ireland. His eldest daughter and heir Mabel married William Agard of Foston, and his second daughter Cecilia married Sir Henry Harrington.[46] John Agard of Foston served as sheriff of Staffordshire in 1640.[47] Three Agards of Foston served as sheriffs for Derbyshire: Henry in 1616–17, John in 1639–40, and Charles in 1660–61. The last named was probably the Charles Agard listed as one of the "Persons who were fit and qualified to be made Knights of the Royal Oak" in 1660, his estate being valued at £2000.[48] Henry was knighted in August 1617. By 1660, however, the Agard house and estate was nearing its end. In 1634, the surviving eldest son of Foston, Sir Henry, arranged in a settlement with his brother John, who had just married Mary Adderley, that the family lands, then in Sir Henry's possession, would pass to his brother John and his eldest son if Sir Henry himself should fail of male issue. This eventuality came to pass. Sir Henry died in or before 1636 and his brother John came into possession. John also failed of male issue. When he died between 1652 and 1657, the family estate passed to a distant Staffordshire cousin and descendant of the Sudbury line, who became Charles of Foston.[49] His son John was the last male of his line. His heiress married John Stanhope of Elvaston, from whom descended the Earls of Harrington. John sold his holdings.[50]

The evidence suggests that the Foston Agards were Royalists, although the degree of their enthusiasm cannot be determined. On 9 April 1652, John Agard of Foston asked that the Committee for Compounding grant him a certificate that he had never been sequestered in England, the Revenue Commissioners for Ireland having seized and sequestered his estate there on information that he had been sequestered in England. The certificate was granted.[51] Charles Agard, the sheriff of Derbyshire in 1661, was named one of the commissioners to seize for His Majesty's use two-thirds of the property of recusants in Staffordshire on 6 March 1674/5 and in Derbyshire on 22 July 1675.[52] Interestingly, another Agard, Henry of Dunstall, Tatenhill, Staffordshire, a descendant of the Sudbury line, served as clerk for the Committee of Stafford on the Parliamentary side. One of his orders, dated 1646, survives among the Royalist Composition Papers.[53] At this point, the Agards and the Rugeleys again come together, for Simon Rugeley of Hawksyard and Callingwood, the latter in the parish of Tatenhill, was one of the leading members of that committee.[54]

Thomas Agar's first father-in-law, Dr. Thomas Rugeley, supplied the king's heralds in 1633 with a record of his ancestry. His father was Simon Rugeley "of Hakesyard, sonne & heire" of Simon Rugeley "of Hakesyard neere Rugely in com. Stafford a 2 sonn out of the house of Hawksyard."[55] The Rugeleys, like the Agards, were a family of antiquity and distinction. Their arms were "Argent, a chevron between three roses Gules." The grandfather of Dr. Thomas Rugeley was the younger brother of the Thomas of Hawksyard who died in 1552; his son Simon was a cousin of the Thomas who was the last of his line; and the London physician was a second cousin of Mary, daughter of the last named Thomas and wife of Richard Rugeley, esquire, of Shenstone and Callingwood.[56] In 1618, the claimants to the Staffordshire lands arranged a property settlement. First, Dr. Thomas Rugeley and his wife Anne, deforciants, remitted all rights in property in Longdon, for which Richard and Mary Rugeley, complainants, paid them £120. Second, Richard and Mary Rugeley, deforciants, granted to Dr. Thomas Rugeley, complainant, manors in "Callengwood, Coxall, Rudloe, Knightley, Tatenell, and Dunstall" to be held by Thomas Rugeley for twenty-one years, rendering 12d. yearly to Richard and Mary and their heirs, for which Thomas gave them £200. Third, Dr. Thomas Rugeley, deforciant of the manor of Hawksyard and property in "Hansaker, Armitage, King's Bromley, Rugeley, Longdon, Brereton, Amerton, Newton, Norton super Cannoke, Kingston, Calohill, Alrewas, Frodeley, Stretehay, and Norton Caynes," remitted all rights to the complainants, Richard Rugeley, Mary his wife, and Katherine Aspinall, Mary's widowed sister, and to the heirs of Richard, for which the complainants gave him £400.[57]

Richard of Hawksyard and Shenstone died in 1623. His son and heir Simon, born in 1598 since he was reported to be sixteen in 1614,[58] married in 1621 Jane Skipwith of Dishley Thorpe, Leicestershire,[59] or Jane, daughter of Henry Skipworth of Leicestershire. He served as undersheriff of Staffordshire in 19, 20 Charles I (1643–44), but joined the Parliamentary side in the Civil War.[60] He was a leading member of the Committee of Stafford and served as an important colonel in the Parliamentary army. He saw the de-

cline of a once flourishing family and had no issue. He first mortgaged and
then sold Hawksyard to Sir Richard Skeffington.[61] He retired to Callingwood
and was buried in Tatenhill in 1665.[62]

There are various records in the Council of State Proceedings mentioning Colonel Simon Rugeley (as well as two letters among the manuscripts of
the Earl of Egmont), but one specific item attests to the financial and personal problems that people encountered during the Civil Wars. There is a
petition to the Protector (Oliver Cromwell) dated 13 February 1654 (*CSPD*,
Commonwealth, 1653–54, 398–99) discussing his estate and asking for discharge of the debt owed him: He "was led by conscience to be amongst the
first on the Parliament side," he writes, clearly telling us of the potential
schism in family attitudes and adherences that would seem to have been
frequent. He gave monies to the Parliamentary side, and his estate, being in
Royalist area, was sequestered by them; further his two years as high sheriff, "a
chargeable and dangerous service," added to his debt. "I have twice petitioned
Parliament, but you being now raised up in their stead, my dead hopes are
revived," and attached are various statements from various people concerning the validity of his claims of such debts (dated from 3 October 1642 through
1643, 1645, 1648, and 17 November 1653). The lack of Parliamentary action
is to be noted, as well as the implied controlling status that the Protectorship
enjoyed. Action was taken on the petition to Cromwell on 8 May 1654 (*CSPD*,
Commonwealth, 1654, 154): entered is an "order granting him 3546/5/9 due
on public faith and 4454/15/11 for personal services."[63]

3

Thomas Rugeley, Agar's father-in-law, was born in or before 1576, since he is
reported as dying as an octogenarian in 1656. Educated at St. John's, Cambridge, he received his B.A. in 1596/7, his M.A. in 1600, and his M.D. in
1608.[64] On 6 February 1607/8, listed as M.A. of Newark-on-Trent,
Nottinghamshire, he and Anne, daughter of Gabriel Odingsells, esquire, of
Epperstone, the same county, were granted a license to marry.[65] Two days
later they were married at Epperstone. About a year later their first child
John was baptized.[66] This son did not survive since he is not listed as a son in
the pedigree devised by Dr. Rugeley in 1633. In this pedigree, Dr. Rugeley
listed as sons Thomas, Luke, and George, and an only daughter Mary, who
was married to "Thomas Agar gent." and was the mother of "Anne only
dau'r." Since Thomas Rugeley was twenty in 1633, he was born in 1613. Luke
was born in 1615 or 1616, according to the records that he was eighteen in
1633[67] and in his eighty-first year in September 1697.[68] He was born in Newark, Nottinghamshire.[69] Thomas and Luke were Royalists with many inter-

connections with the aristocracy, but no records with respect to George have been located. One may only speculate about Mary's date of birth. Since she was already a mother in 1633, it seems unlikely that she was born after 1615 or 1616. The greatest likelihood is that she was born between 1609 and 1613; evidence points to her place of birth also as Newark. No confirmation of the place and date of birth of any of the Rugeley children is offered since the birth records of Nottinghamshire have not been published.

At an uncertain date, Dr. Rugeley moved to London; he later resided in the parish of St. Michael, Bassishaw.[70] In June 1617, he was admitted a candidate of the Royal College of Physicians, the King recommended him as a Fellow in 1621 (HMC, Eighth Report, Part I, / 229), and he became a Fellow on 28 November 1622. He was Censor in 1628 and 1633 and was chosen an Elect 2 September 1641; he resigned that office 24 May 1642. He died 22 June 1656 and was buried two days later in St. Botolph, Aldersgate. He was famed not only as a physician but also as a musician.[71] It is worth noting that his musical interests may have brought him in contact with John Milton, Sr., before the Agar-Phillips connection. Two of his sons (Agar's brothers-in-law) were at Cambridge during the years that Milton was also there (1628–32), which also suggests a relationship before Agar married Anne, since Agar knew and worked with Edward Phillips at this time. The eldest Rugeley son, Thomas, matriculated as a pensioner from Queen's, Cambridge, in 1628.[72] Available records say no more of him, unless he was the Thomas Rudgley who married Jane Dele on 8 May 1652 at St. Bartholomew-by-the Exchange. Luke enjoyed more celebrity. Having acquired his preparatory education in a London private school under Mr. Bell, he was admitted to Catherine Hall, Cambridge, on 14 May 1631 and became a pensioner at Christ's 28 March 1633 at the age of eighteen.[73] He received from Cambridge his B.A. in 1634/ 5, his M.A. in 1638, and his M.D. in 1646. He was admitted a candidate of the Royal College of Physicians 2 November 1649 and became a Fellow on 24 September 1653. He was well known as a medical doctor. He died in his house in Bloomsbury Square in 1697, in his eighty-first year.[74] *A Catalogue of Theological, Philosophical, Historical, Philological, Medicinal & Chymical Books,* from the bookseller John Bullord in 1697(?), offered three of Milton's books that Dr. Luke Rugeley owned: *Epistolarium Familiarium, Paradise Lost, Paradise Regain'd,* 10, 38, 40, as well as Joseph Jane's *Eikon Aklastos,* 48. Little is known of Mary. In view of her presumed date of birth, her marriage to Thomas Agar probably took place no earlier than 1625. It can now be shown that she had died by 5 January 1632, which corroborates the implication in the entry in the 1633 pedigree that called Anne her *only* daughter.

Masson assumed that Mary Rugeley Agar was alive in 1633 and that Thomas Agar married the widow Anne Milton Phillips some time between 1633

and 1637. This dating is inaccurate. In the parish register of St. Dunstan in
the East, London, under marriages appears the entry "Thomas Agar & Anna
Phillips," dated 5 January 1631/2.[75] Agar succeeded Edward Phillips as Deputy
Clerk of the Crown but also as husband and father. Aside from the obvious
benefits of this marriage to a woman recently widowed and burdened with
young children, there was the gain in social position for her and the Miltons.
True, her second husband occupied the same post in the government as
had her first husband, but, as the history of the Agards and the Rugeleys
shows, Thomas Agar's antecedents and connections were ancient, proper-
tied, and of gentle birth.

The new Agar household in January 1632 consisted of Thomas Agar
and his second wife Anne; her two children from her first marriage, Edward
and John Phillips; and Agar's child by his first wife, Anne. The second Mrs.
Agar was to bear two daughters, Mary and Anne.[76] In the parish records of
Kensington appears the following baptismal entry, dated 10 October 1632,
"Mary d. of Mr Thomas & An Egar of Brumpton."[77] Anne's probable year of
birth can be established indirectly through her age given in her marriage
license as twenty-six on 29 December 1662,[78] which yields 1636 as her year of
birth. Thomas Agar is recorded as of St. Sepulchre in this marriage license.
In 1669 he was plaintiff against Tobias Goodwin and Anne, his wife, over
property in St. Sepulchre without Newgate, London, Middlesex.[79] Mary died
very young, and Anne was still living in 1694 according to Edward Phillips
(vii). Anne, the daughter of Mary Rugeley Agar, had died before 1671, the
date of her father's will, and logically in or before 1636 when Milton's niece
of the same name was born. Perhaps she was "Mrs. Anna Eager" buried at St.
Martin in the Fields on 13 November 1633[80] or possibly nine-year-old "Ann
Agor" buried 8 October 1636 as recorded in the parish register of St. Botolph,
Bishopsgate.[81] If the latter, she was born between October 1626 and October 1627, or October 1627 and October 1628 (depending upon the meaning of "nine-year-old"). In this case, Thomas Agar and Mary Rugeley were
married by January 1626-January 1628, a time range that tallies with Mary's
having been born between 1609 and 1613, and allows for the birth of their
first child, Mary, who died before 1633. If "Ann Agor" was Agar's daughter,
then his and Milton's sister's daughter Anne was born in October-Decem-
ber 1636 and probably given the same name in remembrance.

4

Perhaps more important to the Milton-Agar relationship than private family
affairs was the influence of the social position, wealth, and political connections of the Agar family and the governmental post of Thomas Agar upon

Milton's political fortunes. These connections of the Agars during the relevant period, the middle decades of the seventeenth century, must therefore be established. Much can be learned from an examination of Agar's
contemporary family and his immediate descendants, even though some of
what follows deals with events after the death of the protagonists.

A John Agar was associated with a Thomas Agar in 1630 when they drew
up a will for Thomas Harding and then were sued by Awdry Harding.[82] That
John Agar was Thomas's younger brother appears from the fact that Thomas's
nephew Thomas, named in his uncle's will, is listed as the eldest son of John
Agar of the Middle Temple.[83] John was admitted to the Middle Temple as
the second son of Thomas Agar of the Inner Temple, deceased, on 28 May
1636.[84] He became an attorney at common pleas.[85] He and Thomas witnessed
a writ for John Milton, Sr., in the Cotton case on 10 March 1636/7.[86] He was
sufficiently intimate with the Miltons to be present at Horton during the
period of mourning for Sara Milton, who had died there 3 April 1637. The
evidence of the Agars' presence is that they witnessed the signing of John
Milton, Sr., in his answer to the Bill of Complaint of Sir Thomas Cotton on
13 April 1637,[87] and at this time John Milton, Sr., was at Horton according to
an affidavit of Christopher Milton, dated 1 April 1637, stating that his father
was too infirm and of too great age to travel from Horton to Westminster (as
recorded in the previous chapter). This answer of 13 April was received and
endorsed in London on 6 May 1637 "per John Agar gen. . . . Com."

At some date before 1641 John Agar, married Susan, the daughter of
"Thomas" Squire, a preacher at St. Leonard, Shoreditch.[88] This was John
Squire, who was vicar at St. Leonard's. His son, John Agar's brother-in-law,
became rector of Barnes and died 9 January 1663. (See Parker, 810 n61.)
John had acquired a second residence at Barnes, Surrey, by 9 November
1641, the day upon which his eldest son Thomas was baptized in the parish
church.[89] Since Thomas is called the eldest son, John Agar must have had
other surviving sons. He may also have fathered at least three daughters
since his son Thomas refers in his will to his sisters Wyatt, Honor, and Mary.[90]
Records of these other sons and daughters have not been located. References to petitions at the Middle Temple about John Agar's lodgings and
references to his building in Essex Court appear in the records for 20 January 1641/2, 25 June 1652, 2 July 1652, 15 November 1653, 5 May 1654, 22
June 1655, 11 November 1656, 24 June 1657, and 26 and 30 June 1658.[91] He
gave up his lodgings in Brick Court on 26 June 1658.[92] From this combined
evidence, it appears that John Agar removed from the Middle Temple in
1642, possibly to live in Barnes, Surrey, then returned to the Middle Temple
in 1652 to continue until June 1658, when he retired to Barnes. The ten-
year hiatus paralleling the worst of the civil conflict, suggests that John Agar

was a Royalist. A petition of Thomas Willys and Mr. John Agar for a pass to go to Ashe in Hampshire (House of Lords Journal, VI, 557) is dated 17 March 1644, and a Warrant from the Council of State and Admiralty Committee "For John Ager, and Rich. Guilford, his servant (described), beyond seas," dated 16 October 1651, if he is the same person, fills in some of the time and the reason for a lack of records, and suggests something about his political leanings. (See *CSPD*, Commonwealth, III, 535; see also chapter 1, n24.) A number of references to him appear in the records of Surrey from midsummer 1661 to January 1664, two of which are records of fines imposed on him for failure to keep the highway and his wharf from Barnes to Mortlake in good repair.[93] The extent of his holdings is shown by the hearth tax list of 1664, wherein he is listed as having in Barnes one dwelling with thirteen hearths and six empty tenements with twenty hearths.[94] John Agar died around May 1671 and was buried at Barnes,[95] his will being proved in 1671.[96]

Thomas, his son and the favored nephew of Thomas Agar, the Deputy Clerk of the Crown, was admitted to Gray's Inn on 26 February 1657/8;[97] transferred almost immediately to the Middle Temple, entering 30 June 1658,[98] four days after his father's leaving; matriculated at Queen's College, Oxford, on 31 July 1658; was created M.A. 9 September 1661;[99] and was called to the bar in the Middle Temple on 27 November 1663.[100] References to his lodgings in the Middle Temple appear in the records for 21 June 1661, 28 June 1661, 6 June 1662, 13 June 1662, 28 October 1670, 27 January 1670/1, and 18 June 1675.[101] At the age of twenty-three, Thomas Agar, together with John Madden, was appointed on 23 November 1664 Surveyor of His Majesty's Woods and Forest on the south side of the River Trent,[102] an office of heavy and complicated responsibility since it involved the management of the royal forests with respect to preservation, felling, and sale of timber to raise money for royal projects, supplying timber for the English navy, negotiations with various Royal Commissions, especially the Commissioners of the Navy, the institution and management of iron works, and the disbursement and collection of large sums of money to employees, contractors, etc. Thomas Agar held this position under Charles II and James II until his death. The extent of the responsibility and importance of this post is attested by the size of his outstanding account with the Exchequer upon his death, £33,042.[103] A letter to Viscount Hatton requests "a good buck killed for his fee, as Surveyor-General of His Majesty's Woods, South of the Tweed," on 4 September 1684.[104] He also served, according to the inscription on his monument, which bears his arms, as Carver in Ordinary to Catherine, Queen Dowager of England.[105]

This Thomas Agar married twice, but no record of his first marriage has been found. As a widower and resident of the Middle Temple, he was issued a license to marry "Mary Bolles, of St. Clement Danes, Middlesex, spinster, about twenty-two, her parents dead—at St. Martin-in-the-Fields, or the chapel of Clarendon House, in said parish," on 8 June 1674.[106] Mary Bolles was the daughter of Sir Robert Bolles of Scampton, Lincolnshire, baronet, and Mary, daughter of Sir Edward Hussey of Huntington, Lincolnshire, baronet.[107] She was born on 9 October 1648 and baptized at Scampton on 19 October. Her father, Sir Robert, died in August 1663, leaving Mary £1500. "Sir Robert was one of the Grand Jury for trying the Regicides at Hick's Hall in 1660."[108] Her great-grandfather was Sir George Bolles of London, sheriff of London in 1608 and Lord Mayor of London in 1617,[109] who was buried at St. Swithin in 1621.[110] The records indicate no surviving issue for Thomas Agar. In his will, wherein he styled himself "Thomas Agar of the Middle Temple, London, Esq., now living in Gerard Street in S. Anne, Westminster," dated 4 February 1686/7, he mentions no children. He directs that all real estate in Barnes, Surrey, be sold to pay a mortgage on some lands in Barnes of £420 held by Mr. Thompson, this being an old debt of his father. He designates his wife as legatee and executrix. He died 27 August 1687, aged forty-five, and was buried in St. Anne's, Westminster. His will was proved 10 November 1687 by his widow.[111] He was not knighted as was once reported.[112]

One may gain some conception of Thomas Agar's position and property from the fact of his second marriage to a baronet's daughter—two degrees above his own position in the class hierarchy—and an heiress of a Royalist family. More striking still as evidence of the Royalist favor he enjoyed was his appointment at the age of twenty-three to a position of trust and responsibility as Surveyor of His Majesty's Woods and Forests in 1664. Either he had at this time more friends at court than the record shows or his uncle Thomas Agar wielded more influence in the government or among Royalists than his post of Deputy Clerk of the Crown might suggest.

The history of Anne Agar, Thomas Agar's only surviving daughter and John Milton's niece, tells the same story as his nephew's. Her marriage, an alliance with the Moores, landed gentry of Surrey, was no diminishment of her social position. True, the Moore family was not so ancient as her own on the paternal side, but it was a well established county family and Anne's descendants were destined to flourish, to accumulate property, and to form alliances with the sons and daughters of gentlemen.

On 29 December 1662, a license to marry was issued to "David Moore, of Richmond, Surrey, Gent., Bach[r]. 30, * Anne Agar. Sp[r], 26, dau. of Thomas Agar, of St. Sepulchre's, London, Gent., who alleges; at St Sepulchre's or St Gregory's, London."[113] We note again the relationship with St. Sepulchre's for Milton's brother-in-law and with Christopher Milton's daughter Anne's marriage, chapter 1, p. 29. The London Agars no doubt became acquainted with the Moores through John Agar's residence in Barnes, Surrey.[114] According to the pedigree for the Moores of Sayes Court, Chertsey, Surrey, compiled in 1821 from the records of the College of Arms, David Moore was the third son of Edmund of Stratford Langthorne, Essex, and his wife Elizabeth, daughter of Isaac Kilburne of London. The line originated with Robert Moore of Lincoln. A member of the family had been secretary to Anne Boleyn: Robert of Lincoln, or Thomas, his son, or John, Thomas's son.[115]

The Moore pedigree tells us that David Moore's eldest brother was Thomas, seated at Hartswood Park, parish of Buckland, Surrey. Because he was reported as aged twenty-three in 1634, we calculate his birth to have been in 1611. The size of his county seat is shown by his dwelling's being reported as having fourteen hearths in 1664.[116] He seems to have been the Thomas Moore of Chobham in the hundred of Chertsey called to serve as juror in October 1663 and October 1664,[117] indicating that he owned land in Chobham. He appears in the court records also as of Buckland between April 1663 and April 1665.[118] Manning states that by his will, dated 6 July 1676, Thomas left his estate to David Moore.[119] This statement cannot be totally correct. According to the Moore pedigree, Thomas was married to Susanna, who died 29 January 1682,[120] and had by her an only child Susanna, married before 6 July 1676 to Robert Bristow. Susanna certainly inherited Hartswood, for her husband is described on 18 March 1695 as of Hartswood in Buckland, Surrey, gentleman.[121] David Moore may have inherited the remainder of the estate, including holdings in Chobham, since his descendants were landholders there. David had two sisters, Elizabeth and Annabella, married to Daniel Sellin and one Bott respectively, and another elder brother Edmund, living in the parish of Ryegate, Surrey. In 1664, Edmund's dwelling was listed as having five hearths.[122] The Moore pedigree states that Edmund's will, dated 22 July 1670, was proved 22 February 1670/1, at which time his children were minors. His only surviving son Solomon of Chertsey, gentleman, conveyed his estates to his kinsman, Sir Thomas Moore of Sayes, Chertsey; that is, to David Moore's son, and by his will, dated 6 October 1736, but unproved, bequeathed them to his kinsman Edmund Moore, David Moore's grandson. Solomon was buried at Chertsey on 5 November 1736.

David Moore, designated as of Richmond, Surrey, in 1662, eventually acquired a county seat, Sayes Court, Chertsey, Surrey. He appears in the muster rolls for Chertsey in 1675, 1676 and 1684.[123] As already noted, he received but £20 from his father-in-law and had no control over his wife's inheritance. Survived by his wife, David Moore died at the age of seventy-four on either 12 January 1693/4[124] or 12 February 1693/4 and was buried in the Chertsey churchyard. On the south wall of the church appear his arms, an exceedingly complicated shield, which makes unavoidable his gentle blood.[125] The administration of his effects, renounced by his widow, was granted on 13 February 1693/4 to his son Thomas.[126] There is disagreement in the records about David Moore's year of birth. According to his age at his death, he was born in 1620, but according to his marriage license, he was born in 1632. Since his elder brother Thomas was born in 1611, the date 1620 is more likely. He was therefore forty-two, not thirty, when he married Anne Agar. It is worth noting that although David Moore was only a third son of the house, his line benefited by the misfortunes of his two elder brothers. His line acquired the property of Edmund of Ryegate and part of the estate of Thomas of Buckland.

Agar's grandson, Thomas Moore, was born 9 October 1663 and baptized on 13 October in Richmond, Surrey.[127] He was admitted as "son and heir of David M. of Chertsey, Surrey, gent." to the Middle Temple on 19 May 1677.[128] The Milton pedigree reports that he was knighted in 1715 and died in 1735. The Moore pedigree shows that he was knighted at Clarendon House, County of Surrey, on 7 June 1715, the reason unknown, and died in the parish of St. Bride's, Fleet Street. Administration was granted to his son Edmund 12 June 1735.[129] We should keep remembering that David Moore was Edward and John Phillips's brother-in-law, and thus that this Thomas Moore was their nephew. In reading chapters 3 and 4, the reader should consider the position, estate, and politics of each of these close members of the family. The influence of position and financial matters of the extended family raise questions about the often repeated alleged "knowledge" about Edward and John.

Thomas married Elizabeth, daughter or sister of Sir William Blunden of Basingstoke, Hampshire, who survived her husband. Their children were, according to the Moore pedigree: 1) Thomas, baptized at Chertsey 8 March 1686; 2) David, baptized at Chertsey 14 January 1694 and buried there 1 March 1694; 3) Edmund of Sayes, esquire, baptized at Chertsey 31 May 1696, died 12 April and buried 19 April 1756 at Chobham, and survived by his widow Sarah, daughter of William Lee, buried at Chobham 14 October 1768; and 4) Anne, baptized at Chertsey 27 October 1691. Manning's report differs in these details: 1) the second son was Agar, who died in the service of his country in Lisbon, and 2) Edmund died at the age of fifty-four on 12 April 1750, survived by his widow Sarah, daughter of George Martin, who died 5 October 1768, aged sixty-five. The Milton pedigree also reports Sarah's death at sixty-five on 5 October 1768 but her father as William Lee. The son Agar is also included. Further, it reports that Anne Moore married someone named Savell in 1728. Manning adds that Thomas was living in 1712.[130] Independent records settle the question of Edmund's marriage. A license to marry was issued 28 April 1729 to "Edmund Moore, Esq., of Chertsey, 30,

and Sarah Lee of Chobham, spinster, 17; at Purbright," accompanied by a
certificate reading: "These are to certify whom it may concern y[t] my daughter, Sarah Lee, be married to Edmund Moore, Esq[r], of y[e] parish of Chertsey,
in y[e] county aforesaid, witness my hand, this twenty-eighth of Aprill, 1729.—
William Lee."[131] In the marriage license, the ages are incorrect. According
to the pedigrees, Edmund was thirty-two at the time. According to her baptismal record dated 24 April 1702,[132] Sarah was twenty-seven in 1729. She
was sixty-six when she died in 1768. All reports agree that Edmund of Sayes
carried on the line. His elder brother Thomas, in the normal course, would
have been the head of the family and chief landholder, but it is clear he did
not occupy this place. According to the records, he had neither wife nor
heirs. In 1712 he would have been twenty-six. Perhaps he was the Agar who
Manning says died in Lisbon.

Edmund and Sarah had five children, born from 1729 to 1739, all baptized at Chertsey. The first surviving son was William of Sayes and Byfleet,
baptized at Chertsey 10 April 1733. He married Mary Cory *alias* Rafter at
Byfleet 13 April 1757, but died without issue on 7 January 1760, and was
buried at Byfleet on 18 January 1760. Mary Cory Moore, who was buried at
Byfleet on 1 July 1759, is reported by one source to have inherited the Byfleet
property from her late employer. The property deposed to William's brother
Blunden of Sayes and Byfleet, the eventual heir and perpetuator of the line,
who was baptized at Chertsey 2 January 1734. He married Bridget, daughter
of Richard Ford, a brewer. He died in March 1768 and was buried at Byfleet
on 1 April 1768.[133] Blunden's marriage on 28 March 1761 is recorded:
"Blunden Moore of Byfleet, abode many years, Esq. bachelor, 26, and Bridgett
Ford of Chertsey, abode 4 weeks, spinster, a minor, 17; at Chertsey. With
consent of Richard Ford of Chertsey, gentleman, her father."[134] Through
Blunden and Bridget, the Moores continued for several generations. Accounting for at least one continuing branch of the family, Sir John Dashwood-
King married Sarah Moore, great-granddaughter of Milton's sister. French
(V, 139) errs in saying "granddaughter" and gives the date as 1790; Parker
has 1761ff. (II, 1433), but this seems to be a typographical error and probably was meant to indicate Sarah's birth date. We should note, however, that
Elizabeth Foster (Milton's granddaughter by his daughter Deborah) reported
to Thomas Newton (see his edition of *Paradise Lost,* 1749, I, lix) that "She
knows nothing of her aunt Philips or Agar's descendents, but believes that
they are all extinct."

Thomas Agar's descendants clearly maintained their position as gentry,
and one of their number, Thomas Moore, his grandson, rose from the rank
of esquire to knight. The family apparently increased its property holdings.
Sayes Court remained in the family into the eighteenth century, and other

property was acquired. Between 1739, when Edmund's last child was baptized at Chertsey, and 1756, when Edmund was buried at Chobham, the family changed its county seat. Perhaps the Chobham property was acquired through Edmund's wife, Sarah Lee, whose family came from that parish, or it may have derived from Thomas Moore of Chobham, noted before under the date 1663–64. By 1759, the year in which William's wife was buried there, the seat of the family had been changed to Byfleet, and since in his marriage record of 1761 Blunden is spoken of as a resident of that parish for many years, the move must have occurred before 1759. The Agar and Moore families were assuredly, both in class and property, a group representative of a society hardly compatible with what has usually been cast as John Milton's concept of an ideal social structure.

5

It is strange that no investigation has been made of Thomas Agar's possible political and legal connections, since he became the Deputy Clerk of the Crown in Chancery late in 1631 and he came of a family of lawyers, his father being a member of the Inner Temple and his brother and his nephew being members of the Middle Temple. True, there is a dearth of evidence with respect to such connections, yet something of their nature can be observed through an examination of the relevant structure of the government and the courts, the nature of the lawyers' community, and Agar's place in these schemes. True again, so far as is known, Agar himself was not a lawyer, but he must have been surrounded by them and counted many of them his associates and friends by virtue of his family and his post. An examination of the records of English history in the seventeenth century shows that lawyers were rife in the government and many of them held powerful positions.

The posts of Clerk of the Crown in Chancery and of Deputy Clerk were direct lines to the highest sources of power in the courts and the government. Chancery was the highest court of the land next to Parliament and was presided over by the lord chancellor, the chief chancery or equity judge of England. The Lord High Chancellor was the first great officer of the state, ranking next after the blood royal and the Archbishop of Canterbury. He was lord keeper of the great seal of England, privy councillor, and president and prolocutor of the House of Lords. The Clerk of the Crown and his deputy were the Lord High Chancellor's administrative assistants. As Masson notes, they were required continually to attend the Lord High Chancellor for special matters of state, and a place was reserved for them in the House of Lords. Further, the Clerk of the Crown or his deputy produced all writs for summoning parliaments; for new elections of members of the House of

Commons, upon warrant, at the death or removal of any member; for commissions of oyer and terminer, jail-delivery, commissions of the peace, and others distributing justice.[135] The Clerk of the Crown and his deputy were, of course, not high in the Councils of State, but they must certainly have had considerable knowledge of governmental affairs and were known to the Lord High Chancellor and other officers of state with whom he conducted the government's affairs, including the attorney-general and the solicitor-general. Furthermore, administrative assistantships in any government at any time can be powerful positions when occupied by aggressive and skillful men. It is assumed, therefore, that knowledge of the Lord High Chancellors incumbent during Agar's occupation of his post will throw some light on his connections and influence.

When Thomas Agar entered the Crown Office is unknown. He was not there during the chancellorship of the two eminent lawyers, Baron Ellesmere and Sir Francis Bacon. He may have entered the office during the incumbency of John Williams; Edward Phillips was in the Crown Office at this time and became Deputy Clerk in 1625. John Williams (1582–1650) was an exception to the custom that a lawyer should occupy the chancellorship. He was a favorite divine of James I, a former chaplain of Baron Ellesmere from 1612 to 1617, and Dean of Westminster when he became lord keeper of the great seal on 16 July 1621. His position became uncertain with the accession of Charles I (1625), for he had quarreled with Buckingham shortly before. More interested in politics, it seems, than his bishopric in Lincoln, he objected to some of the actions of Charles and Buckingham and so ceased to be lord keeper on 25 October 1625, being banished to his diocese. In the 1630s, he defied some of Archbishop William Laud's rulings concerning visitations, and was suspended and sent briefly to the Tower in 1638. Williams remained a Royalist, fled in 1642 to the king in York, and there was enthroned as Archbishop of York.[136]

The next incumbent was Thomas Coventry (1578–1640). He was a friend of Sir James Whitelocke (1570–1632), member of the Middle Temple and the Society of Antiquaries, justice of King's Bench, who, in 1602, married Elizabeth, eldest daughter of Edward Bulstrode of Hedgerly Bulstrode, Buckinghamshire,[137] and was a frequent visitor at the Manor House in Horton, the favorite seat of the Bulstrodes after 1595.[138] A member of the Inner Temple, Coventry, appointed solicitor-general and knighted in 1617, was next appointed attorney-general in 1621 and lord keeper of the great seal on 1 November 1625. He was created Baron Coventry in 1628. He continued in the post of lord keeper until his death on 14 January 1639/40. His daughter Anne became the wife of Sir William Savile and mother of George Savile, Marquis of Halifax. His daughter Margaret was the first wife of An-

thony Ashley Cooper, the first Earl of Shaftesbury. His sons were ardent Royalists and were favored at the Restoration.[139]

Sir John Finch (1584–1660), a lawyer from Gray's Inn, followed Lord
Coventry. Knighted in 1626, he was appointed chief justice of the Court of
Common Pleas in 1634, where John Agar no doubt practiced. He became
lord keeper on 17 January 1639/40, but his tenure was short-lived, for he
was impeached by the Long Parliament and fled, arriving in The Hague on
31 December 1640. He served as a commissioner at the trial of the regicides
in October 1660, but took little part, dying 27 November 1660. He came of
a family of lawyers. His father Sir Henry (1558–1625) was a member of Gray's
Inn, and both his cousin Sir Heneage (d. 1631) and his second cousin
Heneage, first Earl of Nottinghamshire (1621–1682), were trained in the
Inner Temple.[140]

Perhaps the most important of the Lord High Chancellors during Agar's
tenure was Edward Hyde (1609–1674). After having been called to the bar
in the Middle Temple in 1633, he was first appointed keeper of the writs and
rolls of the common pleas. At first, he was allied with the popular party in
the Short and Long Parliaments, but eventually went over to the Royalist
side, joining the king in York in June 1642. He became the most powerful of
the men about the king, acquiring the chancellorship of the exchequer and
later on 13 January 1657/8 being named Lord High Chancellor. He entered London with Charles II and took his seat in Chancery on 1 June 1660.
Virtually the head of the government, he was created Earl of Clarendon at
the coronation. He surrendered the exchequer office early, but remained
Lord High Chancellor until 30 August 1667.[141]

He was followed by Orlando Bridgeman (1606?–74), a lawyer from the
Inner Temple, who enjoyed a high legal reputation during the reign of
Charles I. He was a Royalist and sat in the Oxford Parliament in 1644. During the Interregnum he was allowed to practice privately, specializing in the
conveyances of property. A week after the king's return he was made a serjeant-at-law and a chief baron of the exchequer and was the first baronet
created. He presided as Lord Chief Baron at the trial of the regicides, taking
a strong position against treason in his charge to the court. He was lord
keeper from 30 August 1667 to 17 November 1672.[142] His successor for a
short while was the first Earl of Shaftesbury, who held the office for about a
year. In his early manhood, Shaftesbury was a member of Lincoln's Inn and
was closely associated with the Coventry family. After a remarkably piebald
career in the Civil War, he was pardoned on 27 June 1660 and sat on the
special commission for the trial of the regicides.[143]

The next holder of this office, who was brought in because of his position at the Restoration, was Heneage Finch (1621–1682), later the first Earl

of Nottinghamshire. Finch, trained in the Inner Temple, went into private practice during the Interregnum. He was a member of the Convention Parliament and was appointed solicitor-general on 6 June 1660. He managed to become the official representative of the court and the church in the House of Commons. He was the Heneage Finch who, Masson reports, remarked that John Milton, having been Latin Secretary to Cromwell, deserved to be hanged.[144] Prosecuting counsel in the trial of the regicides in October 1660, he rose to the attorney-generalship in 1670 and became lord keeper on 9 November 1673 and lord chancellor on 19 December 1674.[145] Finch came from a strongly Royalist family and had distinguished ancestors and relatives. His father, Sir Heneage Finch (d. 1631), a lawyer from the Inner Temple, was elected speaker of the House of Commons in 1626. His grandmother was the Viscountess Maidstone and Countess of Winchilsea. He was the great-grandson of Sir Thomas Heneage (d. 1595), favorite of Elizabeth I, a member of Parliament, privy councillor, and Keeper of the Records in the Tower, whose brother Michael Heneage (1540–1600) was also keeper of the Records in the Tower, a member of Parliament, and a member of the Society of Antiquaries. His second cousin was Sir John Finch, lord keeper in 1640. Another cousin, also named Heneage (d. 1689), who became Earl of Winchilsea in 1639, was a friend of General Mon(c)k and became lord-lieutenant of Kent on 10 July 1660.[146]

It does not seem probable that Thomas Agar was at any time a mere cipher in such governmental circles in view of his participation in the community of lawyers both before and after the Civil Wars; in view of the position and connections of his family, especially of his nephew Thomas Agar; and in view of the opportunities offered by his government post to bring himself to the attention of greater and lesser officials. He must have wielded some influence. Further, that he was a loyal Royalist sufferer reflects his involvement in the general Royalist community, whether that involvement arose from conviction or from the knowledge of what was to be gained from it. The positions and importance of the above-mentioned Lord High Chancellors at the trial of the regicides and the decisions made concerning those connected with the Interregnum government, when the treatment of John Milton is considered, strongly suggests that his brother-in-law Thomas Agar, despite their political differences, may have been one of the most important influences on Milton's disposition.

The date and the manner of Agar's removal from his post during the Civil Wars are uncertain. Masson reports that Agar was ejected from his place some time before the establishment of the Commonwealth.[147] No doubt, this is derived from Edward Phillips's statement that Agar held his office for many years "except some time of Exclusion before and during the *Interreg-*

num" (vii). Agar's own version is that he resigned. In his petition for a return to office in 1660, he asserted that he had "declined [the post] during the troubles to his great loss."[148] This, however, may have been his adroit way of representing his Royalist loyalty to recover his post and so not the exact truth.

The activities of Agar during the Civil Wars and the Interregnum are obscure. He can be located three times during this period. In 1646 and 1647 Sir Henry Ferrers, baronet, of Skellingthorpe, Lincolnshire, was involved in coming to terms with the Committee for Compounding. Thomas Agar was a claimant on the estate. "26 April 1650. THOS. AGARD, late Clerk of the Crown, of Lincoln, claims allowance of a debt due from Sir Hen. Ferrars, for which he has extended his lands in Lincolnshire."[149] Just why Agar lent money to Sir Henry, or even how and when they first met, is impossible to say. Ferrers's pedigree shows that he had London relatives and that his mother was Eleanor, daughter of Edward Ferrers of Warwickshire,[150] and sister of Henry Ferrers of Baddesley-Clinton, Warwickshire,[151] a Roman Catholic, who died in 1633, a descendant of the Earls of Derby and a noted antiquarian, well known and respected by William Camden.[152] However, these connections throw no light on the Agar-Ferrers relationship. Another unsolved problem is why Agar went to live in Lincoln, but as the above indicates, he owned property there. There were Agars in the county, but there is no apparent connection between them and Thomas Agar.[153]

A suit between John Trott and Christopher Milton brought in 1652 and 1653 has an answer from Agar attached, dated 1653; see French, V, 469. In his answer, Agar attests to Christopher's "further answer" denying an assignment of the bill from John Raven to Thomas Willis in 1649. Another deposition of Christopher Milton, this on 25 May 1658,[154] in answer to the seventh interrogative, attests "That hee was present and did see Thomas Agar one of the partyes in this Jnterrien named signe seale and as his act and deede deliuer the deede in this Jnterrien mentioned," Agar's examination bearing the date of 25 July 1657; Christopher deposes only concerning Agar's sealing and delivery of the deed. Suggested, thus, is Agar's presence on occasion in London at least in 1653, 1657, and 1658. He returned to London and took up lodgings in the Middle Temple on 30 June 1658,[155] perhaps in anticipation of the Restoration with the impending death of Cromwell.

In 1660, Agar lost no time in recovering his fortunes. On 22 June 1660 at Whitehall, while Milton remained concealed in Bartholomew Close and Parliament was drawing up the list of regicides and exceptions to the general amnesty, he petitioned the king for grant of the office of Clerk of Appeals in Chancery in addition to his former office. Lord Chancellor Hyde endorsed the petition favorably on 27 June.[156] On 15 July and 11 August, he sought and secured from Hyde the government's favor for other aspirants

to office.[157] On 14 June 1661, Thomas Agar, registrar, and his assistants petitioned for payment of services rendered to the Commission for Claims at
the Coronation, in which they had had the assistance of William Dugdale.[158]
They were granted the money, £200, on 15 July 1661.[159] Agar continued in
his two posts up to or near the end of his life, including Collector of Subsi-
dies to which he was appointed on 8 June 1664. His memoranda, etc., appear among the state papers, the last being dated 26 April 1671.[160] Among
those with whom Agar communicated or had business were Sir Joseph
Williamson, Arthur Annesley, and Sir George Carteret. Williamson in the
mid-1670s deterred the publication of the State Papers, and along with them
De doctrina christiana; he caused both Daniel Skinner manuscripts to be deposited in the Public Record Office, consigned to oblivion until 1823 (and
published in 1825). Other manuscripts of the State Papers, however, were
published in 1676 (and 1690, 1695), 1692 (and other editions), 1700, and
1712. Annesley was Earl of Anglesey, and a friend of Milton; he wrote an
important memorandum on the authorship of *Eikon Basilike,* naming John
Gauden. He was a member of the Council of State under General Monck
and the Privy Council of Charles II, and served on the Commission dealing
with the Indemnity bill and the trial of the regicides. Carteret, who became
a member of the Privy Council at the Restoration, signed himself "Milton"
in a letter to Sir Edward Nicholas, Secretary of State, dated 9 (19) June 1651.[161]
There are also three extant letters from Nicholas to Clarendon, 1652, discussing the Salmasian controversy.

Masson's interpretation of the events leading to John Milton's escape in
1660 from all reprisals provides a framework for the role that Agar may have
played in these maneuvers. Masson asserts that, because of Milton's eminent role in the civil conflict, the Commonwealth, and the Protectorate,
everyone at the time, including Milton himself, expected his death by hang-
ing. Yet when the Act of Oblivion was proclaimed on 29 August 1660, it was
clear that Parliament had not made Milton an exception to the general
amnesty. Masson tries to explain Milton's escape as the work of a powerful
organization on his behalf, including Sir Thomas Clarges, Monck's brother-
in-law; Secretary Morrice, Monck's intimate friend; and Annesley. He interprets events in the House of Commons that seemed to threaten Milton as
evidence of the workings of a plot to save him. In June 1660, Commons,
having determined the identity of the regicides, turned to drawing up a list
of twenty Republicans from the general community who should be pun-
ished short of life. On 16 June, when seven of the twenty were yet unchosen,
the Commons ordered two of Milton's works, *Pro Populo Anglicano Defensio*
and *Eikonoklastes,* called in for burning and resolved that the author be arrested. This order was not acted upon until 13 August. In the meantime,

Commons sent its completed list of exceptions to the amnesty, not including Milton, to the House of Lords. While this body was devising its own list
and working out differences with the Commons, a royal proclamation of 13
August called in Milton's two works. No order for his arrest was issued. Then
on 29 August came the Act of Oblivion and Milton was safe. Masson contends that the order for book burning, the resolution for arrest, and the
royal proclamation were all efforts by Milton's adherents to save him from
the list of exceptions, since by these acts he had already been singled out for
reprisal, a reprisal there was no intention of carrying out. True, Milton was
arrested, between 13 September and 6 November, apparently as a result of
the inadvertent reemergence of the arrest order. An order for his release
came from Parliament on 15 December. The fees he was required to pay for
release were reduced on the complaint of Andrew Marvell; Edward King,
member for Great Grimsby; and Robert Shapcott, member for Tiverton.[162]

Whether or not Masson's conjectures are exactly what occurred, it seems
certain that men were at work to save Milton, men who carried weight not
only in the House of Commons, but also in the House of Lords and the
Clarendon administration. The role that Agar may have played has never
been considered. The pertinent facts are simple. Agar was early upon the
scene in London; he had secured two posts by 27 June 1660; during the
summer his influence secured favors from Hyde; and, above all, the nature
of his post put him in a position that, if not powerful, was strategic. He was
in a position to report to interested persons events leading to the amnesty
and the making of exceptions and in a position to influence the government's
decisions. Records of a later date show that he knew how to use the bribe
discreetly. In a note dated 12 July 1664 to Sir Joseph Williamson, who became Undersecretary of State in 1666, he begs dispatch of the enclosed,
which wants signing, and though it has the face of a pauper, it will be better
than that to Williamson. On 19 July 1664, he follows this up with another
note, in which he hopes the poor woman's pardon is signed and begs for its
delivery. He will give Williamson for doing it "three pieces" that have been
raised by several persons commiserating her sad condition.[163]

To these facts may be added the central contention of this chapter, that
Agar's moderate wealth, gentle blood, immediate family connections, membership in the community of lawyers, and governmental connections were
such as to give him some power and influence that could be wielded in favor
of John Milton. The seven lord chancellors discussed above were but one
segment of Agar's possible political and personal connections, provided by
his post. Of these seven, all were clear-cut Royalists with the possible exception of Shaftesbury. Six were lawyers. Two, the Finches, came from a family
of lawyers. Four and the descendants of a fifth, Lord Coventry, received hon-

ors at the Restoration or shortly afterward and wielded power and influence
in Royalist circles.[164] Four acted in the trial of the regicides, Heneage Finch
being prosecuting counsel. Assuredly they constituted one of Agar's lines of
communication and influence.

3

Edward Phillips
Royalist(?) and Nephew

References to Milton's nephews Edward and John Phillips in the preceding chapters have indicated the acceptance of Edward by his stepfather Thomas Agar, although some uncertainty about Edward's mode of life and financial abilities has been inferred, and implied a favorable relationship with his uncle Christopher Milton, although he was not mentioned in testimony concerning John Milton's will; but John has been viewed as estranged from both. The pattern of acceptance without much enthusiasm for Edward and of dislike and disapproval of John was set in motion by Anthony Wood in *Atheniæ Oxonienses* (Ed. 2, 1721) and developed by William Godwin in The *Lives of Edward and John Philips, Nephews and Pupils of Milton.*[1] It has continued today, particularly in Ralph Hone's dissertation *Edward and John Phillips, Nephews and Pupils of John Milton,*[2] and underlies William Riley Parker's biography of Milton. Only Tilottama Rajan has really put a critical eye to Godwin's work, raising questions about Godwin's motives and the nature and methodology of his interpretations.[3] The usual judgment is that Edward frequently aided his uncle in the recording, correction, and publication of his work, but that Edward wrote a lot that was derivative, was not a gifted thinker or author, and was not much concerned with the politics surrounding him. His connections with those of the privileged class placed him among the Royalist sympathizers and aristocrats, and so he is either viewed positively by those who agree with monarchical principles or disregarded as to political persuasion. The lack of information about his life—his marriage, his residences, his financial condition—has led to inferences that may or may not be valid. On the other hand, John is seen to have left his uncle's home in 1652 after he reached his majority (in October 1651) and "never darkened his uncle's door again," as it were. He is viewed as a most prolific hack writer, with the emphasis upon the "hack" rather than the nature and variety of the writer's many publications, and one who espoused the anti-monarchic cause, but when it was profitable, the Royalist cause. Not so much turncoat as opportunist, he becomes a person of no real principle.

The brothers are epitomized in Godwin's jaundiced eyes: "It also appears from Wood, that Edward Philiips gave to the press A Poem on the Coronation of James the Second,[4] which I have never seen. I own that I feel grieved at this. John Philips might enlist himself among the flatterers of this inauspicious reign; he had already made an obnoxious appearance, and he offered up his Pindaric Odes as a sort of atonement for past political offences; add to which, John Philips was a busy, pragmatic man, and was accustomed to stand forward in some way or other, in every party that successively bore the vogue. But his elder brother was quiet, inoffensive and retired; and it would have been most consistent with his character, as well as conducive to his credit, to be silent, when no lover of his country would have chosen to pollute his lips with words of approbation. It is probable that the Poem he thus produced, was set to music, and that the performance of it by the royal band, made part of the solemnities of the Coronation" (Appendix III, addition to chapter X, 386). For Godwin (310) quoting Wood (II, 1119), John was "A Man of very loose Principles, Atheistical, forsakes his Wife and Children, makes no Provision for them." (See chapter 4 for discussion of John.) Both nephews, Godwin writes, were indebted to Milton for their "reasonable portion of talents," but they had only "a very slender portion of resemblance to the intellectual character of their sublime instructor" (317). Indeed, they "threw off the peculiar and favorite modes of thinking of their uncle" by the time they were twenty-five and twenty-four years of age. Despite the extensive discussion of their literary productions, particularly translations from various languages, and Edward's teaching stints, Godwin allows himself to say, "They were bred to no profession or trade" (329), and that John separated himself from his uncle "so far as we can perceive, for ever" (320).

1

Before looking at John Phillips and his relationship with his uncle, we must examine what we know about Edward and about their familial history, which has many gaps and inferences. (We should also review the manuscripts that Milton left, or may have left, at his death, although Edward may be less involved in their disposition than has been generally thought; see section 3 infra.) Edward was born in August 1630, he went to live with Milton in 1640, and through interpretation of a comment in his "Life" of his uncle, it has been inferred that he left around 1646, later going to Magdalen Hall, Oxford, where he became a student, according to Wood, in March 1649; according to Foster (III, 1156) he matriculated on 10 November 1650, leaving in 1651 without a degree.[5] The period of 1639–1648 offers no strong knowledge of Edward: he tells in the *Life* of his uncle John's marriage to Mary

Powell (1642?) but vaguely; Mary's return to Oxford and some of Milton's friends and relatives in the years before her return; the tutoring that Milton did, its nature and its coverage of certain authors; and some of Milton's publications. But of himself little can be inferred, and any documentary evidence is lacking. However, the years 1641 through 1648 were times when Milton was keeping his Commonplace Book and the Theological Index, perhaps first engaging the Tractate which led to *De doctrina christiana*, almost surely writing what became *Accedence Commenc't Grammar* and possibly *Artis Logicæ Plenior Institutio*, engaging in reading that emerges in *The History of Britain* and *A Brief History of Moscovia*, as well as the published anti-prelatical and the divorce tracts, and *Of Education* and *Areopagitica*. Edward would have been an eye-witness to these scholarly activities, and perhaps a helper. His own future work includes volumes on language and on Latin, historical accounts including material on Russia and Asia Minor, and translation, and further, an apparently successful series of tutorial positions. It is not far-fetched to believe that he learned much from his uncle, not only by way of substantive matter, but also methods and ways of thinking. He does not engage controversy, possibly because of the observable vituperation it brought to his uncle at this time. Possibly these impressionable years left him wary of issues, and so he steered clear of them. His brother, on the other hand, constantly found himself in the midst of "issues" as we shall see in chapter 4, the obverse effect of those impressionable years upon a different personality.

When Edward left Magdalen may be charted by the following deed: some time in early 1651, perhaps after the close of Hilary Term, which was about two weeks before Easter, 30 March 1651. The deed (No. 994) concerned with land long owned by the family,[6] dated 1 July 1651, says he is "of the town of Shrewsbury in the county of Salop gent." The residence property of the family, two messuages, was at 2 Milk Street, but there was also other property in Dog Lane and Mardol. This deed, an indenture between Edward Phillips of Shrewsbury and Andrew Vivers of Shrewsbury, endorsed by John Phillips, leased the family's Mardol property. From 1653 through 1655, there are three further deeds: No. 1230, 25 November 1653, another indenture between Edward Phillips of Shrewsbury and "John Phillippes of Westminster in the County of Midd, gent." and Andrew Vivers, signed by both Edward and John; No. 1460, 25 November 1654, a third indenture between "Edward Phillipps of the towne of Shrewsbury in the County of Salop gent & John Phillipps of Westminster in the County of Middlesex gent" and Andrew Vivers, signed by Edward and John (see Hone, 590–620, for the preceding deeds); and No. 567/2F/2-3, in the County Record Office, recording the sale of part of the Milk Street property to Joseph Prowde, a relative, 4 July 1655, by

Edward and John. These deeds indicate Edward's residence in Shrewsbury during the years 1651–1655, and John's in London. (Milk Street lay between the intersection of the High, Fish Street, and Wyle Cys, and Princess Street. At that intersection on Fish Street was St. Julian's Church, and just off Wyle Cop is "Dogg Pole." "Dog Lane" is now Claremont Street. All are within what was defined as the *burh*.[7] Mardol lies northwest, on the other side of Pride Hill, a short distance from the center of the town.) They also tell us that Edward and John were in touch with each other after 1652, when John is alleged to have left his uncle's home, and probably during these years contact continued with relatives from their grandmother's family, as the last deed evidences. There must have been some financial return for the brothers, as well, from these inherited properties, a matter totally unrecognized by commentators. Edward and John, like their father, grandfather, and uncles, seem to be in situations that would bring some income to them over the years. It is curious, however, that the deeds of 1653, 1654, and 1655 were all witnessed by Gilbert Sheldon, later Archbishop of Canterbury.[8]

It appears that Edward remained in Shrewsbury through at least 4 July 1655.[9] However, we perhaps should not suppose that he was constantly there in those years, but rather that he may have spent some time elsewhere, perhaps in London. His penning of Milton's letter to Hermann Mylius on 13 February 1651/2 indicates one such visit. (See French, III, 174–76.) Around this same time, he entered two citations from Niccolò Machiavelli's *Discorsi sopra la Prima Deca di tito Livio* in Milton's Commonplace Book on p. 197, generally dated between November 1651 and February 1652. Comment is in Latin and quotation is in Italian. Between them is an entry on Dante made by the scribe who penned the manuscript of *Paradise Lost*, Book I. Alongside the second Machiavelli entry is a marginal note by Phillips, "Vide Indicem Theologicum de Religione non cogenda," one of twelve[10] such references to six topics of a Theological Index. The note is clearly to be dated at the same time, although recent arguments about the authorship of *De doctrina christiana* have not referred to this or recognized the significance of the dating.[11]

In 1656, translations of Juan Pérez de Montalván's *The Illustrious Shepherdess* and *The Imperious Brother* were published; they were entered together in the Term Catalogues by "Nath. Brookes" on 30 January 1656, "now Englished by Edward Phillips, Gent." (II, 27). The translations are dedicated to the Marchioness of Dorchester and to the Marchioness and the Countess of Strafford, respectively. They were the daughters of James Stanley, Earl of Derby, and grandnieces of Lady Alice, the Countess Dowager of Derby, for whom Milton had written "Arcades."[12] In the same year appeared Edward's edition of *Poems by that Most Famous Wit, William Drummond of Hawthornden*

(1656), three issues,[13] and other books follow in successive years. Included are a preface signed "E. P." and an encomium, "Upon the Incomparable Poems of Mr. William Drummond," signed "Edw. Philips," as well as thirty-five items not previously published. Omitted are "two or three pieces of scurrility against the republicans, and two or three obscene epigrams, which are to be found among the generally chaste and delicate poems of Drummond in the latest editions" (Godwin, 137); rather, this tells us much about Godwin. It has been suggested by Parker that Phillips may have used manuscripts owned by his uncle; at least we know that he owned a manuscript of "Sir Walter Ralegh's" *Cabinet-Council*, which he published in 1658, and various ones of his own, some dating in the 1640s. The first edition of *The New World of English Words* came in 1658, but in 1662 and 1663 there were two issues of the second edition, both dedicated to Sir William Paston (the Earl of Yarmouth, who died on 22 February 1662/3), and to Sir Robert Bolles of Lincoln (died 1663) and Sir Edward Hussey, the father and grandfather of Mary Bolles who was to become his cousin Thomas Agar's wife. The third edition, in 1671, was dedicated to the Duke of Ormonde (died 1688), as was the fourth in 1678; this latter edition also was dedicated to the Duchess of Grafton, his current pupil. (See later.) Ormonde, of course, was James Butler, who acted for Charles I in making peace with the Irish Rebels and Papists, which provoked Milton's *Articles of Peace* (1649). These aristocratic connections that Phillips evinces make clear that animosity toward Milton as author of two indicted books and Latin secretary during the Cromwell reign did not transfer to Edward. The dedicatees of the translations and *The New World of English Words,* also, manifest his close connections with people associated with his family or actually part of his extended family.

Phillips produced numerous other works that were not devoted to "ideas"/"argument" or to independent "creative" writing from 1658 through 1694. For Godwin, his was a "drivelling style" (123); for Hone, he was engaged in scholarly matters and led the "quiet career of the teacher" (583–84); for Parker, "he evidently had the soul of a hasty hack writer . . lacking any real spirit of scholarship" (655). The quality may not be competitive with that of some memorable authors, but Phillips did produce a number of translations (novels, travels, morals, memoirs, burlesques) and was well versed in Greek, Latin, Italian, French, and Spanish; he edited chronicles, poetry, letters, and literary criticism; he produced anthologies and wrote and published poetry. For these latter-day derogators the "professional" author producing "popular" and "commissioned" work is simply not de rigueur; as Wood remarked, he "wrote and translated several things meerly to get a bare livelyhood." Phillips's *Theatrum Poetarum, or a Compleat Collection of the Poets* (1675),[14] according to Parker, was "a shoddy, slapdash compilation" (655), yet it preceded the less ambitious and most biased William Winstanley's *The Lives of the Most Famous English Poets, or the Honour of Parnassus; In a Brief Essay of the Works and Writings of Above Two Hundred of Them* (1687). Phillips's edition of Johann Buchler, *Sacrarum Profanarumque Phrasium Poeticarum Thesaurus* (1669/1670), Ed. 17, added "Tractatulus de Carmine Dramatico Poetarum Veterum," 357–74, with a separate title page dated 1670. (Edition 18 in 1679 has the addition on pp. 375–402). As Hone (208) summarized: "In the remainder of his publishing ventures he displayed a very remarkable tendency to parallel many of his famous uncle's serious interests: lexicography, history, Latin grammar." Were he the nephew of George Wither or Marchmont Needham, might the evaluation that Hone and Parker place on Phillips be different?

During this period of publication, Phillips also was employed as a tutor and secretary. Not previously associated with Phillips, who had attended Magdalen Hall in 1650–51, is an entry in *The Restoration Visitation of the University of Oxford and Its Colleges*[15] under 6 August 1660, f. 15r, citing "Mr Edward Phillips [one of the] clerks of the said Coll." (i.e., Magdalen College). If the connotation of Wood's words is valid, we may have corroboration of this identification; however, a different person of that name had been a clerk at the College a number of years before. Wood writes (II, 72), in discussing Sir Richard Baker's *A Chronicle of the Kings of England* (1660), that Phillips was "sometimes a Student of *Magd.* Hall." This may refer only to his time there in 1650–51, but the implication is that he was at Magdalen at various times. (There is only one other Edward Phillips cited in *Athenæ Oxonienses* [I, 321–22] and he lived at the end of the sixteenth century-beginning of the seventeenth. However, there was another Edward Phillipps at Magdalen College, who received a bachelor's degree in 1647 and a master's in 1654.[16]) A corroborative fact may be that Edward presented to the Bodleian on 11 June 1656 copies of his translations of Montalván's two novels (as well as Milton's *Tenure of Kings and Magistrates* and *Eikonoklastes,* and probably *Pro Populo Anglicano Defensio Secunda* and *Pro Se Defensio*).[17] From October 1663 through February 1665, Edward was tutor to John Evelyn's son at Sayes Court, Deptford, Kent,[18] but he also worked for Elias Ashmole (of Brasenose College) in Oxford from 18 January 1663 (or earlier) through 16 December 1664.[19] This placement of Phillips back in Oxford in 1660 may thus fill in a gap of years in the late 1650s when he was researching various publications (notably *The New World of English Words,* 1658, and his continuation of Baker's *Chronicle,* published in 1660), and may provide the connection with Ashmole that produced the transcriptions. Hone has suggested, too, that he may have been employed by Ashmole during the years 1667–1672, when Ashmole would have been assembling his book on the Order of the Garter. From

March 1665 through, it is supposed, 1670 he was tutor to Philip Herbert, Earl of Pembroke (in Wilton, Wiltshire),[20] and in November 1677 he became reader to Henry Bennet, Earl of Arlington, the Lord Chamberlain.[21] Again, we have him moving in socially high circles, which were also Royalist.

2

Edward's further publications appear in 1658 (with new editions or issues in 1662, 1663, 1671, 1678, 1696 [and 1700 after his death]), 1658 (and 1685 [and 1699 after his death]), 1660 (and 1665, 1670, 1674, 1679 [2], 1684, 1696), 1670 (and 1679), 1675, 1676, 1682, 1685, 1685, and 1694 (his edition of Milton's *Letters of State* with the life of Milton included). The writing and publication and republication (sometimes involving additions or changes) of these works surely kept him busy during these years. We have noted his connections with those in the Royalist camp, yet we are also told that he espoused the Parliamentarian side in some of his works. Blair Worden emboldens these seventeenth-century interpretations when he comments "The political views of the Phillips brothers were flexible," extending the purported collaboration between Slingsby Bethel and John in the Ludlow pamphlets to Edward. He also reports that Edward used General Monck's papers[22] in his continuation of Sir Richard Baker's *A Chronicle of the Kings of England*, Ed. 3 (1660), through addition of "The Reign of King Charles, I. With a Continuation of the Chronicle To the end of the Year M.DC.LVIII." The "Continuation" is in two parts: Rrr1r-Ggg6v, Charles I; Hhh1r-Lll3v, Charles II; Edition 4 (1665) adds "To the Coronation of His Sacred Majesty King Charles the Second That now Reigneth." The book is entered in the Term Catalogues by George Sawbridge and Thomas Williams on 2 February 1664/5 as "*A Chronicle . . .* By Sr Richard Baker, knight, Whereunto is added *the Reigne of King Charles the first . . .* By Edward Phillips" (II, 352). Wood's reference under his account of Baker suggests that Phillips did this work while he was at Magdalen College. The source of the papers would seem to have been Sir Thomas Clarges, Monck's brother-in-law[23] and, for the 1665 addition, a pertinent section recorded from Evelyn's diary. Milton knew Monck, and Monck would have submitted reports to the Interregnum government, one supposes, but he is surely a good example of those—perhaps like Edward—who reacted against certain matters adhering to the monarchical government and yet who objected to the Cromwellian controls. But there is no evidence that Edward espoused the Parliamentarian point of view in his works, nor that he had anything to do with "Ludlow" (Slingsby Bethel).

In other work, Phillips dedicated his edition of John Speed's *The Theatre of the Empire of Great-Britain* (1676) to Sir Joseph Sheldon; he added the section in "Prospect of the World" concerning "The Empire of the Great Mogul, with the rest of the East-Indies, Palestine, or the Holy-Land, the Empire of Russia." A book dealing with the Latin language and its translation appeared in 1682 and 1685, *Tractatulus de Modo & Ratione Formandi Voces Derivativas Linguæ Latinæ* (which includes *Observationes de Compositis et Decompositis*) translated as *A Treatise of the Way and Manner of Forming the Derivatives of the Latin Tongue*. Finally, a bibliographic problem has been created by Wood's listing: "He the said Mr. *Phillips* hath also written, . . . *Enchiridion Linguæ:* or, a compendious *Latin* Dictionary, equally sufficient, with the largest extant, for all Learners, whether Children, or those of riper Years, &c. To which are added, 1. A Collection of the most usitate [usual] Greek words, &c. 2. A brief *Anglo-Latin* or *English Lat.* Dictionary. 3. Another of the most select proper Names, poetical and Historical, &c. Lond. 1684. oct. [¶] *Speculum Linguæ Latinæ:* or, a succinct and new method of all the most material and fundamental words of the *Lat.* Tongue *Lond.* 1684. oct. These two last were all or mostly taken from the *Latin Thesaurus,* writ by Joh. Milton Uncle to Edw. Phillips" (II, 1118). Neither book was discovered, nor was either recorded in any publishing notice. Has there been some kind of confusion and misreport of *Tractatulus* and its translation? See n33 here for Phillips's comment on Milton's Latin thesaurus, which certainly gives no indication that it was a source for any volume by him, but also n35, which complicates the matter.

We do not know what work Phillips may have accomplished for his uncle after the Restoration. He says he was Milton's chief amanuensis for *Paradise Lost*, but that could mean in the periods when it was being developed before 1660 (or, rather,1661, since little work was probably possible in 1660). His report that "for some years as I went from time to time to Visit him, in a Parcel of Ten, Twenty, or Thirty Verses at a Time, which being Written by whatever hand came next, might possibly want Correction as to the Orthography and Pointing"[24] could lie before or after the Restoration. It is also postulated that he was the "corrector" (proofreader) of the first edition of the poem (1667), and his hand is seen in the manuscript of the extant first book that was used as copytext. But it is manifest that he was far from fastidious in any proofreading he may have done. This is obvious too in the results of whoever the corrector of the edition was (Phillips or someone else), probably working from the manuscript, but also with additional knowledge or information about the desired text.[25] Additionally, it is supposed that Phillips saw the second edition through the press (1674). These times fit nicely into what we have recounted of his employments and own writing; work during the years 1661–1665, however (the poem seems to have been completed by 1665, according to the interpretation of Thomas Ellwood's account[26]), seems more restricted. His hand does not appear in the manuscript of *De doctrina christiana* (usually dated between 1658 and 1660), at which time he was engaged with teaching and secretarial work and his own publication.

Aside from these publications, and inferences from what we know of Milton's life and Edward's aiding Aubrey, only Wood's statement offers information about the remainder of his life, but it is important that we recognize Wood's snobbish attitude noted before: of Edward, in 1651, he writes, "he left the University without the Honour of a Degree." "Afterwards, or about that time [apparently after his association with the Earl of Arlington, 1677–1679(?)], he married a Woman with several children, taught School in the Strand near the May-Pole, lived in poor condition (tho' a good master) wrote and translated several things meerly to get a bare livelyhood, was out of Employment in 1684 and 85" (II, 1117). Because of the frequency of his name, no record of a marriage has been certain. There is no other "evidence" that Edward was married, or that he lived in the Strand, or that he was out of employment in 1684–1685, or in financial straits. If Wood's statement is correct, is it possible that Edward's being located in the Strand can be connected with his father's residence there (noted in the deeds previously cited) many years earlier? Is it possible that the references to John as being in Westminster also indicate this same residence? We do not know specifically what property his father owned there or exactly where his mother and her new husband Thomas Agar lived, although it was in the vicinity of the Crown Office.[27] In any case, Wood—and everyone else!—has not thought of Phillips's possible income from rents from properties he inherited (as in Shrewsbury) or that he might have lived in such a property (usually "tenements" were involved with various rentals). Is it possible that Wood has confused the two brothers, revealed by his final negative riposte concerning John, "forsakes his Wife and Children"—that single added statement is also our only "evidence" of John's marriage—, both references being to only one of the brothers? Perhaps either Edward or John was not married. Perhaps this information in the account of Edward added in the 1721 edition is totally wrong for either brother. However, I question an assumption that Wood apparently made and that has been unquestionably accepted ever since. Aubrey had been doing investigative work for Wood's biographical entries, and Wood indeed pens a sentence in "Minutes of the Life of Mr John Milton," Bodleian MS Aubrey 8, Sheet C, f. 1r: "Why do ye not set downe where Joh. Milton was borne?"[28] On Sheet A, f. 2r, Aubrey writes, "vidua Affirmat she gave all his papers [among wch this Dict. imperfect] to his Nephew, that he brought up, a sister's son: . . . Philips, who lives neer the Maypole in the Strand."[29] (Superscripted is "vidua" and "[among wch this Dict. Imperfect],"and the brackets appear in the original.) On this same page,

Aubrey writes: "Q. his nephew Mr Edw. Philips for a perfect Catalogue of his Writings." A couple of leaves later, Sheet C, f. 1r, Aubrey quotes "from Mr E. Philips" and in the following paragraph talks of "Mr Edw. Philip his, [his Nephew and then Amanuensis] hath"; the bracketed section and the brackets appear in the original. On this leaf also appears "wch E. Ph. remembers." Aubrey's "Minutes" are dated 1681(?) and, importantly, they include material written down by Phillips: "Edw. Philips his cheif Amanuensis" ("cheif" is superscripted) alongside Aubrey's listing of "Paradise {lost 4to. | regaind 4to.," Sheet A, f.2v; the catalogue requested, Sheet B, f. 1r; and a paragraph that specifically speaks of "his sisters two sons Edw: & John Philips ye first 10 the other 9 years of age," Sheet B, f. 1v. It is obvious that Aubrey knew Edward Phillips and knew Phillips's first name, Edward (although Edward's manuscript additions were inserted after Sheet A, f. 2r, was written), and yet he leaves blank the first name of him who lived near the May Pole in the Strand and was married and who received Milton's papers from Milton's widow on the same sheet that he refers to Edward. Only Edward, *later,* indicates his brother's first name. The logical conclusion that arises is that " . . . Philips, who lives neer the Maypole in the Strand" was John, not Edward as everyone has assumed because that's the way Wood has recorded it.[30]

The remainder of Wood's comment at this point— "he married a Woman with several Children, taught School in the Strand near the May-Pole, lived in poor condition"—therefore, also becomes misinformation. This is the only "evidence" that Edward was married and became a stepfather, or that he lived in Westminster some time after 1679. (See the next chapter for consideration of the statement in reference to John.) Wood's statement that he "was out of Employment in 1684 and 85" may simply mean that Edward (if Edward truly is meant) was not known to be teaching for some aristocratic person during those years. Since he did teach in various aristocratic venues, Wood may have inferred the residence in the Strand as a place of further teaching. Edward's impecuniousness is also lacking substantiation, other than his uncle Thomas Agar's will of 10 June 1671, a time when we do not know what Edward was doing between 1670 and 1677 unless he returned to work for Ashmole. (He did publish three new items in this period, as well as three new editions of other works.) The £200 bequeathed him was to be used "in the purchase of an Annuity for his life or some place of imployment for his better subsistence which shall seem most for his benefitt," but this was to be guided by his brother's son Thomas Agar, the executor of the will. The legacy would be void if the uncle procured "the Kings Mts Graunt of my Office of ingrossing of Appealls to be made and passed vnder the great Seale of England to him" (French, V, 33). Instead, it was Christopher Milton's son

Thomas who worked with Agar in Chancery and succeeded to his position
as Deputy Clerk in the Crown Office upon his death in 1673. Perhaps Edward was not interested in this position in Agar's office; perhaps he was considered less fitted for it, and Agar maneuvered his nephew Thomas Milton
into it instead. Thomas Milton, as recorded in chapter 1, became a member
of the Inner Temple in November 1670, but was not called to the bar until
November 1677. The nephew Thomas Agar, as we have seen but which fact
has been ignored by others discussing the will, had been a lawyer since 27
November 1663 and in the important position of Surveyor to His Majesty's
Woods and Forests since 23 November 1664. A codicil to the will on 27 October 1673 does not alter the bequest to Edward. The interpretation of the
will—for example, Parker's "The will is not flattering to Edward; indeed,
Agar clearly does not trust his judgement in handling money" (1148)—is an
extrapolation that is not warranted: the nephew Thomas Agar's legal experience and governmental position suggest instead that some help in acquiring "most for his benefitt" would be wise, and "requiring and enioyning him
my said sonn in Law to be ordered and gouerned herein by him my said
Nephew" ensures that it be followed. It should be needless to say: many
people need advice in making financial decisions, and lawyers are often the
advisers of choice. Agar may have wanted to be certain that Phillips did not
do something such as, apparently, John Milton did with "another great Sum,
by mismanagement and for want of good advice" (Phillips, xliii). Perhaps all
of this information about Phillips is quite wrong: perhaps he was not married, did not have stepchildren, was not in particularly difficult financial
straits, and was engaged in his own writing and publication in the last ten to
fifteen years of his life.

It is impossible to say how much financial support came from all of
Phillips's works and their reappearances, but Edward seems not to have been
idle prior to his work for Evelyn and Ashmole, or around the time he tu-
tored the Earl of Pembroke's son, or in the period between that and employment by Arlington, or during part of the 1680s when he was also consulted
by Aubrey (in London? in Oxford?). Wood's specification of "1684 and 85"
for nonemployment is curious when we remember *Minority of St. Lewis* (1685)
and *A Treatise of the Way and Manner of Forming the Derivatives of the Latin Tongue*
(1685). However, it should be pointed out (and never has been) that he and
his brother (not unlike Milton himself, his grandfather, his uncle Christopher, and his father) may have benefited financially from properties or other
holdings acquired by their father, as I have remarked before. Does Agar's
will suggest that Edward may have made some misguided investments prior
to 1671? At least the employments that we do know of seem hardly finan-

cially rewarding enough to sustain Edward during periods apparently lacking in such employment. Financial sustenance may have come for Edward from the "family's profession."

Edward's death date is uncertain. He is not included in his cousin Thomas Agar's will, 4 February 1686/7, but his edition of the State Papers indicates that he was alive in 1694; apparently he had died by the time John Toland wrote his biography of Milton, 1698. The burial of an Edward Phillips on 12 June 1697 at St. Mary's, Shrewsbury, perhaps refers to the mayor who examined a Michael Ball, whose house, interestingly enough, was in Mardol.[31] There were numerous Phillipses in the area, and this might or might not have been a relative. Yet, aside from publications and conference with Aubrey, we know nothing about Edward's life and movements after 1679. Is it farfetched to think that he might have returned to Shrewsbury as a good citizen who owned various properties there?

3

The question of Milton's manuscripts at the time of his death is a vexing one, but it does bear upon Edward, although perhaps less than commentators have inferred. No one makes any mention of the Commonplace Book. As cited above, Aubrey reported that Milton's widow, Elizabeth Minshull Milton, affirmed that she gave all of his papers to his nephew, but as we have seen, that logically should mean John, not Edward. If I am correct, then all of the constant iteration of Wood and of Godwin, who follows Wood, to the effect that John and Milton parted company somewhere around 1652, is wrong. (Discussion of John will be taken up in chapter 4.) Toland tells us: "I perus'd the Papers of one of his Nephews, learnt what I could in Discourse with the other."[32] Darbishire (342n) gives the standard interpretation: "the nephew whose papers he perused must have been Edward Phillips, then, it seems, recently dead; the other with whom he talked was John Phillips 'the younger Nephew, now alive' (159)." Parker, although he maintains the reading of Edward as recipient of Milton's papers in 1674, is accurate in saying, "We can trace surprisingly few things, and these never directly back to Phillips" (II, 655). Edward will appear here and there in the following survey of the manuscripts.

"I heard that after he was blind," Aubrey records, "that he was writing a Latin Dictionary" ("Latin" being inserted above the line, Sheet A, f. 2r) "in the hands of Moyses Pitt" (added in the margin); and notes the papers given to his nephew "among wch this Dict. imperfect." "Dictionarie—impfect Q+" is also listed on Sheet A, f. 1r. This he repeated on Sheet A, f. 2v, as the fourteenth item in his catalogue of works, "He wrote a Dictionary called

Idioma Linguae Latinae, from Mr Packer who was his Scholar" (Darbishire, 9). Aubrey's thirteenth item is: "Idea Theologiae in MS. in ye hands of Mr Skinner [a merchant's sonne] in Marke Lane" (Darbishire, 9–10; the bracketed phrase is superscripted). Cyriack Skinner (the Anonymous Biographer, an identifying description we really should get rid of) tells us (f. 6v): "It was now [after 1652] that hee began that laborious work of amassing out of all the Classic Authors, both in Prose and Verse, a *Latin Thesaurus* to the emendation of that done by Stephanus. Also the composing *Paradise Lost* And the framing a *Body of Divinity* out of the Bible: . . . & had begun a *Greek Thesaurus.*" Wood, repeating Skinner (I, Fasti, 265), writes: "he began that laborious work of amassing out of all the classic Authors both in prose and verse a Latin *Thesaurus,* to the emendation of that done by *Stephanus;* also the composing of *Paradise lost,* and of the framing a *Body of Divinity* out of the Bible." His listing of published works (264–66) is followed by: "These, I think, are all the things that he hath yet extant: those that are not, are *The Body of Divinity,* which my friend calls Idea *Theologiæ,* now, or at least lately, in the hands of the Author's Acquaintance called *Cyr. Skinner,* living in *Mark-lane London,* and the *Latin Thesaurus* in those of Edw. Philipps his Nephew." He means Daniel Skinner, of course, but his error probably arises because he knew the author of the "Anonymous" life, deposited in the Bodleian, which he used throughout his 1691 entry in *Athenæ Oxonienses,* and assumed that he would have been the Skinner who held what we call *De doctrina christiana* and others, including Cyriack, called "a Body of Divinity." (Cyriack was not "a merchant's sonne," of course. His grandfathers were Sir Vincent Skinner and Sir Edward Coke.) While each commentator—including Phillips and Toland—seems to have added something to these reports, it is clear that one took from another without much, if any, change and, one suspects, without corroboration. Such mere copying nullifies the significance of the number of occurrences of a statement and puts a heavy burden of interpretation upon the words of the earliest biographical statement of any specific detail that has been unearthed.[33] It should be observed that Phillips mentions what he calls "a Tractate which [Milton] thought fit to collect from the ablest of Divines, who had written of that Subject; *Amesius, Wollebius, &c. viz.* A perfect System of Divinity, of which more hereafter" (xix) but he never returns to that "System of Divinity." As we have observed, Phillips was in Shrewsbury in the earlier 1650s and engaged in his own studying, writing, secretarial work, and teaching during this decade. He was in Milton's home when the "System of Divinity" seems to have been begun, at least through the keeping of the Theological Index, and which he noted in the Commonplace Book (CPB) around February 1651. Perhaps his not returning to the subject is a result of his not having any first-hand knowledge of it, for not only does his hand not appear in the manuscript, but he was not around Milton's home when the version that Picard seems to have copied during the years 1658–1660 was developed, nor when Picard did his work and afterward when so many alterations were made in the manuscript by so many hands, including Picard's.

Of the posthumous works, Aubrey lists *A Brief History of Moscovia* (1682) as does Phillips in the catalogue concluding the 1694 "Life" ([xlix-liv]), which also includes *Literæ Pseudo-Senatûs Anglicani* (1676), the source for his translation of the State Papers. Parker (637; 1150 n71) assumes that Milton gave the manuscript of *Moscovia* to Brabazon Aylmer before he died, and that he had Daniel Skinner transcribe the State Papers for publication. Of the former, all that Aylmer's preface remarks is "sometime before his death [he] disposed of it to be printed." Phillips published garbled versions of the four political sonnets omitted from the 1673 edition of the poems (xlv-xlviii, sonnets to Fairfax, Cromwell, Vane, and Cyriack Skinner, all in the Trinity MS).[34] Toland covers the content of the preceding paragraph: "He had leisure enough now [after 1655] . . . to pursue his *History of Britain,* and his new *Thesaurus Linguæ Latinæ*" (112); "MILTON'S *Thesaurus Linguæ Latinæ,* design'd as a Supplement to STEPHANUS, was never publisht, and has bin of great use to Dr. LITTLETON in compiling his Dictionary.[35] He wrote likewise a *System of Divinity,* but whether intended for public view, or collected merely for his own use, I cannot determin. It was in the hands of his Friend CYRIAC SKINNER; and where at present is uncertain" (147–48). Of great importance are two manuscripts that Toland caused to be published in *A Complete Collection* (1698): *A Letter to a Friend,* II, 659–740, dated 20 October 1659, and *The Present Means and Brief Delineation of a Free Commonwealth,* II, 799–800, dated 23 February-4 March 1660. "This ['a Letter to som Stateman'] and another small Piece to the same purpose, addrest I suppose to MONK, were communicated to me by a worthy Friend, who a little after the Author's Death, had them from his Nephew; and I imparted them to the Publishers of the new Edition of his Works in Folio" (117–18).[36] The nephew has been assumed to be Edward, but was he John? Only Phillips and Toland make reference to what became *Mr John Miltons Character of the Long Parliament and Assembly of Divines. In MDCXLI* (1681): "In the year 70 also came abroad his *History of Britain,* . . . we have it not as it came out of his hands; for the Licensers, those sworn Officers to destroy Learning, Liberty, and good Sense, expung'd several passages of it" (138). He continued, "But not to digress too far, our Author bestow'd a Copy of the unlicens'd Papers of his History on the Earl of *Anglesey,* who . . . was his constant Visitor" (139). Nonetheless the published book is not reprinted in the 1698 collection, nor is it listed in Phillips's catalogue. (A variant text to that printed is owned by Harvard University Library.[37])

Further, Toland (23) notes "two *Greec* Letters of his [Charles Diodati's] to MILTON, very handsomely written, and which I have now in my hands" (now in the British Library), and *A Complete Collection* (1698), I, prints the *History of Britain* (with a separate title page dated 1694) as *"Publish'd from a Copy corrected by the Author himself,"* yielding a number of emendations and corrections to the 1670 text. No manuscripts of a Latin thesaurus, a Greek thesaurus, or a corrected *History of Britain* are known; the problem of the theological tract is involved and is taken up elsewhere. Manuscripts accepted as probably authentic that have turned up include some personal letters, State Papers[38] (these have been discussed and/or published in the Columbia Edition of the works and the Yale Prose, and by various scholars—Maurice Kelley, J. Max Patrick, Leo Miller, Robert T. Fallon, amongst them), "Proposalls of certaine expedients for the preventing of a civill war now feard, & the settling of a firme government" (owned by Columbia University Library), the Trinity Manuscript (owned by Trinity College, Cambridge, Library, once the property of Sir Henry Pickering), and the Commonplace Book (now in the British Library, once owned by Sir Richard Graham) with a Latin prolusion and two Latin poems (now owned by the Harry Ransom Humanities Research Center, University of Texas).

The authentic State Papers pose many problems. The belief that the 1676 edition of *Literæ Pseudo-Senatûs Anglicani* (printed in Amsterdam by Peter and John Blaeu, with a basket of fruit device on the title page, and reprinted by E. Fricx in Brussels, with a face device on the title page) presented Milton's texts and was the only text is ill-informed. Parker, for example (1180, n145), says that Moses Pitt(s) "was evidently responsible for the publications," basing that on Daniel Skinner's statement of 28 October 1676 (PRO, SP Dom 29/386/65). Skinner writes: "That Mr Pitts Bookseller in Pauls Churchyard to the best of my remembrance about 4 or 5 moneths agoe told me he had mett withall and bought some of Mr Miltons papers, and that if I would procure an agreement betwixt him And Elseviere at Amsterdam (to whose care I had long before committed the true perfect copy of the state letters to be printed) he would communicate them to my perusall; If I would not, he would proceed his own way and make the best advantage of 'um; Soe that in all probability I not procuring Elsevieres concurrance with him, and 'tis impossible it should be otherwise, Mr Pitts has been the man by whose means this late imperfect surreptitious copy has been publish't." Skinner's transcription of the State Papers is in the Public Record Office, SP Dom 9/194, which does not include thirteen papers given

in *Literæ* but adds fourteen that are not in *Literæ*. The first assumption that
has clouded the issue of these items is that the papers Pitt purchased included the State Papers since that is what Skinner is discussing and since no
volume of Milton's work was published by Pitt. However, 1) Aubrey's "in the
hands of Moyses Pitt" refers only to the Latin dictionary, 2) Skinner does not
specify what papers Pitt had purchased, although he says "som," 3) Phillips
cites only the "thesaurus" and these papers were disarranged. The assumption, in other words, may be false. A second assumption is that the copy of
the State Papers that Skinner communicated to Daniel Elsevier is "the true
perfect copy" since this is what he says it was, and Skinner tells us that what
was published is an "imperfect surreptitious copy." That indicates that Skinner recognized that there were at least two copies of the State Papers. Parker's
statement (as well as French's, V, 70) that Milton had Skinner transcribe
them for publication is inferred from Toland's "The Danish Resident prevail'd
with Milton to get the Letters of State (formerly mention'd) transcrib'd,
and which were publisht after his death" (44). Skinner's "perfect" copy, as
noted above, has fourteen items not in the edition, but it is hardly "perfect"
when it omits thirteen. We do not know that Skinner's copy was made at
Milton's instigation. The third assumption that Parker takes over from Skinner is that Pitt "has been the man by whose meanes . . . [it] has been publish't."
Parker, assuming that the nephew who obtained papers at Milton's death
was Edward, asserts: "It was doubtless Phillips himself who sold to Moses
Pitts the different collection of state papers that was published in two editions in 1676" (656). His "different collection" refers to his citation in the
preceding sentence of the Columbia University manuscript MS X823 M64/
S52, which includes papers in the printed edition with two omissions, ten in
the Skinner manuscript but not in the edition, and ten additional items
although these are not connected with Milton with certainty.[39] This therefore implies at least three copies of a rather full manuscript of State Papers,
and Parker's confusion is to be noted. But there were at least two more
caches of State Papers, those printed by Gregorio Leti in *Historia, e Memorie
recondite sopra alla vita di Oliviero Cromvele* (Amsterdam: Pietro et Giovanni
Blaev, 1692), II, and those published in Johan Christian Lünig's *Literæ
Procerum Europæ, ab Imperatoribus, Electoribus, Principibus, Statibusque Sacri Imperii Romano-Germanici* (Lipsiæ: Apud Jo. Frider. Gleditsch & Filium. Anno
MDCCXII), three volumes.[40] Even though the Blaeus produced the first 1676
edition and Leti's biography of Cromwell, the texts of the State Papers therein,
as well as the texts in the Lünig compilation, differ very frequently and do
not always replicate the same letters. Most often, numerous dates and recipi-
ents—either missing, questionable, or in error in 1676—are supplied by
Leti or Lünig. It is clear that there were at least five manuscripts of Milton's

"authentic" State Papers with significant differences amongst them, and the claims that modern commentators have made for Moses Pitt and especially for Daniel Skinner should be regarded with high skepticism. These five different forms of the State Papers do *not* allow for a clear-cut provenance. There has been *no* full collation of all five collections.

Whatever papers were given to Milton's nephew by his widow may not have been many more than these relatively few, but very important, items noted above. That they were dispersed to and through different people seems clear. But was the nephew Edward or John? That question may be unsolvable, and perhaps its answer does not require that the other nephew did not also have some manuscript or other of his uncle, but if we can rid ourselves of the attitude that John did not darken his uncle's door after 1652 and if we can entertain the possibility that John was not the despicable character that Wood and Godwin make him, there is no reason why he might not indeed be the " . . . Philips, who lives neer the Maypole in the Strand," the recipient of Milton's papers.

4

A critical question for John Milton's biography and for Edward and John Phillips is when did his sister, their mother, die? As we have seen in chapter 2, Anne Milton Phillips Agar's, daughter Anne would have been born in 1636 according to her marriage license, and it seems that Milton's sister was alive when their mother died in April 1637. Milton, of course, went to France and Italy around the beginning of May 1638 and returned around the end of June to the beginning of July 1639. He travelled to Venice via Bologna and Ferrara in April 1639, where he seems to have stayed for about a month. Aside from the allurements of the city, an important English enclave existed at this port, the location of an English Embassy where Sir Henry Wotton earlier held official audience. Wotton, as is well known, advised Milton in April 1638 on his itinerary and gave him introductions to various people. It was Venice that became the last port of call for British travellers, from which one sent home books (as Milton did) and other accumulations of travel, and significantly the one place that family in England would know a visitor would be at some point in the sojourn. Mail thus was sent to Venice in care of the Embassy. Milton's itinerary was not laid out strictly, nor strictly followed, as his impulse to go to Sicily and Greece attests, but he did not go—instead he turned back north from Naples. Mail would not have been certain of reaching him in any of the places he did visit—Florence, Rome, Naples, or Florence again where he returned earlier than he would have had he indeed gone to Sicily. At least most accommodations would also have been uncertain before he left England. Only in Venice—the Embassy operating like an American Express office today—would mail with whatever news was deemed important definitely arrive with the assurance that the recipient would receive it. During May and into June, he travelled from Venice to Verona to Milan through Lombardy and the Pennine Alps to Geneva, where he stayed for a bit at least. Here, he visited the famous and learned theologian Giovanni Diodati, the uncle of his friend Charles Diodati.

Charles died and was buried at St. Anne's, Blackfriars, on 27 August 1638; the cause is not certainly known, but a visitation of the plague apparently took his sister Philadelphia on 10 August 1638. (Their stepmother Isabel died at childbirth on 23 June 1638.) Various scenarios have been advanced for Milton's trip to Geneva: the report of Charles's death received in Naples or in Florence or in Venice, or the speculation that Geneva was on his itinerary and he learned of the death from Charles's uncle.[41] My previous paragraph underscores the lack of logic in his learning of the death in Naples (or Rome) or Florence. That Geneva with a visit to Dr. Diodati was an expected stop is certainly possible, and it is also possible that mail sent to him in Venice told of Charles's death. But would not such information in a letter to Milton—from whom?—be simply included in a letter with more direct import for Milton than a letter especially sent to communicate Charles's death? It should be obvious as to where this thinking is leading me. Was there instead a letter from Thomasin or Christopher or Thomas Agar telling Milton that his sister had died while he was abroad, incidentally also noting Charles's demise? Did Anne also succumb to the visitation of the plague in the middle of 1638? Milton's actions upon his return, a pointed comment in his elegy for Charles, "Epitaphium Damonis," and the Poor Laws suggest the plausibility of that sad event.

Where Milton lived upon his return is uncertain. Before going to the continent he lived at Horton, Bucks, with his father, and probably made many trips to London. He mentions such trips, as well as the possibility of taking rooms at one of the Inns of Court in a letter to Diodati in November 1637, but there is no proof that the plan eventuated. (Various connections with those who were members of one of the Inns of Court as cited in chapters 1, 2, and above, suggest that the plan could have been carried through despite all lack of evidence.) As we have seen, Christopher and Thomasin Milton may have joined the father in Horton in 1637, surely before early 1638, and Milton may have made the trip to Eton to see Wotton perhaps a bit more easily from Horton than from London. However, the family seems to have owned various pieces of property around town (for example, the Ludgate tenement) and the Agar family was located apparently near the Crown Office in Westminster. There were thus various places Milton may have stayed on his trips to London. Whether he stayed in such a place or not before going to the Continent and then possibly upon his return, his "Lodging" in the autumn of 1639 was in the house of "one *Russel,* a Taylor," in St. Bride's Churchyard near Fleet Street.[42] Prior to this, however, it is logical that his first domicile, even if only briefly, upon return from the continent was with his father in Horton. How long he stayed at Russell's is not established, but he seems to have moved to a large house in Aldersgate in 1640. Aubrey's statement or interpretation (see n42) conflicts with Phillips's two remarks (one found in Aubrey's notes, the other in the "Life") and what we know of Milton's marriage to Mary Powell, but perhaps it does add to the probability that the lodging at Russell's was less "immediate" and also longer than formerly believed. What is provocative is that John Phillips (eight years of age in 1639) came to live with him at St. Bride's, and Edward (nine or ten years of age in 1640), a pupil there, joined them later in Aldersgate Street, according to what Phillips says. Phillips, who is frequently confused about dates and time, however, wrote in the statement in Aubrey's notes that he was ten years of age and John, nine, when they went to St. Bride's. Edward was born in August 1630, and John in October 1631; perhaps the move to Aldersgate when Edward joined the household was indeed in later 1640 and the statement (made around 1681), built on that association, to have him report ten and nine. The "Life" of his uncle records that Milton "made no long stay in his Lodgings in St. Brides Churchyard" and he hastened to take a larger place.

Edward Jones has raised a question of the date of the move, based upon the lack of assessment in Aldersgate in 1640.[43] The "lodgings" of Mr. Russell, one suspects, may not have been very amenable for a man and a boy (and a variety of books, which Phillips mentions as a cause for the move). Phillips does not say that Milton took a flat in a house owned by Russell; it sounds more like a couple of rooms. The trip from the Agar home, however, if it were still Milton's first brother-in-law's home in the Strand or one nearby the Crown office, would have been neither difficult nor terribly long. The single man of thirty-one, John Milton, seems hardly the person who would make an ideal foster parent. Yet John, Edward tells us, "had been wholly committed to his Charge and Care" (xvii), and Edward was soon to be so committed as well. Such removal from their mother's assumed nearby presence and the total lack of any further reference to her in their lives point to a clear and logical explanation. We have already considered in chapter 1 an upshot that this situation may have provoked a short while later in 1642— Milton's marriage. A slightly different scenario from the one usually offered may be that Milton returned to his father's home in Horton upon his return from the Continent around August or even September 1639, rather than

July; rather than simply "visits paid to his Father and other Friends" (Phillips, xvi), those visits may have involved a couple of months, during which time arrangements were worked out for John to live with him and, later, Edward; and some time around November or so, he took "a Lodging" at Russell's house. The "no long stay" there that Phillips records may have continued until after May 1640 (see note 43) when a larger place was required so that "not long after his taking this House" in Aldersgate Street "his Elder Nephew" could be "put to Board with him also."[44] (That move may thus have been in June or July 1640; see n43.) Whatever the arrangement had been with Thomas Agar for John's leaving his stepfather's home, the continued presence of Edward there may simply not have worked out well, and it was decided that he too should be "wholly committed to the Charge and Care" of his uncle.

While there is no unassailable evidence to corroborate or to deny it, a cogent answer to the critical question of Anne Milton Phillips Agar's death is "sometime between May 1638 and July 1639," during Milton's sojourn abroad. Perhaps the information was transmitted in a letter Milton received in Venice, with the death of Charles also reported. Perhaps her death, if during this time, was a result of the plague. At least this supplies a more meaningful reason why the Phillips boys came to live with their uncle and an explanation of the lack of information about Anne and any relationship with her sons from autumn 1639 onward. That John Phillips was "wholly committed to [Milton's] Charge and Care" is made sensible only if the mother no longer was alive. Why else is there no reference to their mother in the Phillips boys' lives after autumn 1639? Agar would have had the care of his infant daughter Anne and increasing duties as the Deputy Clerk of the Crown; in contrast, Milton was by himself and not gainfully employed.

In his elegy for Diodati, written perhaps in autumn 1639, Milton writes: "Ast ubi mens expleta domum, pecorisque relicti / Cura vocat" (14–15), "But when his mind was full and the care of the flock / left behind called him home." The reference in 1639 cannot apply to his father or his sister or his brother and family, and surely is not the English people! But particularly in view of what does occur in autumn 1639 and 1640, the reference points to his nephews and the "care" ("Cura") needed, since Christopher's family was growing and since his brother-in-law Thomas Agar was much involved in Chancery proceedings and would have been a single parent of his three-year-old daughter Anne. The reference also indicates that he became aware of the need to supply "care of the flock / left behind" while on the Continent.

If Anne did die in 1638, Edward and John Phillips would have technically been orphans. There is no record of adoption by Agar. The Poor Laws of 1601 raise the issue of orphans but not of stepparents, that is, of orphans who would be considered "paupers." Those who should maintain "pauper" children are parents and grandparents when they have sufficient ability to maintain those children. In this case the Phillips boys had a grandfather, John Milton, and a grandmother, Katherine Phillips, who were certainly able to maintain the "orphans" as well as a stepfather. The Poor Laws extended to married and unmarried people having no means to maintain themselves through ordinary and daily trade of life, and dependent children were apprenticed until age twenty-four for boys and age twenty-one for girls or until they married. No Settlement documents have been found for the Phillipses (although in moving into Milton's home they changed the parish of their births), and the arrangement for the boys may have been a private affair, particularly as a result of Agar's official position, and the affluent financial condition of their relatives obviates "pauperism." (Does the grandfather's joining Milton's domicile shortly after they did also ease the regulation?) Edward became twenty-four in 1654, having been a student prior to that time (and apparently since leaving Milton's home) and by 1650, with the death of the grandmother, becoming a landowner. John turned twenty-four in 1655, again having been with Milton and in 1654 at least being employed in semi-official governmental business, as well as being a landowner in 1650.

The only significant attempt to determine the date of Anne's death has been Ralph Hone's in his dissertation and in an article drawn from his findings.[45] A deed from Richard Burde (No. 1457) dated 29 December 1639 concerning the property that he leased in Shrewsbury (see above) remarks Edward Phillips "late of the Strand in the Countie of Middlesex gent deceased and Anne his wife And Katherine Phillipps of the Towne of Shrewsbury." The citation is a variation on Deed No. 1226 of 18 January 1626/7, "Edward Phillips of the Strand, Middlesex, gentleman, and Anne, his wife, and Katherine Phillips of Shrewsbury, his mother" (a deed signed by Anne and marked by Katherine). The deed of 1639 indicates that Burde was aware of Edward's death, which had occurred more than eight years before. The lack of such a note about Anne leads Hone to argue that Anne was still alive in December 1639 (as was Katherine Phillips). But there are two problems with that inference: first, the deed was not concerned with the Phillipses and is a restatement of a former legal conveyance, becoming thus a copying of the former with acknowledgment of Edward's death more than eight years before; second, Burde is not aware of Anne's marriage to Thomas Agar eight years before, although, as a mere reference to the former transaction, there would be no need to include her new name. The inclusion of the statement in the 1639 deed can be construed as a *pro forma* remark, since the property had been leased originally from the three Phillipses and was still in the ownership of the Phillips family. With Edward's death, however, the ownership would have transferred to his mother according to his will, and thus had ownership been significant in this new deed of 1639, Burde should have said only "Katherine Phillips of the Towne of Shrewsbury," not even mentioning Edward or Anne.

Edward Phillips, then—nephew, somewhat "foster child," amanuensis, frequent visitor to Milton's home, schoolteacher and author and translator—remained in close contact with his uncle and with his uncle's world. And yet Edward's world was involved in the aristocratic world of his day, in a world of Royalists and titled people, but with no evidence of his political leanings or activity. His employment of Monck's papers and his historical survey of the reigns of Charles I and Charles II in bringing Baker's chronicle up to date do not establish his persuasion, which could be advanced as anti-Royalist on the one hand and pro-Royalist on the other. Worden's association of him with his brother John in the production of the Ludlow papers is not evidential. He emerges as one not concerned with the political seesaw of his day, an author who was not given to intellectual inquiries and argument, an author who produced a corpus of useful books—whether translations or dictionaries (and linguistic volumes) or edited materials—that should not be dismissed because they are not on a par with the work of his uncle or not trenchant studies of momentous issues. He shows no penchant in his acknowledged work of strong political conviction or for any religious persuasion. The lack of polemics in his work may thus be understood, particularly in contrast with his uncle and his brother. His associates seem to be on both sides of the political spectrum, but with a greater weight on the aristocratic, plus the world of the press. Perhaps Edward was less sharp of mind, one of average intelligence, but Parker's epitome of him as having "the soul of a hasty hack writer" tells us more about what Parker expected from a product of Milton's tutelage than about Phillips as a person.

4

John Phillips

Nonroyalist and Nephew

The difficulty in dealing with John Phillips has been laid out in the previous chapter. As Rajan remarks in discussing Godwin, "John is the bad boy, while Edward allows legacy to be figured as filiation, continuation, and perfectibility. This binary is unsettled by two elements: John's literary energy, and the almost accidental unraveling in the appendix of the narrativization of Edward. If the former salvages Milton's literary legacy in contingent and unpredictable ways, the latter seems sadly to bring his political legacy to a dead end" (81–82). Godwin assumes John's "unnatural animosity" toward his uncle, and, politically nonobjective as Godwin is, writes of John as turning to royalism, supporting the Restoration, approving of Titus Oates and his charges of conspiracy—all of which Milton would have strongly abominated—and then in an about face of becoming an advocate for Whiggery. "John Philips was thus plunged in the foul and impure stream of politics, such as it was found in the latter part of the reign of Charles the Second" (Godwin, 232). A further side of John, whom Wood implied was a debauchee, given much to drink, bothers Godwin: John is "coarse" and "bawdy," a Rabelaisian, one of the "cavaliers, and *bons vivans,* and demireps, and men of ruined fortunes" (50), one of "impure and lascivious ideas" (50, speaking of *A Satyr Against Hypocrites*). John apparently did frequent taverns, but whether he was often inebriate, a debauchee, leading a "Rabelaisian life," where the adjective is used to describe a life "grossly indecent," may be unwarranted. John did allude to Rabelais frequently and there is coarse humor in some of the works, but the transfer of strategy to character (as well as the prudish evaluation of Rabelais) should be unacceptable. As Parker remarks (657), "noting also the gross indecency of some of his writing, most of Milton's biographers have taken a dislike to John which they have allowed to colour their characterizations of the young man." Though "there is, of course, no real evidence for this, and, evidence or no, it will strike the fairminded as a *non sequitur,*" Parker indicates (and seems to accept) the inference of such commentators as Godwin: "John early became such a coarse writer and 'Bohemian' that Milton must have broken with him in disgust!"[1]

At least the anonymous author of *A Search After Wit* (London, 1691) gives John a positive notice,[2] and John Dunton in *The Life and Errors of John Dunton* (London, 1705) writes, "a Gentleman of good Learning, and well born"; he could write "a Design, off in very little time, if the Gout (or Claret) don't stop him" (241).[3] Giles Jacob in 1720 spoke of *A Satyr Against Hypocrites* as "a very ingenious Performance," a "Forerunner of the Hudibrastic tradition."[4] Parker does not supply a reevaluated reading of John when, first referring to *The Vision of Mons. Chamillard* (1706), he tells us (1169n96):

> Phillips was obviously fond of Rabelais and alludes to him often. Lest my readers think I have overlooked or (worse) suppressed important evidence, let me note here that Phillips exhibits a Royalist bias in his continuation of Heath's *Chronicle* (1676, pp. 519–604), later vindicates *Dr. Oates' Narrative of the Popish Plot* (1680), and still later becomes an advocate of the Whigs. Milton would have relished his vigorous attacks on Sir Roger L'Estrange and Samuel Parker as much as he would have disapproved his association with Titus Oates. He would not have appreciated the brief, slighting reference to *Paradise Lost* in the preface to *The History of the Most Renowned Don Quixote* (1687), sig. Aaa1v. (It must have been difficult being a writer known as the nephew and former amanuensis of a really great writer!)

My reaction is: Did Parker actually read what Phillips wrote?

First, we need to review what we can determine about John's life. He was born in October 1631, presumably in the parish of St. Martin's in the Fields; he went to live with Milton at St. Bride's and then at Aldersgate Street. Traditionally, the rental in St. Bride's Churchyard is placed in autumn 1639, and the move to Aldersgate, 1640, but Edward Jones's research indicates that Milton may not have moved there until 1641, as I have previously remarked: certainly after mid-May 1640, but before 29 April 1641. (See his forthcoming article, "The Loyalty and Subsidy Returns of 1641 and 1642: What They Can Tell Us About the Milton Family.") It is assumed that John was with Milton until he reached his majority in 1651, leaving in 1652; definite evidence for or in denial of this conclusion has not been found. (A remark by Edward Phillips in his "Life," cited later, indicates that he was still with Milton in 1652.) Thus, he should have been with Milton in the Barbican (September 1645 through autumn 1647), in High Holborn (autumn 1647 through March 1649), in Charing Cross and Scotland Yard, Whitehall (March–November 1649, November 1649 through December 1651), possibly in Petty France, Westminster (December 1651 through whenever he left). He lived in Westminster or the City during these years, and the Shrewsbury deeds of 1651, 1653, 1654, and 1655 place him still there. But while there is no evidence about when he left Milton's home, there is also no evidence that he stayed in it until he reached his majority. Edward, we might remember, seems to have left well before *his* majority. For some short time, at least John was in Scotland, for Andrew Sandelands "employed Mr. John Philipps (Mr. Milton's kinsman) to sollicite the busines, both with the judges at Edinburgh, and with the Commissioners at Leith, who by his last letter promiseth to give me a very good account very speedily."[5] The letter is dated 11 April 1654. Phillips was to gather information about the Crown Lands in Scotland. This assignment for John has always been interpreted as the result of Milton's recommendation to his friend, which certainly seems logical, and it is concerned with English governmental business. But the obvious has not been observed: John was in communication with his uncle in 1654 and surely on good terms with him and thought of highly. This in no way suggests a break with Milton when he lived with him, nor at least in the years following.

With probable input from his uncle, he produced *Joannis Philippi Angli Responsio Ad Apologiam Anonymi cujusdam tenebrionis pro Rege & Populo Anglicano infantissimam* (1652), apparently printed in December 1651, in rebuttal of reactions against *Pro Populo Anglicano Defensio* (1651), and most particularly against John Rowland's *Pro Rege et Populo Anglicano Apologia, Contra Johannis Polypragmatici, (alias Miltoni Angli) Defensionem Destructivam, Regis & Populi Anglicani* (1651). (The *Responio* was reprinted in London, Amsterdam, and Leyden in 1652.) The book has been the major reason for placing John in his uncle's home through 1651/52, and then, in 1652 or 53 John, along with his brother, as noted in chapter 3, n9, wrote verses praising Henry Lawes. The attitude toward John by commentators can be seen in Hone's verb and evaluation: "Sometime during the year John was induced to write, in addition to his *Responsio,* twenty-two lines of commendatory poetry, merely conventional stuff, to place above his name in Henry Lawes's *Ayres and Dialogues,* which was to be published in 1653" (135). The poem is not less in worthiness than most of the encomiastic verses prefacing such publications: the words Hone uses aim at putting Phillips down, valid though they may be. But "induced," for the poem and for *Responsio?* John becomes a twenty-one year old "kid" who needs forcing, some kind of parental pressure, to write this important rebuttal. Edward writes that Milton "committed this task to the youngest of his Nephews" (xxxii); "committed" may mean, not only "assigned," but "entrusted." Toland's interpretation of this is that Milton "delegated that easy task to his younger Nephew *John Philips,* now alive." John asseverates in the preface, "I could not refrain from undertaking, even though unasked, to blunt the impudence of this utterly impertinent scoundrel" (Yale

Prose, IV, ii, 891). He precedes this with a statement that is ignored by those who wish to believe his "unnatural animosity" toward his uncle: "likewise bound by many ties of duty to that gentleman whom I have always honored and who is now attacked by this scurrilous fellow." And then there is the comment in his *Montelions Predictions* (London, 1672), 8, that Parker (1169 n95) suggests refers to Milton as "a civil, grave old gentleman whom they know no more than the Pope of Rome." The fact that he would go on to produce more than fifty items in Hone's "Descriptive Catalogue of the Known Works of John Phillips" 'including other poems and political rebuttals' seems to have no significance!

Among documents that may or may not refer to John Phillips are the following, charting or suggesting a charting of the next years of his life.[6] On 29 April 1653 was recorded a "Lease from Richard Moore of Inner Temple, London and Edmund Hopkins to John Phillips, all of London, of 8 rooms above the shop of Richard Holton and the cellar, part of the messuage in Temple Bar, Fleet Street, London, known as Lamb or Holy Lamb, and right of passage thereunto, for 18 years at a rent of £10 per annum."[7] Phillips's residence during the years 1653–1655 seems to be Westminster; however, the deeds may continue only the first reference in the deed of 1651, and thus be incorrect during those years. A letter, dated 10 May 1659, from the same John Phillips, it would seem, to George Bifield is concerned with governmental issues.[8] (See later for Phillips's inferred governmental attitudes immediately preceding the Restoration.) Among the pertinent events of this month, the Rump Parliament was restored on 7 May, its relationship with the Army was explored, and Richard Cromwell resigned on 25 May. A further document may be even more apt. On "16 Nov. 1654, JOHN PHILIPPS, OF Aldersgate Street, London, begs leave to prove his title to a fee-farm rent of 50 l. on land in co. Chester, sold to him last February by Thos. Cotton, of London, and sequestered for recusancy of Edw. Cotton, who was never owner, but received the rent a few years for Thomas" (*Calendar of the Committee for Compounding*, 40 n122). While we cannot absolutely identify this plaintiff with Milton's nephew, it is certainly provocative when we remember Milton's residence (as well as John's) on Aldersgate Street earlier and when we note Sir Thomas Cotton's suit against Milton, Sr., on 28 May 1636 through 1 February 1638. However, this Thomas Cotton (whose brother was John of Fulham, Middlesex) seems to be a painter, whose address was the Compter (prison), London, in October 1654, because of cheating the Prize Office out of money on false warrants for the Admiralty Commissioners.[9] He used an alias of "Miller." A document in the Public Record Office (E179/252/32) records that "John Phillips, schoolmaster, who lived in Aldersgate Street in 1666" was taxed on six hearths; Parker's posthumous note suggests that this was Milton's nephew (see "Additional Notes," 1256, for 1168 n92, in Gordon Campbell's edition of the biography). If these items are in fact citing Milton's nephew, we can place him in a neighborhood from 1654 through 1666, at least, that had been familiar to him and that was nearer to his uncle, who resided in Holborn near Red Lyon Fields from September 1660 through early 1661 and in Jewin Street from early 1661 through 1669(?).[10] Further, such identification would iterate what I have suggested before, that neither nephew was so impoverished as Wood's statement about Edward posits, but rather that, like the rest of the Milton/Phillips family, they were land owners and involved in various transactions that brought in moneys. And a house of six hearths, if indeed that was Milton's nephew's residence, would not be small and suggests rentals of part of it, as was a common practice.

In February 1656, Nathaniel Brooks (that is, Nathanael Brooke, who had published *A Satyr Against Hypocrites* in 1655), publisher of *Sportive Wit,* which has a dedication to [Sir] Ralph Banks signed "J. P.," said "the author of the epistles of the said book" was "John Phillips, who lives about Westminster" (Thurloe, IV, 717–18). The inquiry into regulation of printing, 19 April, found "much scandalous, lascivious, scurrilous and profane matter" in the work, causing the book to be seized; the examiner, Sir John Barkstead, levied fines on John Phillips of Westminster (merely repeating Brooks as to location?), writer of the epistle dedicatory. The book was burned at the Old Exchange on 20 April 1656.[11] On 15 August 1667, a "John Phillips, of St Martin's in Fields, Esq., Bachr, abt 20, his parents dead, & Mrs Margaret Hewes, of St Clement Danes, Spr, abt 18; her mother's consent; at St James Clerkenwell, St Martin's in Fields, or St Clement Danes" is recorded.[12] Parker (1168 n92) notes that a John Phillips married an Elizabeth Ibbitt in St. Giles, Cripplegate, on 4 October 1674. Neither is probably Milton's nephew. Much has been made of his omission from his stepfather's will on 5 November 1673, but dated 10 June 1671. For Hone (147), this omission "was undoubtedly due to disapprobation, on Agar's part, of John Phillips' sympathies or conduct." Agar was a Royalist and John a Parliamentarian (although some have seen a flair with Royalist positions), and John may have led a personal life that Agar disapproved of. Yet we do not know of his financial condition or whether he had made bad investments as perhaps his brother had and which his uncle had. Perhaps he was not poorly off as ownership of lands, which there still may have been, might have countered. However, Hone (148) infers that he may have gone to prison in 1674 as a debtor, from remarks in *Mercurius Verax: or the Prisoners Prognostications for the year 1675* (1675), where he remained until 1677. Yet he published books in 1673, 1675, and 1676, and three in 1677; the inference thus is questionable, a case of overreading. The introductory remarks in the volume are sarcastic toward prognostications alleging good times that cannot be given weight because of the dire economic conditions of the times, and particularly toward those who create and persecute debtors, throwing them into prison for economic problems not in their control.[13] One major cause he says, is women (wives) who force their husbands into debt to keep up with others or simply for extravagant commodities. I suppose that one can read the voice of experience into any remarks that someone makes, but there certainly is nothing that demands that personal reading here and no evidence (in 1674–75) of marriage or impoverishment. Phillips is lashing out at the horrors of indebtedness that plagued the late seventeenth century and the eighteenth century, rendered so graphically by William Hogarth.[14] Phillips does not need to be one experiencing debtor's prison to launch his diatribe.

Agar's omission of John in his will may certainly indicate a breach of relationship or nothing at all. Omission of both Phillipses in Milton's nuncupative will may also be nonindicative of a schism, but instead the questionable reportage of Christopher. A remark in *Modern History, or a Monethly Account*, November 1687, suggests to Hone that John had fallen ill shortly before, and *The Present State of Europe* (London, 1690), I, ii-iii, leads him to consider that John went overseas in August 1689. The preface refers to *Modern History* and its noncontinuance "by reason of the absence of the Gentleman beyond Sea that first began it."

A "Warrant to Thomas Atterbury, messenger, to search for John Philips, against whom information has been given that he has written, published or dispersed several seditious and dangerous pamphlets and libels, and bring him before the Earl of Sunderland to be examined touching the premises" is found in PRO, SP Dom. Entry book 335, p. 219, under 1 November 1684 from Whitehall. Two days later Roger L'Estrange (knighted in 1685) wrote to the Earl (SP Dom. Car. II, 438, No. 74): "Being informed by Mr. Atterbury that one Philips is taken up by your warrant, without conjecturing the cause of his commitment I inform you that he has been very privy to the contrivance of several narratives, which may enable him to make great discoveries. Lest this should escape your knowledge I offer to your consideration the following queries:—1. What narratives or papers about the plot he has at any time written and for whom. 2. Who furnished the materials. 3. Who made any alterations or corrections in them. 4. Who paid him and how much respectively for such and such particulars." The "seditious and dangerous pamphlets and libels" were *Dr. Oates' Narrative of the Popish Plot, Vindicated* (1680); *Mr. L'Estrange Refuted With his own Arguments* (1681); and *The Character of a Popish Successor, and What England may expect from such a one. Part the Second* (1681). These works, and their incompetent interpretations, will be taken up later. The reason for the arch-Tory L'Estrange's entry into the case is obvious; he also was the surveyor of printing presses and licenser of the press. The Earl of Sunderland was Robert Spencer, a member of the privy council and one of the reigning ministers in the first Tory administration of 1680, gentleman of the bedchamber to Charles II, an ambassador, and a major mover in the intrigues of 31 January 1683. Under James II, he became Lord President and principal Secretary of State (for the northern departments) on 4 December 1685. The outcome of this search for Phillips is not recorded.

As cited above, the only reference we have to John's domestic life is Wood's final statement that he forsook his wife and children and made no provision for them. His argument in *Mercurius Verax* suggests an antipathy toward wives (toward marriage?, possibly with influence from Milton's experience in the 1640s). He seems to have lived in Westminster, on or near the Strand, but whether and when he may have moved elsewhere is uncertain. Aside from his numerous publications, to be looked at below, we cannot verify his place of residence or activities. Toland says that he was alive in 1698, and his two last publications, a commendatory poem, a2v, in *Amphion Anglicus. A Work of Many Compositions, for One, Two, Three and Four Voices: . . . By Dr: John Blow* (1700) and *The Vision of Mons. Chamillard Concerning the Battle of Ramilies: and the Miraculous Revolution in Flanders Begun, May the 12th. 1706. A Poem. Humbly Inscrib'd to the Right Honourable John Lord Somers. By a Nephew of the late Mr. John Milton* (1706) and Dunton's remarks in 1705, supply the only information in his last years. It is thus assumed that he died in 1706.[15] For Hone, his was a concern with social and political matters, but it took the form of an "obstreperous career of a dilletante in public affairs" (584).

2

That John Phillips performed scribal work for his uncle has been long accepted; suggestions of the extent of that work, however, have not always been agreed upon. His signature appears on the manuscript of *A Satyr Against Hypocrites* (Bodleian MS Rawlinson Poetical 30) and on the three deeds cited before. What of the text of the dedication "To the Right Worshipfull John Churchill, Esq," the text of the poem itself, and the marginal glosses and corrections? Darbishire argued that the dedication, marginal glosses, and corrections were in the same hand, John Phillips's, the text in the hand of a professional scribe. That seems to be the consensus. The problems are basically two: the formality and the informality of the different pieces of writing, and the fact that the two hands (if we take Darbishire's division) both use differing forms (of r and of e, for example). "Most gratious" in the text (f. 11v, line 21) (are italics intended?) compared with the dedication's letter forms shows them to be suspiciously alike, and when on the same page, f. 11v, we observe the scribe's different capital M̲ in line 12 and t̲'s in the same line and a secretarial r̲ and c̲ in the next line in "preach," we can wonder whether that division is indeed accurate. The hand of the text employs varying letter formations, and the marginal and corrective hand does also; yet those hands seem to be suspiciously the same in both capital and lower case letters. If the autograph of the full manuscript is in one hand and that hand is John Phillips's, then we may have additional reason to assign a number of items written for Milton as penned by his younger nephew.

In regard to John's functioning as an amanuensis, we have the testimony of Edward Phillips in the "Life," xliii-xliv, where he adds "two material passages." The first deals with the preliminaries to the Dutch war in 1652: the Dutch *"Plenipotentiary* could not make such haste, but that the parliament had procured a Copy of their ["Three Embassadours"] Instructions in *Holland,* which was delivered by our Author to his Kinsman that was then with him, to Translate for the Council to view, before the said *Plenipoteniary* had taken shipping for *England."* The kinsman is identified as John Phillips (who was *then with him,* that is, in 1652), and it is supposed "some work was occasionally turned over to him."[16] The second passage reads, "our Author's Kinsman was sent to [an Agent from the Prince of Condé], with an Order of Councel commanding him to depart the Kingdom."[17] No specific item has been identified as the translation referred to. An anonymous note on the title page of a copy of *Responsio* owned by the British Library also calls him "Miltonj Amanvensis"; see French, III, 291.

However, on the basis of accepting the dedication of *A Satyr Against Hypocrites* as being in John's hand, I have previously suggested a number of items that John may have penned for his uncle.[18] These suggestions raise questions and have not necessarily been accepted, but they all date before July 1652, when, perhaps, Phillips was still residing with Milton, or at least close by. The seventeen entries in the Commonplace Book from the *Discorsi* of Machiavelli raise particular problems. Kelley separated these into nine groups: Group 1, pp. 193, 246 (I, 2; I, 4); Group 2, 197 (I, 10); Group 3, 195 and index for Group 2 (I, 2; I, 10); Group 4, 185, 245 (I, 58; I, 59); Group 5, 198, 243, 148, 242 (I, 58; II, 10; II, 12); Group 6, 242, 243 (II, 18; II, 19); Group 7, 242 (II, 24); Group 8, 198 (III, 1); and Group 9, 198 (III, 34).[19] He indicates that "They sometimes show similarities of letter formation and habits of lifting the pen which suggest that in some instances the notes were written by scribes who employed more than one style of handwriting" (124). He states that Groups 1 and 3 are probably the same, and that Groups 4 and 6 and probably 9 are the same. Group 2 is Edward Phillips, and Group 5 is apparently Hands 2 and 3 (that is, if I am correct, John Phillips). That leaves

Groups 7 and 8 entirely unaccounted for. The order of entry is: Group 5 before Groups 8 and 9, the index for Group 2 made with Group 3 and thus Group 2 before Group 3. Further, Group 9 is the scribe who produced letters to Mylius; in Columbia XII these are: L, 348, 350 (7 November 1651); LIIa, 352, 354 (2 January 1652); LV, 360 (8 January 1652); LVII, 362, 364 (20 January 1652); LIX, 368, 370 (10 February 1652); and possibly LXV, 376 (21 February 1652).[20] The CPB entries are dated 1651–1652 based on these letters to Mylius; however, since Edward Phillips was one of the scribes, and it would seem that John Phillips was another, there is no need to restrict the entries to the period of the letters. If we can push up the date a year or two, other entries in the CPB may be dated differently, such as Amanuensis D's material from Dante, 1649–1651 rather than 1650–1667(?).[21] It appears on p. 197 between the two entries by Edward Phillips; it refers to the same 1568 edition that Milton himself recorded in his workbook. Amanuensis D was the scribe of the extant Book I manuscript of *Paradise Lost,* and he also penned the entry from Nicetas Acominate (apparently from the 1647 Paris edition) and its heading on p. 249, dated ca. 1665 because of the *Paradise Lost* manuscript, but this we now may conclude is erroneous. (Certainly, such an isolated entry in the CPB at that time is far-fetched.)

The copy of the *Discorsi* employed probably was from *Tutte le Opere* (1550), which Milton used for his two entries from *Dell'Arte della Guerra,* pp. 177, 182, dated 1640–1642. Although no direct use of these materials from the *Discorsi* has been suggested, except in *The Ready and Easy Way* (1660), some of the ideas seem to lie behind remarks in *Defensio pro Populo Anglicano,* ordered 8 January 1650 and entered in the Stationers' Register on 31 December 1650. Of course, Milton may have read this material well before he had the CPB notes written down, yet it is also possible that his nephews and others made such entries earlier in 1649. On 15 March 1649, Milton was appointed Secretary for Foreign Tongues, a post requiring much time and effort, not only through the clerical duties of correspondent, but also through the commissions of such works as *Articles of Peace* and *Eikonoklastes,* both 1649, and the *Defensio* of 1650–51. Further, his eyesight was failing and he may have been in ill health. Perhaps a professional amanuensis was needed, and perhaps he was Amanuensis D, an unreliable scribe as far as orthography, at least, was concerned; the texts of *Articles of Peace* and *Eikonoklastes* attest to such unreliability of a scribe.

A further suggestion that I have previously made is that Phillips may be Amanuensis A of the Commonplace Book as designated by James Holly Hanford. Assigned to Amanuensis A are entries from Francesco Berni on pp. 71, 187, and from Matteo Maria Boiardo, pp. 77, 186, and the sonnet in Milton's copy of Giovanni della Casa's *Rime et Prose* owned by the New York

Public Library. The notes in the CPB have been dated 1650(?). As with Edward, it is important to remark that none of the hands involved in the above discussion of John's possible scribal work for his uncle appears in the manuscript of *De doctrina christiana*.

3

Phillips's numerous published works, which I look at briefly here, include *A Satyr Against Hypocrites* (1655), *The Tears of the Indians* (1656), *Montelion 1660* (1660), *Don Juan Lamberto* (1661), *Montelions Predictions, or the Hogen Mogen Fortune Teller* (1672), James Heath's *A Chronicle of the Late Intestine War* (1676, continuation), *Dr. Oates' Narrative of the Popish Plot, Vindicated* (1680), *Mr. L'Estrange Refuted With His Own Arguments* (1681), *The Character of a Popish Successor* (1681), *New News from Tory-Land and Tantivy-Shire* (1682), *A Pleasant Conference upon the Observator, and Heraclitus* (1682), *An Humble Offering to the Sacred Memory of the Late Most Serene and Potent Monarch Charles II* (1685), and *Sam. Ld. Bp. of Oxon, His Celebrated Reasons for Abrogating the Test, and Notions of Idolatry* (1688). I have commented on, or will do so below, *Wit and Drollery, Jovial Poems* (1656; perhaps false attribution), *Sportive Wit* (1656), *Maronides or Virgil Travestie* (two parts, 1672, 1673), *Mercurius Verax: or the Prisoners Prognostications For the Year 1675* (1675), *Plutarch's Morals* (1684, 1691), *The History Of the Most Renowned Don Quixote of Mancha* (1687), and poems in *The Gentleman's Journal* (Vol. III, 1694). Other works are: *An Introduction to Astrology* (1661), *Typhon: or, The Gyants War with the Gods. A Mock-Poem* (1665), Matthew Locke's *Observations Upon a Late Book, Entituled, An Essay to the Advancement of Musick, &c.* (1672; Locke's further revision, 1673, includes *Duellum Musicum*),[22] Madeleine de Scudery's *Almahide; or, the Captive Queen* (1677), *La Calprenède's Pharamond* (1677), *The Six Voyages of John Baptista Tavernier, Baron of Aubonne* (1677), *Jockey's Downfall* (1679), *Speculum Crape-Gownorum* (1682), *Speculum Crape-Gownorum, the Second Part* (1682), *Horse-Flesh for the Observator* (1682), *A New History of the Kingdom of Abessinia* (1682), *A Late Voyage to Constantinople* (1683), *The Art of Physick Made Plain & Easie* (1684), *Modern History, or a Monethly Account Of All Considerable Occurrences* (1687–90), *The Turkish Secretary* (1688), *The Dilucidation of the Late Commotions of Turkey* (1689), *The Present State of Europe* (1690–1706?), *The Present Court of Spain* (1693), *In Memory of Our Late Most Gracious Lady, Mary Queen of Great-Britain, France, and Ireland* (1695), *Augustus Britannicus* (1697), *Amphion Anglicus* (1700), and *The Vision of Mons. Chamillard* (1706). There are seven numbers of *The Dilucidator: or, Reflections upon Modern Transactions, By Way of Letters from a Person at Amsterdam, to His Friend in London* (London: Printed for Randall Taylor, MDCLXXXIX), which is also probably by Phillips, although not so ascribed by anyone. *The Dilucidation of the Late Commotions of Turkey . . . Printed in Italian at Venice, and Translated into English by the Author of the Monthly Account. To be Annex'd to Numb. 10. of the Monthly Account* (London, Printed by Randal Taylor, 1689) is, as noted in the title, part of *Modern History*, though treated separately.[23] Parker also lists separately *The General State of Europe* (1692), but this is a variant title of *The Present State of Europe.*

Parker does not include *Montelion 1661, Montelion 1662, A Collection of Several Relations & Treatises Singular and Curious, of John Baptista Tavernier, Baron of Aubonne* (1680), *New News from Tory-Land and Tantivy-Shire,* or *Plutarch's Morals,* all listed as apparently authentic by Hone. As to *Montelion 1661* and *Montelion 1662,* Parker is correct in not citing them as Phillips's work; on the title page of *Mercurius Verax* (1675), Phillips calls himself "*Author of the first* Montelion" only. A seventeenth-century note on the title page of the British Library copy of *Montelion 1660* ascribes it to Phillips on the basis of the remark in *Mercurius Verax* and refutes those who follow. Thomas Flatman also produced a lampooning "Montelion," that of 1662 having a preliminary poem on "The Meaning of the Picture" (frontispiece) by "T. F." It is an imitative burlesque of Phillips's work. There is also nothing to connect *A Collection of Several Relations & Treatises* with Phillips, except that he had translated the first six voyages; the work is by Edmund Everard. (*New News* and the Plutarch are by Phillips.) Hone cites a number of items, such as *A Letter from the King of Denmark to Mr. William Lilly Occasioned by the Death of His Patron the King of Sweden* (1660), which he rejects as attributions; this volume is not mentioned by Parker. Parker lists *Pantagruel's Prognostication* (1660?), *News, from the Land of Chivalry* (1681), *An Anniversary Poem on the Sixth of May* (1683; a broadside), *A True and Exact Relation of the . . . Earthquake* (1688), *Advice to a Painter* (1688), and *The Works of Lucian, Vol. III* (1711), which are noted by Hone. *Pantagruel's Prognostication* does not have a publication date on its title page, and Wing (R106) gives c. 1645; F.P. Wilson shows that it dates after October 1658 and suggests late 1659 or early 1660. (See the reprint in Luttrell Reprints No. 3, pp. vi-vii.) It is dedicated (satirically) to William Lilly (the astrologer) and is signed "*Thine Idolater, as thou art the Stars,* Democritus Pseudomantis" (that is, false prophet). It is learned but ridiculing, a travesty on such prognostications as had become commonplace. It offers an imitation in "Skelton upon Rabelais" (pp. 10–13), signed "Per me *Johannem Skeltonum,* Poetam Laureatum." (Note also p. 119 here for Phillips's possible use of Skelton in another work.) The lampoon may indeed be an example of Phillips's poking fun at all this silliness that Lilly's yearly almanacs presented to a believing public and at the attempt at respectability of some of the "pseudomantes" by citing Rabelais. A well-respected physician, Rabelais, of course, was a satirist, whose work employed impolite language and situations, but Godwin, as well as Parker, uses the term "Rabelaisian" as insult. Others besides Phillips made reference to Rabelais.[24] Perhaps also we should note that Lilly, despite serving Parliament, was an adherent of Charles I.

Parker seems to be correct in listing *News, From the Land of Chivalry. The Pleasant and Delectable History: And, The Wonderful and Strange Adventures of Don Rugero de Strangemento, Kt. of the Squealing Fidle-stick And, of several other Pagan Knights and Ladies* (London, Printed for I.P., 1681), Numb. I. The "I.P." has suggested Phillips, but probably the publisher is someone else, perhaps even John Playford. On the other hand, the tone, satiric wit, and learned allusions do resemble his acknowledged work, and no. 3, chapters V-VI, talks of a "Fool's Paradise," which recalls Book III of *Paradise Lost*. Initials, content, and style (as well as ability to translate Italian) corroborate Parker's assignment *of A True and Exact Relation of the Most Dreadful Earthquake which happened in the City of Naples, and Several other parts of that Kingdom, June the 5th, 1688 . . . Translated from the Italian Copy, printed at Naples, by an Eye-witness of those miserable Ruins* (1688). It is presented to "T.G. Esq." and signed "Your obliged Friend and Servant, J.P." It has a notably informed prefatory statement on earthquakes and classical authors. (In 1688, Randal Taylor also published the third edition of Milton's *Paradise Regain'd and Samson Agonistes*.) The title page of *Advice to a Painter* (1688) also gives the author as "J. P."; it is an anti-papal lampoon against judges. The date, of course, puts it amidst those demanding James II's abdication. Most importantly, Phillips did contribute to the translation of Lucian; see later. Wing assigns *The Jockey's Farewell* (P2089), *Mercurius Pædanus* (P2092A), and *Phœnix Britannicus: or, London Rebuilt* (P2095aA) to Phillips and lists the 1661 edition of *A Satyr Against Hypocrites* separately by its new title, *Religion of the Hypocritical Presbyterians* (P2097). *The Jockey's Farewell* is a broadside, perhaps from 1670, and is signed "I.P."; this and *The Jockey's Downfall* seem to account for that ascription, which is probably wrong. *Mercurius Pædanus* was written by "Johanne Philipps, Mag. in Artibus; Hypodidas. Liberæ Scholæ Civitatis, & Comitatus Norvici" in 1650; this resident of Norwich was certainly not Milton's nephew, despite a noncontemporary note on the flyleaf of the British Library copy. The basis for assigning *Phœnix Britannicus* (1672) to Phillips is not stated. The entry on Phillips in the *DNB* by Sir Sidney Lee is generally drawn from Godwin's account and is most unreliable.

Parker cites *The King's Evidence Justifi'd* (1679), *The Character of a Popish Successour Compleat* (1681), and *The Secret History of the Reign of K. Charles II. and K. Iames II* (1690), as false attributions.[25] However, Hone, like Godwin, assigns *The English Fortune-Tellers* to John, while Parker calls its 1703 edition a doubtful attribution. "The English Fortune-Teller" was published in 1642, 1643, 1686–88, and "The Book of Fortune" was printed by J. Heptinstall, for

Brabazon Aylmer, in 1698 (Wing, B3707); it is a reworking of "Libro di Ventura" (published in 1484, 1508, 1532). The 1642 edition (Wing, E3084) is a six-page "New Almanacke and Prognostication" printed for A.R. and C.A. An imperfect copy, without title page, of "[The English Fortune-Tellers" (London: Printed for P. Brooksby, J. Deacon, J. Blare, and J. Back, 1692?]" (Wing, P2083A) is found in the Wellcome Library and is listed by Edward Arber in *The Term Catalogues,* Vol. II, p. 428, as "The English Fortune-Teller . . . By J.P., Student in Astrology. Printed for P. Brooksby, J. Deacon, J. Blare, and J. Back" and dated November 1692. According to Godwin, there were only two extant copies; he writes: "In conclusion, we must deny to John Philips the merit of originality, and that superior elasticity of mind which he might have laid claim to, if his book had been without an archetype; while at the same time we must admit in it a wonderful facility of labour and perseverance in execution, which are so much the more extraordinary, as he himself must have regarded his work as an empty trifle" (Appendix X, an addition for chapter XII, p. 410). The only reason to assign this work to Phillips is the subject matter, disregarding the earlier dates, and "By J.P., Student in Astrology" if indeed that appeared on the title page, but Godwin's constant antipathy toward Phillips shown in the above comment despite the positive things that he also writes renders Godwin's opinions fatuous. Unlike Godwin, I am sure that we classify good translation as a worthy activity, even profession, and its validity as admirable.

Among the items listed above are translations from Latin, Greek, French, Spanish, and Italian, with a suggestion that Phillips may also have known Dutch. The success of Milton's teaching and the abilities of John Phillips in language should not be ignored. Dedications are also interesting, as we have seen they are in Edward's works. The dedication of *A Satyr Against Hypocrites* is "To the Right Worshipfull, John Churchill, Esq.," a barrister in the Court of Chancery, later Master of the Rolls and knighted in 1670, at which time he became King's counsel and Attorney-General to the Duke of York. (Association through his stepfather Thomas Agar is probable, even in 1655 when Agar, who would have known Churchill through his employment, was apparently around London, as we have seen in chapter 2, although not functioning as Clerk of Chancery at that time. If John Phillips's association with Churchill did come through Agar, a rupture between them is refuted.) Churchill was sent to the Tower in 1675 because of a breach of privilege by the Commons, though it had been approved by the Lords, a situation indicative of the internal strife in which many were caught. This dedication, however, was not printed in 1655, for what reason is unknown. Dedication of *The Tears of the Indians* was to Oliver Cromwell; *Sportive Wit* to [Sir] Ralph Banks, apparently a friend.[26] *Maronides* (1672) is addressed to George

Wharton, another friend and "Treasurer and Pay-master of his Majesties Office of the Ord'nance in the Tower" after the Restoration; Wharton was created baronet on 31 December 1677 for his services to the Royalist cause. As an astrologer (we will examine Phillips's work in this area, below), he produced Royalist almanacs from 1641 to 1666 (except in 1646), becoming involved in a bitter controversy with other astrologers who were opposed politically. John Bradshaw wanted him hanged and he was sent to prison during the years 1649–1650, but Elias Ashmole interceded, and on the stipulation that he produce nothing against the Council of State, he was released. He became Ashmole's agent; astrological papers and letters to Ashmole will be found in the Ashmolean Museum. What seem like interconnections with Milton as Latin secretary, Edward Phillips as Ashmole's employee, and John as student of astrology indicate the strange political bedfellows of this time. The second part of *Maronides* (1673) was dedicated to Dr. Valentine Oldis (or Oldys), a friend, poet, and patron of literary activities, who received his medical degree from Cambridge in 1671.

Particularly indicative of the political jockeying during this time was Thomas Thynne, to whom Phillips addressed *Almahide* (1677). Another friend, he entered the Middle Temple in 1668, was in Parliament during the years 1670–1682, and was attached to the Duke of York's contingent. But then, in early 1680, he denounced the Duke of York as a Papist, petitioning the king "for the redress of grievances and the punishment of popish plotters." He joined the Earl of Shaftesbury's contingent and is represented in Dryden's "Absalom and Achitophel" as Issacher. The dedication of *Pharamond* (1677) to the Duchess of Albemarle is interesting because she was the wife of Christopher Monck, the second Duke of Albemarle and son of George Monck. The first state of *The Six Voyages* (1677) was presented to Sir Thomas Davies (1631–1680), Lord Mayor of London, a bookseller in St. Paul's Churchyard, and a draper. The second state was dedicated to its publisher, Dr. Daniel Cox (also the dedicatee of William Hog's translation, *Paraphrasis Poetica in Tria Johannis Miltoni*, 1690), and associate of Dr. Luke Rugeley, as recorded here in n74 of chapter 2. *The Vision of Mons. Chamillard* was inscrib'd to John Lord Somers, who was generally accredited with sponsoring the very important 1688 fourth edition of *Paradise Lost*. These dedications place Phillips in a world of both significant people, including Royalists and non-Royalists both before and after the Restoration who often also figure in Milton's world, and lesser-known friends.

It seems that Phillips, even as translator, cannot be given a positive review. For Godwin, his production of the fifth and then sixth books of the *Aeneid* "is infinitely the most odious and loathsome performance of the kind I have seen" (148); his reading of reference to "regicides" is called "consummately detestable" (148) and thus Phillips is "a reptile" (149). The title page of both volumes indicates that it is "in burlesque verse," but the monarchist/republican Godwin doesn't understand. Despite "a very liberal portion of praise" for his undertaking of "a giant's pertinaciousness and energy" in the translation of Tavernier's voyages, Phillips is only "a bookseller's drudge" since he has not performed "a great literary labour for the pure love of the occupation" (183). In the second part of *Maronides,* Phillips argues he has "only stript him [Virgil] out of his old Roman dress, and put him into the fashion Alamode" ("The Epistle Dedicatory," iv). While Hone is aware that it had become commonplace in translating some classical texts to present travesty through an updating of references and persons to current English significance (and soon Alexander Pope would be commended for his Horatian poems), he finds vituperativeness, coarseness, abusiveness, and scurrility in the Virgil.[27] On the other hand, the translation of La Framboisière's "De Schola Medecin" in *The Art of Physick* (1684) "By J.P. Gent." "Published for Publick Benefit" is passed over, as are a number of other translations. Straightforward translation most notably appears in Phillips's contributions to all five volumes of *Plutarch's Morals: Translated from the Greek By Several Hands* (1684–1691). These volumes had three or four editions (through 1694). Vol. I includes "Concerning Musick," 122–61, and "Concerning the Fortune or Vertue of Alexander the Great in Two Orations," 561–610; Vol. II, "Concerning the Procreation of the Soul as Discours'd of in Timæus," 167–224; Vol. III, "Plutarch's Conjugal Precepts Dedicated to Pollianus and Euridice," 95–125, and "Wherefore the Pythian Priestess Now Ceases to Deliver Her Oracles in Verse," 191–260; Vol. IV, "Concerning Such Whom God Is Slow to Punish," 167–218, "Of Garrulity or Talkativeness," 252–89, and "Of Love," 290–353; and Vol. V, "Which Are the Most Crafty: Water-Animals or Those Creatures that Breed upon the Land," 91–154. There were thirty-six other contributors, only William Baxter and Phillips having translations in all five volumes. Here Phillips joins others like John Dryden, who is probably the connection with Phillips's contribution to *The Works of Lucian* in 1711; Dryden had written the "Life of Lucian" in 1696 in expectation of the edition.

Phillips's contribution to *The Third Volume of the Works of Lucian. Translated from the Greek By Several Eminent Hands* was "Tragopodagra, or Gout-Farce; a Play on the Gout, which is made a Goddess, and exerts her Destruction, &c. By John Philips," pp. 187–206. The argument is significant for its referenced knowledge and particularly for its attitude toward the quacks that Phillips's "astrological" work also illustrates (see later): "The design of this Drama is either to expose the swelling fustian of the ancient Tragedies, by applying the same Phrases to a more ignoble Subject, something like which has been done in the *Secchia rapita,* and *Boileau's Lutrin,* or (what I rather believe) to ridicule those noisy Empyricks who have the Impudence to pretend to cure all Diseases, and with a little Variation it may still serve for a Satyr upon the Modern German Doctors and Mountebanks" (187–88, reversed italics). The "play" is in blank verse, with some rhyme at times, and unrhymed and sometimes rhymed other meters; its prosodic form, its language, and its classical references are those that one finds in Milton's "Comus." Compare the tone and substance of its ending (p. 206) with lines 966–75 and 1012–23 of the masque:

> Wherefore, most dear Companions, set
> Your Hearts at rest, and Pains forget.
> Or if the Goddess fierce disdain
> To cease the fury of our Pain,
> The Gods, more merciful than she,
> Will find a way to set us free.
> In the mean time let us that share
> Of Miseries the most severe,
> With Patience our afflictions bear,
> Let the Rabble laugh on, and sawcily prate,
> We're happy by knowing the worst of our Fate.

Perhaps the most egregiously misread work is Cervantes' *Don Quixote,* in which Godwin concluded that "The very soul of the translator was gross and fleshly, and loved to wallow in the mire of beastly allusions, and revel in the slang of the vulgar tongue" (253). He, apparently, had not read the Spanish of Cervantes! In chapter XVI of the Second Part, where Don Diego de Miranda offers some literary evaluations, such as of Homer in the *Iliad* and Martial's bawdiness and Virgil's meanings, Phillips's text says Don Diego is "a great admirer of *Horace, Juvenal* and *Persius* [Godwin adds Tibullus] but as for the Modern Poets, he allows very few to be worth a Straw; amongst the rest, he has a particular Peek against *Du Bartas,* and *Paradise Lost,* which he says has neither Rhime nor Reason" (361, Aaa1v). To Godwin, Phillips is "placed at an immeasurable distance from the character and style of Cervantes" (253). Hone offers nothing to disabuse this opaque reading, although he recognized the creation of an English context here and elsewhere in the translation. And William Riley Parker's take on the passage is imperceptive: "He [Milton] would not have appreciated the brief, slighting reference to *Paradise Lost* in the preface to *The History of the Most Renowned Don Quixote* (1687), sig. Aaa1ᵛ." In the original, Cervantes criticizes classic epics and classic epic heroes, and especially the narrow and prescriptive demands of the "literati": surely Don Quixote himself is the antithesis of Don Diego's heroes. Phillips is not snidely lamenting his education from his uncle, nor elevating his own work by odious comparison. The translation reflects in Don Diego de Miranda's positive discussion of poetry ideas as expressed in *Of Education* and perhaps *An Apology* on pp. 362–63. But Phillips is also reacting with great sarcasm against those who discredit the "modern" Guillaume Salluste, Sieur Du Bartas (author of a religious epic, *La Semaine*, on the creation of the world, and who, of course, was a major influence on *Paradise Lost*) and Milton's epic because it was written in blank verse rather than the "correct" heroic couplet. In 1678, Thomas Rymer, in contempt of blank verse, said he was going to present a full discussion of it (see *The Tragedies of the Last Age Consider'd and Examin'd*, p. 143), and Thomas Shipman disavowed blank verse but did not proceed to discuss it because Rymer was going to. (See *Henry the Third of France, Stabb'd by a Fryer*, 1678, pp. A4v-*1r). Rymer never published such a review. And, of course, Andrew Marvell took out after John Dryden for "tagging" Milton's verse in 1674. The argument of blank verse vs. the heroic couplet continued well into the eighteenth century. Phillips sarcastically pokes fun at the Don Diegos who were so numerous toward the end of the seventeenth century (and into the eighteenth century) and who, in their argument of the Ancients vs. the Moderns, showed over and over again their reactionary attitude toward anything that did not fit the "formula," just as E.E. Cummings skewered such "critics" in "Poem, or Beauty Hurt Mr. Vinal." Indeed, the twentieth century has had its Arnold Bennetts who felt that no author or work could be seriously evaluated unless the author had been dead for some time. And it was not long ago that graduate schools would not let a dissertation be written on a living author! No, rather than not appreciating his nephew's ridicule, Milton would have enjoyed it, even though he would probably have known that many would not read the passage cogently, reading it only as Godwin, and Hone, and Parker did. It is perhaps indicative of the acceptance of this opaque reading of Phillips's sarcasm that none of these writers remarks that Phillips, cited specifically as "a Nephew of the late Mr. *John Milton*" on the title page of *The Vision of Monsieur Chamillard* (1706), employs blank verse for his poem. The translation of Cervantes was entered in the Term Catalogues by Henry Cruttenden and Thomas Hodgkin on 26 December 1685, as "By J.P. Gent. The poetry by severall eminent hands. Made English from the Spanish Originall" (III, 297).

Edward Phillips's comment in *Theatrum Poetarum* (1675) is more apt than those in the preceding paragraph: "*John Philips*, the Maternal Nephew and Disciple of an Author of most deserved Fame late deceas't, . . . from whose Education as he hath receiv'd a judicious command of style both in

Prose and Verse, so from his own natural Ingenuity he hath his Vein of Burlesque and facetious Poetry, which produc't the Satyr against Hypocrites, and the Travested Metaphrase of two Books of *Virgil*, besides what is dispeirc't among other things; nevertheless what he hath writ in a serious Vein of Poetry, whereof very little hath yet been made public, is in my opinion, nothing inferior to what he hath done in the other kind" (114–15). John's penchant for burlesque is recognized and approved, but it is seen not to encompass all his poetic endeavors. Some serious poetry has been made public, but according to Edward, not all has been: prior to 1675, there are the poem to Lawes and the epigram on Matthew Locke's *Observations Upon a Late Book* (1672; A2r), as well perhaps as some "Cavalier"-like poetry in *Wit and Drollery* and *Sportive Wit*. There are various poems in the almanacs as well that may strike one as not burlesque; for example, "A Ballad Loyal" in *Montelions Predictions*, 11–15, on the impending war with the Dutch. What "serious" poetry Edward may have known cannot, of course, be determined, but aside from later occasional verse, there are four poems in *The Gentleman's Journal: or the Monthly Miscellany* in Volume III (1694), three of which may have been written much earlier: "An Epigram on the Peruvian Bark, by Mr. J.P." (57); "An Ode on his Majesty's going into Flanders, by Mr. J. Phillips" (91–92); "Horace's 34th Ode, Book I, imitated, by Mr. J. Phillips" (125–26); and "To Phillis by Mr. J.P." with an "Answer, by a Lady" (195–96). ("Peruvian bark" is dried bark from South American trees used medically to reduce fever; it is also called cinchona.) The editor, Peter Motteux, prefaces the last poem: "Here are some Verses by a Gentleman, who doubtless is none of those who are for this inconstant way of Loving." Surely worthy of note is the fact that three of Thomas Power's translations of parts of *Paradise Lost* into Latin verse are printed in this same volume by Motteux: PL III, 1–55, pp. 129–31; PL IV, 440–91, 172–74 [recte 166–68]; and PL V, 153–208, 201–02. Hugh Wilson ascribes another poem to Phillips, that entitled "To His *Friend* Mr. J.T. on the Following *POEM*" (on A2r-v) in *The Search After Honesty. A Poem By Mr. Tutchin* (1697). Godwin had mentioned this poem, but Wilson is the only modern critic to examine it and, quite correctly I think, assign it to Milton's nephew. The poem is signed "*J. P.*" and is in heroic couplets (like Tutchin's poem). John Tutchin (1661?–1707) was a Whig pamphleteer, who took part in the Duke of Monmouth's uprising and was antipapist and pro-William. He was often before the courts as a result of his attacks on governmental actions and sentenced to prison and whipping (but pardoned through bribery) and later again sentenced to prison for further infraction, where he died. Similar political positions can be seen between Tutchin and John Phillips, as well as mutual associates.

What is even more significant for us here in the quoted comment above than Edward's understandably positive view, however, is, first, that through 1675 the brothers were in touch with each other; John was certainly not estranged from Edward. And second, Edward's word "Disciple" should not be ignored (I seem to use this word a lot in connection with Milton's nephew, because so much has been ignored by those writing about him): indeed, John, in his poetical and extensive writing and in his political (and religious) positions, has learned well from his uncle. With that statement, however, there has been fairly unanimous disagreement on two counts: John's coarse and vituperative language, and his alleged seesawing between Royalist and non-Royalist positions.

The years after 1675 saw a number of occasional poems published that show loyalty to the monarch, but should not be thus necessarily cast as "Royalist" (that is, Tory) in political persuasion: *Jockey's Downfall: A Poem on the late total Defeat given to the Scotish Covenanters, near Hamilton Park, June 22, 1679. By His Majesties Forces, under the Command of His Highness the Duke of Monmouth, &c. Written by the Author of The Satyr against Hypocrites* (broadside), *An Humble Offering to the Sacred Memory of the Late Most Serene and Potent Monarch Charles II. By J. Phillips, Gent.* (1685), *In Memory of our Late Most Gracious Lady, Mary Queen of Great-Britain, France, and Ireland. A Poem, By Mr. John Phillips* (1695), *Augustus Britannicus: A Poem Upon the Conclusion of the Peace of Europe, At Rijswick in Holland, upon the 20th. of September, 1697 . . . By Mr. J. Phillips* (1697), *The Vision of Mons. Chamillard* [with a title page quotation of *PL* VI, 86–91] (1706). The prose accounts in *The Present State of Europe* show allegiance to the reigning monarch whether James II or William III. An encomium "To my Friend, Dr. Blow, on his Amphion Anglicus" is printed in *Amphion Anglicus* (1700), iv. He joins such well known people as William Pittis, Thomas D'Urfey, William Crofts (organist at St. Ann's), and Jeremy Clarke (organist at St. Paul's Cathedral). (We should note that "An Ode on the Death of Mr. Henry Purcell," which was written by Dryden and set to music by Blow, is influenced by "Lycidas" and was published for Henry Playford in 1696 and reprinted in *Orpheus Britannicus* in 1698, p. iv, without the music.)

The poem on Charles II's death is instructive in the matter of allegiance to one's king, despite one's political differences. Charles died on 6 February and the poem was published on the twenty-eighth. The Pindaric ode does praise both the late king and somewhat incidentally his father, and it opposes what the Interregnum had become:

> . . . such was our Immortal CHARLES the Great,
>   Embracing now
>   His Father's blessed Soul,
> Whose soft Controul

Three Nations made
The Happy Seat
Of Plenty and Peace, and all our former Storms allay'd.
. . . Long had Three Patent Realms bewail'd
Th'Oppressive Hand
Of Bold Rebellion, pamper'd with Success;
Discord and Slaughter Chaos'd all the Land,
And ruinous Anarchy prevail'd,
Till at length Rebels against Rebels fought,
With deadly feud,
And their own Monstrous Bulk of Strength subdu'd.
But then it was,
Three Kingdoms, bleeding, mangl'd, torn,
In Ruines all forlorn,
Shewing their ghastly Wounds, for swift Redress
Their Exil'd Prince besought:
Who straight appearing, with His Vernal Heat
Reviv'd th'Autumnal face
Of Church and State,
And Wild Disorder became Lovely Grace.

The antagonism toward what the Protectorate had created in the years 1653 through 1659 occurs frequently in Phillips's work, as discussion here shortly will evidence, but this antagonism was widespread among those who would be classified as Parliamentarians. Hindsight cast the uprising that led to the Cromwellian government in 1649 in unfavorable light (the "Bold Rebellion"), and the label of "ruinous Anarchy" that "prevail'd" in the last years of the Commonwealth was widespread as "Rebels against Rebels fought, / With deadly feud": this was not only Phillips's view. The international successes under Charles II and the general improvement of life and church and advancement of liberty of conscience cast a view of "Lovely Grace" in the years from 1660 through 1685. The six to ten years of "ruinous Anarchy" became starkly significant against the twenty-five years of the revival of "th'Autumnal Face /Of Church and State." The poem opposes Charles's competition from the Duke of Monmouth, and calls James, "who now survives Protector of our Laws and Lives," a "parallel" to Charles. "Protector" specifically contrasts with the Cromwells and the nature of "Laws" (like those setting up the Major-Generals) and the people's "Lives" between 1655 and 1659. At this point in history, without evidence of James's actions, Phillips admonishes that the people "Honour and Obey our Second JAMES," for "'Twould be Ingrateful to forget so soon / The Peace and Plenty of His [Charles's] Reign." In 1685, the Scotch ambassador Lord Fountainhall recorded somewhat similar reactions, although he was distressed at the licentiousness of Charles's court and not really happy with James: "The change upon the face of the English court is very remarkable: in the last king's tyme mirth, playes, buffoonerie, etc., domineered, and was incouraged; now there is little to be seen but seriousnesse and businesse." "[T]o flatter the genius of the nation, he tells them in a style vain enough, that he hopes to raise the reputation of England beyond what any of his predecessors had done. . . . Some ascrybed this complyance of the House of Commons with the king more to fear than love . . . For sundry of this House of Commons are disaffected, but are borne doune by the major part, who syde with the king."[28]

The poem shows definite opposition to the Cromwellian regime, approval of the people's life that existed under Charles II, hope that that life would continue under James II, but does not show political turncoating from a liberal position (a kind of "Whig" position—Hone calls it "vestigial Whiggism") to a "Royalist" position (to "Toryism").[29]

4

The negative charges against John Phillips, as intimated above, are his association with astrological matters, his coarse, vituperative, and obscene language and images, and his alleged political fluctuations. The mock almanac *Montelion 1660, Don Juan Lamberto, Introduction to Astrology,* and *Montelions Predictions, or the Hogen Mogen Fortune Teller* lampoon people like Lilly, as noted before, and particularly those who believe such quackery. The almanacs become the vehicle to criticize, particularly political matters and people. Much of the "Fortune Telling" of these works derives from the rumor-mill of the tavern or coffee house, as verse in *Montelions Predictions* attests:

> We further find by the *Hermetick* Learning,
>   (*For so of late our Quacks do call,*
>   *All Tricks if Strange and Mystical.*)
> That *Coffee-Houses* (the Mint of Intelligence, and Forge of Lies)
> Shall bee much frequented . . . (p. 8)

The full title of the first item above should have put anyone on guard to recognize the absurdity being exploited: *or, the Prophetical Almanack; being a true and exact Accompt of all the Revolutions, that are to happen in the World, this present year, 1660. Till this time Twelve-moneth. By Montelion, Knight of the Oracle, a Well-wisher to the Mathematicks.* The "author's" name suggests "mountebank," a charlatan, trickster, quack, and etymologically equals one who "mounts" The Lion (the constellation Leo), with a hint of "eminent person." (Wilson reminds us that the name was well known from Emanuel Forde's very popular prose narrative *The Famous History of Montelyon, the Knight of the Oracle* [1633].) The obscenity in this use should specifically be understood as satiric against the *Rump* that is "mounted." But the belief that Godwin shows—that the Rump Parliament in 1659–60 was as eagerly accepted by non-Royalists as it had been earlier in Cromwell's regime—is not accurate. As Austin Woolrych writes, "To the broad mass of the gentry the return of the Rump was most unwelcome."[30] A rather simplistic division between those championing Charles and those championing the Commonwealth, which Godwin assumes, did not exist. And the separation between the monarch and governmental officers that *still* exists in the United Kingdom must be acknowledged to understand Phillips's writing and political position. One may accept the monarch but reject the governmental organization of which he was (or became) the figurehead.

The uprisings in August 1659 to return the King to his throne failed, yet the Rump was again expelled by the army on 12–13 October 1659. Milton's argument to remedy the anarchy that occurred, as Woolrych tells us, quoting *A Letter to a Friend,* dated 20 October (VII, 121), was, first, "'a senate or generall Councell of State,' empowered to preserve the public peace, conduct foreign relations, and raise revenue," but with liberty of conscience and abjuration of a single person assured. Phillips's "All the Revolutions" in "this Present Year, 1660" casts an analytic eye on the absurdities that were occurring with the jockeying back and forth of people in both camps and indeed the variety of the numerous camps. In February, there is the observation that "Sore designes there are a working against the Parliament and Army; some great persons are discovered, and will be brought to an account. I wish the two great Gyants in *Guild-Hall* to have a care of themselves." Placing this in the genre of the astrological almanac emphasizes the ridiculousness of the numerous "solutions" to the problems that were proposed, but the work also attests to the political subject that is Phillips's concern and to the political maneuverings themselves as being "very scurrilous, and abundant in low buffoonery," and their classification as "obscenity" and "ordure" (Godwin, 107–08). The "Exact Chronologie" of the period pretty much began "Since Oliver Lord Protector tumbled out of the Coach-box at Hidepark corner"; the unsettled war with Spain (despite the actions of 1655) is impugned: "An Envoy is sent to the King of *Spain* to ask him the reasons why he doth not make a peace; & likewise to shew him what a detriment he does the English nation in hindring them their wonted supplies of sauce for their Veal, and new Reasons to make plum porridge"; what seems to be Phillips's anti-feminism appears: "The weather is cold and therefore O *Citizens Wife* who ere thou art, let not thy parson want caudles in a morning. And you O citizens look to your wives, as they go from the *six a clock Lectures,* for I assure you they will not come directly home"; and papal intervention in English affairs is vilified: "The Pope hearing of the beauty of H.M.'s L*asses,* sends him a letter intreating him to furnish him with one of his best to keep him warm this winter, promising him in lieu thereof if he think fit, to send him a boy; withal assuring him that if he please to make trial, he will find no small content in the plesure as he hath often found by experience." (A "caudle" is a warm drink given to sick persons, especially to pregnant women.) One of the remedies offered (many almanacs played the role of apothecary) was "To cure Maids that cannot hold their water, or fear the loss of their *Maidenhead.*" The antipapal ridicule should make us remember Milton's "In Quintum Novembris," which also exhibits sexual innuendo and charges papal homosexuality.

As Hone epitomizes, the mock romance *Don Juan Lamberto: or, a Comical History of the Late Times. The First Part* (which plays upon General John Lambert, who was among those restored in April 1659 and which action weakened the Wallingford House party[31]) is "part of the grisly and gory spirit which animated Restoration reprisals" (352). Here, in 1661, Phillips deals with Commonwealth figures and Fifth Monarchists, and looks back to the intrigues and the problems that the Protectorate created. Anyone who makes a positive equation between pro-Cromwell, "republicanism," and the Major-Generals, like Lambert, in the year 1655 and following, has not understood the political maneuvers and oppositions of the 1650s; see remarks, as well, in the Introduction before. In archaic language and black letter font, chapter 1 explains "How *Cromwel* Soldan of *Britain* dyed, and what befel his Son the *Meek Knight.*" "Sir" Lambert becomes the "Knight of the Golden Tulip"; Sir Henry Vane, "Knight of the Most Mysterious Allegories"; and Charles II, "The Loyal Knight." "Whereas all other Knights fought for their sakes, our Knights fought for Nobody's sakes but their own" (Postscript, p. G3r). The "Forty Tyrants" equate the Council of State (in both parts), and in chapter IV of the second part (1661), we learn "how Sr. *Vane* made Sr. *Lambert* believe that the Moon was made of green Cheese." The lack of stability, the lack of attention to a religious settlement, the lack of liberty of conscience brought forth many proposals (not only Milton's 1659 and 1660 tracts), and General Monck's actions in those years continued the up-and-down reactions. Lambert was apprehended in April 1660 and, avoiding the Tyburn gallows, was imprisoned in the Tower for the rest of his life. Woolrych indicates that when Milton's first version of *The Ready and Easy Way* appeared, February 1660, "anyone who directly and publicly advocated the king's cause still risked serious penalties," but by April 1660, when the amplified second edition was published "there was far more hazard in defending the Commonwealth" (197). Phillips is not defending the monarchy, although the restoration of the king began the movement to settlement, but he is criticizing the schismatics of the previous years, including those (like Hugh Peters) who were on the "right" side. The actions of the "Cavalier" Parliament of May 1661 make clear the continuing problems (religious antagonisms especially) that this travesty was attacking.

A final sally into such a vehicle for political satire is *Montelions Predictions, of the Hogen Mogen Fortune Teller* (1672). The Duke of York was the supreme commander of the Anglo-French naval operations against the Dutch, in the third war for control of sea trade. The tract is presented as patriotic support of the war by a Dutch astrologer, "Hogen Mogen" having been used frequently to poke fun at the Dutch and their language. Normally it would be "High *and* Mighty" with ridicule, however, of the words' presumptions. (Note such as the English edition in Dutch of the 1654 "Articles of Peace" [Shawcross, No. 173]: "Tusschen den Alder-doorluchtighsten ende Hooghsten Heer Olivier, Heer Protecteur der Republijck van Engelandt, Schotlandt en Yerlandt, &c. Ende De Hooghe en Moghende Heeren Staten Generael . . . Copye besloten tot Londen.") The war continued through 1674, but in the battle of Southwold Bay (Suffolk) on 28 May 1672, Admiral Ruyter was forced to retreat by the English and French forces, and on land, three provinces were captured and four others were threatened, with the ensuing defense by the Dutch of opening sluices and dams to stop the invading forces through inundating the land. Phillips's book is pro-English and like others pro-James for his routing of the Dutch. In none of these astrological lampoons is Phillips showing an adversarial position to Milton's, but he is castigating the personal ambitions that had promulgated the instabilities of government and endorsing his nation, and this came to embrace the monarch as figurehead. The attitude of commentators has, I suggest, been colored by their reading of Milton as being relentlessly opposed to monarchy and royalty whereas such a work as *The Tenure of Kings and Magistrates* opposes the failure of certain kings and magistrates, not essentially kingship, and *Eikonoklastes* is not directed against Charles so much as it is against his alleged book, *Eikon Basilike,* and its pervasive influence. Such a work as *The Ready and Easy Way* first attempts to obviate a return to the kind of monarchic control that Charles I represented. Milton, an overview reveals, was consistently opposed to central state authority, whether Royalist or republican, as David Quint has argued.[32] The figurehead of the monarch is not the problem; the lack of personal autonomy for citizens was.

The matter of the astrological in Phillips's oeuvre shows itself, then, as politically involved and as strategically satiric, employing vituperation and what has been cast as scurrilous language. This latter penchant arises in his second publication, *A Satyr Against Hypocrites,* a popular work having two issues in 1655, a second edition the same year, a third with two issues in 1661, and succeeding editions in 1671, 1674, 1677, 1680, 1689, and 1710. It was entered in the Term Catalogues, as noted before, by "Nath. Brooke" on 14 March 1654/5 as being "by Edward Phillips, Gent." (I, 467). The poem undergoes many alterations, but a complete examination of a variorum text has not been made. It is assumed that Phillips made the deletions, additions, and language changes; in any case, attention should be paid to the contemporary political/religious world of those alterations to understand the probable reason for such alterations. Surely 1661 is a very different world from that of 1655, as is 1680 or 1689. At issue in the poem is the question of its intention and the butt of the satire. For Godwin (49–50), it "is an undisguised attack upon the national religion; upon every thing that was then visible in this country and metropolis under the name of religion; and that at a time when it was universally conceived that the religious and political state of the country were inseparably united." His prejudice and ignorance of the state of affairs, particularly after the installation of the Protectorate in 1653, is clear. He seems not to understand the political division between those favoring episcopacy (Anglicanism) and those disavowing it. Masson saw the poem as "anti-Puritan" and "anti-Cromwellian" (V, 228), and Darbishire placed the Presbyterians as the only apparent target (xxii). Beaty specified the Scottish Presbyterians, and included other dissenting groups and Catholics as well. He dwells on Phillips's activities in Scotland in 1654 and his anti-Scots position in the poem, and suggests the influence of Skelton's "The Tunning of Elynour Rumming" in parodying the Puritan hymns of the coarse and common Puritan audience. Leon Howard argued that "The Sunday service which Phillips burlesques shows no signs of Presbyterian discipline," and he goes on to talk about "sectarianism," Fifth Monarchy men, Baptists, and Independents.[33] Significantly, nonetheless, the third edition of 1661 gives the title as *The Religion of the Hypocritical Presbyterians in Meeter,* the edition reported by Godwin and commented upon by Masson. Howard sees the changed title as a ploy to "appeal to the post-Restoration tendency to condemn the strongest of the Puritan sects" (iii), which seems to be on good ground; for the most part after the Restoration "Puritan" and "Presbyterian" became almost synonymous. All of these commentaries, however, avoid the simple and designated subject: hypocrites—hypocrites whether they are Baptists or Independents or Fifth Monarchy men, pro-Cromwell, anti-Cromwell, or whatever. Critics want Phillips to espouse some religious group without the least criticism, and what is surely beside the point, they want him to espouse a religious position that they assign to Milton on the basis of the constantly repeated and age-old epitome of him as a "Puritan," whatever that word is supposed to connote. Hone is right in seeing the poem as satirizing the insensitive people who go to church but not for genuine worship. However, he also seems to delimit that satire: Phillips is "constitutionally unable to appreciate or to tolerate the shallowness, the irregularity, and the irreverence of the emergent Independents and the canting Presbyterians" (306).[34] "Puritan" often seems in these commentaries to mean any calvinist Protestant including the episcopalian.

Howard suggests "a personal offense" to Milton in the reference to St. Mary Aldermary, his evaluation of the poem as "a pointless piece of scurrility which lacked real wit, coherence, or character," and if not seeing it "in open recalcitrance," his recognizing "a young man's departure from the paths of good instruction." The poem thus becomes an "irresponsible outburst of a young man of twenty-three who was tired of discipline, disappointed in his expectations of political preferment, and angry at the sort of people who had taken over the country but who seems incapable of appreciating his peculiar merits" (Howard, iv). My reader can ponder the implied "facts" behind such a statement, the antagonism toward this satire's author, and the dig at a mere twenty-three-year-old youth. The two earmarks that Howard (and others) sees in Phillips's work that condemn it are really foundationless, showing a lack of adequate reading of the literary scene of the day and of Milton, who remains a sanitized and nonspecific "Puritan." Verse satire had assumed a form and certain characteristics, and the invalid but expected coherence of a fully rounded poem rather than a linear organization of only slightly connected episodes which might go on or which might have been curtailed at some other point leads to artistic disapproval for *A Satyr Against Hypocrites*.[35] Likewise, satire along with other poetic expressions, as remarked before, often employed what would be considered obscene. Howard considers that Milton may have tolerated "the violation of the Scriptures and the punning obscenity of his nephew's introduction of the Prophet Habakkuk into the poem" (iii); but Howard is wrong to think them, among others, to be "a pointless piece of scurrility." Just before this passage (see pp. 12–13 of the 1655 edition) the poem talks of Daniel in the lion's den and dates itself in "fifty and four," commenting upon the alleged Millennium that was supposed to occur in 1657:[36]

> now Antichrist, so saies
> My book, must reign three daies, and three half daies,
> Why that is three years and a half beloved.
> Or else as many precious men have proved
> One thousand two hundred and threescore daies,

> Why now the time's almost expir'd, time staies
> For no man; friends then Antichrist shall fall,
> Then down with *Rome,* with *Babel,* down with all,
> Down with the Devil, the Pope, the Emperour,
> With Cardinals, and the King of *Spaine's* great power;
> They'l muster up, but I can tell you where,
> At *Armageddon,* there, Beloved, there,
> Fall on, fall on, kill, kill, alow, alow,
> Kill *Amaleck,* and Turk, kill *Gog* and *Magog* too.
> But who deare friends fed *Daniel* thus forsak'n [?]

(The manuscript differs in this passage in spelling and accidentals, and includes the question mark. "Alow," which is also the manuscript reading, is "halloo," the shout urging dogs on to the kill in a foxhunt.) A marginal note pokes fun at this with "And hey then / up goe we" (not in the manuscript) and another alongside the last two lines above has a pointing hand to indicate its significance. Not only is Phillips lampooning the Fifth Monarchy men, but all the others who have not read Daniel and Revelation well and who take on false hope of the end of the world and the righting of all wrongs (although through slaughter) and the ascent to Heaven for themselves within a few years—even though they are turning their backs on Daniel, who, some lines before have said, "is the Church, the *World's* the Den." The passage pokes fun at the ignoramuses who believe such misread prophecies (including the atheists who worship pride and avarice), but who are the same people that forsake the true believers: Daniel, the Church, remains in the Den. These are hypocrites who are looking out only for themselves and their undeserved salvation: they use the crutch of scriptural prophesy to continue their hypocritical actions, relying on the awaited Millennium to bring salvation in a few years.

The lines then move to allusion to the prophet Habakkuk (known for his prophecy), who complained of the injustice of Judah and prayed for the advent of woe on the unrighteous: in the Lord's words, "Woe unto him that saith to the wood, Awake; to the dumb stone, Arise, it shall teach! Behold, it is laid over with gold and silver, and there is no breath at all in the midst of it" (Habakkuk ii:18), which is followed by the prophet's prayer. Bringing Habakkuk in at this point is appropriate and cogent; countering the "ceremonious" "Pagan Judisme," this one who "sleeps . . . would do well to awak'n." The 1655 text reads: "As 'tis in th' English his name ends in Ock/ And so his name is called *Habacuck.*" But the manuscript reads: "ends in Cock," with allusion, thus, to someone who has resisted the "Kings and Governours, / These Byshops too, nay all superiour powers," and whose name ends in "-cock." They "are Lyons, Locusts, Whales, I [ay, MS] Whales," who beset Daniel, Job, Jonah. "But woe unto you Kings! woe to you Princes." The printed version's inaccuracy removes a pun and nonaesthetically creates a repetition two lines later. In print there is a break before the next line, but not in the manuscript:

> But in th' originall it ends in Ock
> For that dear sisters calls him have-a-Cock.
> And truly I suppose I need not feare
> But that there are many have a cocks here:
> The Laud increase the number of have a coks,
> Truly false Prophets will arise in flocks.

Howard is disturbed, obviously, by the reference to the penis, which addressing the "dear sisters" emphasizes, signifying "have a cock"'s manliness but also his hedonism. The Laud (here and throughout the poem, meaning Archbishop William Laud, who thus is caricatured as thinking himself the Lord) can increase these "arisen men" (with pun) who are but false prophets, not like Habakkuk of the Bible, and ultimately, at least, who subrogate advocates of Laudian autocracy, regardless of their specific sect. The marginal note, "The Doctrine of Generation," emphasizes the "manly" importance of the "have a coks." He who sleeps and would do well to awaken has not been identified, but a possibility is Dr. Edward Pocock, a Professor of Orientalism at Oxford (particularly of Hebrew, and later he became Regius Professor of Hebrew—and thus the play on the English form and the "original" form of the name), until being ousted for refusing the engagement to the Commonwealth in 1649. He aided and was aided by Laud. In 1655 (although the appendix is dated 1654), he published the six prefatory discourses of Maimonides on the Mishna with Latin translations and notes, the first Hebrew text printed in special type at Oxford.

Phillips is punning on the name "Habakkuk," which in Hebrew (as Pocock of course would know) means "embrace" or the "clasping together of the hands," but this is formed from "Châbaq" and the reduplication of "qûwq," which Phillips apparently is relating to a Hebrew word for "decree, law," "qûwq [kokh]." The "original" ending of "Ock" is perhaps intended to signify that the name is "Habak-uk," but a misreading leads to the licentious "have-a-cock." The "False Prophets" should embrace one another through abiding by the edict, but instead they exhibit only their "manliness." What they should do, his "glowrious truth" exhorted to "old men and youth" asserts, is to "Be sure to feed young Daniell, that's to say, / Feed all yoʳ Ministers that preach & pray." Yes, the pun is obscene but it is also appropriate and involved and meaningful in creating a number of criticisms of the religious factions and adherents of the day, those who do not stand up for their convictions even against the new Laud's disciples.

The opprobrium that readers like Godwin and Howard express at the vituperation and obscenities of the poem ignores their prevalence in the literature of the period, a frequency that evoked a Council of State order on 28 August 1655 (executed on 9 October) to suppress all "scandalous books and pamphlets." The vilification that Milton often enough heaped on his opponents[37] and his own obscene punning as in *Paradise Lost* VI, 568–90, which connotes penis, testicles, semen, and anus, are actualities that commentators have either ignored or not realized—probably because Milton has been viewed as above such ribaldry.[38] In all, I find the readings of *A Satyr Against Hypocrites* that have been offered inept and the negative accusations against its author of coarse language unrealistic and unenlightened.

5

The translation of Bartolomeo de las Casas's *The Tears of the Indians being An Historical and true Account Of the Cruel Massacres and Slaughters of above Twenty Millions of innocent people; Committed by the Spaniards* (1656), appearing one year after *Scriptum Dom. Protectoris Reipublicæ Angliæ, Scotiæ, Hiberniæ &c. Ex consensu atque sententi, Concilii Sui Editum; In quo hujus Reipublicæ Causa contra Hispanos justa esse demonstratur,* Milton's translation of Cromwell's declaration against Spain, cannot be mere happenstance. The work is dedicated to Oliver Cromwell and "To all true English-men" and is signed "J. Phillips." Again we have a probable positive connection between uncle and nephew, and Milton's *Observations on the Articles of Peace* and the subject of the Irish massacres compares significantly with the atrocities of the Spaniards against the Indians.[39] Commended are Cromwell's actions against the Spaniards *and the popery they represented:* "there is no man, who opposes not himself against Heaven, but doth extol Your just Anger against the Bloudy and Popish Nation of the Spaniards, whose Superstitions have exceeded those of *Canaan,* and whose Abominations have excell'd those of *Ahab,* who spilt the Blood of innocent *Naboth,* to obtain his Vineyard" (A4v). The numerous illustrations of the Spanish atrocities included depict truly inhumane and horrible acts. The "true English-men" are urged "*not uow* [now] *to fight against your Country-men, but against your Old and Constant Enemies, the* SPANIARDS" (b3v–b4r). That these twin enemies—Spain and the Papacy—were anathema to Phillips and to other Englishmen we also read in the references cited from *Montelion 1660* and in lines quoted before in *A Satyr;* that they continue enemies is seen in the re-publication of the Declaration in 1738–40 when economic

wars, reemerging after the Treaty of Utrecht in 1713, brought the defeat of
Prime Minister Robert Walpole.[40]

While some of the previously discussed items in their political interconnections have seen Phillips on the side of the Commonwealth and Cromwell,[41]
but without attention to his attitude toward what was soon to be assessed as
Cromwell's power play with the 1653 Protectorate,[42] the next work to be
discussed has placed him on the Royalist side,[43] but without consideration
that an acceptance of the monarch did not make him a Royalist or (in 1679
when the label became commonplace) a Tory, a point I posited before.[44]
George McFadden tells us that, "In Restoration politics, it is now understood that personal connections or class sympathies were much more significant, especially during the earlier decades, than 'Whig' or 'Tory'
affiliations" (11). In 1676, John published a continuance of *A Chronicle of the
Late Intestine War in the Three Kingdoms of England, Scotland, and Ireland . . . to
the happy Restitution of our Sacred Soveraign K. Charles II . . . By James Heath,
Gent. The Second Edition. To which is added a continuation to this present year
1675. Being a brief Account of the most Memorable Transactions in England, Scotland and Ireland, and Forreign Parts. By J.P.* Phillips' work appears on [517]-
604, XXX1r-Iiii1v; the separate title page is: *A Brief account Of the most Memorable
Transactions in England, Scotland, and Ireland, and Forein Parts: From the Year
1662, to the Year 1675* (London: Printed by J.C. for T. Basset, 1676). It was
entered in the Term Catalogues as a separate work by Thomas Bassett on 18
April 1676, as "by John Phillipps." His work has generally been mentioned
as pro-Royalist and anti-Milton; it is anti-papal, anti-Spanish, and anti-Dutch,
all enemies of the British nation. It is decidedly pro-national. Its organization is different from Heath's, proceeding year by year as "*Anno Dom.* 1663"
and "*Forein Affairs,* 1664," etc., but its content is reportage of what occurred
on the national scene (in Parliament and such) and on the foreign scene
(usually treating the European nations individually) set up as a kind of log.
It is not really exposition or argument. The preliminary and the closing
statements, however, are what have led to the work's being labelled pro-
Royalist and anti-Milton. "There is a justice due to the Memory of Actions,
as well as the Memory of Men; and therefore since the times of Usurpation
have had the favour done them, as to have the Transactions of those times,
that had nothing but Enormity to signalize 'em; with more justice may we
assay to take a short view of those great and Noble Actions, perform'd in the
succeeding Years . ." (519). The statement is not Royalist, but it is decidedly
antagonistic to the Protectorate ("the times of Usurpation") as were many
on the Parliamentarian side, as has already been recorded. Positive national
actions since the Restoration included the defeats of the Dutch in 1664 and

1665–1667, the Triple Alliance of 1668, and Charles II's second Declaration of Indulgence in 1672, which then led to the Test Act. These transactions were not without their negative aspects, but they did advance the nation within the world, particularly the world of commerce and imperialism, and they did effect some curtailment of the Popish incursions into British government and society. Milton's *Of True Religion* written a few years before (1673) comes immediately to mind for its arguments against Catholic influence and for its suggestion of "what best means may be us'd against the growth of Popery."

The after-statement should be read with the rule of the army and the impossibility of a freely elected parliament that 1653 ushered in as backdrop: "And thus you have an account in brief of all the most memorable transactions since the greatest act of Providence that has been observed for many Ages, the happy Restauration of his Majesty" (604, all italics). His next sentence, I believe, backs up my contention: "And we may aver, that here is nothing but Truth, if all the publick Intelligence of so many years have not fail'd." The near-anarchy of 1658–60 also hangs heavy over what the Restoration averted. Phillips is not plumping for Royalism; he is saying that Charles II's restoration put a stop to the abuses of Cromwell and his autocratic and arbitrary rule, a situation made worse for Englishmen of all stripes by a kind of primogeniture promotion of the weak Richard to the Protectorship, and by the actions of the Army and particularly of Lambert. Fairfax, indeed, came out of retirement to lead the forces against Lambert. Further, Phillips asserts that the intelligent and cognizant public, remembering life under the Protectorate from 1653 to 1659, will recognize the truth of his statement. Phillips has not turned his back on Parliamentarianism (which will soon transform into Whiggery), but he has recognized the failure of Cromwell's regime, commended the improvements and successes that came with the Restoration, and accepted the king as national leader.

The Exclusion Bill ushered in "Whig" in 1679 as one opposed to accepting a Roman Catholic on the throne of England (the insulting label meant a Scottish whey-eater), with "Tory" as one supporting the church and the crown party (that insulting label means an Irish bog-trotter). The bill was passed after a new Parliament gave Whigs a majority, the election being fanned by the frenzy that Titus Oates had stirred up with his *True Narrative of the Horrid Plot and Conspiracy of the Popish Party . . . With a List of such Noblemen, Gentlemen, and Others, As were the Conspirators* (1679). Oates's trumped up tales and lies, proclaimed the year before, were accepted as truthful by many—for a while, a result one now understands as the apprehension accumulated through alleged Catholic "plots" over the years from Charles I onward and Charles II's relationships with France. James, who was the obvious successor to his brother Charles, had acknowledged his Catholicism, and the support given to the Duke of Monmouth, Charles's illegitimate son, brought concerns for the rejection of hereditary succession and for the possibilities of another civil war. Amidst that frenzy a number of tracts were produced, among them Phillips's *Dr. Oates' Narrative of the Popish Plot, Vindicated: In an Answer to a Scurrilous and Treasonable Libel, Call'd, A Vindication of the English Catholicks, from the pretended Conspiracy against the Life and Government of His Sacred Majesty, &c. By J.P. Gent. Humbly presented to both Houses of Parlament* (1680). (Note Phillips's Miltonic spelling of "Parlament"; and Cockerill had also published Oates's book, in a number of issues.) During this period, the epithets "Whig," Scottish king-killer, and "Tory," Irish robber, became honored badges.

After one has read Phillips's tract, the thought has to cross one's mind that those who have written about it have not read it, including Parker, who seems to repeat only the title when he says that it "vindicates" Oates's narrative (implying approval of Oates) and when he alleges Phillips's "association" with Oates, unless he is not using that word to imply any kind of personal relationship. What Phillips is doing is arguing against Roman Catholicism and its purported interconnections with English governmental affairs, and specifically against (as his title says) *A Vindication of the Inglish Catholiks from the Pretended Conspiracy against the Life and Government of His Sacred Majesty. Discovering the cheife falsities & contradictions continued in the narrative of Titus Oates* ([Antwerp], 1680), accusing "This Patent Vindicator" of being foremost a "*Roman Catholick*" on the defense (2). The author was John Warner, a Jesuit priest, although this was not known by Phillips at this time. Addressing "the Lords and Commons of England Assembl'd in Parlament," he charges the Papist aim is "to vilifie and render insignificant that Evidence ["which you have adjudg'd and voted Real, I mean the Popish Plot"], which you have both approv'd and justifi'd" (iii). The dedication, which he signed "J. Phillips," continues (iv): "However, that they might not triumph in the conquests of their Pens, as in the success of their busie Councils, I undertook this brief Essay to stop the career of the first, leaving the greater work to a more mighty Power." According to Phillips, the Papists "confess there was a Plot, but they say it was contriv'd by others, and not by them" (6); he also remarks, "For certain this was not the first detection that ever was made of Popish Conspiracy and Treason in *England,* and therefore not singular in its kind" (7). He is not championing Oates: he is arguing that indeed there has been a plot, and had been plots, by Catholics, and that the attacks on Oates were executed by Catholics. Phillips is vindicating the narrative of the Popish plot by arguing that there have been many papist "plots" and that the "Patent Vindicator" of the Catholics, that is, Warner, is untruthful. The

Vindicator, Phillips says, is offended that Oates "Charges the late *unnatural War* upon the *Papists*. But 'tis very true, for all his Ale and History; for had not the Papists perpetrated that Inhumane Massacre in *Ireland,* those other heats of a few violent Spirits had soon been overmaster'd. But when the Papists by that bloody means had conjur'd up the fears and jealousies of the nation for the common safety, 'twas high time to disarm Papists, and put Priests and Jesuits to death" (16). (The Irish problem keeps rearing its head constantly, and here we again hear the charge that it really was the Papists who provoked the massacre.) His rebuttal of the Vindicator's accusation against Oates's information that the *Narrative* was presented to the King on 13 August and sworn on 6 September is based on logic and possible explanation; the Vindicator says, with no logic or "proof," "'Twas not so, because it was not so—'twas not so, because it could not be so—and it could not be so, because they themselves say so—Ergo" (20). Rather, "To say the truth their Religion it self is a Religion of no Credit. A Religion founded upon forgery. A sort of Devotion that no man of reason can admit into his Belief or Conscience. A Religion in the practice of its Professors so Diametrically contrary to all the Precepts of the Founder of Christianity that nothing can be more" (48). As far as Oates and his book are concerned, Phillips asserts, "So that if the Narrative be so like those Fables [Homer, Ovid, Aesop, as Warner charges], it follows that there is a great deal of Truth couched in the Narrative" (40).[45]

In rebuttal, Warner published *A Vindication of the English Catholiks . . . The 2. Edition with some Additions: & an answer to two Pamphlets printed in defense of the Narrative. Jtem A Relation of some of Bedlow's pranks in Spain, & Oate's Letter concerning him.* Permissu Superiorum. M:D.C.LXXXJ. He says little about the anonymous pamphlet in "A Preface to Mr. I. Phillips" (3–7) or the "Courteous Reader" (8–73), which is largely built upon quotations from Phillips and Warner's reactions to those quotations; included are Attestations and an appendix. He corrects some of Phillips's statements and argues against the rest, and takes him to task for his "sucurrility and Billingsgate language" (7, *sic*). At no point does he imply that Phillips was in Oates's employ or a friend.

In all, there is no real evidence that Phillips was associated with Oates: he vindicates the narrative of the Popish plot by arguing its possibility, its precedent occurrences, and its fictive rebuttal by Warner. Nothing in his text indicates any relationship with Oates whatsoever. One suspects from *Of True Religion* that Milton would not have doubted that a Popish plot existed.

The question of succession remained a burning issue for some years. *The Character of a Popish Successor, and What England May Expect From Such a One. Part the Second* (1681) follows Elkanah Settle's pamphlet of similar title on the Exclusion Bill: *The Character of a Popish Successor, and what England may expect From such a One. Humbly offered to the Consideration of Both Houses of Parliament, Appointed to meet at Oxford, On the One and twentieth of March, 1680/1* and *The Character of a Popish Successour Compleat: In Defence of the First Part Against Two Answers, One Written by Mr L'Estrange, called The Papist in Masquerade, &c. And another By an Unknown Hand* (1681), which has sometimes been assigned to Phillips and sometimes to Settle and Phillips. Phillips takes off on those who talk of the succession as if Charles II were already dead, with "his Herse design'd to make a Bridge for Roman Catholick Ambition to walk over his Blood to the destruction of their [the people's] Religion, their Laws and Liberties" (2). The thrust is anti-papal, with hope of Parliamentary action to settle the question, and a learned summary of British history such as we can observe in Milton's tracts in the 1640s is the primary content for evidence of his contentions. He is not exhibiting Toryism in not attacking kingship or in espousing Church of England affinities. He is not taking sides about the Exclusion Bill or hereditary principles of kingship anymore than his uncle did in *Tenure of Kings and Magistrates*. Settle, incidentally, in the second tract cited above, observes that the Protectorate was "ten times worse" than Kings "by woful Experience" (Preface, [vi]). L'Estrange countered Phillips with *A Reply to the Second Part of the Character of a Popish Successor* (1681).

   L'Estrange No Papist: In Answer to a Libel Entituled L'Estrange a Papist &c. (1681) provoked Phillips's *Mr. L'Estrange Refuted With his own Arguments. Being a Reply to his late Impertinent Pamphlet Entituled L'Estrange No Papist. In farther Justification of the Informations sworn against him, before the Lords of the Secret Committee. By J.P. Gent.* (1681). L'Estrange's sarcasm toward Dissenters is answered by a toleration not unlike Milton's, excluding only the Papists. Phillips is bothered by L'Estrange's licensing and accusations against writers, and, of course, the reader will be reminded of *Areopagitica*. L'Estrange confesses "himself to be a Catholick of Rome in a harmless fashion" (23), whatever that is supposed to mean; and the reader suspects that Phillips is thinking of the *Index Librorum Prohibitorum*. Also, Phillips's correction of L'Estrange's classifications (and those of some people even today) should be noted: "Protestant" is the general term, under which are "species" called Episcopacy (which is not unqualifiedly the same as the Church of England), Presbytery, and Independency. (Some adherents of the Church of England accepted Episcopacy, others did not. Rather, they, like Milton, rejected prelacy as a lingering Catholicism which the incomplete Reformation had not expunged.) He concludes: "Thus Mr. L'Estrange, I have done. I have only said this to tell you, that your Answers to the affadavits against you are frivolous and impertinent, and that you must bring better proofs of your Innocency, or else you will never be believed among Rational Men . . ." (36). We might wonder whether in the back of his mind was remembrance of L'Estrange's criticisms of his uncle in such as *L'Estrange His Apology* (1660), *No Blind Guides* (1660), *Treason Arraign'd* (1660), and *Considerations and Proposals in Order to the Regulation of the Press Together with Diverse Instances of Treasonous, and Seditious Pamphlets, Proving the Necessity Thereof* (1663).

The political and religious problems continued during the 1680s, with clearer sides being taken by Tory and Whig, and Phillips pursued his attacks on those favoring Roman Catholicism, thus many who would espouse Toryism and thus exhibiting what has placed him among the Whigs for later critics. His next tract is a lampoon—anti-Pope, anti-Heraclitus (a name adopted by Thomas Flatman), anti-Observator (a name adopted by L'Estrange).[46] *New News from Tory-Land and Tantivy-Shire* (1682) puns on those at full gallop, mounted on the Church of England, riding to Rome behind the Duke of York—such as Flatman in his periodical *Heraclitus Ridens*. It informs its readers, with unhidden irony, that "The *Presbyterians* are *Traitors,* and *Fanatick,* and the Kingdom is to be dispeopl'd with their utter Extirpation" because they "*had no hand in bringing in the King*" (5). L'Estrange and Castlemaine and "that *Wizard, Gadburies Astrological Jargourie*" (8) iterate "*Periuries, Forgeries,* and *Subornations* of the Papists" (6). "Can the *Sons of the Church of* England so Passively hear the Reformed Religion abroad, and all its pious Professors derided, and their Reputation blasted by a Vermin of a *Figure-Caster,* and not give one gentle admonition to their *Great Guide,* to bestow one cast of his Office upon so infamous an Enormity?" (8–9).[47]

In *Horse-Flesh For The Observator: Being a Comment upon Gusman, Ch. 4. V. 5 Held forth at Sam's Coffee-House. By T.D.B.D. Chaplain to the Inferiour Clergies Guide* (1682) Phillips's impugning of L'Estrange and Catholic Spanish connections continues. Gaspar de Guzman, Duke de San Lucas de Barameda, Count de Olivares, fell into disgrace in Spain because of his secret negotiations with Richelieu. (Phillips is picking up on the popularity of Mateo Aleman's prose narrative, *The Rogue: or the Life of Guzman de Alfarache. Written in Spanish* [first published in 1622].) In *A Pleasant Conference upon the Observator, and Heraclitus: Together With a breif Relation of the Present Posture of the French Affairs* (1682), he points his finger at "*Lucifers* Emissaries" who "counterfeit sometimes *Tory,* and sometimes *Whigg.*" The tract is a dialogue playing off against a decade-old treatise: *ΠΛΑΝΗΣ ΑΠΟΚΑΛΥΨΙΣ. Popery Manifested, Or, the Papist Incognito made known, By way of Dialogue Betwixt A | Papist Priest, | Protestant Gentleman, and | Presbyterian Divine. In Two Parts. Intended for the good of those that shall read it. By L.B.P.* (1673). (The Greek title means the "deceiving Apocalypse"; compare my previous remarks on *A Satyr Against Hypocrites.*) The two speakers in *A Pleasant Conference* are Belfager and Pluto: "all the vast Army, and all the numerous Captains that *Miltons Paradise lost* musters up for ye, they'l all do you not a pins worth of good," Belfager (the war-maker?) tells the ruler of the underworld (3). Of "The Character of the *Observator* and *Heraclitus Ridens*" he comments, "The one is a meer *Fidler* in Dialogues, the other plays the *Treble* to his *Base*" (14), for "before the *Grand Plot,* the *Whiggs* were accounted good subjects . . . But no sooner was the *Grand Plot* of your *Highnesses Nephew the Pope* discovered, but up starts *Forty One* in a Winding-sheet" (18). The blame for the continuing questions about the succession is determined: "And all this proceeds from the Animosities which are daily blown up and cherished by the Pamphleteers, those Tools of the *Jesuits,* the *Observator* and *Heraclitus*" (25).

Religious/political problems flared in the 1680s, particularly through the effects of the Test Act (29 March 1673), which ostensibly attempted to rout out Catholics, and through what was looked upon as a Tory/Catholic juncture by the Whigs. Indeed, the Test Act was amended on 1 December 1678 to expel all Catholics from both houses of Parliament, and the denial of James II's request to suspend the Act in 1685 led to his proroguing Parliament. Milton's adversary, Samuel Parker (see his acrimonious references in *A Reproof to The Rehearsal Transprosed, in a Discourse to Its Author,* 1673), wrote *A Discourse of Ecclesiastical Politie* (1670) and *A Defence and Continuation of Ecclesiastical Politie* (1671), and *Reasons for Abrogating the Test* (1688). The act ordered those holding civil or military office or receiving remuneration from the king to "take the several oaths of supremacy and allegiance, which oath of allegiance is contained in the statute made in the third year of King James, by law established" and to partake of "the sacrament of the Lord's Supper according to the usage of the Church of England," while also declaring "that there is not any transubstantiation in the sacrament of the Lord's Supper, or in the elements of bread and wine, at, or after the consecration thereof by any person whatsoever." Parker's important church position is cited in Phillips's animadversion entitled: *Sam. Ld. Bp. of Oxon His Celebrated Reasons for Abrogating The Test, And Notions of Idolatry Answered By Samuel, Arch-Deacon of Canterbury. It's better to Indulge Mens Vices and Debaucheries, than their Con-sciences. Sam. Park. Eccles. Pol. Pag. 54.* (1688). To Hone, the work is more political than religious and was "calculated to increase his ingratiation with James II" (516). This is certainly not informed criticism and decidedly opaque: it was through James II that Parker, who became Archdeacon of Canterbury in June 1670, assumed the presidency of Magdalen College, Oxford, in 1687 over the protests of all others concerned and through forcible action by the King's men. Through the mandates of James, Parker admitted Roman Catho-lic fellows to the College, including several Jesuits, and was seen as an en-abler of Roman Catholic projects against the Church of England, to the point of being regarded as avowedly Romanish. Indeed, the College was looked upon as a Roman Catholic "seminary" by many. (There were three reprints of Parker's volume in 1688; he died in mid-1688.) Phillips is not championing James; he is incensed by Parker's "most bitter Invectives against the *Nonconformists,* and his temptuous Indignation against *Dissenters* in general; so diametrically opposite to the Serene and Pious Desires and Resolutions of His Majesty, to make His Subjects happy, and unite them to Him as well by Inclination, as Duty" (1). (The Test Act, of course, had been first passed under Charles II and though James was not happy with its Catholic intolerance, it was still in force under his reign. See also remarks on this issue in chapter 5.) Parker is also accused of making "a Plea for *Transubstantiation,* and his own new Modell'd Notions of *Idolatry*" (1). His writings "run so apparently counter to His Majesty's *Gracious Declaration for Liberty of Conscience*" (2) and "He boasts his having prov'd, *That* Indulgence *and* Toleration *is the most Absolute sort of Anarchy*" (4). According to Parker, "*governours must look to the Publick, and let* Tender Consciences look to *Themselves.*" He had earlier in *Ecclesiastical Politie* asserted that the position of dissenters is untenable and ridiculous; he discourses enthusiastically upon "the Pretense of a Tender and Unsatisfied Conscience" and the "Absurdity of Pleading it in opposition to the commands of Publick Authority." The problem of liberty of conscience had loomed as a major bone of contention from the 1640s onward, and underlies much that Milton wrote between the years 1641 and 1673. With the oppositions revolving around the Papacy, the monarchic interconnections with it, the Test Act to force out those of such religious persuasion, and the difficulties over succession of kingship, the buzz term "Tender Conscience" associated with dissenters and other naysayers arose frequently at this time.[48]

Phillips believed that Catholicism should be extirpated from national government and even, like his uncle, from religious existence in England. Phillips reads Parker as recommending loss of conscience, of misequation of nonconformity with papal thinking, and of actually submitting to Catholic concepts. "He appeals to all then, whether *Liberty of Conscience* be any better, than a License for *Anarchy* and *Confusion*" (19). A doctor of divinity in the Church of England and Lord Bishop of Oxford, he supposedly "fears the Return of Popery into the Nation, should the *Nonconformists* joyn with the *Papists*" (22). But Phillips, speaking of "the Church of *Rome,* and her Adherents," interprets Parker's words not to rid Rome's influence but "to furnish them with better Arguments of his own, than any they have Themselves, to vindicate *Transubstantiation,* and clear them from *Idolatry*" (22). Phillips is not arguing for or against the Test Act (Hone sees him as not opposed to abrogating it): he is arguing against what he sees as Parker's misunderstanding and, because of Parker's religious office and influence, his potential advocacy of Catholicism.[49]

In all, then, Phillips has been misread, ignorantly maligned, and unreliably dissociated from Milton, personally and ideationally. William Riley Parker raised questions concerning the dissociation, but certainly misreads at times and does little to set the record straight. A major concern in all of John's work is to argue against Roman Catholicism and to argue for a Church of England position that did not include episcopacy. He is impatient with clergy (and political figures) who weaken the "people's" rights, who write against liberty of conscience and toleration (except for Roman Catholics), who are hypocritical, and who favor censorship. All of this sounds much like his uncle. Phillips in the last years of the Interregnum and in the early years of the Restoration is highly critical of and antagonistic to the Protectorate and what he, and other Parliamentarians (other republicans), conceived as Cromwell's tyranny and improper dynastic leanings. The actions of the Army, as under the leadership of John Lambert, were deplored. The approbation of and allegiance to the king and achievements under his reign, whether Charles II or James II, do not demand a Royalist political philosophy, and do not elicit it from Phillips. Milton's position in this issue is complicated, but the assumption that he accepted the Protectorate wholeheartedly may need much modification and the contention that he was consistently dead-set against a monarchy (which has been under revision lately) should be rethought. Milton's religious "classification" has again recently run into op-positions, largely over the matter of his burial at St. Giles, Cripplegate, if indeed he was not a practicing member of a calvinistic church or was the Arian that hindsight has reputed him. "Quite simply," I have urged, "Milton was Calvinist, agreeing with election and predestination but also accepting renovation (and vocation) as the means to restoration through the redemption of Christ. . . . 'Ingrafting in Christ' defined regeneration for Milton, as the former person is destroyed and a new inner man emerges, restored to God's image, sanctified in soul and body, to God's service and to good works."[50] No agent is required for such renovation/regeneration, only the individual working through Faith in God and Charity to Others. Comparing Phillips's work to this kind of thinking will lead to overwhelmingly different readings of both his own writing and thought and his relationship with his uncle after 1652.

Phillips, like so many other writers of the day, engages in vituperation, obscenities, and scurrilous language; his is a satiric vein, a burlesque style, an impatience with such a palterer as L'Estrange and such an illogical musi-cal charlatan as Thomas Salmon. That Milton would have "disowned" him for such attacks is hardly creditable. There is no certain evidence of his visiting his uncle after, perhaps, 1654, and aside from his writings and their receptions, we can say nothing with certainty about the rest of his life. But the story of John and his uncle has been a flagrant example of a main point of this book: time present has simply taken over the foundationless and prejudiced assertions of time past, superannuating them, and ignoring or misreading whatever evidence there has been that would lead to at least defensible opposed judgments. The following chapter will iterate much that has been looked at in this chapter, although it has here been seen only in application to John Phillips (such as the state of religious/political affairs in the Interregnum and Restoration and such as the economic/social world of Milton's time). It will not be employed to relate uncle and nephew: it does, however, indicate the worlds that both reacted to and often unfortunately found themselves in. It does imply that the past's refrain that "Milton must have broken with him" is stridently wrong. Earlier chapters on Milton's brother and his family and his brother-in-law and his family will also bear on our consideration of Milton's political and religious self. Family matters do matter.

Part 2

John Milton

It has often been observed that the British seventeenth century is a transition period between the Renaissance and the early modern period. And it has long been my view that what happens then is a vying between open patterns of life and an increasing closed pattern in the way people came to think. By "open" and "closed," I mean a truly free situation that allowed at least consideration of ideas in all endeavors of life from all groups of people in life, or a situation that did not allow this. A "closed" pattern implies a delimitation of possibilities, a definite and unswerving and unmodified way of doing anything. In literature, that analysis has been seen most readily and clearly through the prescriptive rules of composition, genre, and dramatic structure that came to dominate through the influence of people like Castelvetro interpreting Aristotle (1570) and Roger Ascham ignoring Aristotelian concepts of mimesis and offering in its place imitation of authors (1570, though written much earlier), and then through such descriptions of literary types as Thomas Hobbes's in his preface to Sir William Davenant's *Gondibert* (1651). The later seventeenth century, of course, saw the beginnings of the hegemony of what has been called neoclassicism, as well as restatements of the Hobbesian delimitation as in William Wollaston's preface to his *Design of Part of the Book of Ecclesiastes* (1691). Neoclassicism not only "imitated" the classical authors, primarily Homer and Vergil, and eschewed the "romantic" (and more modern) ones like Ariosto, Boiardo, and Tasso, but it also expected "standard" prosody (dominated by the heroic couplet or lyric stanzaic forms), a "standard" genre with at least most of its expected elements and structure in place, and an effect that satisfied an acceptable intentionality for that work. Needless to say, there were important authors and works that did not follow these "rules" and "principles," and that did develop other technical and qualitative poetics. Closed patterns found opposition by a few whose nonconformity emerged not only in literary matters, but in religious, political, and social life. That continuance through literary productions is the burden of N.H. Keeble's book on nonconformity; Keeble concludes, "It was a literature which in its premises and procedures dissented from evolving literary canons as did nonconformists themselves from the developing values of what came to be called Anglicanism."[1]

As the century began, the argument over the decline of the Earth, with its Deistic relationships, posed the problem the end of the century would debate over the Ancients and the Moderns. In literature, negative criticism was cast on those of nonconforming nature (such as Milton, with his disliked blank verse) or those whose treatment of certain themes was not what a critic thought it should be (such as John Donne, whose lyrics John Dryden, in his opaque misreading, saw as "perplex[ing] the Minds of the Fair Sex with nice Speculations of Philosophy, when he shou'd ingage their hearts, and entertain them with the softnesses of Love"[2]). The effect of this underlying change in attitude (perhaps anchored in certain ways by the success and spread of Ramism and Ramistic categorizations and classifying) can be seen in the antagonisms in political thought, philosophic concepts, the advancements of science, educational theory, and sociological and economic thought, as well as the arts. Despite the continuing of open patterns (even with, once in a while, a dominance of open pattern), the history of modern life since the mid-seventeenth century has been the triumph of closed thinking, of reduction of life to constitutions and principles of motion. Owen Barfield expressed it a different way: a systematic forgetting of the past, for he argues that with the Cartesian dichotomy, the Aristotelian conception of *potentia* was eliminated, leaving only demonstration, quantification, "Uniformitarianism."[3]

5

Royalist Connections, but Parliamentarian

1

In this chapter, I first glance at the 1640s and 1650s in England, a time when Milton is solidifying his political and religious thinking. I then proceed to examine that side of his life *and thinking* that may be called "royalist" despite his republicanism and parliamentarianism. Previous chapters have disclosed the entwined familial and social interfacings of Milton and the Royalist world. The intertwining of the political and the religious requires consideration of his religious position (and its theological beliefs), which reaffirms his life's early *and continued* vocation and which comes to combat some accepted interpretations of his prose and poetry and to assert a middle state, as it were, in the debate that has been wrought through the investigation of the authorship of *De doctrina christiana,* which I firmly believe Milton wrote. Those who say he did not write the treatise misunderstand his religious beliefs (among other problems) and those who say he did write the treatise misunderstand his religious beliefs as well. I am constrained to take up this complicated subject in a separate, more thorough book.

Those years of 1640 to 1659 constitute a period that gave rise to the Leveller Petitions called *Agreements of the People* (1647–49), the Diggers' platform, expressly recorded in Gerrard Winstanley's work, and Utopianism. The problems that these social and economic reforms faced—as all reform always seems to—were those of the closed thinking gaining strong ground in religion, politics, and the social order; yet solutions the reformers themselves proffered also created a closed world. The example of the Massachusetts Bay Colony is only one case in point of the religio-political situation: colonists who fled from oppression of thought in expectation of freedom of religion soon enough ostracized any and all who did not conform to the theocratic state that had been set up. While the 1662 Act of Uniformity, which required uniformity to the Church of England and its Book of Common Prayer (something Archbishop William Laud had attempted to enforce in the 1630s, although now a new Book of Common Prayer had been developed[4]), dispersed further dissidents to America, it was not a tolerant world they found themselves in.

Much of the political action of the seventeenth century was essentially religiously interrelated: the overarching movement was to separate the Church and the State, or its countermovement, to maintain a fusion, with obvious sallies into Erastianism. With monarchs on the throne who believed in a divine right of kings, such separation became a sacrilegious action. The century's inheritance from the middle ages was an equation of the law of nature with the law of God as handed down in the Bible. Natural law was common to all humankind, but man-made law, as Hobbes and others saw it, limited natural rights. Arguments therefore flourished over what natural rights existed as given through God's natural law, and whether the king was a David who understood, better than others, those natural rights.[5] The variety of interpretations of natural rights and the means to enjoy them led to widespread sectarianism. Most opposition arose, as one commonly would expect, over what was conceived as an abrogation of natural rights as in political actions, taxation, judicial recourse, economic matters, and especially in tolerance of religion. The Petition of Right, passed on 28 May 1628, asserted the rights of the people over royal prerogative, especially as seen through the influence of George Villiers, Lord Buckingham (assassinated by John Felton on 23 August 1628), and restricted the king's powers. The Third Parliament declared among other planks that, "They do . . . humbly pray your most excellent majesty, that no man hereafter be compelled to make or yield any gift, benevolence, tax, or such like charge, without common consent by act of parliament; . . . that no freeman, in any such manner as is before mentioned, be imprisoned or detained."[6] Note that word *compelled;* it is significant for both political and religious thinking,[7] but also note that the king is still "your most excellent majesty." While the king had condoned actions that were reprehensible to the peers of Parliament, he remained an exalted and superior being. Hierarchy was not shaken among titled men, and those who were not "freemen" remained in their subjected and poor circumstances.[8] Many of the succeeding struggles between the king and the people revolved around religious matters, and the Civil Wars that ensued in the 1640s had more to do, for many people, with religion than with economics. What should be salient is that these arguments attempted to alter the closed patterns set up by royal prerogative through review and approval or rejection, not really through unrestricted actions applied to all people. That designation of "freeman" was not an indication of equality for all people of all social standings or backgrounds, or for both genders. The "people" for whom the petition was written were the middle and upper classes (almost exclusively the men), who held the franchise. Attention was not paid to revisions of the franchise.

While the Civil Wars promoted schismatic groups, they also unified certain religious positions to a point of intolerance toward other groups, a fact borne out by the prosecution of the Friends (or Quakers) and of such itinerant preachers as John Bunyan (whose writings Keeble discusses as a mainstay in the continuance of nonconformity). The continued economic problems created by the enclosure system, spread from medieval times onward, added to the increase in debtors and a shifting of social standings. The agricultural land of the earlier middle ages increasingly became enclosed for sheep raising, thereby setting up the important wool staple, and putting in motion demands for agricultural products from outside the British Isles. Ensuing, of course, was an explosion of commerce and the naval force needed to maintain trade routes and to delimit foreigners' trade routes and colonization. Along with this came a sharp population shift from agricultural areas to the cities and the accompanying growth of an impoverished lower class. We have heard much of debtors' prisons in the eighteenth century, but a work like the anonymous *The Malady and Remedy of Vexations and the Unjust Arrests and Actions* (1646) is directly concerned to repeal the enforced laws bringing imprisonment for debt. I have already raised this issue in looking at John Phillips's *Mercurius Verax*.

These seemingly open ways of life—changes in economic structure, expansion into other cultures, an alteration of social identifications and expectations—also led to even stronger stratifications. Remedies were sought in the *Agreements of the People* in 1647–49, much of which was penned by John Lilburne. The documents, approved by a popular vote of the so-called Levellers, who advocated popular sovereignty with parliament as the People's representative, hoped to establish a government without a king or a House of Lords, the single ruling house to be elected by "the people" (Article III, but the term is undefined). It aimed at redistribution of the franchise, legal reforms, abolition of a state church, and abolition of the privileges of peers. While the results of the Civil Wars were the Rump's establishment of a Council of State and the abolition of monarchy and the House of Lords, the new government also imposed a series of "Blue Laws" in 1649 requiring, as one "closed" way of life, observance of Sunday (in repeal of James I's 1617 Declaration of Sports, reissued by Charles I in 1633), and punishment of adultery, swearing, and blasphemy, among other matters. Oliver Cromwell, Protector of the Commonwealth in 1653, enacted further laws in 1655 and tried to enforce them through the rule of the Major-Generals over ten presbyteries (later eleven). The Instrument of Government promulgated in 1653 reverted to a constitution declaring "That the supreme legislative authority of the

Commonwealth of England, Scotland, and Ireland, and the dominions thereunto belonging shall be and reside in one person and the people assembled
in parliament," "That there shall be a parliament summoned to meet at
Westminster . . . once in every third year," and like articles, including a still
restrictive religious toleration: "That such as profess faith in God by Jesus Christ,
though differing in judgment from the doctrine, worship, or discipline publicly held forth, shall not be restrained from, but shall be protected in the
profession of the faith and exercise of their religion; so as they abuse not this
liberty to the civil injury of others and to the actual disturbance of the public
peace on their parts; provided this liberty be not extended to Popery or Prelacy,
nor to such as, under the profession of Christ, hold forth and practice licentiousness."[9] Particularly to be noted, of course, is the outlawing of episcopacy
from the so-called "Church of England"; the anti-prelatical arguments of such
people as Milton in the early 1640s, and episcopacy's assignment as a remnant
of Catholicism, had their desired result.

Countering closed patterns has brought seemingly equalizing concepts
that thence become closed again in their own way. Milton's and Smectymnuan
arguments against prelacy in the early 1640s are reaffirmed, and his future
arguments against popery in *Of True Religion,* 1673, should not be seen as
only personal intolerance, as so many students of Milton have viewed it. The
word "compelled" in the Petition of Right in 1628 remains the telling argument in *Of True Religion* against popery, which Milton says compels action
and thought by adherents of Roman Catholicism.[10] Yet the Instrument of
government in its seemingly republican concepts has denied certain "free"
practices of religion for all those *not* "under the profession of Christ" (such
as Jews[11]) or to those acceding to church hierarchy as in Catholicism or as in
its remnant of existence in Church of England prelacy. (Today some people,
like those in the United States who think that their country was founded as
a "Christian" nation, echo the same kind of intolerance and ignorance.)
And in clarion defiance of the rebellion against monarchy that led to the
"new" government, the Instrument of Protectorship set up a single Protector, and was to set up a new primogenitureship with the appointment of the
less than competent Richard Cromwell in 1658, upon his father's death.

The Army Debates of 1647–49 between Cromwell and Henry Ireton and
the Levellers, the ordinary members of the army, argued over property qualifications as the base for suffrage (a base maintained in the United States,
incidentally, until only very recently) and the doctrine of natural rights. The
Levellers seem to espouse (but do not) the equality that Fredric Jameson
lamented as missing from *Paradise Lost,* which instead "illustrates and documents, not a proposition about human nature, not a type of philosophical
or theological content, but rather the operation of ideological closure."[12]

Demanded by the Levellers were suffrage, biennial or annual parliaments, changes in the electoral process, social reforms, maintenance of the poor and aged, abolition of commercial monopolies, direct tax on real and personal property, and, significantly, restoration of enclosed lands. Underneath these demands is an assertion of the individual against the group;[13] such an assertion aims to establish the natural (inalienable) rights of the individual, and thus it undermines the social order based on class distinctions. The Levellers, however, seemed not to realize this aspect of "equality" in their planks until Ireton pointed it out, and one must pause to wonder whether full equality lay in their hopes. Ireton was appalled at the upshot of the natural claim to political rights demanded by the Levellers because it would lead to a claim to economic rights, a rejection, that is, of the significance of land ownership or corporation membership. (The dichotomy between the Left and the Right, of course, continues to be unsolved and to propagate injustice and inequality.) Particularly to be noted is the Levellers' (and especially the Diggers') antagonism to the enclosure system seen in their revision of land laws to include revision of inheritance: although the eldest son might inherit two-thirds of the land, the rest should be divided equally among the remaining sons—an inheritance procedure that hardly seems to allow for "equality" for progeny. And, yes, daughters were not included!

Behind such ideas is the thinking of William Walwyn: suffrage for all men (women are neither mentioned nor implied), abolition of the lords, the supremacy of law as a written constitution insuring the rights of man, and free trade or "common right," that which promotes the welfare of the community. As he wrote in *The Compassionate Samaritane* (1644): "if ever there be [an agreement of judgment], in all probability it must proceed from the power and efficacie of Truth, not from constraint," and "The greatest glory of authority is to protect the distressed."[14] Lilburne's *An Outcry of the Young Men and Apprentices of London* (1649) suggests the beginnings of trade unionism in the schism between employers and employees underlying his rejection of current practice of appointing masters and wardens and of the suppression of the workers.

The first manifesto stating the position of the Diggers was *The True Levellers Standard Advanced: or, The State of Community opened, and Presented to the Sons of Men* (1649). Gerrard Winstanley's contribution is dedicated to the cause of "the common people of England [who] have begun, and [have] consent to digge up, manure, and sowe corn upon George-Hill in Surrey."[15] Believing that political revolution must be based on social revolution, that the land should be restored to the people, and that all religion is internal, Winstanley, in such works as *The New Law of Righteousnes* (1649), *The True Levellers Standard Advanced, A Declaration from the Poor Oppressed People of En-*

gland (1649), *The Law of Freedom in a Platform* (1652), consistently attacked the forcing of people to work for a miserable and insufficient wage while the idlers (landlords, gentry, employers) enjoyed the Earth's riches. But he is not arguing for a decent wage: his is a communistic (in the basic meaning of that word) appeal. In *The True Levellers Standard* he asserts to those idlers, "Take notice, That England is not a Free People, till the Poor that have no Land, have a free allowance to dig and labour the commons, and so live as comfortably as the Landlords that live in their Inclosures. . . . making the Earth a Common Treasury . . . and having a comfortable livelihood in the Community of one Earth their Mother" (15). The proposal looks toward a "utopian" social and economic world that rejects stratifications in that world. Later he will write, "Jesus Christ who is that powerfull Spirit of Love is the head *Leveller*."[16] The subtitle of *The New Law of Righteousnes* indicates the apocalyptic vision that T. Wilson Hayes examines in his study of Winstanley,[17] and suggests the conflation of apocalyptism and positive utopianism: "Or a Glimpse of the new Heaven, and new Earth, wherein dwels Righteousnes."

Utopianism is, of course, what underlies so many of these proposals; that is, the speculative or constructive type of utopia, although the satiric may also emerge. Positive utopianism begins with ideals for society, one of which has often been a social equality even though analysis points out that proposers have seldom thought that through. Seventeenth-century utopias or utopian proposals counter what is viewed as the individual versus the institution, and the germ lies in conceived religious oppression, political and government structures, and in the 1640s and 1650s economic disjunctures. Samuel Gott's *Nova Solyma, the New Jerusalem* (1648), or Richard Baxter's *A Holy Commonwealth* (1656), or John Eliot's *The Christian Commonwealth* (1659) represents such religio-political criticisms of the existing institutions; and James Harrington's *The Commonwealth of Oceana* (1656) offers a kind of economically utopian world based on agrarian law that ensures the perpetual distribution of land and prevents its being inherited and accumulated by the few. He moves into an electoral and parliamentary system that predates, of course, not only Milton's *The Ready and Easy Way to Establish a Free Commonwealth* (1660) but, significantly, the constitutionalism of Montesquieu and the American colonies. People, here, are classified according to age, fortune, quality, and residence, the aristocracy being distinguished from other citizens by merit and fortune. That sounds good, but is it equality? There are various civil units with various officers, the ballot being used to vote in such officers from the candidates picked by lot. There is rotation in public office. And while there is liberty of conscience, toleration is not extended to Papists, Jews, or Idolaters. Harrington defines types of government according to the distribution of property, and argues that equality of estate causes equality of power, which in turn creates a republican commonwealth. He is clearly an advocate of the idea that economics should determine government, and its source is in the recognition that during this period, because of the shifts in population and wealth, there have been shifts in political life, most notably in the conflicts between Royalist types and parliamentarians.

The theme of Winstanley's *The Law of Freedom in a Platform* (1652) is that the earth and its products should belong to all; therefore, the land should be returned to its original owners, the people. The near-communistic system advocated is to be controlled by laws strictly enforced, so that true freedom, being where humankind receives its nourishment, will be maintained in the free enjoyment of the earth. Michael Wilding reminds us that the spirit of Winstanley's assertions is echoed by Milton, who reasserts the primacy of the inner light in *Paradise Regain'd*, with its "stress on the primacy of the individual conscience over the pressures of external authority, the stress on the accessibility to all men of 'the Spirit of god.'"[18] Wilding so incisively understands "the contradictions that arose when [Milton] renounced the attempt to establish by military means a radical Kingdom of Heaven on earth, and turned instead to the private preparation of the soul for the paradise within" (258). While this is an acceptance of political status quo, it is not a rejection of anti-authoritarianism or the love of liberty or the desire to establish a new society.

The latter-day theories of Robert Owen, Henry George, or 1970 communes indicate the continuance of such thinking. Rejection of certain closed patterns, however, creates new closed attitudes that doom all New Harmonies to ultimate defeat. With the Diggers, we have clear indication of the change from Revelation to Manifestation of God as guiding principle, which is to emerge in the centuries immediately following. Joseph Glanvill in *The Agreement of Reason and Religion* (1676) epitomized what had occurred philosophically: he argues that "the Being of a God, the Foundation of all, is proved by Reason," not by Revelation, for "*Revelation supposeth* the Being of a God, and cannot prove it, . . . The *Knowledge* of his Being must *precede* our Faith in revelation; and so cannot be deduced from it." "Reason proves the Divine Authority of Scripture . . . and there is no distinct Revelation that is certain and infalliable to assure us of it; so *Reason only* remains to demonstrate the Article." Reason "demonstrates the *divine* Authority of the *Testimony* that declares . . . the Truths of *pure* Revelation" and is thus in harmony in its teachings with the teachings of nature.[19] Here, in the last quarter of the seventeenth century, just shortly after Milton's death, Glanvill in 1676 argued deistic principles and the rationalism that was to characterize the oncoming century at the same time that sectarianism burst into renewed vigor and new schisms arose. "*The denial of Reason in Religion,*" he argued, "*hath been the principal Engine that Hereticks and Enthusiasts have used against the Faith*" (25); such denial leads to the "follies and impostures" of Arianism (including Socinianism), Apollinarists, Donatists, Ubiquitarians, Macedonians, Enthusiasts, and to advantage to the Church of Rome (25–26). Churchmen like Richard Cumberland, Lord Bishop of Peterborough (1631–1718), though antagonistic toward Deism, accepted Reason in religion, but at the same time maintained the significance of Revelation as the pantheistic view of nature continued to spread and begin to dominate. For him, "GOD, the Author of Nature, has imprinted Characters of His independent Power, Wisdom, Goodness, Providence, &c. upon his Works; he has given us Reason, by which we cannot but discover, if we attend, these his Attributes, and the Relation we have to him."[20] But "Revelation was useful and necessary for the Reformation of Mankind," even though "*some* cry up *Reason, and the Light of Nature,* at such a rate, as to think them alone *sufficient Guides,* in consequence of which they think all Revelation useless and unnecessary . . . *Others,* with a mistaken View of magnifying Revelation and Faith, undervalue and *vilify Reason* and the *Light of Nature* most immoderately."[21]

Perhaps the various utopian schemes that flourished in these years would have done well to heed Robert Burton's thinking on the subject in his "An Utopia of Mine Own," from Democritus Junior's address to the reader in *The Anatomy of Melancholy* (1628): he is basically materialistic and utilitarian, presenting a world not concerned with communal living or justice, but with security and a decent standard of living for all its citizens. His is a planned and thus regulated economy, one clearly acknowledging the need for closed patterns in some things. Perhaps a fusion of Reason, Revelation, and Manifestation, although it posits the existence of a godhead, would have served sociological, political, and religious life better than the internecine war of words.

2

Looking back on the preceding century, John, Lord Hervey, referring first to those arguing against prelacy (but not including Milton, I trust), asserts:

> Anti-ministerial Writers . . . have as often prostituted the Name of Liberty, as they have abused the *Enjoyment* of it.
> They always talk both of Liberty and Frugality in government; as if any Society could be form'd without some Restraint on natural Liberty . . . [I]t must be granted, that all Peace, all Order in Society is maintain'd by some Restrictions on natural Liberty, and that the Anarchy of natural Liberty wholly unrestrain'd, would be as great an Evil as the Slavery of no Liberty at all allow'd.[22]

In the language I employ at the beginning of this chapter, Hervey argues that a totally open system will not work, nor does a closed system. Milton, of course, had said what is tantamount to that in Sonnet 11: "Licence they mean, when they cry liberty." It is not only divorce that is involved, but politics and religion that need freedom of thought, the freedom of conscience that Walwyn spoke of. Let there be some moral laws like those promulgated in 1655 and some constitutional legalities, republican although restrictive in certain ways from allowing one to run roughshod over all life.[23] But also let there be free thought. For Milton, this could not condone Roman Catholicism because the Pope *compelled;* nor could this accept the tyrant or a king or magistrate who served himself and not the people. Yet as one looks over the years of the Interregnum from Hervey's point of view and from Milton's involvement in those years, particularly after the Instrument of Protectorship in 1653, one must pause before assigning a label to Milton of Cromwellian or Parliamentarian if either means an adherent to all that occurred in those years, or a label of Republican without making clear what that includes and what it may not.

Hervey, who shows acceptance of much in Leveller philosophy, commends the strength that the people gained through the Revolution and laments the world of Charles II and James II, but he recognized what the Commonwealth became: "Those who pretended at first only to reduce and bound the Power of the Crown, and curb him who had abused it, became themselves, after they had destroy'd the King, such intolerant Oppressors of the People, that they straiten'd every chain they pretended to loose, and doubled every Evil they pretended to cure" (33). The central figure in creating what the Commonwealth became was, of course, Cromwell—and this involved his actions and the opposed reactions from almost all quarters. The attitudes toward Oliver Cromwell during the years 1649–1660 are confused and inconsistent, sometimes positive and often negative, and Milton's opinion of him has been much debated. As J.C. Davis elaborates,[24] Cromwell was viewed as a paradox, one with great skills as a leader, one who achieved numerous successes, but one who also was blamed for the massacre in Ireland and the war with Spain, one who ultimately divided and demoralized the church establishment, and one, especially, who saw himself as a kind of king. That he rejected the Humble Petition and Advice of 25 May 1657 did not erase the concept of Protector, and of course, his son Richard's succeeding to the title only exacerbated the problems of the "commonwealth" and aided in settlement of the Restoration. "Cromwell's valour and clemency are justly praised, as are his political skills, which held the country together when the military failed, and which eventually made England a more formidable international force than she had been for a century," as Graham Parry points out in talking of the poetic views of Andrew Marvell, Abraham Cowley, and John Dryden.[25] "To his contemporaries Cromwell was a figure larger than life, military hero, godly ruler, or, to Royalists, Machiavellian schemer. Those who opposed his principles and policies still exhibited grudging respect for his forceful determination and political skills," Kevin Sharpe epitomizes.[26]

Aside from the execution of the king, which even those opposed to Charles I found abhorrent, negative reactions against Cromwell arose from the founding of the Protectorate (note the representative letter cited before, chapter 4, n6), the Spanish War (declared in October 1655), the institution of the Major-Generals' rule, and the assumption of the Protectorship by his son Richard and the fast deterioration of government thereafter. According to Blair Worden, the Rump Parliament between 1649 and 1653 was "essentially conservative," aiming at the removal of a particular king, not kingship.[27] But then, according to S. Mewce, a lawyer, writing to Elizabeth, Lady Hatton, on 21 April 1653, "The long sitting parlament was dissolved in a trice, without noyse [the day before] . . . Wee must nowe every day looke for newe things. God knowes what will follow; but generally this change is not unwelcome to the people."[28] That last phrase should particularly be noted. One reason was Cromwell's emphasis on toleration, such as can be seen in his use of Whitehall Chapel: Mewce wrote to Lady Hatton, 5 January 1653/4, "Wee say 12 chaplains are nowe chosen, 6 Presbiterian, 6 Independents. I doubt not but hee may find sects enough to make up 48 and not exceed six of a sort, and yet not troble himselfe with popish or prelaticall people" (10). "The nonprelaticall people," like Milton, welcomed the tolerant attitude that the Protectorate brought in as well as the exclusion of Roman Catholics, and many did disavow the "Popish" remnants that prelacy was seen to retain in the Church of England. Further, Cromwell did put an emphasis on the relevance of prayer in daily life, a conviction Milton thoroughly agreed with. Yet the Protectorate also saw Cromwell looked upon as Caesar, "His Highness," with hegemony by the Army, and autocracy.[29] The "symbols of monarchy," in fact, accompanied the pomp of his accession as Lord Protector. "Rumors about Cromwellian kingship circulated in oral and manuscript form throughout the Protectorate."[30] Contributory was Cromwell's assumption of Whitehall (the principal monarchic residence) in April 1654 as his official residence, and of Hampton Court as his nongovernmental residence.

In the last half of the decade, fear of Catholic Spain and a possible coalition with Catholic France demanded keeping the two nations separate, and especially in 1658 the threat of a Royalist uprising and Spanish invasion loomed. It could not be forgotten that Charles I's wife was French, that Charles II's court-in-exile was in France, and that relationships with the Spanish and Portuguese thrones were strong. (He was to marry the Portuguese

Catherine of Braganza in 1662.) Looking back, we can accept that "the Spanish war, however deeply ideological a conflict, is understood primarily as a defensive war driven by the threat of Catholic aggression in general and Spanish power in particular" (Norbrook, 387), but for many in the 1650s it represented Cromwell's tyranny in creating an intolerable political/economic situation. For Milton, it had a different cast: *A Letter to a Friend Occasioned by the Ruptures in the Commonwealth* (May 1659) stresses that the alternate to the Rump Parliament is not the army, but the king and his Spanish allies. Milton, it appears almost certain, translated the Declaration against Spain for Continental audiences (*Scriptum Dom. Protectoris Reipublicæ Angliæ, Scotiæ, Hiberniæ* in October 1655), and in it Spanish atrocities are cited. As we have seen, his nephew John Phillips translated Bartolomeo de las Casas's impugning of the Spanish massacre in the New World in 1656, and dedicated it to Cromwell. The influence of uncle on nephew seems assured, and Phillips's comparison with the Irish massacres by Pope and by Cromwell (see chapter 4, n39) is surely meant to sway opponents of the Spanish War to justify any action that might ensue. "The arms of the family" work both ways, and for Milton and for Phillips an overwhelming element is religion. In the massacres of the Irish, it makes a difference to both whether it's by Catholic forces on non-Catholic people or by Protestants against those construed as instruments of the Papacy; in the massacre of the Vaudois, it was Catholics killing those "who kept the truth so pure of old"; in the massacre of the American natives, it was again the action of the followers of "the triple Tyrant." Milton contributed to the relief of the Protestant Irish in 1642 (see chapter 3, n42) and accepted the assignment of Charles I's "complotting" in the massacre.[31] Yet we should not ignore as cause in the English/Spanish war Cromwell's "Western Design" (his global vision) and the difficulties encountered in the New World at this time, primarily with Spain in both colonization and mercantile interests.[32]

The intolerance of Cromwell and the government, and of Milton and Phillips, and of most of the people toward Roman Catholics, as well as the intolerance by some toward those who accepted the Church of England's rituals and hierarchical administration, or on the other hand toward dissenters, does not make for real tolerance on the part of any of these people. In the case of Catholics, the intolerance was both political and religious, and that of other groups—including Friends (Quakers), itinerant preachers, and other sectarians—religious. Many classified Nonconformists with Catholics as having the same ends, the disestablishment of the Church of England, putting a political cast over this religious intolerance. During the 1650s, there was also much discussion of readmission of Jews into England; it did not become a burning issue for most people, as I have noted elsewhere,[33] which in turn suggests a prejudice of the people in general against Jews by omission of any attention: they were not even worthy of consideration. Official readmission did not take place until the early nineteenth century. Yet, as widespread as these kinds of intolerance were, we are not pleased in looking at such statements by Milton as Sonnet 18, on the massacre of the Vaudois or the way in which the situation in Ireland is seen only from an English Protestant point of view. This inconsistency, this intolerance on the part of Cromwell and of Milton (and we should add John Phillips) is examined by Elizabeth Sauer,[34] who remarks, "The rhetorical dexterity in fulminating against the Catholics, while justifying the colonization of the Irish and the internal colonization of the sectarians and, in the same year [1655], the Jews, marked the agendas and writing of the nationalists."

While his stand against the Catholic massacre in Piedmont in May 1655 put Cromwell in good favor with many in England and on the Continent, the creation of the Major-General rule in August-October, coupled with the declaration against Spain on 26 October, caused sharp deterioration of that high esteem. We have remarked how the classic government (though short-lived) created antagonism toward and rejection of Cromwell's leadership in discussing some of John Phillips's work. The point is that this move looked like a centralization and control of government on local levels, and the intended reformation of manners found no roots among the local parishes or counties. Any religious reformation was dispersed and enervated by the demoralized church establishment and the lack of ecclesiastic discipline. "The system's performance and effectiveness were patchy and it became a public relations disaster of some magnitude" (Davis, 39). At first there were high hopes for this action for many, including Milton, but by July 1656 it was totally rejected. The ardent republican Lucy Hutchinson reflects what both the Protectorate and the institution of the Major-Generals evoked from even the most avowed anti-monarchist: "Allmost all the ministers every where fell in and worshipt this beast [Cromwell], and courted and made addresses to him. So did the City of London, and many of the degenerate Lords of the land, with the poore-spiritual gentry. The Cavaliers, in pollicy, who saw that while Cromwell reduc'd all the exercise of Tiranicall power under another name there was a doore open'd for the restoring of their party, fell much in with Cromwell, and heigth'ned all his disorders; who att last exercis'd such an arbitrary power that the whole land grew weary of him, while he sett up a companie of silly meane fellows, call'd Major generalls, as Governors in every county, who rul'd according to their wills, by no law but what seem'd good to their owne eies, imprisoning men and obstructing the course of justice betweene man and man and perverting right through partiality, acquitting some that were guilty and punishing some that were innocent as guilty." Negative remarks on John Lambert follow at some length.[35] The altered attitudes of John Phillips toward the end of the 1650s, contrary to the ill-informed opinions of critics of the past like Godwin, iterate the views of people like Lucy Hutchinson. That the Restoration might, and in some ways did, remove the economic and social blights that many felt from Cromwell's rule, or Lambert's disturbing power-play, and the incompetence of Richard in controlling the seesawing of 1658–59 has evaded the comprehension of some writing about Milton (and of all writing about Phillips).

Milton's opinion of Cromwell up to the end of the Interregnum is difficult to gauge, and it has been variously read. David Norbrook reminds us that "Milton's early poems . . . make their political points not so much by direct comment as by modification of generic expectations. The lack of explicit political statement need not be too surprising."[36] Robert T. Fallon argues against any subtle criticism of Cromwell in the encomiastic statement in the "Second Defense" (1654), which some have discovered in it, but it is noteworthy that hereafter Milton does not even allude to Cromwell. That is telling, I think, of what appears as an avoidance of the issue of Cromwell a year after the institution of the Protectorate because of a wish not to criticize him and his actions, and because a statement would, in all probability, be negatively critical. Fallon sees in the statement in the *Defensio secunda* an agenda for reform through action unfinished or neglected by Parliament, finding Milton "in full accord with the radical sects' proposals to separate church and state, but . . . unequivocally opposed to their political agenda, in particular to their demands for manhood suffrage."[37] Again that, if true, as it seems to be, portrays a Milton who is not the "republican" that some today would seem to argue he was. Sauer attests in "Milton's Peculiar Nation," that "Milton too deflated the image of the elite [compare *Of Reformation*, I, 556–79], but as a defender of the 'middling sort,' he placed the burden of responsibility for national change on Parliament rather than the lower orders."

In contrast to Fallon's reading of the situation, Sonnet 16 (May 1652)—perhaps even Sonnets 15 (August 1648) and 17 (July 1652)—does suggest an uncertainty about Cromwell, and alongside the Protectorate of 1653, we should consider the translations of Psalms 1 through 8 (August 1653). The Committee for the Propagation of the Gospel, actually begun to be established in 1651, met most importantly on 10 February 1652, continuing work on fifteen Proposals from petitioning Independent ministers, which were published as *The Humble Proposals of Mr. Owen and Other Ministers Who Presented the Petition to Parliament*, dated by George Thomason 31 March 1652. Cromwell was a member of both the larger Committee of forty and a subcommittee of fourteen. On 29 April 1652, the matter of tithes entered the picture, and it is this action that must have specifically moved Milton to compose Sonnet 16, which, like *Considerations Touching the Likeliest Means to Remove Hirelings out of the Church,* apparently first written at this time (1653) and revised later for publication in 1659, attacked the concept of tithing. The poem does not criticize Cromwell's military victories at the battle near Preston in 1648 or that at Dunbar in 1650 or that at Worcester in 1651, but it does emphasize the need for victories in peace against "new foes," a need he remarked in the sonnet to Fairfax that puts down wars even though they may be needful for independence of a commonweal,[38] and that pleads that Truth and Right be separated from Violence. A similar dichotomy between war and peace and their achievements appears in the Vane sonnet, where Milton commends Vane's "civill" sword for his advocation of religious toleration (Liberty of Conscience) against the demands made to the Committee. While laudatory, Sonnet 16 cites "detractions rude" that have been leveled against Cromwell (2) and raises a curious note in saying, "Guided by faith and matchless Fortitude / To peace and truth thy glorious way hast plough'd" (3–4). He does not subscribe to those "detractions," but his mention of them does raise their potential validity: they are "rude," not "false." Line 4 points us to Luke xi:62: "And Jesus said unto him, No man, having put his hand to the plow, and looking back, is fit for the kingdom of God." That is, Cromwell should not rest on those successes in war, necessary though they may have been construed to solidify the Commonwealth, and should not look back at his victories and his trophies, for "much remains / to conquer still." "Peace" (as admonished in Sonnets 15 and 17) may raise a different kind of war, one against those who would "bind our souls with secular chains" by controlling "free Conscience." The fact that Milton thinks he must call to Cromwell's attention this problem from "new foes," that he implies a possible backsliding because of conceit of past achievements, and that he raises the existence of any viable detractions (which are given validity by the way in which the reference is made) does not attest to total trust in Cromwell to do the "right" thing. His life before the 1649 political coup (much pitted with rumors of less than moral behavior in a Puritan's eye[39]), coupled with inferable acceptance of tithing that his presence on the Committee for the Propagation of the Faith allows, may lie behind that biblical allusion.

In *Defensio secunda* Milton is concerned to "examine the principal crimes" that are charged to Cromwell (Yale Prose, IV, 662ff.) and that he finds petty and without weight in themselves. He then turns to Cromwell's positive self and "how worthy of all praise" he is. Proceeding in time, he records that "Another Parliament was convened anew . . . The elected members came together. They did nothing. . . . considering themselves inadequate and unfit for executing such great tasks, they of their own accord dissolved the Parliament" (671). Thus Cromwell's becoming Lord Protector is accepted, for "On you alone has fallen the whole burden of our affairs." His following remarks, however, do seem to show anxiety over the significance of such a title, and particularly of the title of king, which increasingly was urged (by Lambert, for example, in December 1653). While he is not explicit, Milton may be recognizing the problem of one-man rule that he had objected to with Charles I and was to reject at the end of the decade with Charles II. A note of apprehension sneaks in when he concludes, "honor yourself, so that, having achieved that liberty in pursuit of which you endured so many hardships and encountered so many perils, you may not permit it to be violated by yourself or in any degree diminished by others. Certainly you yourself cannot be free without us" (673). In his judgment, the momentous ends desired and "our liberty" can be accomplished best "by admitting those men whom you first cherished as comrades in your toils and dangers to the first share in your counsels" (674). It is not a denial of "single rule" ("leadership") but it certainly disclaims single action and control. There is defense of Cromwell by rejecting criticisms of him and by expressing excellences in him, matters I have cited above from modern commentators. But there is too an apprehension that Cromwell will err, will move toward sole rule, will reject the "republicanism" that has been the ideal in the overthrow of Charles I.[40]

The Council of State was declared abolished on 20 April 1653, and from 29 April through 4 July an interim Council of Thirteen ruled, the "Barebones Parliament" being called for on 6 (or 8) June and holding its first session on 4 July. It remained in force through 12 December. On 16 December, the first Protectorate began and was formally proclaimed on 19 December. In the midst of the months when the Barebones Parliament sat, Milton translated Psalms 1 through 8 (7?, 8, 9, 10, 12, 13, 13, 14 August; the eleventh was a Sunday). They experiment with meter, rhyme schemes, rhythms, perhaps as prefatory exercises for renewed poetic activity—*Paradise Lost,* it has been suggested. But, and it is an important "but," there is in these particular psalms an undertone of anxiety, of the need for God's help and protection: "For the Lord knows th' upright way of the just, / and the way of bad men to ruin must" (I, 15–16); "Princes in their Congregations / Lay deep their plots together through each Land, / Against the Lord and his Messiah dear" (II, 3–5); "And thou O Lord how long? turn Lord, restore / My soul, O save me for thy goodness sake" (VI, 7–8); "O're the works of thy hand thou mad'st him [Mankind] Lord, / Thou hast put all under his lordly feet" (VIII, 17–18). Is Milton sensing a loss of religious concern and freedom in these months preceding the Protectorate? Is this not the same apprehension he feels in 1660 when he calls "Free Commonwealths . . . fittest and properest for civil, vertuous and industrious Nations, abounding with prudent men [note the plural] worthie to govern" but then understands that "monarchie [is] fittest to curb degenerate, corrupt, idle, proud, luxurious people"? If the latter rears up because we despair "our own vertue, industrie and the number of our able men, we may then, conscious of our own unworthiness to be governd better, sadly betake us to our befitting thraldom: yet chusing out of our own number one who hath best aided the people, and best merited against tyrannie, the space of a raign or two we may change to live happily anough, or tolerably."[41] Cromwell's assumption of a Protectorate (or in 1660, Monck's assumption of power) became acceptable—for "a raign or two" at most, and monarchy itself is not rejected.

Additionally, a further contemporary belief and hope entered the picture of the Protectorate, and that was the Millennium, with prognostication that it would occur in (or around) 1657.[42] One requirement (as Marvell's "To His Coy Mistress" reminded his lovers who should succumb to love before their world has disappeared) was the conversion of the Jews, a factor in the continuing agitation at that time for their readmission. The need for what was advanced as the Protectorate, and its promised reform of religious life and of manners, and the impending rule of Christ on earth lie behind those psalms, I would urge. But by May 1654, the Protectorate had not achieved its potential; it had, instead, shown some dangerous cracks, and the Millennium was approaching fast. "Milton made the best of this bad bargain [the Protectorate], as is evident later in this tract [*Defensio secunda*], but it is apparent also that, though Milton accepted this *fait accompli* and genuinely admired Cromwell, he did not really like such absolutism and hoped for a change in the direction of broader-based power" (Donald Roberts, ed., Yale Prose, IV, 638 n380). As Worden has told us, "Milton was almost alone among the republicans again in his willingness to support and serve the semi-monarchical protectorate of Oliver Cromwell, a regime bitterly condemned by most of the others as a usurpation" ("Milton's republicanism," 226).

When, in April 1655, a clarion call to "true" believers in Christ was sounded because of the actions of Roman Catholic adherents against the Vaudois, Milton may have become hopeful again, the intervening years not having advanced his early hopes. When, in August-October, an allegedly reformative action was enacted by Cromwell through Major-General rule, Milton engaged a further positive hope as the Millennium further neared, and rationalized the way in which his worth would be demonstrated to God: by standing and waiting. This move, in creating the Major-Generals' controls, was aimed at completing the Reformation of the English Church, which people like Milton believed to be incomplete. Such complete Reformation of religion from the doctrine and discipline of Roman Catholicism was deemed necessary before Millennium would proceed. Still, we should not ignore that in Sonnet 19 the poet asks, "fondly" (that is, foolishly, naively), whether God exacts "day-labour"; Patience "prevents" that murmur (anticipating the question and countering it before it is asked). The reference, it has not been noted, is to "The lowest Member, the Feet of the Body Politick, are the Day Labourers."[43] Milton's casting himself in such a role in 1655 indicates more than just his lack of ability to act as this "reformative" action was being put into operation: it suggests his naive understanding of what was supposed to be done and its results, and his desired position as one attached to the Army in some kind of more meaningful and leader-related situation. With the hindsight of history, at least, we recognize Milton's lack of perspicacity when it comes to the real as opposed to the "ideal." As we have seen, the classic rule of the Major-Generals failed on all counts—as should have been expected by the astute, and the position of people like Cromwell, but also Lambert, was reassessed (or reasserted), and Cromwell becomes a "beast" to Lucy Hutchinson and Lambert a major culprit. Phillips's altered attitude from that in *Tears of the Indians* (1656) to that in *Don Lamberto* (1661) is reflective of a general reassessment of those involved in these governmental affairs during these years. And perhaps we can infer from Phillips Milton's unstated but nonetheless similar revision of political evaluation in those years. Did he come "to share the belief of other republicans that the protector had sacrificed the revolution at the altar of his own ambition"? Worden asks (241). The "New Jerusalem" that Milton's allusion to Isaiah 65:20 in line 2 of the sonnet envisioned through the actions of the Major-Generals was certainly obliterated as the last years of Cromwell's life came. Keeble reminds us that "during the final four years of Cromwell's life, Milton has nothing more to say of him, nor is there any elegiac tribute at his death. It appears that finally Cromwell, too, may have disappointed Milton."[44]

Prior to Cromwell's death on 3 September 1658, there were discussions and consultations, concern and anxiety about who would take over the reins of government, as figurehead at least.[45] With his death and his son Richard's assuming the title of Protector, overt and subversive reactions, most of them aiming at removal, led to near anarchy and rapidly changing conditions, a seesawing between Army action, "republican" action, Royalist advancements, and mixed allegiances. Parliamentary assemblies before and after that date evidence the uncertainties clouding over the government: Parliament was summoned on 10 July 1656, met on 17 September through 26 June 1657, then again on 20 January through 4 February 1658 when it was dismissed; it did not meet again until 27 January 1659 and then was dismissed on 22 April 1659 after an Army coup. At this point Richard was no longer the Protector, the Rump Parliament being reconvened by the Declaration of the Officers of the Army on 6 May 1659, and sitting from 7 May through 13 October. The Declaration invited the approximately hundred members of the Long Parliament who continued sitting until 20 April 1653 to return. Richard resigned as Protector on 25 May 1659 and the Rump reestablished the Commonwealth. The Army's action on 13 October prevented Parliament's sitting, but this was reestablished on 26 December, continuing until 16 March 1660, when it dissolved by its own action. Presbyterian members excluded in Pride's Purge (1648) were excluded in the Long Parliament of 26 December 1659, but were recalled by the Rump Parliament on 21 February 1660. A new summons came on 16 March with assembly on 25 April. This Parliament was in session until 13 September 1660 and again in 6 November through 29 December when it was dismissed. Earlier, General Monck and his troops had entered London on 3 February 1660, and on 25 April he called for a Convention Parliament to consider Charles II's Declaration of Breda, 4 April 1660, in which he promised general pardon and religious toleration. In May he was invited to be king with limited powers, on 8 May his restoration was proclaimed, on the twenty-fifth he returned and entered London four days later. Against all this indecision and confusion, we have Milton's apparently reduced work as Latin secretary, his publishing of *The Cabinet-Council* (May 1658), a revised edition of *Pro Populo Anglicano Defensio* (October 1658), *A Treatise of Civil Power* (February 1659) to be joined by *Considerations Touching the Likeliest Means to Remove Hirelings out of the Church* (August 1659), *Letter to a Friend Concerning the Ruptures of the Commonwealth* (October 1659), "Proposals of Certain Expedients for the Preventing of a Civil War" (November? 1659), The *Present Means, and brief Delineation of a Free Commonwealth, Easy to be put in Practice, and without Delay. In a Letter to General Monk* (March? 1660), *The Readie & Easie Way To Establish a Free Commonwealth* (8 March 1660) and its second edition (April 1660).

3

The evidence of *Tenure* and *Eikonoklastes* in 1649 has not always been recognized: Milton argues against what he and others classified as tyranny and thus against Charles I's misuse of power. *Tenure* discusses kings AND magistrates, and *Eikonoklastes* is aimed at refuting *Eikon Basilike* and the idolatry for Charles, not Charles per se. As cited above, he admonished Cromwell that "Certainly you yourself cannot be free without us" and that there was need to admit others "to the first share in your counsels." He does not argue against kingship (or the latter-day Protectorate), nor against kings: he argues against tyranny, which a Protector could exhibit as much as any king.

Norbrook's reminder is most important for us to understand: "Milton's God, then, is a king with distinct overtones of a republican founding legislator. He is a king nevertheless" (*Writing the English Republic,* 477).[46] Even Algernon Sidney, who ran afoul of Cromwell because of his strong republican demands, and who was executed in 1683 for his part in the Rye House Plot, maintained that "Nothing is farther from my intention than to speak irreverently of kings," and he quoted sentences from Milton's *Tenure* in his *Very Copy of a Paper Delivered to the Sheriffs* upon the scaffold on Tower Hill.

While Milton's argument in *Tenure* often finds substance in Aristotle's *Ethics,* Book VIII, and *Politics,* Books III-V, there seems to be no specific influence from Machiavelli's *Art of War* or the *Discorsi.*[47] Between 1640 and 1642, he is struck by Machiavelli's preference of a commonwealth to a monarchy and observation that "kingdoms that have good rule do not give their kings absolute power"—ideas consonant with this earlier political tract. During the years 1651–1652, after there has been some experience with the Commonwealth but before the troubles associated with the Protectorate, he records, among other items, that Machiavelli prefers a republican form of government since it makes fewer mistakes than a prince does in choosing its magistrates or councillors, since a republic may enact good laws and reduce magistrates to the ranks of ordinary citizens, and since controls are restored to the people (CPB, 198). Yet Milton did *not* actively seek "to argue for the English republic in terms derived either from classical models or from Machiavellian political theory."[48] Quentin Skinner's examination of the question concludes that other writers—and this is not in opposition to Corns's statement concerning Milton just given—attest that "the best form of constitution for a commune or civitas must be of an elective as opposed to a monarchical character" and that "government by hereditary princes or *Signori* must at all costs be avoided; some form of elective and self-governing system must always be maintained."[49] These views of the meanings derived from Machiavelli's work and of Milton's position do not remove single person rule from acceptance, and thus we can understand his acceptance of the Protectorate in 1653, and the continued possibility of a monarch governing in the public interest in the first edition of *The Ready and Easy Way* (compare Corns). However the second edition is read with good reason as a total rejection of single person rule (by Worden and by Warren Spehar[50]).

The period between *Defensio secunda,* May 1654, and Cromwell's death, September 1658, is difficult to assess in terms of Milton's beliefs and assessment. Aside from his continued work for the government and his defense against his critics, what we can interpret as Milton's reactions to the Dutch, Swedish, and Spanish negotiations, to the Piedmont massacre and the creation of Major-General rule, to the ups and downs of controls and Oliver's death suggest, to me at least, a continued hope in the Commonwealth, a continued acceptance of one person as leader of that Commonwealth but perhaps with some nonstated recognition of abuse by Cromwell, and perhaps some vague understanding of the divisiveness and misuse of power that organized group opposition can bring. Some critics have seen Cromwell reflected in Satan in *Paradise Lost;* perhaps some of the reading of Satan-as-hero and Milton's being of the Devil's party hangs over that identification. In general, at least, we can read in this period Milton's approval of Cromwell's foreign policies and action, and continued hope that domestic matters (the reformation of manners) can be altered and the separation of church and state, within a strong Protestant church, can be maintained.

Just before and after the questions of succession, Milton published "Sir Walter Ralegh's" *The Cabinet-Council* (May? 1658) and a revised edition of *Pro Populo Anglicano Defensio* (October) with an important postscript. Martin Dzelzainis has presented the former as an attack on the Lord Protector and his tyrannical regime,[51] and Paul Stevens has refuted this interpretation.[52] "The best context in which to understand *The Cabinet-Council* and Milton's relationship with Cromwell is not so much his now widely emphasized return to republicanism [in 1659–60] as his unfolding and remarkably durable Protestant nationalism" (Stevens, 365). Instead, Stevens argues that this editorial action is "a timely reminder of the justice of England's foreign policy—a policy in whose articulation in the spring and early summer of 1658 Milton was immediately involved" (367). (Reference is to the numerous letters of state that Milton produced during that period.) The problem for Milton during those years of the Protectorate continued to be the question of liberty of conscience, of toleration—although limited to Protestant groups. His silence on Cromwell and certain issues that we analyze as delimiting liberty of conscience and as autocracy may indicate a lack of astuteness in recognizing what was happening, or, I think more likely, a continued naive hope that things would right themselves over time. The loan to Maundy in 1658–59, which was discussed in the Introduction, seems a clear case of Milton's lack of recognition of what was happening and what would ensue. As Dzelzainis writes, "only in a flurry of published and unpublished works shortly before the Restoration did he express opposition to monarchy in terms approaching the unequivocal."[53]

The "anarchy" of April 1659 through May 1660, and Milton's publications within those months are to be read against the growing discontent against the Rump Parliament in February 1660; against the belief that the political chaos developed since Cromwell's death would be resolved by bringing in the King; and against the Declaration of Breda issued by Charles II on

4 April 1660, promising a general amnesty and religious toleration. There were worries about continued anarchy and about Lambert's moves. Edmund Ludlow saw in Lambert's action the advancement of only personal interest, not public.[54] His expelling of the Rump in October 1659 and rule by the Committee of Safety provoked *A Letter to a Friend* (20 October) and "Proposalls of certaine expedients" (autumn). Herein we find a "senate or generall Councell of State" proposed, elected annually or perpetually, to "sitt indissolubly" and to "retaine their places during life." But almost uppermost in Milton's mind, it would seem, was the religious settlement and toleration and the Protestant national state, under England's providential role in securing salvation, particularly against the Catholic menace in these years when the Millennium was hoped for.[55] As Puritans envisioned political recovery during these months, "it became all but impossible to disentangle religious from political motivation among those who opposed the Caroline regime" (Keeble, 132). Milton proposed two qualifications for members of his Council of State: belief in "Liberty of conscience to all professing Scripture the rule of their faith & worship, And the Abjuracion of single person."[56] Norbrook reads the situation as Milton's distancing himself from the Protectorate around 1658, and producing *Civil Power* and *Hirelings* in 1659 to insist on separation of church and state (which is what Milton had particularly called upon Cromwell to maintain in *Defensio secunda*). Through the religious—Christian—public result would come the nourishment of civic virtue, as well as secular controls to ensure that religious world. While Milton's attitudes have led scholars to align him with sectarianism, he is silent about sects and radical religious or political groups. And as David Loewenstein makes clear, "he remains fiercely opposed to *any form* of institutionized religion"; rather, "In his late writings . . . Milton exhibited sympathy toward radical sectarians and their controversies, but he also maintained his independence, and at tense political moments, silence."[57]

The indecisions and changes of position on certain issues (such as whether the Council should be "an annuall democracy or a perpetuall Aristocracy") can be justified by the rapidly changing course of events of those months in 1659 and 1660 and the relief that was seen in accepting Charles II as king and taking his word for amnesty and toleration as certain. How we read *The Ready and Easy Way* in its two versions (along with *The Present Means, and brief Delineation of a Free Commonwealth,* known as "Letter to General Monk," written in between those two versions) offers the most significant concepts of where we place Milton ideologically, of what his political strategies may have been in these works, and of how his future oeuvre may have changed because of the political realities he (finally?) faced.

4

The dates of writing and publication of the first edition of *The Ready and Easy Way* (18–21 and 23–29 February 1660), of *The Present Means* (23 February–4 March; published in 1698), and of the second edition of *The Ready and Easy Way* (16–27 March and 1–10 April)[58] indicate the changing political picture and Milton's developing and reactive responses in an attempt to have some influence upon the settlement that was so fast approaching. Concepts may, on the one hand, not have been very carefully thought out, or on the other, immediate expedients to modify what loomed as return to pre-Interregnum times. While edition one of *The Ready and Easy Way* denounces the bondage of kingship to which the people should not return, it proposes a perpetual senate, which, though this would not be one-person rule, would undoubtedly set up a stagnation that in time would calcify into a type of bondage. He seems not to recognize this, but a possibility of limited rotation is held out. Beneath such concepts of a "perpetual" government are the lures of utopianism and a closed society, which, as discussed earlier in this chapter, are at best naive and intolerant. Milton seems not to recognize this in his aim of expediency. I have referred above to similar advocations by Lilburne and Harrington. The "kingship" Milton speaks of ("if we return to kingship") he equates with "the tyrannie which we then groand under," "the same bondage." A king should be "but a cypher," for he is "a mischief, a pest, a scourge of the nation, and which is worse, not to be remov'd, not to be contrould, much less accus'd or brought to punishment." And they are "madd or strangely infatuated" who put their happiness or safety into the trust of "a single person" (5).[59] This development in Milton's thought, which lies unacknowledged, unrealized to himself, in *Tenure* and *Eikonoklastes,* has been exposed through "the frequent disturbances, interruptions and dissolutions which the Parlament hath had partly from the impatient or disaffected people, partly from some ambitious leaders in the armie" (7).

The "Grand Councel" (and the "Councel of State" elected out of their constituency), "being well chosen, should sit perpetual" because successive parliaments unsettle what has been accomplished and are subject to the ambition of individuals. The possibility of changing the constituency of a hundred or so every two or three years is noted, but not advocated. Either politically naive or pushing thoughtlessly to back up this suggestion or with his seemingly constant belief in moral honesty of some people, he continues, "And the government being now in so many faithful and experienc'd hands, next under God, so able, . . . and abundantly sufficient so happily to govern us, why should the nation . . . seek change, and deliver themselves up to meer titles and vanities, to persons untri'd, unknown, necessitous, implacable, and every way to be suspected" (11). Those he assigns to the governing group he equates with—I think unbelievably even though it be thought a strategic move—"all these our Patriots." To these he adds "all the wisdom or force of the well affected joind with them," but all of them together never "can deliver us again from most certain miserie and thraldom" *if* there is return to kingship. Monarchy represents anarchy since it allows private interests to overrule public good. But we should make trenchant note of "well affected," hardly a term suggesting democratic rule or social equality. The term pervades the Leveller literature and seems to mean only "well-disposed toward" or "well-conditioned toward (mentally)."

"The whole freedom of man," he contends, "consists either in spiritual or civil libertie" (14). The spiritual will exist under a Protestant Church with the "supream judge or rule in matters of religion" being only "the scriptures themselves." The civil "consists in the civil rights and advanc'ments of every person according to his merit," and this may be best achieved through every county's becoming "a little commonwealth" with controversies amongst them being settled in "the capital citie." (In *The Present Means* he iterates a Leveller proposal for "the full and absolute Administration of Law in every County," Yale Prose, VII, 395.) Behind this view seems to lie the same concept that Cromwell tried to manage through the Major-Generals and that Harrington proposed. And like Harrington's discussion, Milton recognizes stratifications, economic and social, but Milton writes on the side not only of a "meritocracy" but of a continued inequality. Note that his "chief town" in the counties is "where the nobilitie and chief gentry may build, houses or palaces, befitting their qualitie," and that those "to be chosen into the Grand Councel, according as their worth and merit shall be taken notice of by the people" (16). Perhaps we remember "the indolent rabble" he shuns in "Ad Patrem" and the "insolent speech of the multitude and even the vicious throng of readers" that he castigates in "Ad Joannem Roüsium," the ignorant misspellers of Sonnet 12,

> And what the people but a herd confus'd,
> A miscellaneous rabble, who extol
> Things vulgar, and well weigh'd, scarce worth the praise,
> They praise and they admire they know not what;
> And know not whom, but as one leads the other;
> . . . Of whom to be disprais'd were no small praise? (*PR* III, 49–56)

and perhaps his comment about, "The vulgar only [who] scap'd" in *Samson Agonistes,* an addition to the biblical text. His type of toleration which specifically excludes Roman Catholics (and thus the Irish), which would seem to exclude "Anglicanism" (that is, the form of the State Church that included episcopacy), and his silence concerning the Jews disavows a modern sense of equality and even "democracy." As Merritt Y. Hughes found himself forced to say, "he was no egalitarian" (Yale Prose, III, 28).

The Present Means, addressed to Monck, works on these same proposals and tries to direct how the County/City Council and how the Grand or General Council will be elected, avoiding the "Danger and Confusion of readmitting Kingship in this Land," backed by "a faithful Veteran Army, so ready, and glad to assist you [Monck] in the prosecution therof" (393, 395). Yet, the emphasis on the "chief Gentlemen" and the "ablest Knights and Burgesses," as well as the possible impress from the Army, bothers us. In the revised *Ready and Easy Way* there is an elaboration of the perpetual senate, an expansion of the evils of kingship, a prophecy of what backsliding will bring, a warning of Catholicism and its sumptuous court entourage, including the French queen mother, Henrietta Maria, and a new queen, undoubtedly Catholic and "outlandish," that is, foreign (perhaps anticipating a Spanish consort, although the new queen—in 1662—was Portuguese). (To stress the Catholic menace, he cancelled the earlier section on the separation of church and state.) The epigraph on the title page adapted from Juvenal is apparently directed toward Monck, who had not in this last month acted as Milton sought, though the "way" was "ready" and "easy," but who had instead made contact with Charles on 19 March, following the annulment of the Engagement Oath of members of Parliament to remain faithful to the Commonwealth on 13 March, and the dissolution of Parliament on 16 March. The epigraph translates: "We have advised Sulla himself, advise we now the People" (Masson's translation). The additions and deletions of this second edition can be read to measure Milton's disappointment and his continued hope that those "in the midst of our Elections to a free Parliament" and "sitting to consider freely of the Government" will "have all things represented to them that may direct thir judgment therin" (VII, 408).

Within a few years Milton finished *Paradise Lost,* and Hong Won Suh argues that this supposedly "ready and easy" way, rejected, is ironically put into the mouth of Satan when he baits Eve, "Empress, the way is ready, and not long" (IX, 626) and into Michael's counsel that the Israelites' path to Canaan is "not the readiest way" (XII, 216).[60] "The time the Israelites gain in not choosing the readiest way is to be spent in establishing, among other things, a 'great Senate' of their choice. . . . 'Ready' and 'easy' meet in *Paradise Lost* to define the high-arching bridge that leads humanity to Hell" (411–12; compare "a passage broad, / Smooth, easie, inoffensive down to Hell," X, 304–05, and "this glorious Work, . . . made one realm / Hell and this

World, one Realm, one Continent / of easie thorough-fare," X, 391–93). In a sense, as Suh suggests, there is another way implied in the tract of 1660, one that is "chosen out of ignoble ease and peaceful sloth by the people of England" and this leads "to certain destruction" (412–13). Belial's "words cloath'd in reasons garb [that] / Counsel'd ignoble ease and peaceful sloath, / Not peace" (II, 226–28) epitomize the worthlessness (the meaning of his name) in not acknowledging that God's "yoke is easy, and [his] burden is light" (Matthew xi:30), which return to placing "responsibility" in the hands of one person subverts and replaces with only a superficial "peace."

The study by Blair Hoxby, dealing so significantly with an otherwise forgotten aspect of Milton's concern, economics, irrefutably shows that in *The Ready and Easy Way* the proposals are "more coherent and creative, more important in the history of ideas, than even Milton's most general readers have recognized"; its agenda helps us to understand why the tract's famous renunciation of the claims of trade in its peroration is not merely a rhetorical dismissal of arguments that could no longer serve the cause of the republic, but the record of a deeper intellectual crisis that left its mark on *Paradise Lost.*[61] Milton is not really proposing a "utopian" or "ideal" society, despite the implications in his scheme,[62] as some seem to read this work. Influence of ideas may be found in the writings of Gerrard Winstanley, John Lilburne, and James Harrington, or in Cromwell's hopes for Major-General rule, but such "utopianism" that underlies those works is not the goal of Milton's practical and *changeable* scheme. Only the "perpetuity" of the senate that is advanced seems to contradict that goal, a result of fear on Milton's part, I suggest, of nonrepublican influence in altering the constituency of that senate and of rapidity of possible alteration, as in the immediately preceding months. He does consider rotation, specifically partial rotation. Milton's basic federal system of government sets up a central authority and a multiple local jurisdiction that allows for variations in locale, way of life, social and religious differences, and means of livelihood, without a superimposition of one way of life or way of thinking dominated by the powers of a central government and especially of a single king. The similarity to the experiment of the American colonies is striking, along with the partial rotation, on different bases, for the two houses of government.[63] The tract is not, I contend, a "jeremiad whose rhetoric of lamentation is more important than its proposals";[64] rather, it is in the mode of Isaiah foreseeing a new existence: "I create Jerusalem a rejoicing, and her people a joy" (65:18). "And they shall build houses, and inhabit them; and they shall plant vineyards, and eat the fruit of them . . . They shall not labor in vain" (65:21, 23).

5

What is the republicanism of Milton? Modern critics seem to want to read it as "democratic" in the sense that the Levellers appeared to advance political, social, and economic reforms. They are bothered by the lack of "equality" for all people and particularly for women; yet Milton does argue in various tracts for and demonstrates in *Paradise Lost* a more equal position for human beings and specifically for woman than was (and still today is) truly commonplace. On the one side, there is a disregard for and even a dislike of the "rabble": a snobbishness seems to enter toward those of lower economic position, of less education. And we must ask, who are the "well-affected"? There is the problem of toleration where attitudes toward the Pope and his power and influence cast everything and everybody with relationship to Catholicism into opprobrium. The lack of regard for the Irish and the sharp contrast that his words concerning the treatment of the Vaudois proclaim do not offer a Milton who was philosophically "politically correct" or fully "egalitarian," but instead a person who was dominated by his own beliefs, which, though they encompass variations rather than demand uncompromising adherence, color his thinking. As I have argued in connection with John Phillips's entry into the Titus Oates affair, Milton views any situation that involves the Papacy and thus Roman Catholicism as anathema: that involvement dominates any position he might take on any issue. (I look at the religious aspect of Milton's thinking in chapter 6.) We can classify Milton as "tolerant" but only up to a point. His position on Jews is difficult to assess because of his silence on the subject, particularly when it was such an issue in the 1650s and when it was believed basic to the advancement of the Millennium. He would seem to praise the Hebrews of the Old Testament as the chosen people of God with analogies to the people of England as the Chosen Nation of God. But the Jews, because of their crucifixion of Jesus, become hated—this bifurcation is not exclusively Milton's, and it is not uncommon during this period. It leads to strong prejudice against Jews in all economic arenas. His position on the Irish is tempered by reports of actions by Charles both with the Catholics and Charles's alleged inciting of the attacks upon them by Protestants, and with action against the Anabaptists and other sectaries in the early forties. Primarily, it is dominated by anti-Catholicism and hopes for a spread of Protestantism through indoctrination of those following the Pope. The problem becomes a political one, of course, but for Milton it is basically a religious one extended into theological belief. The question of the Divine Presence at Mass and transubstantiation is a major issue in the century, as well as sacramental rethinking and

rejection of Marianism, much of this antagonism from non-Catholics arising from attitudes toward the papacy and papal bulls *ex cathedra.*

The family, the extended family, and the friends and acquaintances that
I have paraded before the reader in previous chapters of this study place
Milton solidly in the midst of the well-to-do, the "significant" people of England (some with hereditary titles), professional and educated men. I have
noted that Milton's move to the Barbican in 1645 placed him as a neighbor
to the Egertons (the Earl of Bridgewater and his family); it was a most affluent and privileged area. But even earlier the move from St. Bride's to
Aldersgate Street is a social and economic "improvement." And while his
residence in Petty France placed him close to his employ with the Council of
State, it too was in a very well-to-do area, his neighbor being Lord Scudamore,
and I have also noted that John Jackson and Anthony Wilson were residents
there. Edward Jones has discovered records in St. Margaret's Overseer Rate
Books citing Milton for 4 shillings, in toto 16 shillings, in each year from
1652 (document E166) through 1659 (E173); and in the Army Assessments
for St. Margaret's in 25 December 1651–24 March 1652 (E1595) and successive documents (to E1603) through 24 June 1654 (later immediate records
are no longer extant), for 0/5/0 (rents) and 0/1/6 (estates) in the first
year.[65] These sums, in comparison, indicate a decidedly impressive domicile. Listed immediately following Milton is Thomas Herbert (his residence
was where York Street is today), a Commissioner of Parliament residing in
the Army under Fairfax, and appointed early in 1647 to attend the king
during his confinement at Holdenby House.[66]

Milton is well placed financially throughout most of his life, and well
situated as to where he lived and who his neighbors were. He is surrounded
by family and friends who are adherents of the kingship, but also those who
can be called Parliamentarians even when their criticism of Cromwell, particularly during the later 1650s, was strong. He does not seem to have broken with those who thought differently from him, although some coolness
may have existed with his brother and some of his family and with his brother-
in-law. Through most of the forties, he is little attentive to governmental
issues, arguing rather on the religious issue of conceived Catholic remnants
in the State Church, on social problems like censorship and divorce (which,
of course, were more religious issues, as they remain today in the Roman
Catholic Church). He is not anti-monarchy or anti-Royalist, and even in *Tenure* he is largely theoretical about the demands upon any king or *magistrate,*
not antimonarchic. Behind his argument is an assessment of Charles as one
who should be removed because he does not abide by such demands of
leadership, but it is not a diatribe to throw over single-person rule or, most

importantly, a king. As Worden, quoted before, expressed it, he was not different in this political thinking from others in the new government that followed. A king's centralizing leadership or the figurehead that the king becomes later and is today are not rejected, and through most of the 1650s that position seems not to change overtly: it is not kingship, but who is the king. Differences with family and friends lie in the assessment of Charles, in the justification of his execution, then in austere demands by the Cromwellian government, and in the reading of what the Protectorship was vis-à-vis kingship. As cited in chapter 3, n42, even Robert Russell denied antagonism toward the "king," illustrating the same kind of thinking that I have urged for John Phillips. There is no sharp incompatibility that many commentators seem to require for Milton or Phillips between accepting the king and rejecting kingship: the theoretical concept of republican establishment and action for them does not insist on the removal of kingship, although the removal of a specific king may be insisted upon.

Milton's position on single-person rule during the 1650s, as we have seen and as various critics have viewed it, does not reject it, per se, but does expect controls over that person. Such controls set up a republican (not a "democratic") structure and do not disallow a "King" or "Protector" as an active leader (not just a figurehead). As in *Paradise Lost*, God as the Father is in command of everything: all, even God the Son and the Holy Spirit are subject to him. In the family, it is the Father who is in command; indeed, the mother is almost ignored. All else turns on *a kind of* equality, a toleration at least, but it stops with God and with Pauline dicta about husbands and wives. Much as we do not like the thought of "Hee for God only, shee for God in him," the relationship approved for Adam and Eve is that of the Father in his house and God in his Heaven. God, however, takes on a totally separated and unassailable presence, whereas a father (apparently) and/or a husband— that is, any human being—can be subject to repudiation and removal, thus including a "King" or a "Protector." Milton's republicanism lies in government by the many, but his thinking is not refined until the disasters of the 1650s hit home with the anarchic 1659–1660 period. At this point, he comes to recognize that single-rule of even a "Protector" can nullify representationalism of the "people," and that not everyone is capable of competent representation. There is choice involved, but the choices are somewhat limited. The "federalist" proposal that emerges in *The Ready and Easy Way* results from such recognition finally, but it is also an attempt at a stop-gap to avoid return to a monarchy that could echo that of the immediate past. And, as a stop-gap, it is less fully explored than perhaps it might have been: justification of the council in perpetuity is argued and some modification with rotation grudgingly allowed, but the naive concept that times remain basically the same—particularly socially and economically, thus with no necessity for change—is ultimately the lure of utopianism.

Milton has not understood that the "closed" position that a senate in perpetuity would create is really an underlying "ideal," a kind of utopia, with all the certainty of failure that time will bring, let alone poor "choice." Lilburne, Walwyn, or Winstanley also offer unthought-out utopianism. It becomes a "closed" political world, one that would control the social and economic and thus, unacknowledged, with expectation that those worlds would not change or be allowed to change. It is built on a social structure of stratifications, a not surprising element for the Milton we have seen in his surroundings of family, friends, and personal life. He is far from radical when it comes to social consciousness. A definition of "people" is as lacking as it is in Lilburne's tracts. While the economic and trade propensities that Hoxby examines are discernible in Milton's 1660 work, we do not find evidence of attention to the franchise for everyone, certainly (like Lilburne and Walwyn) not for women; we do not discover any "communistic" aura such as Winstanley espouses; we do not find sympathetic understanding of all the "people"—the "rabble," "the insolent speech of the multitude." The network of influence (or possible influence, at least) from the "well affected" strikes one today as potentially capable of setting up acts that could be prosecutable, acts smacking of nepotism or of prejudicial influence (though "influence peddling" may not have occurred). Yet, he does not argue for a transfiguration of that society of which he is a part. As far as what evidential writing is known, he at no time questions the nepotic world of the Crown clerkship or other governmental positions (like extended family member Thomas Agar's position as Surveyor of Forests); or the advantages gained from people like Henry Lawes or the Earl of Anglesey or John Evelyn. There is nothing in his arguments that takes on revisions of class structure or truly meaningful economic reform.

Milton's lack of economic acumen and his strong loyalties in the face of equivocal circumstances like those that occurred around 1659–1661 hardly make him an astute adviser for "constitutionalism" (which became such a hot topic a few years later) beyond the scaffolding of the governmental central and deployed structure he proposes. While the Lady in "Comus" may say,

> If every just man that now pines with want
> Had but a moderate and beseeming share
> Of that which lewdly-pamper'd Luxury
> Now heaps upon som few with vast excess,
> Natures full blessings would be well dispens't
> In unsuperfluous eev'n proportion (768–73),

we do not find him following through with further thought on this socialis-
tic concept. (I use the adjective in its basic, general meaning.) The same
awareness of inequality is expressed in the "Ode to Rouse"—"if we have
atoned sufficiently for our former offences / and the base idleness of our
unmanly extravagance" (27–28), but had he proceeded to understand his
own placement socially and economically? We have nothing to guide an
answer; even John Phillips's attention to the plight of the debtors didn't
come until 1675. From Milton, there is silence, which may be attributable to
various reasons, of course; with John the discrepancies with his own social
milieu and possible economic standing don't seem to show either. Although
Milton's way of life is not "lewdly-pamper'd Luxury," and although his station could be classified as "moderate" or "middle" or perhaps "upper middle"
class, we must admit his position as that of the landed gentry, and one living
off rents and loan interests, with no "worker" experience, not even with
"business management" within his activities. School-teaching and governmental secretarial work are quite different from the livelihoods of Lilburne's
"Young Men and Apprentices" or Winstanley's "Diggers" for both Milton
and his nephews.

John Milton over the full range of his life exhibits the kind of anal reten-
tive personality that is always a bit behind other people in recognition and
in doing. He is not the radical, cutting social and economic or even political
roots, not even after the return of monarchy in 1660. He is still concerned
with religious matters and the Catholic menace and, to him and others, the
superstition and idolatry of this belief. The full implication of toleration
does not really strike him; the inequalities of class, residence, gender do not
fully strike him. The need for "open" aspects of political life at the same
time that "closed" structures are proposed to correct what is condemned as
tyrannical action and unacceptable "manners" is not articulated in the way
that Lord Hervey realized a few years later. Milton's republicanism is not
fully thought-out and certainly not egalitarian.

We should not equate Royalist and monarchy in these years of the seventeenth century, for the first term, first used in William Prynne's *Soveraigne
Power of Parliaments* (1643), shows in *Eikonoklastes* (Milton's first use of the
word) a more specific meaning of adhering to Charles, not just any king.
"From such learned explications and resolutions as these upon the Covnant,
what marvel if no Royalist or Malignant refuse to take it, as having learnt
from these Princely instructions" (Yale Prose, III, 496); "To give account to
Royalists what was don with thir vanquisht King, yeilded up into our hands,
is not to be expected from them whom God hath made his Conquerors"
(III, 559). His nephew's convictions demonstrate the same bifurcation: a
king, even a Charles II or a James II, may be looked on positively for what he

has accomplished for the nation, but this approval does not extend to that same king for other acts (for example, for their Catholic support), nor should it evoke the label "Royalist" as if no qualifications (or limitations) of the term were possible and needed.[67]

Von Maltzahn reviewing the last years of Milton's life concludes that "Milton could only be a Whig of a peculiar kind. . . . The Whig *Milton* who emerges in the bitter controversies of the Exclusion Crisis and the Glorious Revolution is the ancestor of the very different Whig Milton, at once polished and sublime, whose poetry would find such elegant notice in the essays of Addison's *Spectator*" (231, 230). The emphasis in this "Whiggery," however, is upon the interrelated religious question rather than the strictly political. Protestant toleration at the time of the first Test Act (1673) showed bitterness about Presbyterian impositions in matters of faith. *Of True Religion* is the result of rearticulating toleration, most specifically against the Presbyterians. George Sensabaugh explained the phrase "that grand Whig *Milton*" as the result of the emphasis in their platform built on liberty of conscience; Milton thus served to argue against licensing acts and the divine right of kings, and for toleration, a free press, and the theory of compact.[68] John Phillips, like his uncle, can be labelled the same kind of Whig; his constant subject is anti-Catholicism but liberty of conscience otherwise. His thinking spills over into political areas but government is not really one of his missions. Edward Phillips, not overtly like his uncle or brother, eschews direct confrontation with these issues and more patently moves in what come to be called Royalist circles. We can only infer attitudes, and those seem to be inexplicit. Despite the lack of evidence of relationship with his brother-in-law, we cannot assume that Milton distanced himself from Agar or Agar's extended family; there is certainly nothing to suggest that he was severed from them or their influences. We should not forget (that is, if we ever knew!) that Milton's niece Anne Agar Moore and her family were among the gentry with extensive landholdings. Just because documents do not place him in propinquity with the Agars and Moores does not deny familial relationships. The question of Christopher, however, does make viable both Milton's and his father's disjuncture with Christopher over religion, and even early on in 1642 over politics. Our reading of Milton's last years of life has been colored by the depositions in conjunction with the nuncupative will, and as we have seen, they raise many more questions and suspicions than should have existed in a straightforward inheritance.

In all Milton was a Parliamentarian—which does not mean nonacceptor of monarchy, which does not mean consummate theorizer about the "people" and government, which does imply a Republican advocating controls by the "people" (the "well-affected" in any case), which does mean acceptor of action against Charles I in the 1640s and of the theocratic oligarchy of the 1650s and even of the Protectorship as ostensibly intended. His Royalist connections are not broken because of his political positions and they seem to be helpful to him in 1660 when retaliation against those who engaged in regicide and those who were significant in the Cromwellian government were prosecuted. That Lord Bridgewater commented that Milton should be hanged for his work for the Interregnum government, despite, as a youngster, his having participated in the first production of "Comus" and having been his neighbor, indicates the strange position that Milton found himself in in 1660, but the lack of action against him (except for the brief imprisonment) exemplifies the confused state of affairs and friendships and associations. His association with adherents of the restored monarchy and with titled folk continues: he remains "Parliamentarian" with "Royalist Connections."

6

Protestant and Familial Literary Implications

Religion has played a significant part in the relationships of John Milton and his family and associates. It has played a major role in attitudes toward him through the interpretation and appreciation of his literary work. Many of those attitudes clearly arise from readers' differences of opinion about religion—their own religion, a most notable case being William Empson's rejection of Milton's God. In his book *Milton's God*, Empson is most constrained by the figure of the Father, especially in Book III of *Paradise Lost*. But also assuredly a disbelief in what is conceived as Milton's heterodox position is still currently driving antagonisms concerning the import of *De doctrina christiana*, its authorship, and its "gloss" on the epic. Part of the problem is that Milton is thought incapable of uncertainty or of variance from "standard," but generally undefined, unthought-out, and stereotyped, classification. Indeed, the belief that he could not err seems to arise.[1] Yet his religious position is significant in its underlying influence on how and what he presents when writing creatively—a basic *Affekt* that one is not necessarily conscious of but that exists nonetheless. While personal worlds have been seen to enter his literary work, such as political issues and even descriptions of people and events, and such as his first wife's being cast as Dalila in his dramatic poem—which I strenuously disbelieve—the fundamental (and psychological) attitude concerning family that we are all subject to as a result of our upbringing has not been generally considered. But, I contend, it is significant to recognize the familial play of relationships and actions that occurs in Milton's three major poetic works, as well as others. In this chapter I look at what appears to be Milton's religious persuasion, and its sources in the familial—only glancing at his theological precepts, which is such a complicated subject—and then briefly at the literary implications of family in *Paradise Lost, Paradise Regain'd*, and *Samson Agonistes*.

1

Milton was raised a Protestant by a father who was severed from his father, it would seem without any further contact, because of religious issues. The Roman Catholicism of Milton's yeoman grandfather, Richard, clashed with his father's religious beliefs in the early 1580s. The grandfather was "an Under-Ranger or Keeper of the forest of Shotover near to the said Town of Halton and Thame in Oxfordshire" (Wood, I, Fasti, 262). He was excommunicated for recusancy on 11 May 1582; his son was disinherited, or put away, or cast out (verbs employed by Skinner and Aubrey, Wood, and Phillips) "for embracing, when Young, the Protestant Faith, and abjuring the Popish Tenets" (Phillips, iii-iv) around this time. The move of Milton's father to London is thus speculated to have been around 1583 or a year or two later. The grandfather died in 1601. The religious issue was clearly an important one for Milton's father, and its transmittal to his son John was as clearly effective. We have seen the antagonisms of John Phillips, brought up by Milton, to the Papacy, but Edward has not been considered as to religious issues. Significantly in 1694 in the life of his uncle, he calls his great-grandfather "a bigotted Roman Catholick," an adjective that suggests that Milton's education of his elder nephew was also effective. As is always pointed out, the intertwining of religion and politics during the seventeenth century could not have been ignored and could not have failed to have substantial effect on everyone. Edward was also stepson to Thomas Agar, was employed by those like Evelyn who was Protestant, but was also employed by those who were Catholic like the Earl of Arlington. Perhaps religion was a less vital issue for him than it was for his brother, but he too appears to be of Protestant persuasion.

On the other hand, there are Christopher and his family. By all accounts Christopher, though professionally he follows what probably had his father's early and continued approval unlike John's decision as expressed in "Ad Patrem,"[2] theologically and probably politically rejected his father's teaching. His children Thomas and Richard by all accounts reflect the religious divergences of the period and of their father's "teaching." Thomas gives every indication of rejecting his father by his long delay in becoming a lawyer, by being an adherent of the Parliamentarians, and by following Protestantism. The lives as far as we know them of his daughters Anne, Mary, and Catherine likewise suggest Protestant affiliation. But Richard, early to become a lawyer and to join his father in various business transactions as we have seen, and one to reflect Royalist affinities, was a Catholic and overtly so with his move to Ireland with the forced abdication of James II in 1688. Is it ironic that Christopher and Richard had so much to do with Milton's last days and nuncupative will, or was it manipulation, or is there no religious correlation with "family" blotting out all ruptures of conviction?

Milton was early intended to the church, that is, the State Church which was calvinist and episcopal, but in an uncertain position because of the influence of Arminianism and because of attacks on its maintenance of "Popish" elements, its incomplete "Reformation." "With the Puritans we are still in the full flush of the Reformation," Patrick Collinson tells us, "not in some post-Reformation atmosphere of orthodoxy or unorthodoxy."[3] Trained to become a minister of the Church, Milton signed the subscription books of Cambridge University in both 1629 and 1632, which demanded allegiance to the State Church and its Thirty-nine Articles. With certain Arminian influences, such as Archbishop William Laud in the 1630s reflected, Milton would have agreed, but with his formalism, demands in the use of the Prayer Book, and full acceptance of episcopacy as the decade proceeded, Milton was "church-outed." Early in that decade, when Milton was still in university, "Arminian doctrine and Laudian formalism . . . appeared strange and novel in the 1630s, whereas what we take for Puritanism would have been widely equated with orthodoxy" (Collinson, 535). What comes to be called Anglicanism at a later age provoked a schism of Separatists and Nonseparatists within the Church, the first group rejecting the Church of England, though both agreed with certain demands for reform. Milton, of course, knew the liturgy and employed it connotatively in his earlier poetry (most notably through the 1630s), but the early 1640s brought published arguments against episcopacy and the increasing emphasis upon eradication of further "papist" elements and upon the individual as communicant with God and upon the Bible. The minister had a function, but the function of the "Church" was quite different from the years before 1641. The principle of the indivisible church, the Church Universal, led to mistrust of traditional discipline, and for Milton at least a questioning of received doctrine. In my discussion of John Phillips I urged that Phillips was anti-Catholic as his uncle also showed himself to be. The starting point of this animosity for many people seems to have been the Papacy's political intrusion into the world of national governments and the world of secular life. The Pope wielded military and diplomatic controls and influences; actions and beliefs became, for the adherent of the religion, unquestioned—or so it seemed. Financial matters, too, were involved, for monies did go to the Vatican for support of papal activities and leaders of governments resented the loss of funds for their own endeavors. In exercising his position as earthly overseer of people's lives—socially, familially, religiously—the Pope made pronouncements that became tantamount to canon law—or so it seemed at least on the surface. This situation persists today, of course, in such areas as marriage and divorce, sexual life, abortion, the position of women in the clerical hierarchy, and so forth. Many Catholics accept papal rulings; many do not accept them but do not turn from their beliefs and church adherence; many not only do not accept them but hypocritically engage in acts directly in opposition while alleging to be Roman Catholics. For Milton, as I have remarked and have contended elsewhere, the position of the Pope, and thus the Catholic religion, was to compel followers of the religious (and theological) precepts to accept these intrusions into world and personal affairs or run the risk of committing sin and of excommunication thereby. It was, perhaps, an easy step to move to a rejection of the religion itself, from that to the theology of that religion, and thence to a lampooning of it as being built on superstition and idolatry. Milton and Protestants question and reject as sacraments most of the sacraments, assign following the Pope and the church leaders to idolatry, and cast as superstition and illogic the Divine Presence at the mass and the priest's ability in transubstantiation.

Vestiges of the clerical hierarchy of the Catholic religion continued as prelatical structure in protestant reforms, and as Milton's earliest published prose work argued, that obviated a complete reformation.[4] The clerics who made up Smectymnuus were not breaking with the calvinistic principles of reformation, but with the division that the State Church had established between adherents of a ministry that maintained prelatical hierarchy and adherents of a ministry that emphasized a relationship between a single person and God, with the minister being a helper to better that individual union, to interpret the Scriptures for those needing such help, and to guide the parishioner to maintain that individual faith. The preface to *De doctrina christiana* makes it clear that Milton thought that all one needed was the Scriptures, but that most people were incapable of fully understanding them, and thus that some need guidance. He sees himself engaging in "restoring religion to something of its pure original state, after it had been defiled with impurities for more than thirteen hundred years, [which] dates from the beginning of the last century" (Yale Prose, VI, 117). "[T]he only authority" is "God's self-revelation" and this is found in "the Holy Scriptures." "God has revealed the way of eternal salvation only to the individual faith of each man" (VI, 118); "I advise every reader, and set him an example by doing the same myself, to withhold his consent from those opinions about which he does not feel fully convinced, until the evidence of the Bible convinces him and induces his reason to assent and to believe" (VI, 121–22). Such stress on individual faith rejects the Catholic emphasis on confession and penance. Nothing but the study of Christian doctrine "can so effectually wipe away those two repulsive afflictions, tyranny and superstition, from human life and the human mind" (VI, 118). (The translation is inaccurate: Milton says "slavery and fear," not "tyranny and superstition.") This stated position will lead Milton in his poetry to stress the "paradise within" and the "inner light" (as Michael Wilding has explored this radical position). But we should recognize that Milton himself finds the Scriptures sometimes contradictory and perhaps misleading (as in the question of Trinity).

Added to the Protestant view that Catholics were superstitious were rituals, robes, rings, kneeling—the externals of Catholic practice, which one faction of the State Church maintained. Here too was evidence, for people like Milton, that a true or complete reformation had not taken place. For people like the Smectymnuuans and Milton, the Church of England had taken two roads, one espousing more reformation from Catholic discipline than the other; to follow that espousing more reformation was *not* to divorce oneself from the State Church of England despite the position of the Church of England during the 1640s and 1660s and beyond. And thus Edmund Calamy, Thomas Young, Milton. That Milton interrogates Christian doctrine and presents his uncertainties and "answers" openly does not remove him from membership in that Church; it separates him from the "high" order of what two centuries later will be called "Anglicanism," but his thinking proceeds later to distinguish him from a "low" order as well. The basic division remains today in "Low" Episcopalianism and "High" Episcopalianism. The alleged heresies of *De doctrina christiana* cannot be investigated here—it is much too involved a subject; let it suffice to quote the preface again: "some irrational bigots . . . condemn anything they consider inconsistent with conventional beliefs and give it an invidious title—'heretic' or 'heresy'—without consulting the evidence of the Bible upon the point" (VI, 123). The meaninglessness of the recent questioning on the Internet of how Milton could be buried at St. Giles, Cripplegate, when he was allegedly an "Arian," is clear: he was an adherent of a protestantism from his early childhood and he followed the example of his father on through his university training and the antiprelatical tracts that remained "calvinistic," "anglo-protestant," and opposed to the "Roman Catholic" and its remnants found in some "anglo-protestant" disciplines. Keeble is correct in stating that "Milton was certainly no Calvinist," instead being "committed to the freedom of the human will" (135). He does show acceptance of Arminian positions—Arminius maintained that he was a Calvinist—but he was not one who should be labelled "an Arminian": the opposition to Archbishop Laud's extreme position is one piece of evidence; his position on predestination is another separating him from strict Calvinism and Arminianism. (Laud's literal interpretation of predestination, and other rigidities, brought increased belief, by, among others, General Baptists and those who would soon be called Friends, that all could attain salvation.) Milton's comment in *Doctrine and Discipline of Divorce* certainly denies that he was "an Arminian," in spite of the basic Arminian principle of possible salvation: "The Jesuits, and that sect among us which is nam'd of Arminius, are wont to charge us of making god the author of sinne in two degrees especially, not to speak of his permissions" (II, 293). In *De doctrina christiana*, Milton is also clear about "predestination," although many commentators have tried to make him agree with Arminius: the word "is habitually used to refer to reprobation as well as to election," but "in scripture, specific reference is made only to election. . . . When other terms are used to signify predestination, the reference is always to election alone" (VI, 168–69). "PREDESTINATION, then, must always be taken to refer to election" (VI, 171). As God the Father says in *Paradise Lost* III, 183–84: "Some I have chosen of peculiar grace / Elect above the rest; so is my will." But he also says:

> I will cleer thir senses dark,
> What may suffice, and soft'n stonie hearts
> To pray, repent, and bring obedience due.
> To prayer, repentance, and obedience due,
> . . . Mine ear shall not be slow, mine eye not shut.
> And I will place within them as a guide
> My Umpire *Conscience*, whom if they will hear,
> Light after light well us'd they shall attain,
> And to the end persisting, safe arrive. (III, 188–97)

According to Doran and Durston, defining English Arminianism, "bishops insisted that the parish clergy should incorporate into their church services a number of ritualistic features regarded by ministers and parishioners alike as 'popish': these included bowing at the name of Jesus, genuflection, kneeling to receive communion, and the insistence that women should wear veils while being churched following childbirth," and they note the use of altars.[5] Laud's attempts at uniformity drove moderate Puritans to join Presbyterians and Separatists, and by 1640 there were some ten separate congregations in London. Before the end of the 1640s episcopacy and the Book of Common Prayer had been abolished, leading to an Interregnum characterized by a fusion of Presbyterians, Particular Baptists, and Independents (generally "Congregationalists"). The official liturgy of the new State Church was that in the Presbyterian Directory of Public Worship (1645), although there continued a popular attachment to the old Prayer Book. The "toleration" of the Cromwellian rule nonetheless placed adherents of the episcopal system into the classification of "dissenter." Such dissenters as Catholics, episcopalians, and followers of the old Prayer Book were tolerated. For officials, however, there was an Oath of Adjuration, dated January 1655: a parish officer was required to "abjure and renounce the Pope's supremacie and authority over the Catholique Church in generall, and over myself in particular, and I doe believe that there is not any transubstantiation in the Sacrament of the Lord's Supper"; he also had to reject crucifixion, religious images, and Purgatory.[6]

The compulsory and "uniform" State Church that was restored with the return of monarchy led to the so-called Clarendon Code with the passage of the Corporation Act of 1661, the Conventicles Act of 1664, and the Five Mile Act of 1665, making unauthorized meetings for worship illegal. The 1662 Prayer Book, with a preface dismissing Puritan objections, returned to such incendiary matters as vestments and "priests" rather than "ministers." The 1662 Act of Uniformity returned to acceptance of all Thirty-Nine Articles and of the Prayer Book. The rise in dissent and increased sectarianism was an obvious result, and the intertwining of government and one's religious life returned with a vengeance. Many left England rather than submit to Uniformity, as we know, and many were imprisoned, like Bunyan, for their activities and defiance. As remarked before in looking at Phillips's *A Satyr Against Hypocrites,* after 1660 "Puritan" and "Presbyterian" became almost synonymous. One can understand Milton's and Phillips's positive reaction to the Test Act (1673), despite misgivings. While it ordered those holding civil or military office to partake of "the sacrament of the Lord's Supper according to the usage of the Church of England" and specifically declared "that there is not any transubstantiation in the sacrament of the Lord's Supper, or in the elements of bread and wine, at, or after the consecration thereof by any person whatsoever," it also opposed toleration of one protestant group against other protestant groups and *compelled* through prohibition, thereby obviating the inner reformation—the Inner Light that various sects (the Antinomians, the Quakers, the itinerant preachers) maintained—that Milton came to champion. Its "several oaths of supremacy and allegiance," harking back to "the statute made in the third year of King James," almost nullified what advances had been made in shifting controls from king to people. Indeed, the Declaration of Indulgence of 1662 yielded legislative sanction for the exercise of royal dispensing power, although Parliament refused to rescind the laws against dissenters, which was its focus. It was not until James II's reign that both Roman Catholics and Protestant dissenters began to find some toleration with the Declaration of Indulgence of 1687, which suspended penal laws against those refusing to conform to the rigidities of the State Church, and with the Toleration Act of 1689, under William III, which allowed worship by Trinitarian Protestant dissenters. Charles II's attempt at such "freedom of worship" in the Declaration of Indulgence of 1672 was declared unconstitutional by Parliament; the Bill of Comprehension of 1672 tried to redefine "Anglican" doctrines and practices by including sectarians in toleration. What it did was provoke the Test Act in 1673. James II's 1687 proposal for tolerant action was declared illegal by one judge, and was reintroduced in 1688. It should be clear why John Phillips was able to commend both Charles II and James II for some of their acts, even with his hatred of Catholicism and the "tyranny" that monarchy often exhibited.

Yet after the Restoration, the authority of Parliament, rigidly episcopalian, increased, and thus the Clarendon Code came into existence. In religious matters the poor condition of parishes and the lack of education of the new parochial clergy aided in creating the Bill of Comprehension of 1672, whereby all ministers were to subscribe to all the Articles of Religion "which only concern the confession of the True Christian faith and the doctrine of the Sacraments," a somewhat relaxed demand. An alliance of episcopalians and Presbyterians was deemed necessary against the inroads of both Sectarians (dissenters) and Recusants.[7] For Milton, the possible spread of Catholicism and the rumors of Charles II's secret actions needed a way to inhibit the growth of popery.[8] His answer to this is: "The last means to avoid Popery, is to amend our lives: it is a general complaint that this Nation of late years, is grown more numerously and excessively vitious then heretofore; Pride, Luxury, Drunkenness, Whoredom, Cursing, Swearing, bold and open Atheism every where abounding: Where these grow, no wonder if Popery also grow a pace" (*Of True Religion*, VIII, 438–39). In this same tract he writes, "[W]e have no warrant to regard Conscience which is not grounded on Scripture . . . Let them bound their disputations on the Scripture only . . . The next means to hinder the growth of Popery will be to read duly and diligently the Holy Scriptures" (VIII, 432–33). In *De doctrina christiana* he again stresses the reading of scripture and presents his reading of theological matters, which reading offers no acceptance of Catholic dogma but also no specific classification into religious or sectarian grouping. It is a Protestant reading, and that's the best label that can be assigned. "Puritan spirituality was Bible-centered"; there was "no unmediated union with God, least of all any absorption into God, apart from Christ."[9] While Catholic emphasis lies in the love of God and Christ, "the emphasis in Puritan poetical spirituality is on the role of Christ in power, not on his tenderness"; "Catholicism glories in the sacred humanity, Puritanism in the divine powers of God as man" (Davies, 88). Love, and its many forms in human and divine worlds, dominates *Paradise Lost,* but it is the mediation of the Son, of the Christ he becomes, and thus the Son's (Christ's) power that is heralded in the epic (though sometimes unrecognized) and in *Paradise Regain'd.*

By all accounts, with the exception of his brother Christopher and at least his nephew Richard, Milton's relatives and close friends were not Catholics. Yet there were associations, for example, Edward Phillips's dealings with the Earl of Arlington, and the question of his relationships with his brother and nephew looms when we observe the lack of evidence of close association from the early 1640s through the end of his life, since the main information for Christopher's visiting his brother comes in the depositions concerning the nuncupative will. Further, the background to their father's move to Aldersgate Street to reside with his elder son may involve only security from possible military action and what seems to have been Christopher's unsettled residence, but one must wonder whether religious factors did not also enter in. For one who left his father's home—apparently without further contact—because of religious differences to come to reside with a son who was apparently exhibiting that same kind of religious belief suggests that religion did play a role in his joining his elder son, despite what might have been inconveniences because of the latter's bachelorhood and foster parentage of two young boys. Indeed, this does lead to the possibility that such a move was the catalyst for Milton's marriage in mid-summer 1642, as I have suggested before: provision of a wife to attend to husband, "sons," and father-in-law.

The subject of Catholic existence and significance in the seventeenth century has generally had only biassed and cursory attention by those dealing with the political issues or such literary figures as Milton. Even Richard Crashaw and John Dryden, though examined from religious points of view, both pro and con, have not generally been set against the broad canvas of their periods. A Latin work such as John Warner's manuscript discussion of *The History of English Persecution of Catholics and the Presbyterian Plots* (1683–86) offers a counterstatement to most (Protestant-oriented) commentaries on the period, and supplies significant statements (seemingly accurate) concerning Charles II and James II.[10] That Milton is not a minority voice, however, can be seen in such later comments as Edward Chamberlayne's in *Angliæ Notitia: or, the Present State of England* (1700):[11] "[I]n those Countries where the Roman Catholick Religion is National, Ignorance is the Mother of Devotion" (Part III, p. 249); "the dissenters from the Church of England are these five sorts, Libertines, Papists, Anabaptists, Independents, and Presbyterians" (and despite some seeming flirting with Independency and Presbyterianism in the past, Milton does not belong to one of these groups; Part III, p. 250). Chamberlayne remarks that "all Protestant Dissenters from the Church (except Antitrinitarians) are tolerated" and he notes that "The Number of Jews and Socinians among us is still more inconsiderable" than Libertines (Part III, pp. 250, 251). (Milton has been labelled an antitrinitarian, but toleration of all dissenters is an aim in *Of True Religion*.) Shortly after this, Major

Richardson Pack states in "Essays on Study and Conversations," Letter I section of "Of Study": "RELIGION may be divided into *Natural* and *Revealed*. The Former hath been more generally Agreed among Mankind than the Latter. . . . As to Revealed RELIGION (I mean the *Christian*) . . ." (See *The Whole Works,* p. 90.)

Milton's religious "affiliation" is significant because of the Erastian component seen in the State Church and the relationship of that affiliation with the political issues impending within all the discussions of this study. As Keeble remarks (126), Milton's "puritanism" particularly urged "The acceptance of toleration as a religious and civil duty" and determination "not to submit their consciences to the dictates of ecclesiastical or state power." Liberty of Conscience is a driving force in his thinking, and the theocratic proportions of Cromwell's administration caused problems for him, as we have seen, even if he did try to avoid confronting them. His nephew John shows himself to be an excellent "disciple," contrary to the past's iteration. Early on, Milton's education and career expectation pursued a protestant goal, and as Graham Parry tells us, "Milton appears sympathetic to a ceremonious Anglicanism in poems such as the elegy on Bishop Lancelot Andrewes and 'Il Penseroso', and . . . *Comus*."[12] The masque of 1634 (revised around 1637 and published in 1638) offered a form associated with the court and the aristocracy, and, for others at least, a bid for a career in court circles.[13] With the impositions of Archbishop Laud upon clerics, including the Book of Common Prayer, in the 1630s, Milton found himself "church-outed." With the Irish Rebellion in October 1641 and the negotiations of Charles I with the Irish Catholic rebels during the 1640s,[14] political and religious issues merged for Milton, and the equivocal position of the Presbyterians in the Westminster Assembly of 1643 onward represented the forcing of "our Consciences that Christ set free" and a pluralism (in its system of provinces and classes) that showed the "New Presbyter is but old Priest writt large." He seems to have naively separated the two issues until it became quite clear that they were not separate issues. Nonetheless, he continued to argue for separation of church and state, a church of one's own, as it were, and a state representing and created by the "people," one that looked out for its constituents. We might compare the equation of government and religion and their distinction in different people's minds by a letter from Thomas Hearne to White Kennett, dated 12 December 1711, which was provoked by one from Kennett to Hearne on 3 December. Kennett had snidely remarked, "if you had inquired after truth, and avoided that party where it is seldom to be found." Hearne remonstrates: "I never took the Church of England to be a *Party,* and therefore I espouse the Doctrines she maintains (as I hope I shall always do) and happen to write any thing in behalf of her, or of any of her friends. I think 'twill be very *improper* (not to say *uncharitable*) to censure me as striking in with, or writing on purpose to serve, a *Party*. And whereas you add *a party where truth is seldom to be found*, I must own to you that I think there is more truth on the side you have left, and now call a *party*, than on the other to which all the Dissenters are joined and linked in interest."[15]

Thus, of the various Protestant sects that had emerged in opposition to Catholicism, Milton has been seen as a Puritan, one opposed to Presbyterianism (although there has been suggestion of acceptance around the beginning of the 1640s) and finally by 1640 opposed to those who espoused prelaty. Perhaps his church-outing by Laud's actions and position on prelates, which finally brought him to reject his intended, though unrealized, vocation as a minister and turn to the world of poetry, caused his negative analysis of the prelatical system. He seems not to have thought previously of the interference and indirectness that that system maintained for an individual with his God, or of its Catholic descent. Laud's own exercise of power as archbishop created more than just repudiation of one man: it evinced how the prelatical system removed an individual from any direct union with God and was thus to be extirpated. This belated awakening in the early 1640s led to Milton's reexamination of what was, or should be, Christian doctrine, and he began to keep a "Theological Index." The "System of Divinity" which grew out of these concerns and index was set down in some kind of organized fashion prior to 1658–1660 when, apparently, Jeremy Picard made a copy of what has come to be called "De doctrina christiana," as we noted in the Introduction here. That it was not finished and in fact was augmented and altered in succeeding years is obvious from the manuscript and its numerous revisions. But this we should expect, for the Interregnum and the Restoration brought religious (as well as theological) issues to the fore to lead many, and including Milton, to revised perceptions about God and his "children." The disciplines that resulted from the sectarianism that developed were to be tolerated because all essentially believed in a God unhampered by the trappings of Catholicism.

The surface of the Interregnum's religious world offered toleration—although not outright to Catholics and Episcopalians—and this, in contrast with the years of Charles I and Archbishop Laud, separated church and state. The reaction of the state against the Irish and the Italian perpetrators of the Waldensian massacre was acceptable because of the Catholic underpinnings. But Milton is otherwise not negative toward the Irish, not with friends, former students, nor extended family all participating in Ireland's affairs. We should remember, too, Edward Phillips's dedication of *The New World of English Words* to James Butler, Duke of Ormond, in the third and fourth issues of 1671 and 1678. This suggests not only the alterations among political friends and foes that the Restoration brought, but possible recognition that Milton was doing his job in 1649 when his commissioned "Observations" on Charles I's Irish peace, orchestrated by Ormond with the Irish Rebels and the Papists, appeared. The confusions of politics and religious beliefs of the people during Milton's lifetime, and the almost impossible clear-cut classification of most of them, is reflected in Milton's changing thought 'or maybe it is only awareness' from his days at Christ's College to his final days on Artillery Row. What rises above all is that he was a Protestant, abjuring all Catholic doctrine and practice or their incomplete eradication in the so-called Reformation (there were, of course, many Reformations in the fourteenth through sixteenth centuries); he was not an episcopalian nor a Presbyterian; he was a Puritan, but perhaps more outwardly than truly. He was not an Arian although his position on the Trinity is uncertain and has caused him to be labelled "antitrinitarian." These will have to be only glanced at here because of the involved substance and the need to pay very close attention to the Latin text of *De doctrina christiana.*

Both words—Arian and antitrinitarian—have been loose terms assigned to anyone who did not (does not) adhere to the unqualified "God is three persons indivisible." The denial of this was not strictly said by Arius, and Arius's position included much, much more than just this one, albeit basic and telling, concept.[16] Likewise, one is cast as an "antitrinitarian" ("nontrinitarian" might be better) if any specifications are attached to "three persons indivisible." Logic, of course, says that is an impossibility; accepters of the phrase without explanation of it must take it on faith as a great miracle generated by God. While Milton early exhibits a belief that God is three persons—becoming God the Father with the generation of God the Son, and both presenting the Holy Spirit[17]—who is a unified God, he does examine in *De doctrina chrisitiana* the "personness" of the three forms in which God appears, with acceptance of the analogy between a father and a son in an ultimately "subordinationist" relationship. *That* part of the matter is quite clear in *Paradise Lost.* (He does exemplify in the epic three different *essentiæ,* or "personalities," essences, in the characters of the Father and of the Son and in the godly Spirit that hovers over the poem.) A major complication is that God the Father becomes coterminous in many ways with God, although the person of the Father refers (or should refer) only to situations where the Son, who is *generated* from the *substantia* of Godhead, and all others (like the angels, whom Satan calls the "sons" of God), who are created from the substantia of Godhead, are involved. The Holy Spirit, which pervades the epic although, logically, is not a character in it, imbues and is defined by God the Father and God the Son.[18] In the treatise (Book I, chapter VI), however, the discussion of the Holy Spirit does raise uncertainties. Milton writes that "the whole doctrine of the TRINITY seems to have been wrested primarily from this one sentence, which is almost the only foundation for it" (that is, I John 5:7: "there are three witnesses in heaven, the Father, the Word and the Holy Spirit, and these three are one").[19] Immediately before this statement, we should note, he says that there have been considerations "which make a lot of people increasingly suspicious of the passage in question." He had begun the chapter by remarking that "The Bible, however, says nothing about what the Holy Spirit is like, how it exists, or where it comes from—a warning to us not to be too hasty in our conclusions. . . . The spirit, then, is not said to be generated or created, and it cannot be decided, from biblical evidence, how else it exists. So we must leave the point open, since the sacred writers are so noncommittal about it" (VI, 281–82). Attempting to explain everything theological by the Bible, Milton runs into a kind of stone wall where the Holy Spirit is concerned, and finds that the one sentence proclaiming a trinal God is held with suspicion by others. His examination of the texts does not confirm a Trinity for him.

These last matters are theological, dealing with doctrine rather than the discipline of religious sects. That theological differences appear amongst the various Protestant sects has not been the main divisive element in arguments for or against episcopacy or Presbyterianism or Anabaptism. Milton comes to disagree, it seems, with all sects on certain theological grounds and to agree with many of them on various religious issues, but the three constants that characterize "Protestant" are the disavowal of Catholic doctrine and discipline (even when remnants would seem to remain), the primacy of Scriptures, particularly the New Testament, and closeness of communicant with his God rather than through the intercession of a Pope, despite the infrastructure of such as the episcopal church. What occurs in the seventeenth century is a greater emphasis on that closeness as seen in Quakerism, Antinomianism, and itinerant preaching. For Milton, it takes the form of the "paradise within," the inculcation of the attributes of the Christ, the "inner light" with its radical overtones in social and military life, should it ever become the standard for all people, the "church of one" that ultimately can be its only end.

2

The relationship between God the Father and God the Son in *Paradise Lost* reflects a religious position that has been seen as acceptable by many who believe in the teachings of Christianity concerning the godhead. It has also been questioned by many others who do not separate the actions and abilities of the godhead into the subordinationism that occurs in the poem. For here it is only God the Father who possesses omnipotence and omniscience and omnipresence, who makes decisive laws and directs decisive actions. The Son acts for the Father, becomes his delegate on the third day of the War in Heaven, in the Creation of the universe, in the Judgment devolved on the disobeying Adam and Eve. He may be granted omnipotence. Most telling is that Milton presents the Son in his victory over Satan and the rebellious angels in Book VI as ascending in the Chariot of Paternal Deity, employing the Hebraic Merkabah of Ezekiel as a testament to that familial relationship, although no other biblical authority—Christian or Hebraic— had alleged any such an affinity for the chariot. Throughout *Paradise Lost*, Milton goes out of his way to place the Son as subordinate to the Father, to extol the Father as All (the text of 1 Corinthians 15:28 pervades the poem), to render a consanguinity between Father and Son that is more than just physical generation as the terms "Father" and "Son" would require. The critical impasse that has developed is largely a result of nonacceptance of any kind of defining or elaboration of what the concept of God the Father and God the Son, as well as Trinity, can mean. Any deviation from an unexamined iteration of a trinal concept has led to charges of a heretic position.

Book III has bothered many readers because of the Father's simple and unambiguous voice of truth, leading to a casting of him as harsh and unloving, and the Son's role in ameliorating the punishment that the future disobedience of humankind's grandparents should demand.[20] The commonplace metaphoric reading of the Trinity as representing Truth (the Father), Mercy or Love (the Son), and Justice (the Holy Spirit) lies behind this subordination in Book III, and the language and rhetoric employed for Father and Son reflects that.[21] While the Spirit is everywhere in the poem, it obviously cannot be an anthropomorphic character, and by the time *Paradise Lost* was completed, Milton had (as *De doctrina christiana* shows) come to question the orthodox relationship of the Spirit to the Trinity. (The author's, Milton's, basic argument is that there is only one reference to the Holy Spirit as the separate trinal essence in the Bible. The author even questions the canonicity of that text.) In Book III, therefore, we have a Father who speaks Truth and who exacts some kind of retribution for disobedience and lack of faith and love toward him, and a Son who offers a means to alter what might be retribution by obedience and faith and love toward the Father. The predicament, though somewhat conflictual, receives a religious resolution that echoes the mundane argument Milton advanced to his father in "Ad Patrem" with hoped-for persuasion of the father/Father to accept filial action for discharge of a seeming difference of opinion. Such acceptance extended, it is submitted, in the

mundane world "will preserve [his] praises and the name of the father /
sung again and again, as an example to a future generation" (119–20), and
in the world of theological belief will bring "the multitude of [those who will
be] redeemd" to "enter Heav'n . . . ,

> Father, to see thy face, wherein no cloud
> Of anger shall remain, but peace assur'd,
> And reconcilement; wrauth shall be no more
> Thenceforth, but in thy presence Joy entire. (III, 260–65)

The religious and filial relationship between Milton and his father drives
the ideas and language of this major section of the epic. It keeps being reit-
erated throughout the poem:

> Go then thou Mightiest in thy Fathers might,
> Ascend my Chariot, . . .
> O father, O Supream of heav'nly Thrones,
> First, Highest, Holiest, Best, thou alwayes seekst
> To glorifie thy Son, I alwayes thee,
> As is most just; this I my Glorie account,
> My exaltation, and my whole delight,
> That thou in me well pleas'd, declarst thy will
> Fulfill'd, which to fulfil is all my bliss. (VI, 710–11, 723–29)

And in this filial contrast lies the antagonisms of another son, Satan, who
disrespects the Father, religiously and politically, setting himself up in a position that tries to imitate the Father's being and world. But whereas the
Father's throne is simple, easy to approach, with attendant angels who "freely
. . . serve / Because [they] freely love" (V, 538–39), this other "son" assumes
a position "High on a Throne of Royal State," which outshines "the wealth
of *Ormus* and of *Ind*, . . . the gorgeous East . . . [and] her Kings *Barbaric* Pearl
and Gold" (II, 1–4). He purports that Heaven first created him the Leader
of those "Deities of Heav'n" that now stand below him looking up. Exerting
that leadership, he "whom the highest place exposes [as] Formost" (II, 27–
28) imperiously allows a debate to proceed: "who can advise, *may* speak"
(42, italics added). The difference between the Son of God and the sons of
God, such as Satan and the rebellious angels, is made clear in the epic: the
Son is God.[22] Yet the familial relationships of all characters to God the Father revolve around what Milton perceives and accepts as the authority and
prerogative of a father and, accordingly, the obedience and duty of a son.

I do not wish to imply any conscious equation between the rebellious Satan and the conflictual Christopher in their relationships with the Father or with the father, but vestiges of such familial disruption do seem to lie psychologically for Milton underneath the change of Lucifer (the light-bearer) to Satan (the Adversary). The emulation of being like the father, and thereby the expected recipient of fatherly preference, emerges in Christopher's actions and conduct in his pursuit of law and in his early marriage and fathering of children, actions that place him as a kind of patriarchal "light-bearer" when compared with his brother's lack of such achievement and even familial tendency during the years 1637–1641. But politically (apparently) and certainly religiously he becomes an adversary to his father's attitudes and beliefs, an adversarial position that seems to produce no contact between them in the ensuing years of 1642–1647, a period when the older brother has shown political and religious concurrence as well as establishment of family and home. Whatever Christopher's legal work was in those years is not easily established since political activities are the only evidence we have until his return to the Inner Temple in 1646, after the first Civil War. Records do not offer inferences of actual cases or legal commitments during the last years of the 1640s. In the meantime, the father had moved in with the brother, who has achieved success (and notoriety) as poet and advocate for religious, sociological, and educational convictions that do not seem to diverge from what may have been the father's, and who has established a home with two "foster children" and wife, and who has sired a daughter of his own.

The concept of Satan as parallel and opposite to the Son has been argued by Carl Jung, who saw concealment of the quaternity in the orthodox dogma of the Trinity. While the Son is identified with the light of the Logos, Jung opined the need for an archetype of the Brothers, the Son and Lucifer, to render the wholeness of Deity.[23] This "brothers archetype" has reared up in such popular venues as motion pictures showing us the good guy or even ministerial brother who must lead the gangster brother (or sometimes just friend who is like a brother) into the path of righteousness and repentance (even penance in some tangible way). The dualism that the archetype sets up creates oppositions as in the story of the twins Esau and Jacob with such oppositions taking on negative or positive attributes. Jung in his archetypal theorizing is registering what study of civilizations evinces and applying it here to what he conceives as a quaternity with the "son" between the Father and the Spirit as two warring figures. We might heed the acknowledgment of Northop Frye: "there is one theme that recurs frequently in the early books of the Bible: the passing over of the firstborn son, who normally has the legal right of primogeniture, in favor of a younger one. . . . In later literature, the theme is carried much further back: if we look at the fifth book of *Paradise Lost,* for instance, we see an archetype of the jealousy of an older son, Lucifer or Satan, at the preference shown to the younger Christ" (180–81). Frye, of course, is referring to the impression in Book V that Lucifer and the other angels had been created before the "begetting" (that is, exaltation or generation) of the Son; but Milton counters such misreading in Book III: "Hail holy Light, ofspring of Heav'n first-born" (that is, the Son who is the first-born offspring of Heaven, being the "Coeternal beam," the "Bright effluence," that is not created ["increate"], of the "bright essence" of God [III, 1–6]). Lucifer, created, bears the light, but the Son, generated, is the Holy Light. That John was the older and Christopher the younger should not obscure the age-old ubiquity of the brothers archetype and the problems of sibling rivalry and parental preference, first seemingly accorded by John Milton, Senior to the younger.

I have not raised the issue of Milton's mother in this book, although some of her relatives, Hester and William Blackborough, for example, are extremely important in his biography. Hester née Jeffrey was the daughter of Richard and granddaughter of Richard, uncle of Milton's mother (and thus Milton's second cousin). She died in 1657 and had borne at least five children. Her husband was a leatherseller who died in 1646; Milton witnessed his will the year before. From at least 1638 the Blackboroughs owned a home in St. Anne and St. Agnes parish in Aldersgate, the precinct in which Milton lived in 1640 through September 1645, and "hard by" his residence. Phillips (xxvi) says he visited these relatives in the 1640s, their home being in St. Martin le Grand Lane, and here reconcilement with his estranged wife Mary was effected. Milton's references to his mother, however, are few. In *Defensio secunda* (81–82), he says he was "of an honorable family. My father was a man of supreme integrity, my mother a woman of purest reputation, celebrated throughout the neighborhood for her acts of charity," soon noting that "my mother having died," he undertook his continental trip. The psychological import of the mother/son relationship is explored by William Kerrigan in *The Sacred Complex* (passim), where he particularly emphasizes the mother's weakness of eyes and Milton's problems with his eyesight and finally his complete blindness, and the way in which mother fixation emerges in Milton's Muse in *Paradise Lost*. Refer also to my remarks in *Self and the World*, 177–78, 185–92.

An additional reference to his mother, not previously cited, it seems, lies in "A Post-Script" to *The Judgement of Martin Bucer, Concerning Divorce* (1644): "But this [epitome], I hope, will be enough to excuse me with the meer *Englishman,* to be no forger of new and loose opinions. Others may read him in his own phrase on the first to the *Corinthians,* and ease me who never could delight in long citations, much lesse in whole traductions; Whether it is natural disposition or education in me, or that my mother bore me a speaker of what God made mine own, and not a translator" ([25]). This encomium to his mother places her—not just his father as seems to be the usual assignment—as the fashioner of the independent thinker who does not merely put someone else's ideas into more readily understandable words.[24] (I might suggest, "Here let the deniers of Milton's authorship of *De doctrina christiana* take notice," to paraphrase a line from *Ars Logicæ Plenior Institutio* [19].) This reference indicates a religious influence upon her son that has not previously been assigned to her. And, by all accounts, her religion was Protestant, although anything more specific cannot be determined; she and her relatives that we know of all attended parish churches of the State Church.

Perhaps what overrides what could have been a more *observable* position of his mother within his life and work are the Pauline admonitions, which place the wife subordinate to the husband (an attitude not to be rejected by Milton since a similar subordinationism appears between God the Father and God the Son) and indeed woman as an inferior being to the man. That she does not appear often within his work does not demand that we read her as unimportant in his eyes or in what he creates and thinks. In *Tetrachordon,* as frequently has been recognized in recent years, while he argues for a compatibility in marriage and is not unaware or opposed to a focus on the woman as deserving of release from marriage, he weakly— "religiously" overthrowing logic and reason—writes: "But St. Paul ends the controversie by explaining that the woman is not primarily and immediatly the image of God, but in reference to the man" (3). He continues by paraphrasing 1 Corinthians 11:3, 7, "*The head of the woman . . . is the man: he the image and glory of God, she the glory of the man*: he not for her, but she for him. Therefore, his precept is, *Wives be subject to your husbands as is fit in the Lord, Coloss.* 3.18." But his position modifies the misogyny of Paul and raises the stature of woman.

The masculinity and individuation that separation from the mother may release generally leads to an attempt to identify with the father. This we observe in "Ad Patrem" less than a year after his mother's death. It likewise can lead to such assertion of patriarchal dominance as St. Paul espoused, and Milton, strong believer in the Scriptures, ran into this contradiction, but nonetheless accepted it as his tract on divorce exhibits. Still, mothers are cited often in the prose works and in some of the poetry, appropriately either in acclaim or in reproof. In *Paradise Lost* it is the Virgin Mother of Jesus or Eve as the Mother of Mankind or Mother Nature who usually appears. It is through the Virgin that God unites with man (XII, 375–85) and enables the defeat of the Serpent, and it is thus womankind that is praised as the conduit for ultimate salvation, which is the focus of Milton's concern. Mary is the second Eve, who is hailed as the Mother of Mankind (V, 388), indeed "Mother of all things living, since by thee / Man is to live, and all things live for Man" (XI, 160–61). Here "Man" means humankind, and the enunciation of the protevangelium (here and in X, 179–81) that Eve / Mary / womankind conduces towers over all human concerns and actions when the Son of God as Jesus defeats Satan, Sin, and Death in his Crucifixion and Resurrection. It cannot be too often stressed that the last speech of the poem bestowed upon Eve reprises this means of redemption and fulfillment of the Father's promise in Book III, and alludes to the last of things when God will again be All in All. The figure of the mother is positive and intertwined with religious resolution of the adversity and wickedness that beset human beings. His speaking of these matters that "God made mine own" are to be credited to his mother.

However, the one actual mother in *Paradise Lost* is Sin, who can be looked upon as the mythic Terrible Mother but also as woman overpowered and abused by a male, whether her father Satan or her son Death or (apparently) the dogs that are her offspring; a woman nonetheless who enables her father/consort to proceed to what will be his false kenosis and his "defeat" of God through his deceit of Eve, and thus his forcing of the Son's Incarnation. The infernal dialectic that Sin contributes to (despite any sympathy we have for her mistreatment by male figures) places her as antithesis to Eve and especially to Mary. The relationship of Death to his Father is not unlike that of his Father to his Creator, until that Father collapses opposition between them through his own egoism and pride. This son does not emulate his father and he would soon devour his parent mother, were his end with hers not involved (II, 723–34, 803–13). Milton's literary strategy is to set up antitheses where one is built on positive (and observably personal) familial relationships and the other one as a diametric opposite, thereby to enhance the positive by sharp contrast. The contrast of women persists in such passages as the narrator's "Hail wedded Love" remarks (IV, 750–75) where Milton's mother's "purest reputation" and "acts of charity" may be seen to underlie the "Perpetual Fountain of Domestic sweets, / Whose bed is undefil'd and chast pronounc't" and her opposite seen in the "bought smile / Of Harlots, loveless, joyless, unindeard" who are "best quitted with disdain." I cannot agree with Kerrigan's attempt to find a negative effect on Milton's relations with women from an association of blindness with maternal inheritance (see 177–80). Rather the mother fixation produces the morality of "domestic sweets" and the abhorrence of "bought smiles."

The companion poems of 1671 engage a different kind of contrast in terms of appearance of a mother, and yet a similar contrast between women. This antithetic strategy of joining *Paradise Regain'd*, dealing with the Incarnated Son as Man, and *Samson Agonistes*, portraying an all too human man, has been affirmed often. While the brief epic presents the mother figure as a character and as a referent in all of its four books, the mother is ostensibly absent from the dramatic poem. The only reference to "parents" in the former is found in line 235 of Book I, where Jesus remembers his mother's telling him that he is "no Son of mortal man, / Though men esteem thee low of Parentage." In the latter, the mother appears only within two references to Samson's parents, lines 25, 220, although the biblical story of Samson has much to say about the mother. (The word is used with different significance in lines 886 and 1487.) Of Milton's own parents, there is the often cited statement in *The Reason of Church-Government* (41) about his vocation in "the Church, to whose service by the intentions of my parents and friends I was destin'd of a child," which also points to his mother's role in his religious self. Often the prose quotes and discusses the biblical statements in Genesis and in Matthew positing the man's leaving father and mother, or parents, and cleaving to his wife, with Milton's notable remark "that nothing is done undutifully to father or mother" upon such a move (*Doctrine and Discipline of Divorce*, 1644, p. 62).

I have previously discussed the organization of the brief epic as a separate book followed by three continuous books, the relationship of that ternary and quaterny structure with the import of the first unitary book, and the Son's identity of himself in Book I, where the energy associated with the father is established in his rejection of purported bodily needs and of the falsity of Satan, and the development of the form that that energy will take in Books II-IV.[25] "Energy, an attribute of the father, implies action and wisdom; form, an attribute of the mother, implies tangible structures or patterns through which energy will work" (63). Books II-IV show the energy of Book I being employed in various ways, as in the banquet or the storm, or especially "the highest Pinacle" of "the glorious Temple" of "*Jerusalem*, The holy City." The psychological substruct that thus emerged from Milton's own relationships with his father and his mother, especially as noted just above, is clear: "my mother bore me a speaker of what God made mine own." The Son returns at the end of the epic to his mother's house: the womb symbolization is important to emphasize his emergence from that house/womb after the poem ends[26] to undertake his ministry as the anointed Son of God, the Christ, who has up to this point been Man and who is now the Man-God. The temptation in the wilderness ends in Matthew at 4:11, in Mark at 1:13, in Luke at 4:13, and his ministry begins in the immediately following verse in each. As Matthew 4:17 states, "From that time Jesus began to preach, and

to say, Repent: for the kingdom of heaven is at hand." Milton's addition of
the mother's presence between the temptation and the ministry emphasizes
the significance of the mother-child identity, particularly through the "meekness" of the mother, the "softness" and "Grace" associated with the female,
the love "celebrated" in his own mother's "acts of charity," which Michael
declares "the soul / Of all the rest."[27]

Looking at the Son's soliloquy in Book I, and the remarks cited above
concerning Milton's mother (as well as the father's endowment), we can
read added meaning in his words:

> These growing thoughts my Mother soon perceiving
> By words at times cast forth inly rejoyc'd,
> And said to me apart, high are thy thoughts
> O Son, but nourish them and let them soar
> To what highth sacred vertue and true worth
> Can raise them, though above example high;
> By matchless Deeds express thy matchless Sire. (I, 227–33)

Of Mary's soliloquy, the narrator of the brief epic notes her "thoughts /
Meekly compos'd" and her patience as she "awaited the fulfilling"; and how
"her Son . . .

> Sole but with holiest Meditations fed,
> *Into himself descended, and at once*
> *All his great work to come before him set;*
> *How to begin, how to accomplish best*
> *His end of being on Earth, and mission high.*
> (II, 107–14; emphasis added)

Her ruminations (II, 66–104) stress her "troubl'd thoughts," those of any
mother for the future of her child, though in this case fed by prophecy for
Jesus of "fall and rising"; her not understanding his current absence from
her home, though he has gone probably, as once before, "about His Father's
business," she endures, "wait[ing] with patience . . . inur'd." It is tempting to
see in this a reflection of Milton's own life uncertainty during the years 1632–
1637, after graduation from Christ's College and rejection of a ministerial
career, and a lack of expectation from him of paternity up to his mother's
death in April 1637. But foremost is the inveterate familial dilemma of the
future of children, their welfare, and their selves.

The figure of the father in *Paradise Regain'd* is not much different from

that in *Paradise Lost*. God the Father's address to the "full frequence bright /
Of Angels," having "pre-ordain'd and fixt" the intended temptation of Satan upon his Son, "by merit [so] call'd," predicts that the Son's "weakness"—
his "Humilitation and strong Sufferance"—"shall o'recome Satanic strength
/ And all the world, and mass of sinful flesh," in order "To earn Salvation for
the Sons of men" (I, 126–67). *If* there is a personal note sounded here, it
implies that Milton has come to view his father's recognition of him as one
whose strength lies in the meekness and virtue of the mother's influence in
him and the rejection of sinful carnality—an eventuality that may have developed in the years 1642–1647. What God the Father proposes is action
against the Adversary—Satan—akin to that of Job, who is actually named in
line 147, by "This perfect Man," who "shall first lay down the rudiments / Of
his great warfare" through that temptation. Only then—that is, after he has
returned to his mother's house and later to emerge to begin his great ministry—shall he be sent forth "To conquer Sin and Death the two grand foes."
The Son, like the human Milton, will engage in a "great duel, not of arms, /
But to vanquish by wisdom hellish wiles" through "his filial Vertue" (I, 173–
77). The upbringing and energy that his father afforded him Milton had,
early on, seen in divine terms:

> What father could bestow a greater gift, or Jove himself,
> with the exception of heaven, if he had given all?
> He bestowed no more preferable gifts, however many might have been
>   prudent,
> who trusted to his young son the common light,
> the chariot of Hyperion, the reins of day,
> and the tiara waving about with radiant brightness.
> ("Ad Patrem," 95–100)

The Satan of *Paradise Regain'd*, on the other hand, is not the Satan of
Paradise Lost, except in little ways in his address to his constituents shortly
before the starkly contrastive speech of the Father.[28] Herein he boasts his
bad success with Adam and Eve and portends like success in confronting
and nullifying the "ill news" of the appearance as "man" of the "first-begot"
of "the Monarchy of Heav'n." There is nothing in the full poem to suggest
any *sibling* rivalry.

The absence of the mother in *Samson Agonistes*, which has been noted
especially by feminist critics, may be a purposeful maneuver by Milton rather
than a sign of negative attitude toward woman.[29] As the text stands, the son,
Samson, shows none of the maternal qualities that I have elaborated above,

qualities that Jesus manifests. The contrast in these two companion poems is striking. The "omission" emphasizes his nature: his lack of humiliation and strong sufferance until he is shackled in the grist mill; his being a kind of *miles gloriosus* driven by overweening pride; his carnal desires, a pursuit of "domestic sweets" with both the Woman of Timna and Dalila. It is the mother figure (and notably that which we discern as Milton's epitome of his own mother) that defines what Samson is not and thus, as opposite, what he is. At the same time the absence of the mother within sets up the need for development within of those attributes that will provide Samson's achievement of his destiny, his being the Great Deliverer of his people.[30] That his people are not delivered through their own inaction and acceptance of the ease of security, even if in bondage, does not negate the role that Samson has finally played. The movement within the drama is the alteration that Samson undergoes, a self-awareness and its resultant renovation, not a regeneration as some former critics have advanced.[31] The energy of the father has to be channeled to action that is not aimed at self-aggrandizement or at gratification of the libido only; its action will involve humiliation.[32]

Contrast (or dialectic or antithesis) is replete in Milton's poetry as meaningful literary and ideational device, as has so frequently been shown in scholarship primarily on *Paradise Lost*. In *Samson Agonistes,* a major use of the trope lies in the irony created by the contrast of Manoa the "father" and God the "Father." It underscores Manoa's self-concern rather than religious belief as in lines 444, 446–47 where he is lamenting the magnification of Dagon: "Which to have come to pass by means of thee, / . . . Of all reproach the most with shame that ever / Could have befall'n thee and thy Fathers house." Here Manoa means himself, but we understand that Milton means God the Father and what seems to be the exultation of Dagon's "house." The capitalization of the word in the original text suggests some kind of input in producing the text that has been received from Milton himself (for which various answers can be made). In the *kommos* Manoa will again twice present the same irony unrecognized by him, lines 1714–17 and 1728–37. The latter is patently a signifier of Manoa's crassness and self-centeredness and his negligence of Samson's prophesized role: "he shall begin to deliver Israel out of the hand of the Philistines" (Judges 13:5). "I with what speed the while," he says,

> Will send for all my kindred, all my friends
> To fetch him hence and solemnly attend
> With silent obsequie and funeral train

> Home to his Fathers house: there will I build him
> A Monument, and plant it round with shade
> Of Laurel ever green, and branching Palm,
> With all his Trophies hung, and Acts enroll'd
> In copious Legend, or sweet Lyric Song.

His boorish view of renown as resting in monuments would seem to obliter-
ate Milton's early exhortation from Phœbus Apollo to himself that "Fame is
no plant that grows on mortal soil." The end of Samson (ambiguous though
it has seemed to many) can be and has been read as a faithful act bringing
him home to his divine Father's house where the "pure eyes / And perfet
witness of all-judging Jove" will reward his renovation. He has taken on the
energy of the true Father in his final resolve and action, linking with God
the Father in the way that humans (as opposed to the Son as man in *Paradise
Regain'd*) can: "so God with man unites" (PL XII, 382).

The Manoa of *Samson Agonistes* is not the father-figure Milton knew
and praised: he is the slow and obtuse Manoah of the Bible, Judges 13:11–
23. Far from representing "energy," Manoa confirms his etymological being, *m'nuach*, meaning "rest."[33] This kind of reverse play that I have argued
for the absence of the mother and now in the characterization of Manoa
as father extends to the presentation of Dalila. I have noted the antipathy
that Milton shows toward the harlot, toward her who has not been like his
mother of "purest reputation." Dalila enters as a ship of Tarsus, a symbol
of the prostitute,[34] and appears to the Chorus as a "Matron," a most interesting epithet for someone who has been looked upon in terms of the
Bible and other renditions of the seduction story as attractive and "young."
Milton makes Dalila Samson's wife, implying that theirs should be "wedded Love," and setting up ironic contrasts with those engaged in "loveless,
joyless, unindeard, / Casual fruition" (*PL* IV, 766–67). As "matron" she is
particularly contrasted with what she has been and offers contrariety with
those who truly are part of a familial environment. While Dalila, in her
plea to have the blind Samson return to her domestic care, has been read
by some few commentators as sincere, including her psychologically understandable counter stance toward what she has done after his abusive
rejection of her, she has been one who has contravened the familial expectations of wife and is, continuingly in her "bedeckt, ornate, and gay" appearance, one "best quitted with disdain."

The literary (as well as ideologically meaningful) use of this trope of
antithesis becomes the integral component in a reading of the dramatic
poem. It points to the alteration over the course of the poem of Samson's
self-awareness and final resolution and action, uncomprehended by him

though it is, through the rejection of false father, the taking on of the expectations of the true father without reasoning out those expectations, and through the assertion of the mother within that self-awareness and the rejection of the nonfamilial dominance that carnality brings. The "foul effeminacy" (410) that Samson says he has succumbed to in the past by letting in "the foe / Effeminatly vanquish't" (561–62) is the lack of strength of the father, the metaphoric masculine attribute of mind over Self, and a weakness, not of humiliation or meekness or charity associated with the mother, but of "the snare . . . / Of fair fallacious looks, venereal trains, / Soft'n'd with pleasure and voluptuous life" (532–34). In *Paradise Lost* (XI, 632–36) Michael corrects Adams charge that Man's woe begins through Woman: "From Mans effeminate slackness it begins, / . . . who should better hold his place / By wisdom, and superiour gifts receav'd." In *Paradise Regain'd* Jesus counters Satan's lure of licentious and extravagant Rome:

> Nor doth this grandeur and majestic show
> Of luxury, though call'd magnificence,
> More then of arms before, allure mine eyes,
> Much less my mind . . . (IV, 110–13)

and its imperial ill-governing of "Nations under yoke" with its accompanying "daily scene effeminate" (IV, 135, 142).

　　Family matters in all three major poems, the concentration being on father and mother. Its manifestation emerges in positive and in contrastive negative characters and events. It is reified for Milton through the religious world that his father and his mother tendered him—a religious world that was Protestant, a world emphasizing the individual's direct relationship with his God, a world in which Liberty of Conscience is the driving force and Conscience is the Umpire implanted in Humankind by God as guide (*PL* III, 194–97). All three poems demonstrate the need for and means of obtaining the "paradise within," the precedence of the Scriptures for Milton, and the continuing place of father and mother in his total world.

Afterword

In *Genograms in Family Assessment* (New York: W. W. Norton, 1985), Monica McGoldrick and Randy Gerson present the way to create and interpret a genogram format schematizing a family tree and the interrelationships of its members.* They indicate the importance of birth order and sibling position, patterns of repetition across generations, which patterns are not necessarily linear, and the closeness or conflicts among individual members. These interactions and relationships are highly reciprocal, patterned, and repetitive; a genogram is a family therapist's version of a family tree.

Families repeat themselves. What happens in one generation will often repeat itself in the next; i.e., the same issues tend to be played out from generation to generation, though the actual behavior may take a variety of forms (5). Redundancy of pattern not only may predict tentative future action but may allow for analysis of existence within any present time when absolute proof is lacking. *Once we have drawn the family structure, the skeleton of the genogram, we can start adding information about the family, particularly: a) demographic information; b) functioning information; and c) critical family events* (9). In addition, *triangling* (98 ff.) may exist for two against a third, creating high tension, or it may express a healthy development among the three: *The behavior of any one member of a triangle is thus a function of the behavior of the other two.*

The accompanying genogram of John Milton and his immediate relatives indicates patterns that I have presented in the chapters of this book and suggests, further, that some postulated relationships may indeed have existed. The conflictive nature of John Milton, Sr.'s relationship with his father over religion would seem to play out in the conflict in the next generation with his son Christopher. The elder son, John, on the other hand, exhibits very close relationship with the father in terms of religion as well as other matters. The pattern continues with Christopher's relationships with his sons: a very close relationship with Richard—and religion would certainly be a major element in that closeness—and a distant, if not conflictual, relationship with another son, Thomas, who was older. Interestingly, all of Christopher's sons became (or apparently intended to become) lawyers, following their father's profession. Yet Thomas made that decision quite late, even after his younger brother had completed his law studies. Is not the conflictual being seen here ultimately relented or at least altered when Thomas did pursue legal study? Christopher seems to have followed a career that had his father's approval, and John, at least at first, did not. Those are conclusions that can be drawn from "Ad Patrem," in which John uses the argument that he, pursuing poetry, is following a career akin to his father's avocation of music and is not forced into such as law (the intended profession of his younger brother at the time he wrote the poem). (See chapter 6, n1, for evidence of this contretemps.)

Birth order and sibling rivalries would seem to lie behind some of these life events, with the implication that John, in preparing to follow a ministerial Protestant (or Puritan) role, was doing something that his father, who had become estranged from his own father over religion, would highly approve; initially, however, he chose a role that his father disapproved. John displayed no defiance, but from 1637, with the death of his mother, Sara, he is able to assert himself, first with his European sojourn, which was embarked in terms of education and writing to advance that career decision, and then to set up bachelor quarters in London in order to try to come to the full circle of his studies and to write. Conflict is not the word to describe what would be the relationship between father and son but what were surely the father's expectations from his older son in terms of life experience, livelihood, and family, were not being fulfilled. Milton scholars may be thinking of the portrait of God the Father and God the Son in *Paradise Lost,* particularly in the consult in Heaven and with the Son's ascent in the Chariot of Paternal Deity to defeat Satan and his cohorts: a son who is "independent" of thought, yet dependent upon father and ultimately executing what will make him proud. (See discussion in *Self and the World,* especially pp. 269–71 and 312–13 n46.)

The contrast with Christopher is sharp: a son who follows what his father would seem to have wished for, a son who marries young and produces sons and daughters and settles into a family life. Christopher and his family joined the father around 1637 in Horton and that family group moved for a short while to Reading in late 1640 or early 1641. Did conflictual problems from Christopher's emerging Catholicism and his Royalism and Royalist activity arise to cause the father soon to return to London to live with his other son? A repetitive pattern had emerged. Christopher pleased and rivaled through vocation, displeased and defied by contrast with his sibling in religion and politics. John pleased by religion and probably politics, but displeased (for a while only?) by vocation. Milton's antiprelatical tracts from 1641 should have reconciled father and son on the score of a return to religious matter and by producing writing that was more than just the poetry of published "Comus" or "Lycidas." John's life choice was establishing pride for the father, and precisely at a time when the younger son's beliefs and political actions would be disturbing to the father.

Yet another point of sibling rivalry and possible parental reaction was family. Christopher married early, apparently produced children early and continued to present his father with grandchildren. John, though older, did not marry or show (as far as we know) intentions of marriage, had bachelor quarters (but was soon to provide a domicile for his nephews), seemed at age thirty-three not soon to be a father. Were pressures on John to marry in 1642 so that the father would join him (could better join him?) around this time? The possible conflictual relationship seems not to be in evidence now, perhaps because of Milton's prose writing of 1641, perhaps because of his provision for his nephews, perhaps because of his marriage in 1642. Did the desire of the father to move in with his elder son prompt (along with foster parenthood) John's becoming married—a quick marriage and without much buildup—to a girl half his age who was therefore an excellent prospect for motherhood? A repetitive pattern of John Milton, Sr.'s leaving his father's home because of conflictual relationships emerges in his separation from a son, who, in Toland's words, "more resembling his Grandfather than his Father or Brother, was of a very superstitious nature, and a man of no Parts or Ability." There is no evidence of any kind of contact between father and Christopher or his family, it is certainly important to recognize, after the father left that son's home. A conflict between the brothers seems graphed by the questions of religion and politics: legal activities in between the years 1654 and 1657 offer some evidence of contact, although the closeness of Christopher and John's brother-in-law Richard Powell may hint at coolness, and testimony over the will—if indeed honest—weakens the significance of such conflict.

The family matters that Christopher's daughters point to are a close relation with their brother Richard and a possible distance from their brother Thomas, who, indeed, is in only one instance meaningfully associated with Richard. However, Anne and Thomas are cited in the same parish, St. Dunstan's in the West, allowing for some contact or even more, and a reference by Thomas's widow Martha concerning John Younger, as has been speculated, may mean contact with Thomas. There is nothing to imply that the daughters were not Protestant, and Anne's marriage to Pendlebury would seem to confirm that religion in her case. Yet Mary and Catherine, and perhaps the others, appear to have been close to Richard and still in touch after he moved to Ireland.

What amounts to a triangling that may obtain with Milton and his two nephews accords with my arguments in previous chapters. Rather than estrangement there is closeness between Milton and John Phillips, and tradition has always seen closeness between Milton and Edward Phillips. The source of Aubrey's statement that Mary Powell Milton "often-times heard his Nephews cry, and beaten" (Sheet C. f. 2) is unclear; it is not documented elsewhere. It is easy to imagine circumstances in which a twelve- or eleven-year-old child might be spanked and cry, but regardless, there is nothing in Edward Phillips's account to suggest real conflict with his uncle even as a child. (Mary in 1642 was seventeen; that age perspective is undoubtedly to be taken into account.) In *Milton and the Culture of Violence*, 204 and nn4–6, Michael Lieb remarks the frequent *plagosum* that schoolmasters imposed on their students (a practice that long existed in English public schools) and Milton's ironic use of reference in *Defensio secunda* to have Salmasius turned over to his students for their flogging him. Milton's tone here (and his regimen in *Of Education*) indicates a disapproval of this practice, which apparently he himself endured from William Chappell at Christ's in 1626, who "whip't him," according to Aubrey. As Lieb comments, the quip against Salmasius complicates how we take this report of Milton's beating his nephews.

The evidence presented in chapter 3 does indicate that Edward and John were close and not rivals or estranged or distant. And we have seen John following his uncle strenuously in his arguments against Catholicism and in favor of Parliamentarianism; a negative attitude toward Cromwell develops in the late 1650s for Phillips and seems hinted at for Milton. But we do not find conflict. We cannot define Edward's religious position any further than to say he was Protestant, although hints of disapproval of Catholics exist, as we have seen. Nor can we determine his political position any further than to say he had friends and patrons in both major camps. Edward does not exhibit conflictual positions: he offers no portrait of a person with strong convictions. John, quite differently, reflects the kind of rebellion that his grandfather showed in his estrangement from his father, the kind of strong commitment in things religious and political that his uncle showed. The triangling that can be surmised for Edward and John with their stepfather in the household of Thomas and Anne Agar from 1632 through 1638 if Anne died then, but definitely through 1639/40 when they came to live with Milton, is most uncertain. The future evidences no real conflict for Thomas Agar with Edward and the interpreted conflict with John has been argued here not to be demonstrable but the result of later critics' animosity toward John. We cannot conclude anything about their relationship with their half-sister Anne because of a lack of information, but she was only three or four when they went to live with Milton. The possibilities of significant familial connections with Anne's husband David Moore and his well-to-do siblings might prove interesting, but without any hints as to what they may have been does not allow speculation. At least Agar and the Moore family were Protestant, but they also seem to be Royalist, thus suggesting some distancing from Milton and from John Phillips.

Milton's relationship with his daughters and theirs with their stepmother Elizabeth Minshull are reputedly conflictual; relationship with their stepmother Katherine Woodcock has no evidence to support any hypothesis. What accounts there are come, first, out of depositions concerning the nuncupative will: Christopher's statement about Milton's reference to his "unkind children"; the statement from the interrogation that he "only complained, but without passion, that his children had been unkind to him" (French, V, 214); another response that "touching his the deceased's displeasure with them, he [Christopher] only heard him say at the tyme of declareing of his will, that they were undutifull and unkind to him, not expressing any particulars, but in former tymes he hath herd him complaine, that they were careless of him being blind, and made nothing of deserteing him" (V, 214); and the servant Elizabeth Fisher's statement that Milton remarked to her "that hee had made provision for his Children in his life time and had spent the greatest part of his estate in provideing for them and that hee was resolved hee would doe noe more for them liveing or dyeing" (V, 220). One wonders why the latter story might have come up in 1673/74; it sounds strange to have been related to a twenty-eight year old servant. Fisher was in Milton's employ only for thirteen months (October 1673–November 1674) according to her testimony. Christopher's answer to one of the interrogatories says that the daughters left Milton's home "four or five yeares last past," and Parker (1124–26 nn3–6) reviews the reason for dating their departure around 1670.

Four pieces of evidence, although doubts should be raised about full and literal actuality since they come from indirect and past "remembrances," point to conflictual relationships, and then estranged relationships, between Milton and his daughters and strongly between the widow Elizabeth and her stepdaughters. Fisher deposed that "a former Maidservent" told the daughters of Milton's impending third marriage to Elizabeth Minshull, which occurred on 24 February 1663, and had the response from Mary "that that was noe News to heare of his wedding but if shee could heare of his death that was something." The source, according to Fisher, was Milton himself who told this tale (which report would thus be a decade later in 1673/74). Mary would have been fifteen, and not to deny the difficulties that Milton may have caused his offspring or a less than endearing personality, we should nonetheless remember the (it seems "normal") rebellious teens against parents and against anything expected of them. Fisher's further report of Milton's account to her tells of "all his said Children [who] did combine together and counsell his Maidservant to cheat him the deceased in her Markettings, and that his said children had made away some of his bookes and would have sold the rest of his bookes to the Dunghill women" (French, V, 222). Anne, a mentally and physically challenged person, was aged seventeen; Mary, fifteen; and Deborah, eleven. Has the time of this alleged action been implied incorrectly? Has some alteration occurred in the account such as the continued words of the summary statement suggest ("or hee the said deceased spoke words to this Respondent to the selfe same effect and purpose")? The triangling here of daughters (with domination of Mary, it would seem) against the father (and especially against the—against a—stepmother) is a pattern that socio-culturists frequently find in family groups.

Edward Phillips presents pertinent material: "excusing only the Eldest Daughter by reason of her bodily Infirmity, and difficult utterance of Speech . . . the other two were Condemn'd to the performance of Reading, and exactly pronouncing of all the Languages of whatever book he should at one time or other think fit to peruse . . . it was endured by both for a long time; yet the irksomeness of this imployment could not always be concealed, but broke out more and more into expressions of uneasiness"(xlii). Backing up these conflicts and estrangement are two statements from Elizabeth Foster, Deborah's daughter. One related to Thomas Birch (*Complete Collection*, "Life", I, lxii, ed. 1738) was that her mother, "meeting with very ill treatment from Milton's last wife, left her father, and went to live with a lady whom she called Merian." Another which Birch reports is that Foster "gave me a particular account of the severities of her grandfather's last wife towards his three daughters by his first, the two eldest of whom she bound 'prentices to workers in gold lace, without his knowledge, and forced the younger to leave his family. Mrs. Foster confessed to me that he was no fond father, but assured me that his wife's ill treatment of his children gave him great uneasiness, though in his state of health and blindness he could not prevent it" (British Library MS Additional 35397, f. 321r-v, in a holograph letter to Philip Charles Yorke, Earl of Hardwicke, dated 17 November 1750). Family therapists have heard these kinds of stories repeatedly. That Anne, mentally and physically challenged, and Mary were "bound 'prentices to workers in gold lace," and teaching Mary and Deborah—females!—foreign languages, however, should not receive the disapprobation they have from later writers. In mid-seventeenth century England a nonaristocratic woman's lot was marriage and children, or some kind of employment such as seamstress or servant, or poverty. Apparently all three daughters were able to fare adequately as a result of their father's upbringing and their stepmother's action.

Other reports of Deborah's interviews with people like Joseph Addison, John Ward, and George Vertue do not imply antagonism toward her father, and perhaps Foster's statements apply for Deborah, if not for Mary, only to the stepmother. Whatever the causes for conflict and the extent of such conflict, even to estrangement between Milton and his daughters in the last four or so years of his life, and even while we recognize the frequent pattern of parent/children antagonisms, there is a pattern that the genogram reveals of rebellion against parents or at the least oppositions and distancing as between Richard Milton and his son John; that probably between John Milton, Sr., and his son Christopher; some shortlived dissension between father and John, Jr.; that possibly between Christopher and his son Thomas; and as seen with Milton and his daughters and their conflict with their stepmother.

The genogram is also helpful in picturing the kinships that can often be unrecognized, such as that of cousins like Edward and John Phillips and Christopher's children. Or between uncle and nephews. There are no direct contacts that we can cite although demographically contact would be easily possible: an unusual life experience, I would suggest. Or think of Richard Powell, who is a kind of stepuncle for them, something closer than (although in actuality the same as) Powell's kinship with Christopher's son Richard. Yet Powell and Christopher and Richard Milton repeatedly interface. The speculations that loom in looking at this genogram with John Milton as Index Person expose just how much we do not know about the intricate family relationships in his life, relationships that do matter.

. . . .

Symbols employed on the genogram are: square = male; circle = female; X = dead, usually with date; 08:74 = birth date:death date with the century understood; m.42 = marriage date; two or three horizontal lines = close or very close relationship;–||– = estranged or cut off relationship; ^^^^^ = conflictual relationship; circular line = household.

*I thank Ilana Flinker for alerting me to this important book and sociocultural field of study.

GENOGRAM: JOHN MILTON, INDEX PERSON

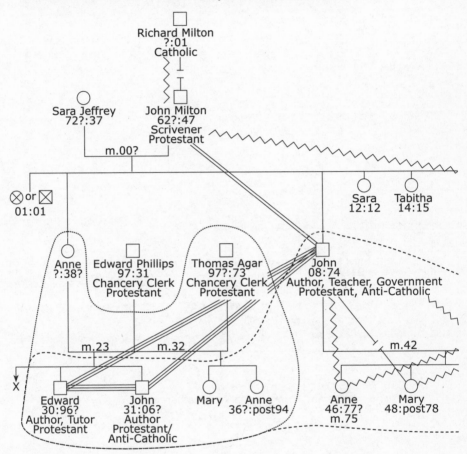

Continued

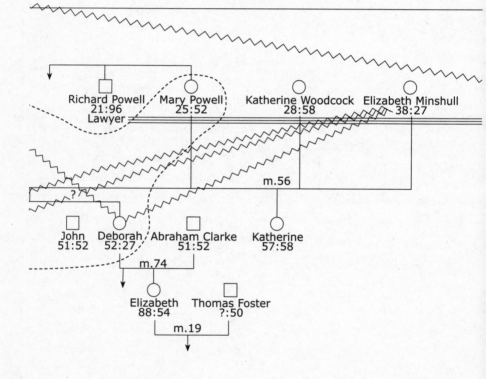

Richard Powell
21:96
Lawyer

Mary Powell
25:52

Katherine Woodcock
28:58

Elizabeth Minshull
38:27

m.56

? ?

John
51:52

Deborah
52:27

Abraham Clarke
51:52

Katherine
57:58

m.74

Elizabeth
88:54

Thomas Foster
?:50

m.19

Genogram, part 2

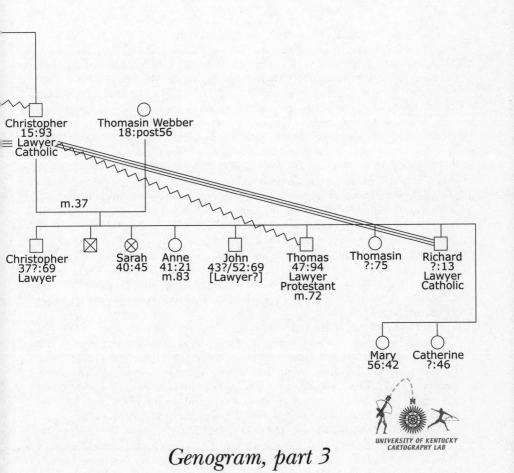

Christopher
15:93
≡ Lawyer
Catholic

Thomasin Webber
18:post56

m.37

Christopher
37?:69
Lawyer

Sarah
40:45

Anne
41:21
m.83

John
43?/52:69
[Lawyer?]

Thomas
47:94
Lawyer
Protestant
m.72

Thomasin
?:75

Richard
?:13
Lawyer
Catholic

Mary
56:42

Catherine
?:46

UNIVERSITY OF KENTUCKY
CARTOGRAPHY LAB

Genogram, part 3

Notes

Introduction

1. For bibliographic references, consult "Works Cited." *The Early Lives of Milton*, ed. Helen Darbishire, includes "Minutes of the Life of John Milton" by John Aubrey, "The Life of Mr John Milton" by Cyriack Skinner (the so-called Anonymous Life); the entry in *Athenæ Oxonienses* (1691) by Anthony Wood; "The Life of John Milton" by Edward Phillips in *Letters of State* (1694); *The Life of John Milton* by John Toland (1698, 1699); and "The Life of the Author" by Jonathan Richardson in *Explanatory Notes and Remarks on Milton's Paradise Lost* (1734).

2. See also such studies as Leo Miller, *John Milton & the Oldenburg Safeguard* (1985), and such articles as von Maltzahn, "Wood, Allam, and the Oxford Milton" (1994).

3. See J. Milton French, *Life Records*, IV, 200–11, and Parker, 1053–54. These "land" actions raise many questions about the rise of capitalism and private ownership. Indeed the matter of lands—the king's, the common people's, the individual's—will arise frequently in this book but cannot be pursued here. See, however, the important study by Mary C. Fenton, "Hope, Land Ownership, and 'Milton's Paradise Within,'" where we can remark, "British land law was being so radically revised and modernized during the mid-seventeenth century that for the first time in British history a 'land market' evolved, and with it a renovation in the fundamental nature of aristocracy, in ideas about social mobility and individual identity, and, ultimately, in notions of power and liberty" (154). That state of socioeconomic life underlies much that is taken up here.

4. The person who signed Milton's name to the 1665 indentures was the person who signed a 1669 receipt for payment for *Paradise Lost*, from Samuel Simmons, the person who signed Milton's name on the 1667 contract for *Paradise Lost* with Samuel Simmons, and the person who added a sentence in the *De doctrina christiana* manuscript on p. 372. I have identified this person as Thomas Ellwood; the items noted here show variations in handwriting (a very common practice, of course) but also great similarities in a number of capital and lower case letter formations.

5. See *The Diary of Bulstrode Whitelocke 1605–1675*, 479 and n. We should note that Whitelocke was Sir Robert Pye's attorney in his suit against the estate of Richard Powell, dated 11 February 1647; this suit demanded that Milton appear in the high Court of Chancery to answer questions about the premises in Forest Hill involved. See French, II, 177–79, and *Milton in Chancery*, chapter VIII.

6. See *Calendar of Treasury Books,* VII, part III, 1582.

7. See Gordon Campbell, *A Milton Chronology,* 95 (under April), for discussion of date.

8. "The Swedes Ambassador again complained . . . that when he had desired to have the Articles of this Treaty put into *Latine,* . . they . . sent it to one Mr. *Milton,* a blind man to put them into *Latine;* who he said must use an *Amanuensis* to read it to him, . . . and that it seemed strange to him there should be none but a blind Man capable of putting a few Articles into *Latine.* . . . . The Imployment of Mr. *Milton* was excused to him, because several other Servants of the Council fit for that Imployment were then absent."

9. Other listings in the *PRO Lists and Indexes* that should be looked at involve "Thomas Ager (Agar, Agarr)" from Middlesex (bundle 268, item 62), from Middlesex and Hertsfordshire (219/34), and Middlesex and Surrey (268/22). Series, No. IV, list Thomas Maunde (B.64/6), John Milton (P.44/4), Richard Milton (M.58/12), Edward Phillips (C.21/26, C.29/2, C.77/33, C.78/4, C.80/20, P.2/40, P.23/9, P.38/20, P.55/16, P.64/32), Katherine Phillips (P.7/12, P.33/11), Richard Powell (A. 4/6, 14, A.6/15, A.10/29, A.47/2, A.50/14, M.3/18, M.49/23, P.6/18, 21, P.13/32, P.16/12, P.26/17, P.42/13), and Thomas Ridgley (P.7/7, P.12/25). I have not been able to ascertain whether these references involve people important to Milton's biography; one or two may, indeed, already be cited in these chapters.

Another item, however, that has not been recorded in Milton's life records involving his father is a note in the Seymour papers that concerns the debts of Edward Seymour, Earl of Hertford (1539–1621). On June 1612 we find the following: "[His lordship, Sir G. Prinn and Jas. Kyrton bound to Wm. Haslefoot in 300l. for payment of 180l. at Jo. Milton Stow [*sic*] in Brodstreete London, due to the Lady Stone. *Cancelled:* paid 5 June.]" Apparently "Stow" was written for an abbreviation of "scrivener." See HMC, MSS of the Marquess of Bath, Vol. IV: Seymour Papers 1532–1686, 213, from Vol. XI of those papers, f. 285. Parker (1075 n136) notes that an owner of a house adjoining Milton's building the Rose was "William Haslefoot, whose tenant was one Bard." The reason for the indebtedness to "Lady Stone" is not given, but the sum is rather considerable. Is this the same Anne Stone to whom Thomas Shelley (gentleman), John Alford (gentleman), and Henry Goring (knight) 'all from Sussex' were indebted for £400. in December 1615, paid and discharged on 27 June 1616 by payment of £210? (See French, I, 9–11.) However, in this document she is called "Sempster" (seamstress), an odd occupation for such high debts and in conflict with "the Lady Stone."

Chapter 1

1. Among such hiatuses and puzzles have been Milton's first marriage to Mary Powell, the reasons for his not pursuing an actual career as a minister and his decision to become a poet, the death of his sister and his assumption of the education (really guardianship) of his nephews, and the authorship of *De doctrina christiana.*

2. He was not excepted in the Act of Indemnity in August 1660, despite his position in Cromwell's government and his political publications and despite some apparent opposition to his not being excepted. An order for his arrest was given but then squelched until around October when he was imprisoned until 15 December,

apparently through some unexpected reemergence of the order and action by an uninformed officer of the law. His release was effected by payment of a small fine, negotiated, it would seem, by various friends such as Andrew Marvell.

3. It is interesting to note that the review of Jane Lane's book *The Reign of King Covenant* in *Seventeenth-Century News* (Summer 1957), makes the following pertinent observation: "The book is of signal importance for an understanding of the English Puritan Revolution . . . The frequent Scottish practice of protecting family interests by aligning different members of a family on opposite sides makes one ask how far Englishmen did the same. It is noteworthy, for example, that the Miltons managed to have secure feet in both camps. Was it an accident that on the eve of a revolution John Milton rather precipitately married into a royalist family? Was his hospitality to the Powells the result of an agreement for mutual security? At first the idea seems preposterous. Then one remembers that later on John's brother Christopher became a Roman Catholic favored by James II & that their nephews were more royalist than Puritan."

4. The prejudiced account of John Phillips and his numerous works by William Godwin is a strident example.

5. See Masson, I, 40, 98, 103, 60, 243, 327, 562, 564, 631, 735 and n; II, 72, 488–90; III, 485–86, 632–33 and n, 674n; VI, 449, 727–28, 735–40, 742–43, 761–63.

6. French, *Life Records,* I, 11. Milton recorded his brother's birth in the family Bible thus: "Christofer Milton was born on Friday about a month before Christmass at 5 in the morning 1615"; that is, 24 November 1615 (French, I, 9). But note that Christopher himself gets the year date wrong three times in the depositions dated 25 May 1658, 17 February 1663, and 13 May 1672. Since Christopher's memory is so important to what we think we know about John, such errors cast the reports of this lawyer into doubt: this cannot be overstressed. Documents are referenced here from French; those not recorded there are cited in full usually from the printed editions of the original sources. References to French are given in parentheses immediately after the item under discussion. While a number of additions to Milton's life records appear in Gordon Campbell's *A Milton Chronology,* none alters our knowledge of Christopher and his family.

7. John Peile in *Biographical Register of Christ's College,* I, 406, gives the entrance date to Christ's incorrectly as 14 February, and the date cited for entrance into the Inner Temple. French (I, 257–58) lists Christopher's entry into the Inner Temple as November 1631, providing as sources Students Admitted to the Inner Temple, 1547–1660, 270, and Edward Foss[e], 446, but later altering it to between this date and October 1632 (V, 378). Apparently unaware of this notation from Peile, French questions Ernest Brennecke's citation of the 22 September 1632 date, 121, which, however, was probably quoted from Masson, I, 562. Masson wrote that he had taken the date from the Inner Temple books. John and J.A. Venn give admission as 30 June 1632, III, 193.

8. Masson, I, 244.

9. Christopher was restored to commons at the Inner Temple, 26 November 1637 (French, I, 351), perhaps signifying his absence just before when he may have been in Horton.

10. John Webber was buried at St. Clement Danes, 5 June 1632; his will was proved on 11 July 1632, including a residuary legacy to his daughter of a half share

in a lease of lands in Devonshire (I, 358). According to Perceval Lucas, the Webbers came from Broadhempston, Devon.

The parish of St. Clement Danes, lying just outside the City but near the Inns of Chancery, was an important location with relatively rich residents. It seems to have had a conservative religious climate, and even during the Puritan era clergymen of the State Church (those still adhering to episcopacy) reappeared to conduct services in the church. See Tai Liu, 132–33.

11. See Parker, 814 n90. Parker's biography extensively updates and corrects Masson's work and incorporates French's. Gordon Campbell's edition of this biography (1996) provides recent scholarship and discussion on various matters. The more recent large biography of Milton by Lewalski does not engage new biographical information. If Christopher were not born at this time, July-August 1642 would appear to be the likeliest time. But as Parker conjectures John Milton would not, in November 1637, have been able to contemplate a move to the Inns of Court, or early in 1638 his continental sojourn, unless some adequate arrangement for his father had been made. The marriage of Christopher and Thomasin and their moving to Horton around the time of the mother's death or soon afterward provides a solution.

12. Questions have been raised as to why the father did not live with his daughter Anne after his wife's death. First off, he remained at his own home in Horton in 1637–1640; it was Christopher who joined him. Anne Agar at this time had a husband, two young sons from her first marriage, and at least one daughter from her second. Secondly, while the date of her death is unknown, evidence suggests that she died after 1637 but before 1639; see chapter 3 here.

13. See HMC, Eleventh Report, Appendix, Part VII, 209.

14. Based on Phillips's statement in "The Life," vi. The Commissioner of Excise is the same as the Commissioner of Sequestration; BL MS Harleian 6802, f. 280v, calls Christopher "his Ma^{ts} Com:^{r} of Excise for the County of Somerset at Wells this present," dated 7 November 1644, and PRO document SP Dom 23/187, p. 193, says, "he was a Commissioner for the Kinge, vnder the greate seale of Oxford, for sequestringe the Parliaments ffreinds of three Countyes, and afterwards even to Exeter," dated 25 August 1646.

15. In the early, 1640s Parliament established a system of heavy taxation, including forced loans and confiscations of goods and land; it levied a new, more remunerative, and fairer assessment (for the commoners), and imposed an excise on the sale of several articles of common consumption. A Committee for Compounding (that is, the Committee of Parliament for the Composition of Property Owned by Delinquents) was formed to compound with those who had not paid the assessment (that is, to come to some kind of agreement for payment other than prosecution). As a Parliamentary committee, it was particularly concerned with Royalists' payments and compromises.

16. See Parker, 748–49 n11.

17. See an affidavit from 16 May 1646 (French, II, 144–45).

18. This information comes from Joseph Hunter (writing in the earlier nineteenth century) citing British Library, MS Additional 24501, f. 23, but Parker (877 n28) speculates that this may be an error for Mrs. Isabel Webber, Christopher's mother-in-law. Payment to one's mother-in-law seems strange, however. The alleged original has not been located.

19. Naming practices, to be cited again in a moment, would name the first-born son with the father's name; thus Christopher's birth in late 1637 or early 1638 is reasonable. If the unnamed son buried in March 1639 had been named Christopher, the next born son should have been he who was named Christopher, thus the suggestion of his birth in July-August 1642.

20. French, II, 144, from PRO MS SP 23/187, p. 199, where Christopher is cited as of London; Composition Papers, Series 2, XIV, 193, gives 20 April as the date and Reading as Christopher's residence. Reference here is to the Solemn League and Covenant, to which he subscribed. It was enacted in 1643 between England and Scotland to maintain the Scottish Reformed Church and the reformation of religion in England, which was to root out Catholicism and prelacy. This is not the Oath of Engagement that was signed by Charles I on 26 December 1646, and came to precipitate the second Civil War. Taking the Covenant was expected of all in any kind of official capacity; if Christopher had Catholic predilections when he took the oath (1646), the oath was expedient.

21. At least a check mark against his name in the record may be so interpreted.

22. See Phillips's "Life," vi ("his composition made by the help of his Brothers Interest, with the then prevailing Power"). It seems unlikely that John Milton's "help" would have been political in 1646; perhaps Phillips means financial help. But then why was the fine lowered? A note added to the document of 25 August and the report of John Man, p. 16, confirm the amount of the actual fine.

23. Cookson, 82. Interestingly, Roger Young, second son of Milton's tutor Thomas Young, became the pastor of St. Nicholas.

24. For four of these records see French, III, 324, 338, 366, and V, 469. The last concerns a bill of John Trott in 1652 and 1653; Christopher answers this "further" on 16 May 1653. Assignment of the bill from John Raven to Thomas Willis in 1649 is denied, and the significance of answers from Willis and Christopher's brother-in-law Thomas Agar in 1652 and 1653 is uncertain. Note that Willis figures in a certificate along with Dr. Luke Rugeley (Agar's brother-in-law), dated 23 September 1668; see chapter 2, n74. Willis was a friend of John Agar (Thomas's brother) as their petition for passage in 1644 indicates; see chapter 2, p. 60.

25. Her petition to the Committee for Compounding dated 20 October 1652 in the Duchy Court of Westminster (see French, III, 265–66) was witnessed by Anthony Wilson, who was Milton's neighbor in Petty France at this time. There are two documents, the petition and a summons to witnesses to appear before the commissioners, both attested to by Wilson "gent." St. Margaret's Overseer Rate Book, E166 (1652) through E170 (1656) lists his rate at 1 shilling, with a total assessment of 4 shillings. He may be the Anthony Wilson buried at St. Margaret, Westminster, on 8 January 1666; see "The Registers of St. Margaret's, Westminster Part III," 5.

26. Hyde Clarke, 536–37, 566.

27. A manuscript letter that is undated, unsigned, undirected, and uncertain of meaning, found with materials concerning John Milton has been noted (IV, 199–200); its leave-taking says, "J am Yor euer lo: bor."

28. Copinger, VII, 112–13. The later provenance of this manor is not taken up by Copinger.

29. G.R. Clarke, 438; see Vincent B. Redstone for further information about Sparrow.

30. *Inner Temple Records,* III, 1.

31. They were Thomas Foster and Sir Richard Hopkins, 1 May and 3 November 1664; *Inner Temple Records,* III, 23, 24. Later he was attendant for Christopher Goodfellowe, 8 November 1668 (III, 52).

32. *Inner Temple Records,* III, 36; also 6 May 1666 (III, 39), 5 November 1666 (III, 40), and 28 April 1667 (III, 45). See French, IV, 400–01, 421, 426, 433. French prints a bill and two receipts for payment of accounts incurred (IV, 432–33). The first appears in the printed *Inner Temple Records,* III, 53; the second does not appear; and the third III, 65 (which French repeats on IV, 450).

33. Vincent B. Redstone, 137.

34. Suffolk Green Books, 165. His tax was nine shillings.

35. A Justice of the Peace was appointed by commission of the King and held office at his pleasure; he would have to take the oath of office and of the King's supremacy. Christopher also acted as Justice of the Peace in 1680, and as Deputy Recorder through the charter of July 1685, both noted in the next paragraph; according to Richard Canning, 60, it was affirmed that "Robert Brooke . . . and Christopher Milton . . . may and shall be our Justices . . . to preserve and keep Our Peace" (French, IV, 268). See Trotter, 201–31, for duties and responsibilities of Justices of the Peace. After 1660 the Court of Quarter Sessions—after Easter, after the translation of St. Thomas (3 July), after the Feast of St. Michael (29 September), and after Epiphany (6 January)—was held every year except for 1688; usually sessions lasted three days.

36. Lilian J. Redstone, 137; Wodderspoon, 121.

37. British Library, MS Additional 19142, f. 79v.

38. *Inner Temple Records,* III, 51, 84 (2), 94, 95 (2), 96, 100 (2), 101, 102, 105 (2), 106 (2), 110, 111, 122, 123, 131, 132, 137, 146, 159 (2), 161, 162, 163, 173, 174, 175 (2), 185, 186 (2), 201, 203 (2), 206, 218, 230; these sittings occur between 24 May 1668 and 26 November 1685. Records of the Inner Temple of 25 November 1666 also cite him (French, IV, 427, not in Inderwick; however, compare *Inner Temple Records,* III, 242 and 249). He also requested special admission for John Haughfell, "in respect of his reading," on 22 November 1668 (III, 59).

39. Matthews, 205.

40. HMC, *Manuscripts of the Duke of Buccleuch & Queensbury,* I, 253–54.

41. G.R. Clarke, 59. The Recorder is given as Sir Robert Brooke and Town Clerk as Thomas Brook.

42. He is listed in various editions of Edward Chamberlayne's *The Second Part of the Present State of England* and reprinted in *Angliæ Notitia: or, The Present State of England Compleat;* e.g., see the thirteenth edition of the former, 1687, 105 for the Court of the Exchequer (Sir Christopher Milton, Baron), the sixteenth edition of the latter, 1687, 172 (Sir Christopher Milton, Kt.), and the seventeenth edition, 1692, 148 for "other Sergeants at Law" (Christopher Milton, Esq.).

43. See HMC, *Manuscripts of the House of Lords,* Vol. II (New Series), for 1695–97, 402, under date of 6 March 1696/7. (See also remarks on the Bulstrodes in the Introduction and in chapter 2.)

44. See HMC, *Manuscripts of the Marquess of Ormonde,* New Series, Vol. VIII, 353.

45. Evelyn, IV, 514. The Test Act (1673) debarred Dissenters and imposed heavy fines for infractions; it was aimed at Catholic officeholders and influence.

Christopher's not passing the Test implies much about his religion; at the least it suggests that he was not an adherent of the Church of England, regardless of possible variations thereon. We also should remember that Edward Phillips was in Evelyn's employ in 1663 and thus Evelyn's knowledge of both uncles may have been enhanced by discussions with Edward.

46. The ascription to Christopher of *The State Of Church-Affairs In this Island of Great Britain Under the Government of the Romans, And British Kings* (London, 1687) has no cogent basis for acceptance; it has also been ascribed to John Milton. The author is clearly Roman Catholic but the work is influenced heavily by *The History of Britain,* thus perhaps showing reason for the ascriptions.

47. *Inner Temple Records,* III, 249. A portrait of Sir Christopher appears in a stained glass window in the Hall of the Inner Temple (V, 293).

48. Register, 167.

49. See HMC, *MSS of the Marquess of Ormond,* N.S. 8 (1920), 353.

50. Let it also be noted that Christopher and his children are said to have used the same coat of arms as his brother, which appears to be that of their father. See *A Display of Heraldry by John Guillim, Pursuivant at Arms. The Sixth Edition* (London, 1724), 210; of course, this does not appear in the seventeenth-century editions of Guillim (1610 ff.). Specifically, Joan Corder reports the arms of "Milton of Ipswich" as "Arg. an eagle with two heads disp. Gu. armed Az.," VII, 119). This has differences from what is reported as the father's coat of arms; see French, V, 198–200.

51. Register of St. Margaret's Church, Westminster, 615.

52. Inderwick, III, 74. Yet it seems strange that "the eldest son" would have entered the Inner Temple after his three brothers (see later) if indeed he were the "eldest" (but see later).

53. Ibid., III, 119.

54. Masson, VI, 763. The source of some of Masson's statements is not known. A money warrant for £144/13/6 to "Thomas Milton, gent., deputy clerk of the Crown: without account: for fees and charges due to himself and others in passing two commissions appointing Treasury Commissioners" was passed on 15 December 1679 and paid the next day. See *Calendar of Treasury Books* (VI), pp. 305 and 310. British Library MS Egerton 2387 records the signature of Thomas Milton, Deputy Clerk, to the Roll of Fines in 1681. On 15 June 1683, Henry Guy wrote to him as Deputy Clerk of the Crown, to send to Mr. Langford at the Treasury Chambers a list of the several Lords Lieutenant of England and counties under their respective care (ibid., VII, Part II, p. 841).

55. Bannerman, *St. Mary le Bone,* 26. Inaccurately Charles Fleetwood, William's brother and friend to John Milton, has been identified as Martha's father (the error appears in Masson among other places). R.W.B., *Notes & Queries* XI, No. 7 (8 February 1913): 113, corrects this but confuses who Charles was. Sir William, George, and Charles were sons of Sir Miles Fleetwood. George became a Swedish general and was made a Baron by Queen Christina. Charles was a member of the House of Commons from Marlborough in 1646; a member of the Council of State in 1651–59; Commander-in-Chief in Ireland in 1651; and allegedly Oliver Cromwell's nominee to succeed him as he approached death in 1658. (He had been Colonel in the New Model Army, Lieutenant-General, and one of the Major-Generals of 1655.) Charles's

second wife was Cromwell's daughter Bridget whom he married in 1652; she died in 1662. He was one of the twenty nonregicides excepted in the Act of Indemnity, yet through the influence of the Earl of Lichfield and others, he escaped punishment but with "perpetual incapacitation from all office of trust." He had not taken part in the trial of Charles I and, curiously and suspiciously, he was adjudged not to be politically dangerous. More indicative of popular pro-Royalist sentiment are such verses in *Rump Poems* as

> If in utter darknesse there should be a failing
> Of Horror, the *Rump* may furnish it with
> Squire *Fleetwood* to help out the weeping and wailing,
> And Sir *William Brereton* for gnashing of teeth.
> ("The Rump roughly but righteously hand-led," p. 65)

and

> Charles Fleetwood is first and leads up the Van,
> Whose counterfeit Zeal turns Cat in the pan,
> And dame *Sankey* will swear he's a valiant man,
> *Oh blessed Reformation.*
> ("The Committee of Safety," p. 99)

The Fleetwood family clearly confirm Jane Lane's remarks (see n3) concerning Royalist and Parliamentarian associations within the same family. Those Royalist connections saved Charles, who died 4 October 1692 and was buried in Bunhill Fields cemetery.

56. French gives December (V, 296), and Parker says, "November (possibly December)," 1176 n134. An inventory of Thomas's estate dated 27 October 1694 accompanies an answer to a suit brought against them in 1695 by William Hoskins (see later). Martha married Dr. William Coward of Ipswich, licensed 27 May 1696, and proved her brother William's undated will (but with a codicil of 6 February 1699/1700) on 2 March 1699/1700; see Prerogative Court of Canterbury, Noel 46. Coward's will, dated 16 March 1724 and proved 20 April 1724, left various items and money to his "Loveing wife Martha" (Ipswich and East Suffolk Record Office, Beccles Register 1723–27, f. 3). No children are mentioned in the will. Does that mean that none of her children with Thomas survived her? Martha's date of death or burial has not been discovered.

Coward translated John Dryden's "Absalom and Achitophel," which is pervasively influenced by *Paradise Lost*, into Latin in 1682, and wrote *Licentia Poetica Discuss'd: or, the True Test of Poetry. Without which it is impossible to judge of, or compose, a correct English poem. To which are added, Critical Observations on the Principal, Ancient and Modern Poets. Viz. Homer, Horace, Virgil, Milton, Waller, Cowley, Dryden, &c. as frequently liable to just censure. A Poem* (London, 1709). Among his observations on Milton are discussions of rhyme, blank verse, versification and prosody, and language, with quotations from Milton's epic and Dryden's version, *The State of Innocence*. Coward speaks of the advantage of blank verse.

57. I thank for the foregoing information Dr. Carol Barton and Mr. Philip Birger, former Curator of the Milton Cottage.

It might be noted, too, that John Adams in *Index Villaris* places the parishes of St. Nicholas and St. Margaret in Bury St. Edmonds. Has Rogers done some kind of research, but faulty research, in order to place Thomas Milton there? These ancient parishes are duly noted under Ipswich in Youngs's *Guide*.

58. *Inner Temple Records*, III, 3.

59. *Catalogus Graduatorum.*

60. *Inner Temple Records*, III, 49.

61. Register, 153: "Cristofer Sonn of Mr. Melton esquire."

62. *Inner Temple Records*, III, 21. This identification is to be rejected; the record gives "John Melton," and the editor, F.A. Inderwick, gives no reference in the index but instead lists this entry under Christopher Milton, the father.

63. Cambridge University, *Catalogus Graduatorum.* At admission he was said to be 15, an error for 25? Or was he born in 1652, not in 1643 as reported?

64. Register, 154. Although the entry is "John Melton gent.," there is no problem with the spelling for most of the entries in the register concerned with Christopher, including his own burial, employ the spelling "Melton." John is called "gent." probably because he was Christopher's son. The term, we would think, would not have been applied to him if he were only of the age of a student at Pembroke.

We can dismiss from connection with the poet's family the marriage of a John Milton to an Anne East on 13 December 1670 (*Calendar of Marriage Licences Issued by the Faculty Office* [British Record Society: London, 1905], 54).

65. Aubrey, in Darbishire, 8; I reference Bodleian MS Aubrey 8. See Lucas, 21–22. See also the sometimes erroneous genealogy in British Library MS Harleian 5802, f. 164. William Godwin includes as Appendix I Aubrey's minutes with the genealogy given on p. 347. However, it is frequently inexact or incomplete; e. g., Richard is not noted.

66. *Inner Temple Records*, III, 49.

67. Ibid., III, 109. He apparently was the Richard Milton who was taxed for two hearths from Cockfield in Babergh, Suffolk, in 1674; Christopher Milton was taxed for nine hearths from St. Margaret, Ipswich. See n34 and pp. 77 and 165 respectively. The "Paper-buildings" were lodgings, eastward from the garden of the Inner Temple, built after 1609.

68. Chetham Society Historical Remains, 18; see also "Sir Christopher Milton and Richard Milton."

69. *Calendar of Treasury Books*, 1685–1689, Part 3, 1803–05.

70. The marriage of Richard Milton and Anne Garland, therefore, on 24 June 1706 cannot be pertinent here (*Calendar of Marriage Licences issued by the Faculty Office*).

71. I quote Lucas; the italics indicate deletions. French (V, 305–07) prints the Latin and an English translation. See Prerogative Court of Canterbury, Administration Act Books, 1713, ff. 184v-86.

72. Register, 157.

73. *Allegations for Marriage Licences*, 165. See chapter 2 for other references to St. Sepulchre.

74. Prerogative Court of Canterbury, 74 Buckingham; see French, V, 311–12. It would seem to be that she was older than her sisters and thus the 1661 birth date cannot be true.

75. Masson, VI, 763. The various locations cited here are not really far apart, just outside the walled City and part of London today, although they appear to be quite distant in references from the seventeenth and eighteenth centuries. Highgate is in the area called Camden Town, north and slightly west of the City, within the parish of St. Pancras; Lower Holloway is in Islington, north of the City and not far from Highgate. Spitalfields where Elizabeth Foster formerly lived was built over the fields behind St. Mary's Hospital, Bishopsgate, around 1700, east of the City, in the area called Stepney. It was governmentally incorporated in 1729.

76. Most of the materials concerned with Anne, Mary, and Catherine are discussed from Lucas, who gives no printed sources for his remarks. All unprinted sources that he cites are given here.

77. Prerogative Court of Canterbury, 126 Edmunds.

78. Has someone writing to the *Gentleman's Magazine* simply picked up some of this information from *Lloyd's* or such source and altered it? A Martha Milton was married to a John Wandsor at St. Botolph, Bishopsgate, on 25 April 1719. Dr. Thomas Secker (1693–1768) was a medical doctor who later took holy orders and became Bishop of Bristol and of Oxford, then Dean of St. Paul's in 1750 and Archbishop of Canterbury in 1758. He has been labelled "Jesuistical."

79. "The Life of Milton," I, lxxxiii–lxxxiv, in the seventh edition of *Paradise Lost* in 1770.

80. The legal difficulties with the term "next of kin" are discussed in Henry Swinburne's *A Treatise of Testaments and Last Wills . . . The Sixth Edition, corrected and very much enlarged* (In the Savoy [London], MDCCXLIII), 490–94.

81. See Parker, 1176 n138; Richardson, xciv; and Register, 231.

82. Williamson, 160; the occasion of the exhibit is referred to as the Milton Tercentenary.

83. See French V, 39, 132–33, and Parker, 1096, 1293.

84. A problem in classifying one's religious affiliations or beliefs during this period, aside from the rampant sectarianism, is the antagonism toward Roman Catholicism from all political groups, the treatment of those who were professed recusants, and the kind of closet Catholicism that one can infer in the courts of Charles I and Charles II. Queen Henrietta Maria, of course, was a French Catholic with a basically French Catholic retinue, and Charles II ran into many religious confrontations in the confused days of the 1660s and 1670s, when such as the Conventicle Act, the Five-Mile Act, and the Test Act were passed. Thus, Christopher's connections with parishes of State Church affiliation may not be salient. He would seem to be a kind of a "Church Papist," that is, one "who obediently appeared at the compulsory Sunday services of the re-established Church of England, but nevertheless continued to adhere tenaciously and instinctively to the faith in which they had been baptised, to the Catholicism of their ancestors" (Walsham, 1). As noted before he had connections in a Catholic stronghold, Reading; the delinquency warrant there (1643) and later the lack of satisfaction the Committee for Compounding exhibited iterate the possibility; the relations with his son Thomas, an adherent of the State

Church, and with his son Richard, a Roman Catholic, invite pertinent implications; and there is the matter of Charles II's royal charter in 1685 and the advancements Christopher received with the ascent of James II.

85. See *The Publications of the Harleian Society*, VIII (1873), 402.

86. See HMC, Seventh Report (1879), Part I, 244.

87. Ipswich and East Suffolk Record office, Ref. No. XI/5/4.2.

88. Ibid., but Ref. No. XI/5.4.1. The mischronological order of these two documents in the Record Office should be noted.

89. A Thomas Milton, widower, married Martha Spencer, widow, of Coleman Street on 14 July 1690 (Parish Register of St. James Church, Duke's Place). Somehow has there been a confusion of different cases reported in this document with reference instead to this couple? Interestingly, Richard Milton, scrivener (son of Thomas Milton, yeoman, of Cheltenham, Gloucester), was an apprentice of Milton's father from around 1614. Documents record his activities during the years 1621–1636, one of which was his witnessing of the will of Francis Spencer, a brewer, buried at St. Giles, Cripplegate, on 7 April 1636. Both surnames are commonplace, but perhaps there was descent on both sides of these families leading eventually to this marriage. The only Mrs. Martha Spencer recorded in Foster's London Marriage Records is a widow of St. Paul, Covent Garden, about 26, who married John Stonhouse of Radley, Berks, gentleman, bachelor, about 29, on 10 October 1668 at the chapel of Lincoln's Inn.

90. *Cases Argued and Decreed In the High Court of Chancery*, 192. Warton's statements cited above may have come from such a work as Henry Swinburne's noted above. See, for evidence, nuncupative wills are "commonly made when the Testator is very sick, weak, and past all Hope of recovery" (58); however, it "may be made not only by the proper Motion of the Testator, but also at the Interrogation of another" (59); yet it must be made "before a sufficient Number of Witnesses. . . . [H]e must name his Executor, and declare his whole Mind before Witnesses" (58). "But it is not sufficient for the Testator to leave a Sound in the Ears of the Witnesses, unless he do leave some Understanding also of his Will and Meaning" (354).

91. Cyriack Skinner (the Anonymous Biographer) confirms much of this in his life written prior to Phillips's: "His moderate Estate left him by his Father was through his good Oeconomie sufficient to maintain him. Out of his Secretary's Salary hee had sav'd two thousand pounds, which beeing lodg'd in the Excise, and that Bank failing upon the Restoration, hee utterly lost. Beside which, and the ceasing of his Imploiment hee had no damage by that change of Affairs" (Bodleian MS Wood D.4, ff. 144v-44r [mismarked second 143]). Wood (I, Fasti, 266) copies this: "The Estate which his Father left him was but indifferent, yet by his frugality he made it serve him and his. Out of his Secretary's Salary he saved 2000 l. which being lodg'd in the Excise, and that bank failing upon his Majesty's Restoration, he utterly lost that Sum." Wood also notes the loss of the house on Bread Street in the Great Fire, which he says "was all the real Estate that he had then left."

The Excise was instituted in 1643 under Charles I and continued with even additional taxes during the Interregnum. But the dismissal of the Long Parliament and the dissolution of bonds led to an ineffective control over economic affairs. Slingsby Bethel's *The Worlds Mistake in Oliver Cromwell* is one account that contrasts the economic changes felt by the people. The problems in maintaining the Excise Act in the period immediately before the Restoration can be seen in reports in the *CSPD* (Commonwealth, Vol. XII), on pp. 42 (under 1 June 1658) and 385 (under 22 June 1659); see also Vol. XIII, 389 ([10] March 1660), 437 (11 May 1660), 445 (25 March 1660), 446 (26 March 1660). A new Act was proposed and passed giving additional powers to the Excise Commissioners on 7 and 8 September 1660, and see 26 September and 24 December 1660 (*CSPD*, Charles II, Vol. 1, pp. 260, 261, 276, 423).

A complication exists in the statement in "To The Reader," appearing in *Mr John Miltons Character of the Long Parliament* (1681). The author of the statement is uncertain and may be whoever saw the text through the press (with its numerous alterations from what is found in the manuscript "Digression") or the publisher, Henry Brome. Suggestions that the editor was James Tyrrell or the Earl of Anglesey, Arthur Annesley, are most unlikely. First off, the statement refers, it would seem, to the time of 1670 when *History of Britain* was published; then the writer, who seems not to know Milton personally, says, "It is reported . . . that Mr. *Milton* had lent most of his Personal Estate upon the Publick Faith; which when he somewhat earnestly and warmly pressed to have restored [observing how all in Offices had not only feathered their own Nests, but had enricht many of their Relations and Creatures, before the Publick Debts were discharged] after a long and chargeable Attendance, met with very sharp Rebukes; upon which at last despairing of any success in this Affair, he was forced to return from them poor and friendless, having spent all his Money, and wearied all his Friends." While this corroborates Skinner's and Phillips's reports for the period of the Restoration, it also implies that Milton's loss and attempts to recoup investments were well known. The final sentence in "To The Reader" is a political and accusative barb: "And he had not probably mended his worldly condition in those days, but by performing such Service for them, as afterwards he did, for which scarce anything would appear too great" (A2v; reverse italics). "Them" apparently means "his Friends," who, in the political context of this "digression," are those who became or were "Whigs"; neither after 1660 nor after 1670 did Milton perform "such Service" except for *Of True Religion* and/or *Declaration*. The writer would thus be identified with one of Tory persuasion, perhaps a Catholic, and almost certainly a Jacobite. Nonetheless, "as afterwards he did" seems to say he mended his worldly condition (financially) by "such Service," although there is nothing to back up that imputation. Von Maltzahn has argued that the "editor" of this *Character,* as well as the writer of the prefatory statement, may have been Sir Roger L'Estrange, who fits such identification on all counts.

92. Parker (638) includes Milton's need for money in the last year of his life as a reason for his translating *A Declaration, or Letters Patents of the Election of this present King of Poland, John the Third, Elected on the 22d of May last past* (1674): "Aylmer . . . doubtless offered Milton a small sum to provide an English version. Milton certainly needed the money. . . ." Doubtless, rather, it exists because of Milton himself, politically motivated amidst the exclusionary action that was fomenting at that time, leading to the first Bill of Exclusion in 1679. As Nicholas von Maltzahn writes, "Milton also anticipates Whig concerns in *A Declaration, or Letters Patents* (1674), which contests the Catholic succession by proposing the merits of elective kingship. As Exclusion became an issue, publications favouring elective monarchy came under severe scrutiny: hence the value of this 'neutral' translation of a Polish advertisement for the value of such an election" (231), and in a note remarks, "The pertinence of

Milton's translation of the *Declaration* to English politics is therefore quite clear."—
see "The Whig Milton, 1667–1700."

93. See David H. Stevens, 7–13; Parker, 870–74 nn14–23; and Roland Mushat
Frye.

94. In 1653 the Barebones Parliament abolished church weddings; yet on 22
October 1656 the first banns were published for Milton's second marriage to
Katherine Woodcock at St. Mary the Virgin, Aldermanbury; the second on the twenty-
seventh, and the third on 3 November. On 12 November they were married by Sir
John Dethicke in a civil ceremony (perhaps at the Guildhall). Thus Milton abided by
Parliament's order, but followed the procedures for marriage of his religion. It seems
logical that in 1642 such procedures were also followed. Further, marriages were not
allowed by the Church in the period between Rogation Sunday (the Sunday before
Rogation Day, the third day preceeding Ascension Day, which is forty days after Easter) and Trinity Sunday (the Sunday after Pentecost, or Whitsunday, which is the
seventh Sunday after Easter). In 1642, Easter was on 10 April and these interdicted
dates were thus, 16 May through 5 June. The saying of the banns may therefore have
occurred on 12, 19, and 26 June, and the marriage sometime shortly after that (in
very late June or early July).

95. He is not Sir Richard Powle (sometimes Powell), Knight of the Bath, whose
activities after the Restoration included appointment, signed by James, Duke of York
(who, of course, became James II), on 20 December 1667, to the Commission for
regulating the expenses of the Household of his Royal Highness the Duke of York.
See HMC, Eighth Report, Part I, p. 280, reporting the manuscripts owned by Lord
Braybrooke retained at Audley End. This Sir Richard Powle was a member of the
Royal Society. Probably referring to the member of the Royal Society, Robert Hooke
has a report on the health of "Powell" and his wife on 12 March 1678/9-*Diary*, 402.

However, he is referred to in "The Diary of Henry, Earl of Clarendon" on 9 May
1688: "The Queen-dowager's motion was again put off, Baron Powell not being well.
And my Lord Chief Baron said, this was a cause of great weight; and therefore it was
fit to have a full court: and so it was left sine die"; see *Correspondence of Henry Hyde,
Earl of Clarendon*, II, 171. A letter from the Lord Chancellor, Sir George Jeffreys,
Chief Justice of the King's Bench and Baron of Wemme, to the Earl, dated 27 May
1686 (ibid., I, 409) recommends "your old acquaintance Mr. Richard Powell, because I apprehended him to be a person both loyal and one for whom your Lordship
had a friendship," as one of the Irish judges. He would thus seem to be the "Mr.
Powell" who came to Windsor on 16 December 1688 with Sir Robert Howard (Milton's
friend and Dryden's brother-in-law) "and had been a long time in private with the
Prince" (James Stuart, the Old Pretender); see ibid., II, 228.

96. HMC, Manuscripts of the Marquess of Ormonde, New Series, Vol. IV, p. 448.

97. *CSPD*, William III, July–December 1695; see Addenda, 1689–1695.

98. Poole Powell, a second son of Milton's brother-in-law, was admitted to the
Inner Temple as "eldest son of Powell of the bench, specially admitted as of Easter
Term, 1682" (III, 207), but this is entered under the Parliament of 6 November
1684. Perhaps "eldest" here is again a loosely used term or perhaps it is recognizing
the brother's death prior to November 1684.

99. *A Catalogue of the Names of the Dukes, Marquesses, Earles and Lords,* under "A
Copy of a List of all the Cavaliers of his Majesties Marching Army," shows "Captaine

Fleetwood," that is, "William Fleetwood, afterwards a colonel in the royal Army. Son of Sir William Fleetwood of Aldwinkle, co Northampton, cupbearer to James I. and Charles I, and Comptroller of Woodstock park. He was half brother to George Fleetwood and Charles Fleetwood the Parliamentary officers" (see Peacock's edition, 10 and n50).

Chapter 2

1. This chapter presents the combined research and writing of my friend and collaborator Dr. Rose Clavering and me. Much of the work reflected here and many of the insights are due to her diligence and analytic skills.

2. [Edward Hatton], *A New View of London*, II, 567. The Register of burials at the Temple Church records that "Thomas Agar, gent., and clark of the Crown Office, was buried out *of the Midle Temple in the long walke* the fourth of November, 1673" (*Inner Temple Records*, III, 449). Another citation from the Inner Temple tells us that in the Christmas Account Book for 1667–68, at the 25 December Christmas Parliament, an order was passed "that Agar be admitted into Commons" (III, 55); specific identification is lacking.

3. Sir Charles Young supplied the information that Agar attended St. Paul's—Milton pedigree accompanying "The Life of John Milton" by John Mitford, *The Works of John Milton* (London, 1851), I. Agar was some eleven years Milton's senior.

4. Masson, I, 637–38; II, 100–01; VI, 763, 770–75. Hopwood, 124, reports his death on 3 November 1673.

5. Hopwood, II, 850; and Bannerman, All Hallows, Bread Street, 188.

6. Hatton, I, 131–32.

7. *Calendar of the Proceedings of the Committee for Compounding*, II, 1453; hereafter, *CPCC*.

8. Dugdale, *The Visitation of the County of Yorke*, 217.

9. Burke and Burke, I, 8.

10. Sir Bernard Burke, I. Burke also records a different coat of arms for another Lancashire Agard, but the records of visitations to the county show no Agards.

11. Joseph Hunter, *Hunter's Pedigrees*, 2–3; and J.W. Walker, 2.

12. *Collectanea Genealogica*, ed. Joseph Foster, III, 4. Hereafter, *CG*, with subject and editor noted, if different.

13. Dugdale, *The Visitation of Derbyshire*, 16.

14. Tilley, II, 310.

15. H. Sydney Grazebrook, in *Collections for a History of Staffordshire*, III, 5, 27. These collections will henceforth be cited as *CHS*, with editors noted if different.

16. Erdeswick, 230–31.

17. Carter, in *CHS*, 280–81.

18. G. Wrottesley, "Extracts" in *CHS*, 129.

19. Carter, 291.

20. *CHS*, "The Staffordshire Sheriffs," 318.

21. Carter, 287.

22. Shaw, I, 146.

23. Jeayes, "Calendar of the Longdon, Lichfield and Other Staffordshire Charters," in *CHS*, 112; and Shaw, I, 212.

24. Burne, in *CHS*, 121.

25. Wrottesley and Boyd, in *CHS*, XII, 233.

26. PRO, *Index of Chancery Proceedings* (Series II) #7, 6.

27. Boyd, in *CHS*, XVI, 206.

28. Glover, I, Appendix, 20.

29. Metcalf, 171.

30. Cox, III, 263.

31. Ibid.

32. Tilley, II, 34.

33. Cox, III, 265.

34. Jeayes, *Descriptive Catalogue*, 290.

35. Cox, III, 263. Masses were to be said for the souls of the founder; his wife Joan; George, Duke of Clarence; William, Lord Hastings; Catherine his wife and their children; Walter, Lord Mountjoy; John Stanley; Lady Elizabeth his wife and their children; and Sir John Ferrers and his wife Matilda.

36. Shaw, I, 146.

37. Tilley, III, 17.

38. Shaw, I, 146.

39. Tilley, II, 34.

40. Cox, III, 266.

41. Jeayes, *Descriptive Catalogue*, 344.

42. Tilley, II, 34.

43. Glover, I, Appendix, 21.

44. There is a record of an "Arthur Agarde" admitted to Gray's Inn on 5 August 1608, but the year is too late; CG, III, 4.

45. Chester, 112; Tilley, I, 123, note; *Biographia Britannica*, I, 64–66; *Index of Wills Proved in the Prerogative Court of Canterbury*, XLIII, 5; *Calendar of State Papers, Domestic Series, of the Reign of Charles I*, II, 305, and IV, 548; and *Alumni Cantabrigienses*, ed. John Venn and J.A. Venn, Part I, I, 9. Hereafter *CSPD*, with years or reigns given, indicates the *Calendar of State Papers, Domestic Series*.

46. Carter, 286; "Members of Parliament—Ireland" in CG, I, 6; and Shaw, I, 145–46.

47. *CHS* (1912), 287.

48. Glover, I, Appendix, 20–21, and PRO, Lists and Indexes, No. IX.

49. Shaw, I, 146–47.

50. Tilley, II, 34.

51. *CPCC*, IV, 2982.

52. *Calendar of Treasury Books*, IV, 697, 792.

53. Dugdale, loc. cit.; Carter, 288; Wrottesley, in *CHS*, 177–78.

54. Shaw, I, *213.

55. Howard, 216. Noted in the pedigree are Luke Rugeley, Thomas Agar's brother-in-law who is named in his will, and Mary, designated as married to Thomas Agar, gentleman.

56. Erdeswick, 231.

57. Boyd, in *CHS*, n.s. VI, Part I, 54, 57, 60.

58. H. Sydney Grazebrook, in *CHS*, V, Part II, 258.

59. *Alumni Cantabrigienses*, Part I, III, 457.

60. A letter from Robert Harsnett to Lord Loughborough refers to "Capt. Ridgley," 20 October 1644; see HMC, *Manuscripts of Reginald Rawdon Hastings*, II, 134. "Captaine Ridgley" is also listed in Peacock, under "A Copy of a List of all the Cavaliers of his Majesties Marching Army" (in 1642) as being in the eighth regiment (14). On the Parliamentary side is "The List of the Troops of Horse, under the Command of William Earle of Bedford," where we find as part of Troop 75, Colonel Simon Rudgley (53). Another letter from Captain Henry Stone and others to William Lenthall, Speaker of the House of Commons, dated 14 November 1645, requests a new sheriff be appointed for Staffordshire in place of Colonel Rugley, "who had been sheriff above a year and a half"; three persons are suggested as fitted for the office. See HMC, *Manuscripts of His Grace the Duke of Portland*, I, 311.

61. Shaw, I, xxxvii, *213. See also the House of Lords, Calendar, 16 February 1641 and 25 May 1641; HMC, Fourth Report, IV, 52 and 67. There are three entries in Chancery Proceedings, Series II, Vol. III, 1621–60, that should be remarked: 1) Bundle 413, No. 144, p. 220, under the Lord High Chancellorship of Sir Thomas Coventry (Lord Coventry), 1626–39, Simon Rugeley, plaintiff, and Edward Eyre and Elizabeth his wife, defendents, over property in Handsacre and Armitage, Staffordshire (note p. 55 above); 2) Bundle 428, No. 70, p. 270, under Sir Edward Littleton, Lord Littleton, 1640–42, Simon Rugeley and Jane his wife, plaintiffs, and Sir John Skeffington, Baronet, of Leicester (cf. above); and 3) Bundle 459, Nos. 81 and 82, p. 365, under the Commissioners, 1642–60, Simon Rugeley, plaintiff, and Hugh Sawyer and others, defendents, over "money matters" in Staffordshire; and a second mutilated document also on "money matters."

62. Idem, n58.

63. A request for a patent attached to the last item states that Rugeley "discovered, and proved by records before the Commissioners of Accounts, marsh lands in cos. Norfolk and Cambridge, drained by the late King. . . ." The Commissioners denied him possession, and now he begs "an order to put me in possession of the land." Further documents from 1654 are cited, and later approving actions will be found (see also *CSPD*, Commonwealth, 1654, VII). The King is reported to have drained these lands in 1638. Perhaps here we have a more personal reason for Simon's opposition to the Crown. But Rugeley did not get satisfaction, and on 4 December 1656 Cromwell caused the Council "to write to the Lord Deputy and Council of Ireland, recommending them to consider Col. Simon Rugeley, and give him a fit employment in Ireland" (*CSPD*, Commonwealth, 1656–57, X, 188). On 10 February 1657 the Protector wrote to his son Lord Henry Cromwell about Rugeley's activities in the Commonwealth cause, "almost to the ruin of his estates," but since he has not received satisfaction "We therefore recommend him to you as well qualified for some employment in Ireland, whether civil or military" to be given lands and to wait for a vacancy if none is immediately available (X, 276–77). Passes for travel were approved for Simon and Captain John Rugeley on 19 February 1657 (X, 587)—to Ireland(?). Payment was made between 30 August 1658 through 11 February 1660, as we learn from HMC, *Manuscripts of the Marquess of Ormonde*, N.S., Vol. III, under "State of the Revenue of Ireland for 1661," "Payments made of arrears to the Foot," 429. (Of the £862/4/10 payment due, £585/0/6 1/2 was paid.) A holograph letter from Simon to Richard Cromwell on 27 September 1658 (Oliver Cromwell had died on 3 September) from London expresses his gratitude for past favors and his prayer that

"Infinite Goodnes to poure down vpon yor Excellence multitudes of blessings both here & hereafter" (BL MS Lansdowne 821, now p. 112).

64. Munk, I, 180. He was the author of Latin verses subscribed "T.R. de Col. Joan." in a collection on the death of Dr. William Whitaker, 1595; see "Epicedia in Obitum ejusdem Theologi a variis Doctis viris Græce et Scripta," in Whitaker's *Opera Theologica*, I, 706–14. Harris F. Fletcher noted that no one has examined the possibility of Whitaker's background significance for Milton through Richard Stock, who was the rector of All Hallows Church. Stock had been a student of Whitaker and translator of one of his treatises. Fletcher suggests that Whitaker's antiprelatical views may emerge in Milton's early prose tracts even more than those of Thomas Cartwright, as often cited. See *The Intellectual Development of John Milton*, I, 55. There is also a holograph letter from Thomas Rugeley, dated 7 June 1595, in BL MS Lansdowne 238, item 3, f. 80.

65. Blagg and Wadsworth, LVIII, 34. See also Nottinghamshire Visitation 1662–1664, XIII, 57. Parker (1479) has the name in error as "D'Oclingsells." Anna Rugeley's grandniece Elizabeth (daughter of Isabella who was the daughter of Anna's brother John) was married to Edward Millington. She was the daughter and heir of "Sam Clud de Aruall" and died in 1653. Millington was the son of the regicide Gilbert Millington, a member of Parliament in the forties and fifties, who signed the warrant for the execution of Charles I. He had been admitted to Lincoln's Inn on 19 October 1614, before Justice of the Peace for Nottinghamshire by 1635 and deputy lieutenant for the county on 1 July 1642. His sentence of death was commuted and he died in prison in Jersey in 1666.

66. Phillimore and Blagg, XII, 61.

67. *Alumni Cantabrigienses*, Part I, III, 457.

68. Munk, I, 267–68.

69. Peile, I, 425.

70. In a letter to John Chamberlain dated 20 October 1607, Sir Rowland Lytton says he has an affection in one of his eyes and requests Chamberlain to tell "Doctor Ridley" about it; see *CSPD*, James I, XXVIII, 375. There are four pertinent records in "The Booke of Accompts of Fraunces Vincenntt, gentleman, receavor for the Righte Hon. Fraunces, Earle of Ruttlande, . . . beginning the xxviij[t] day of Julye, 1614, *anno regii Domini nunc Jacobi Regis duodecimo*" (see HMC, Fourteenth Report, Appendix, Part I, Vol. IV): "Delyverd, the xj[th] day of October, 1614, to Doctor Rudgeley, by my Lorde's comaundemennte, £iiij" (501); "Delyvered, the xiiijth daie of November, 1614, unto Doctor Rydgeley, of Newarke, for vij daies beeinge at Belvoyre with my Lord Roasse, £vij" (502); "Payd, the xix[th] day of September, 1615, to Doctor Ridgley, of Newarke, by my Ladie's comandement, beeing at Garradon with my Lorde Roose when he was not well; payd to him for vj daies, in goulde, £vj xijs" (507); and in the Account of William Sexton, Receiver, "Paymentes of money from my Ladie's comand. Paid, the 24th of August, 1616, to Doctor Ridgsley, for mynistringe phisicq to my Lord Roose at Belvoir, the som of £3" (510). The move to London occurred, therefore, between late 1616 and early 1617. "Dr. Tho. Ridglie a physitian" was assessed for £26 in 1638 from St. Michael, Bassishaw; see Dale, 142 (MS, p. 246a). (A Thomas Ridgeley was assessed £6 from St. Helen's Within Bishopsgate, 69 [MS, p. 131].)

71. Munk, I, 180. Notes to M. Sylvaticus's "Pandectæ Medicinæ" by the "Father

of Dr. Luke Rugeley" are included in British Library MS Sloane 254. Sloane 3310, ff. 135–40, records his medical theses from the seventeenth century.

72. *Alumni Cantabrigienses,* Part I, III, 457.

73. Peile, loc. cit. Milton had been at Cambridge until 3 July 1632, at least, when he received his master's degree. A reference will be found to Luke Rugeley, M.D., dated 2 July 1646, in Dr. John Worthington's almanacs; Worthington became Master of Jesus College and Vice Chancellor of Cambridge University. See *The Diary and Correspondence of Dr. John Worthington,* XIII, 26.

74. Munk, I, 267–68. A letter from Viscount Conway and Kilultagh apparently to his son, dated 26 April 1653, reads: "Your wife called twice to see me when I was from home, but I met her at Lady Northumberland's, where she told me that Dr. Ridgley had given her some medicine for her headache, and I now begin to have some hope, since she will consent to take physic from another" (*CSPD,* Commonwealth, 1652–53, V, 298). And a warrant for a pass "For Edw. Conway, Anne his lady, Fras. Finch, Dr. Ridgley, and 3 servants, Sarah Bennet, Fred. Houbert, and Nich. Bally, beyond seas," was granted on 24 November 1653 (*CSPD,* Commonwealth, 1653–54, VI, 445). These records indicate the aristocratic circles in which Milton's brother-in-law's brother-in-law travelled. Conway had been a lay member of the Westminster Assembly (1643) until he defected from the Parliament's side in April 1644. *CSPD,* Charles II, VIII, 598, records a certificate by Joseph Hinton, Luke Rugeley, and Thomas Willis, dated 23 September 1668, that Lady Moreland had incurable dropsy, in reference to her request to return to her native France. Elias Ashmole (1617–92), the prominent antiquarian and astrologer, recorded in his diary that "Dr. Ridgley (my old acquaintance) gave me a visit" on 20 July 1685—*The Diary and Will of Elias Ashmole,* 134 (Bodleian MS Ashmole 1135, f. 85). He remarks that Ridgley is acquainted with William Lilly (Bodleian MS Ashmole 240, f. 350); that and his note concerning the death (actually the probate of the will) of John Agar's son Thomas (see n111 here) suggests that Thomas was the witness to Lilly's will, 5 January 1674/5, mentioned in MS Rawlinson D.864, ff. 83–84v. (Ashmole also often refers to a Thomas Agar who was an apothecary from Kingston.) Possibly it was through his stepuncle Luke that Edward Phillips worked as a secretary for Ashmole in 1662–64, copying and translating some of the important materials now housed at the Ashmolean Museum and the Bodleian Library in Oxford. (See also chapter 3 here; for the alleged association of Lilly with John Phillips, see chapter 4.) Ashmole's diary indicates his acquaintance with various people significant to Milton's biography: Henry Oldenburg, Arthur Annesley, and Samuel Morland, as well as Justinian and Thomas Pagitt, who were fellow students at Christ's College with Milton. Ashmole likewise was a friend of Sir Ralph Skipwith (see p. 59, 22 May 1657); as recorded before, Colonel Simon Rugeley had married Jane Skipwith.

The medical case of Sir M. Hales was communicated to Dr. Rugeley in 1676, according to British Library MS Stowe 745, f. 117, and some medical prescriptions for him in 1676 appear in Sloane 4078, f. 360. The reference is to Matthew Hale, a lawyer in Cromwell's first parliament and yet one of the judges at the trial of the regicides; he became Chief Justice under Charles II. The connection between Hale and Rugeley may have come through Christopher Milton. Sir Joseph Williamson on 9 July 1677 wrote from Whitehall to the Earl of Northampton that the persons "to be necessary to" the Earl of Shaftesbury includes "Dr. Ridgeley, his physician" (*CSPD*, Charles II, 1677–78, 236). Lady Fitzjames wrote to her sister, Lady Harley, on 2 October 1680, that "Dr. Ridgeley is in town. I went to him and gave him a fee, but he sent me a letter and my fee in it and he will not 'come at me' so I am constrained to make use of Dr. Cox but find no good yet" (apparently she was approaching her death); see HMC, *Manuscripts of the Duke of Portland*, III, 366. On 12 December 1682 Sir Edward Harley wrote to Ridgeley concerning head pains and "vertiginous fitts"; ibid., 373.

He is listed in Edward Chamberlayne's *The Second Part of the Present State of England*, the sixth edition in 1676, p. 248, under "Present Members of the Kings Colledge of Physitians in London" (as is Milton's friend and doctor, Nathan Paget, who died in 1679), and in the eleventh edition in 1682, p. 277. Likewise, Robert Hooke refers to him in his diary, 27 March 1675.

75. A.W. Hughes Clarke, 115. The parish records of St. Dunstan in the East indicate that Agars were located there. Most important, they contain the baptismal records of two sons of a Thomas Agar, William and James, baptized respectively 25 October 1599 and 29 September 1601 (32–33). They could be brothers of Milton's brother-in-law.

76. Phillips, "Life," vii.

77. MacNamara and Story-Maskelyne, 25.

78. Armytage, 67.

79. See "Bills and Answers in Chancery" in the "Bridges' Division," PRO, Bundle 436, No. 121.

80. Mason and Kitto, 280. Since a George Agar, perhaps her husband, was buried there on 26 April 1642, it is less likely that this person was related to our Thomas Agar.

81. Hallen, II, 32.

82. J. Milton French, *Milton in Chancery*, 164, from the Middle Temple Records.

83. *CG*, III, 4.

84. *Middle Temple Records*, II, 850. The editor, Hopwood, III, 1125, apparently errs when he prints that John was admitted to his chamber in Brick Court only on 28 May 1638. French misleads the reader into thinking that John, like his father, entered the Inner Temple and that the date was 27 May 1636—*Milton in Chancery*, 163. Parliament was held on the twenty-seventh, but John was admitted on the twenty-eighth.

85. Smyth, 91.

86. French, *Life Records*, I, 314; PRO, Req 2/630.

87. French, *Life Records*, I, 337; PRO, Req 2/630.

88. Smyth, loc. cit. Is it possible that this was John's second marriage, his first being to a Mary, sometime before 1634, with whom he lived in Kensington, at a time when his brother was there and the Miltons but a short distance away in Hammersmith? At least there was a daughter Ann born to a John and Mary Ager, baptized 14 November 1634, at Kensington (*Parish Register*, 29). Through the archival work of Edward Jones we now know that the Milton family moved to Hammersmith sometime between April 1630 and April 1631; they were still there through mid-1635. We should note that a Mr. Ager of St. Andrew, Holborn, was assessed £20 in 1638 (Dale, p. 187; MS, p. 318a) and that a "Thos. Young" lived in the same parish at this time, being assessed £6 (Dale, p. 189; MS, p. 320).

89. "Register of Admissions to Gray's Inn, 1521–1881," in *CG*, III, 4.

90. *Miscellanea Genealogica et Heraldica*, Series 4, I, 132. These were not members of his second wife's family—Ibid., Series 5, IX, 272. They may, of course, have been his brothers' wives or his sisters-in-law from a first marriage. Hereafter, *MGH*. Perhaps significantly a Honoria Agar was witness to the baptism of Honoria Bridel (was the child named for her?), daughter of Pierre and Jeanne Bridel on 18 December 1692 at l'Église de Londres, Threadneedle Street; see Colyer-Fergusson, 118.

A Thomas Agar who received an A.B. in 1677 and an A.M. in 1681 from Pembroke College, Cambridge, and a John Agar who received an A.B. in 1679 from Sidney Sussex College, Cambridge, may or may not have been related in some way. Perhaps the Richard Agar, Esquire, of the Middle Temple, who married Elizabeth Tregenna, on 9 October 1707 (Foster, 12), was also related.

91. "Agar's building" is also referred to on 29 June 1677 when Parliament approved an addition on the left side (Hopwood, 124); in error Hopwood's index lists the 1655 entry for the building under Thomas Agar.

92. *Middle Temple Records*, II, 917; III, 1038, 1039, 1053, 1055, 1059, 1081, 1101, 1111, 1125, 1304.

93. *Surrey Quarter Sessions Records*, XXXV, 186; XXXVI, 88, 169, 196, 202, 238; XXXIX, 101, 146.

94. *Surrey Heath Tax*, 1664, XLI-XLII, D 4.

95. Smyth, loc. cit.

96. *Index of Wills Proved in the Prerogative Court of Canterbury*, LXVII, 2.

97. *CG*, III, 4.

98. *Middle Temple Records*, III, 1125

99. Foster, *Alumni Oxonienses*, I, 10.

100. *Middle Temple Records*, III, 1191.

101. Ibid., III, 1163, 1164, 1176, 1177, 1251, 1253, 1291.

102. *CSPD*, Charles II, IV, 87. See also *CSPD*, Charles II, I, 357, for reference to a grant to Daniel Treswell of the Office of Surveyor of the King's Woods and Forests, dated 17 November 1660, for £50 a year; there are notes of enrolment from 28 February and 6 March 1662, with endorsements later for a warrant of the same office for John Madden and Thomas Agar. For further entries, see *CSPD*, IV, 206 (17 February 1665) and 262 (20 March 1665); X, 560 (November 1670) and 696 (23 November?). A letter to Joseph Williamson, 1664(?), reports that he cannot find some requested document (IV, 142), and one from Agar to Samuel Pepys, dated 3 February 1679 from Somerset House, dealing with the forest of Dean, is found in Bodleian MS Rawlinson A.181. The Diary of Lieutenant-General Lyttelton Annesley notes that "the Clerk of the Crown, Mr Agar" was in attendance when Annesley took the oaths of allegiance and supremacy and the oath of Privy Seal at the Lord Chancellor's office on 24 April 1673 (see HMC, Thirteenth Report, Part VI, p. 275). SP Dom. Car. II, 414, No. 153, refers to him as surveyor (10 December 1680). A letter from Colonel Edward Vernon to Secretary Leoline Jenkins, dated 9 April 1684, claims that he has been falsely charged in connection with forests and deer by "Mr. Agards" (*CSPD*, Charles II, October 1683–April 1684, 374.) A group of letters dated through 1688 from Agar are preserved in the Marquis of Ormande Collection at Kilkenny Castle (see HMC, *Third Report*, 428).

CSPD (1 January 1697–31 December 1697), in a dispatch from Whitehall, 20

July, 256, indicates that "Mr. Agar, one of the Victualling Commissioners, died last week"; the *CSPD* (1 January 1699–31 March 1700), p. 410 for August 1699, records the revocation of the commission granted to John Agar as Commissioner for victualling the navy. There are other references to him in 1696–1699. Could this be a younger brother of Thomas? It seems that there were other boys born to John Agar (Thomas's father), and this kind of position for this John Agar could have transpired because of his brother's influence.

103. *Calendar of Treasury Books,* I (1904), 602, 671, 673, 717; II, 177, 500; III, Part I (1908), 8, 63, 101, 109, 112–13, 122, 126, 173, 204, 208, 244, 380 (2), 385, 408–09, 429, 460, 478, 481, 524, 531, 537, 626, 630, 648 (2), 682 (2), 692 (2), 700, 729; III, Part II (1909), 774, 801, 803, 804, 855, 1204, 1231; IV (1911), 98, 124, 150 (2), 168, 191, 228 (2), 279, 369, 382, 420, 486, 497, 503, 529, 543, 562, 605, 625, 637, 652, 662, 678, 689, 693, 709, 733, 766; V, Part I (1911), 10, 27, 59, 92, 163, 303, 310, 333, 410, 412, 430, 432, 489–90, 534, 575, 636, 765, 767, 822; V, Part II (1913), 948, 1188, 1338, 1395, 1402, 1405, 1408, 1409, 1415, 1437; VI (1916), 17, 96 (2), 122, 125, 184, 193, 196, 199, 217, 222, 242, 268, 290, 311, 392, 395, 429, 444, 445, 470, 532–33, 551, 601, 623, 641–42, 652–53, 656, 682, 738, 746, 791, 796; VII, Part I (1916), 23–2S4, 82, 102, 108, 139, 147, 176, 207, 209–10, 281, 290, 297, 342, 380 (2), 392, 402, 403, 404, 414, 455, 463, 464, 506, 547, 569, 578, 579, 613, 619, 642, 654 (2), 658; VII, Part II (1916), 681–82 (5), 682, 701, 707, 720, 722, 727, 731, 742, 745, 755, 759, 772 (2), 785, 859, 962–64, 964, 967, 983 (2), 985, 1019, 1021, 1021–22, 1025, 1026, 1026–27, 1066, 1095, 1107, 1112–13, 1119, 1208, 1209, 1240, 1289, 1291, 1391, 1404, 1424, 1446, 1448 (2); VII, Part III (1916), 1498, 1508, 1511; VIII, Part I (1923), 12, 14, 67, 95–96, 142, 157, 161, 166, 172, 180, 185–86, 241, 243, 272, 326, 371, 404, 451–52, 463, 485 (2), 486; VIII, Part II (1923), 518, 573, 588, 598, 655, 673, 675 (2), 680, 687, 709, 726, 751, 771 (2), 772, 793, 807–08, 839, 840, 872, 936, 983, 994, 1002, 1005, 1027, 1033, 1051–52, 1057, 1059, 1076, 1078, 1096, 1107, 1117, 1135; VIII, Part III (1923), 1210, 1229, 1254–55, 1363–64, 1443–44, 1454–55, 1549, 1568, 1604, 1648, 1652, 1722, 1736, 1882.

VIII, Part III (1685–89), 1568, 1604, 1736, 1843, 1882, all raise the issue of the accounts upon Thomas's death through communications with or relating to his widow Mary. VIII, Part IV (1685–1689), 2099–2100, informs us of the monies involved. A Treasury warrant to the auditors concerned to pass the accounts of Mary Agar, relict of Thomas Agar, late Surveyor General of Woods, South Trent, dated 18 October 1686, indicates the monies owed, the monies paid, various charges and reductions; the amount allowed by the Chancellor of the Exchequer left Mary indebted by £91/ 14/11. Various additional entries after Thomas's death, involving warrants concerned with Mary continue in Vol. IX (1689–92), 193, 263, 516–17, 1592, and Vol. X (1693–96), 9. An entry dated 15 April 1696 includes a £20 payment previously promised to "Thomas Agar, gentleman" (among others) as a reward for apprehending conspirators (Vol. XI, 93).

Again the matter of land, land ownership, and the rise of capitalism (here most obviously in the preservation of forests or their deforestation for income) may rear up in assessing Milton's position on economic and social issues. How influential and informative might Thomas Agar—favored nephew of his brother-in-law—have been? Royal ownership and disposition of land rather than the private or public ownership, such as the Interregnum had fostered, may have been a bone of contention.

Further, the long-standing difficulties with the enclosure system, which accelerated during the seventeenth century, and the position of women in relation to "land" and ownership (of them and by them) must also be broached in considering this important social and economic matter. See Lynne A. Greenberg, "Paradise Enclosed and the *Feme Covert*," which examines the question as seen in *Paradise Lost.*

104. See "The Hatton Collection. Correspondence," HMC, *First Report,* 15. The letter to Lord Hatton, a former attendant on the Queen Mother Henrietta Maria and a member of the Royal Society, is now found in British Library MS Additional 29560, f. 354.

105. *MGH,* Series 4, I, 131. The monument also records his office as Surveyor of His Majesty's Woods and Forests this side Trent.

106. Foster, *London Marriage Licences,* 1521–1859, column 12. Mary Bolles was actually twenty-five according to her date of birth. The town residence of the Bolles family about the period of the Restoration and for some time afterward was in the parish of St. Giles in the Fields, then a fashionable part of London.—Illingworth, 48n. Perhaps the family moved after the death of Sir Robert Bolles in 1663. Interestingly, Thomas Agar and Mary his wife, plaintiffs, sued Sir John Bolles, baronet, defendant, in 1674 over lands in Newton Mulgrave Manor, &c., and York, &c.; see PRO, Bundle 436, No. 159. Sir John was Mary's brother.

107. *MGH,* Series 5, IX, 272. Edward Phillips dedicated *The New World of English Words* (1662 and 1663) to Sir Robert and to Sir Edward. He, of course, was a stepcousin of Thomas Agar, and the dedications indicate the closeness between these members of Milton's extended family. The Bolles of Lincoln were "well-beloved" of Charles I, according to a statement from him dated 27 December 1642. Thomas Agar's move to Lincoln during the Interregnum may have been effected through familial connections.

108. Illingworth, 28, 48, 49.

109. Gibbons, 40.

110. Fisher, 13.

111. *MGH,* Series 4, I, 131–32. On 7 August 1689, a petition from a Mr. Agar was presented for the Office of Surveyor-General of the King's Woods and Forests, South of the Trent, as his kinsman, Thomas Agar, formerly held it. Compare n102 above. The request was referred to the Treasury. See PRO, SP Dom, Petition Entry Book 2, p. 120. Elias Ashmole is confused in his notation (Bodleian MS Ashmole 1136, f. 124) that "This day Mrs. Agar died about 5 H.P.M." under 10 November 1687.

112. *The Marriage, Baptismal, and Burial Registers of the Collegiate Church or Abbey of St. Peter, Westminster,* 28. Mary Bolles Agar married secondly Sir Miles Cooke on 20 June 1689, a Master in Chancery from 24 December 1673 until his death. He was knighted 25 January 1673/4. The report in *Collectanea Topographia & Genealogica* (VII, 170) says that Mary was the "relict of Sir Thomas Agar, of the Temple." Cooke died suddenly at his house in Chancery Lane and was buried at St. James, Westminster, on 21 February 1698/9. Mary married thirdly Thomas Turner, esquire, of Kingston, Kent, also a Master in Chancery, who died 1 April 1715. Her will, dated 22 December 1714, was proved by her son Robert Cooke, sole legatee and executor, on 26 June 1731. John Le Neve's "Pedigrees of the Knights Made by King Charles II, King James II, King William III and Queen Mary, King William Alone, and Queen Anne" (BL MS Harleian 5801) spells the name Cook, does not cite Agar as "Sir," and says that her son was "Peter Cook esqr

1696 [who] in a plott agt King William 3d tryed for his life & condemned but repreived";
see *The Publications of the Harleian Society* (1873), VIII, 290.

Provocative is a letter from Richard Thompson (who refers to his "rank") to his
brother Henry in March or April 1689 concerning the possibility of his buying "a
chamber in ye Inn," "a convenience of one just under L. Agar, which I might be able
to compass" (British Library MS Egerton 2429A). Thomas Agar died in 1687, but
this seems to be a reference to him as "Lord Agar."

113. Armytage, 67.

114. It is possible that the London Agars had connections in Surrey before 1641,
although the evidence is by no means conclusive. There was a Henry Eger in Ewhurst,
Surrey, in 1585 (*Wills, Prerogative Court of Canterbury,* XXV, 139). Various Agars were
scattered throughout the county. There were two Agars of note in Kingston, John, a
Commissioner of the Navy, who died in 1697; and Thomas, twelve times bailiff and
once mayor in 1686 of Kingston, who died in 1703, aged ninety-four (Manning, III,
371). One of them was listed as having a dwelling with eight hearths (*Surrey Hearth
Tax,* 1664, 4). Thomas, listed as a bailiff and as a gentleman of Kingston and Elmbridge,
appears in the court records for October 1663, January 1664, April 1664, July 1664,
and January 1666 (*Surrey Quarter Sessions Records,* XXXIX, 120, 136, 153, 172, 265,
277, 294). On 3 March 1664 Sir Edward Brett wrote to Williamson that "Mr Agar, an
honest bailiff of Kingston," has complained about a matter of licensing (*CSPD,* Charles
II, III, 504). No doubt, John and Thomas were brothers. Thomas's age of ninety-four
in 1703 gives as his year of birth 1609. It is possible that they were cousins of the
London Agars. However, no connection can be established on the basis of available
records. A tenuous possibility suggests itself: John Agar of Kingston's position as
Commissioner of the Navy may have brought him in contact with Thomas Agar, the
Surveyor of His Majesty's woods.

115. *MGH,* Series I, I, 312–13; Manning, III, 229; and Rylands, *Grantees of Arms,*
LXVI, 174.

116. *Surrey Hearth Tax,* 1664, 108. A provocative note in *CSPD,* Charles II, 1660–
61, dated 8 February 1661, indicates an order that Thomas Moore of Hartswood,
Surrey, was "to remain free from all molestation about the Oath of Allegiance, so
long as he remains faithful to the government" (506). This implies some objection
to the Oath and perhaps some antagonism toward Charles II's restoration.

117. *Surrey Quarter Sessions Records,* XXXIX, 314.

118. Ibid., XXXIX, 39, 85, 103, 165, 229.

119. Manning, II, 222–23.

120. Aubrey, *The Natural History and Antiquities of the County of Surrey,* IV, 216.

121. Watney, 180.

122. *Surrey Hearth Tax,* 1664, 108.

123. *Surrey Musters,* XI, 345, 377. Sayes Court was leased from the Crown by
David Moore in 1673. Chertsey is in the hundred of Godley; Byfleet adjoins Chertsey;
Chobham is six miles WSW; and Buckland in Reigate hundred is SE.

124. Manning, III, 236.

125. Aubrey, III, 178, 182–83.

126. Milton pedigree by Sir Charles Young.

127. The exact baptismal entry is "Oct. 13 1663 Thomas, son of David Moore &
Anne his wife" and underneath "(born Oct. 9)."—J. Challenor C. Smith, I, 54.

128. Sturgess, I, 195.

129. The *DNB* reports on Sir Thomas Moore, playwright, said to have been a native of Surrey, who wrote a tragedy in blank verse, *Mangora, King of the Timbusians, or, The Faithful Couple*, published in 1718 and played at Lincoln's Inn Fields 14 December 1717. This account states that he was probably Thomas, son of Adrian Moore of Milton Place, Egham, Surrey, who matriculated from Corpus Christi, Oxford, on 19 June 1674, aged twenty-two, having previously, on 13 May 1670, been admitted a student of Gray's Inn. He was knighted by George I in 1716 and died at Leatherhead on 16 April 1735. This identification is in error in one respect and is open to question in others. The error lies in identifying the knight-playwright with Thomas Moore of Leatherhead. Thomas Moore of Leatherhead died, according to one source, on 16 March 1735 (Musgrave, 228). According to Manning, there was a Thomas Moore, colonel of a regiment of foot in the reign of Queen Anne, paymaster of the land forces in Minorca and in the garrisons of Dunkirk and Gibraltar, who was a brother of an Arthur Moore of Fetcham, Surrey. This Thomas died 25 March 1735 (II, 689–91). At another point Manning states that this Thomas Moore died on 16 March 1735, unmarried and aged sixty-seven (I, 483). This latter date agrees with that given for Thomas Moore of Leatherhead by Musgrave. Thomas Moore of Fetcham, the colonel, was in fact Thomas Moore of Leatherhead. Fetcham and Leatherhead are less than a mile apart. Furthermore, in discussing the inhabitants of Fetcham, Aubrey speaks of "*Arthur Moor,* Esq., one of the Commissioners of Trade and Plantations in 1713, with fine gardens towards *Letherhead*" (II, 263). The identification of the knight-playwright with Thomas, the son of Adrian of Egham, is only supposition. The material in Frederick Turner's article does not settle the question. Another candidate is Thomas Agar's grandson; indeed, Parker takes him to be David Moore's son, saying he "wrote some wretched plays" (I, 654). The evidence against his candidature is that he was knighted on 7 June 1715, whereas, according to the *DNB*, the playwright was knighted in 1716. However, this date could be in error. More evidence against his candidature is that the Moore pedigree does not mention any such claim to fame. On the other hand, his background and presumed education fit him for the part and the date that administration of his effects was granted to his son Edmund, 12 June 1735, tallies with the death date given by Musgrave for the knight-playwright.

130. Manning, III, 229, from a manuscript in Richard Gough's possession.

131. Box, 38.

132. The baptismal entry is "1702 April 24, Sarah d. of Mr William Lee" (*Parish Registers of Abinger, Wotton, and Oakwood Chapel, Co. Surrey*, XXV, 148). That this is the proper William Lee is proved by the gravestone in Wotton churchyard, recording Sarah Lee, wife of William Lee of Wotton, gentleman, who died 21 April 1702, leaving as issue only one daughter named Sarah (Aubrey, IV, 143).

133. The Milton pedigree in Mitford; *MGH*, I, 313; and Manning, III, 181.

134. Box, 428. Bridget Moore died in 1783, having married as her second husband, George Tate, who died in 1822.

135. Masson, I, 104. On 28 July 1644, for example, Colonel Lewis Chadwick of Stafford, discussing the advancement on Chester, wrote: "There hath beene strict questions put to Mr. Agard concerning the votes and questions upon them as if he had strayed and corrupted the sence to t[h]wart these designes, but wee tooke him

of [off] by referring it to those p'sent at the votary." A Postscript adds: "The[y] were angry the votes and answers were entred in the booke of orders and mr. [John] Swinfin [later a member of the Council of State in 1659–60] tooke a paper and formally would have taken Mr. Agard's answer and examinac'on like a delinquent wch when wee would not suffer, Capt Stone s^d it should been done to purpose in an other place" (see the Earl of Denbigh's manuscripts, HMC, Fourth Report, Part I, IV, 269–70). Agar's actions, if Stafford's inference is correct, smacks of his Royalism in an attempt to belay the disastrous siege of Chester by the Parliamentarians.

136. *DNB* s.v. "Williams, John."

137. Ibid., s.v. "Whitelocke, Sir James."

138. Masson, I, 556–59. There is an extant letter that Milton sent Bulstrode Whitelocke, President of the Council of State and son of the aforementioned lord, on 12 February 1652, in his capacity as secretary, concerning a request from Hermann Mylius about the Oldenburgh safeguard. Other such correspondence is probable. We may also remark Sir William Davenant's release from prison in 1652, which has been attributed to Milton and others and especially to Lord Whitelocke; see the discussion in French, III, 255–57.

His *Parliamenti Angliæ Declaratio* (1648/49) was influenced by the *Tenure of Kings and Magistrates* and employed state papers drawn up under Milton's inspection. But unaware, the author of *The Censure of the Rota* (1660), directing his remarks to Milton about *The Ready and Easy Way*, speaks of its contents: "but this, he said ['a Gentleman of your acquaintance'], you stole from Patriot *Whitlock*, who began his Declaration for a Free State with the same words" (pp. 5, 4). Whitelocke was also a member of the Committee of Safety created by the Army officers at his home, Wallingford House, in the last days of the Commonwealth. In a derisive poem "The Committee of Safety," printed in the second part of *Rump Poems* (1662), we find a different view of him but one that thereby seems to be a justified epitome (p. 101):

> *Whitlock* that mischievous dangerous Elf
> Never sticks to turn sides to promote his own Wealth,
> And hath Wit enough, Law enough to damne himself.

His *Journal of the Swedish Embassy,* his *Memorials of English Affairs,* and his Diary all have references to Milton or his works. Note also his relationship with Milton's mother-in-law Ann Powell, cited in chapter 1.

Whitelocke, who was born on Fleet Street, 6 August 1605, was christened at St. Dunstan's in the East, became an important lawyer and governmental official, and with Hyde represented the Middle Temple on the committee for the four inns of court in charge of the masque presented before the king and queen in 1633. Whitelocke had the whole care and charge of the music, which, it is said, excelled all other before it. His uncle Edward (1588–1659) was a member of the Inner Temple, as was his cousin Sir Richard (1610–1711), who became a bencher in 1649.

One's mind runs immediately into various speculations: were the Miltons and the Bulstrodes well acquainted since both resided in Horton? did Milton, Sr. acquire his property through them? is Whitelocke's association with music and masques in 1633 in any way connected with Milton, Sr.'s avocation and friends, and with Milton,

Jr.'s production of "Arcades" and "A Masque" ("Comus") in 1634? We just don't know, but the possibilities are there.

139. *DNB* s.v. "Coventry, Thomas."

140. Ibid., s.v. "Finch, Sir John," "Finch, Sir Henry," and "Finch, Heneage."

141. Ibid., s.v. "Hyde, Edward."

142. Ibid., s.v. "Bridgeman, Sir Orlando."

143. Ibid., s.v. "Cooper, Anthony Ashley."

144. Masson, VI, 195.

145. *DNB*, s.v. "Finch, Heneage."

146. Ibid., s.v. "Finch, Sir Heneage," "Heneage, Sir Thomas," and "Finch, Heneage."

147. Masson, VI, 770.

148. *CSPD*, Charles II, I, 63.

149. *CPCC*, II, 1453. (Note also the connection by marriage between Agar(d)s and Ferrers in Staffordshire, p. 53 above.)

150. Maddison, L, 351.

151. Rylands, *The Visitation of the County of Warwick*, 1682–1683, LXII, 166–67.

152. Colville, 281–82.

153. Additional speculation is tempting because of Agar's residency in Lincolnshire. Perhaps through his connections in government and with the Royalists—here notably Ferrers—he was introduced to the Bolles family and later became the link between his nephew and Mary Bolles.

154. PRO, Chancery Town Depositions, C24/825/89.

155. Hopwood, III, 1125.

156. *CSPD*, Charles II, I, 63. His request was granted on 8 July to enroll "all Commissions and Appeals in the Court of Chancery," I, 140.

157. Ibid., I, 120 (for Edward Love), and IX, 189 (for Sir Richard Raynesford). Rainesford (1605–80) was a judge from Lincoln's Inn; he was called to the bar on 16 October 1632, elected treasurer in 1660, and was in both Charles II's and James II's first parliaments. He was sworn serjeant-at-law on 26 October 1660, raised to the Exchequer Bench on 16 November 1663, and transferred to the King's Bench on 6 February 1668/9. He was also a colleague of Sir Matthew Hale. Agar's recommendation to Williamson certainly implies his significant position in Chancery, and Rainesford's probable interconnections with both Christopher Milton and Luke Rugeley are to be noted.

158. Ibid., II, 8 and 48 (31 July 1661).

159. *Calendar of Treasury Books,* I, 263.

160. Ibid., III, Part II, 818; and *CSPD*, Charles II, II, 38, 66, 381, 589; III, 159, 235, 238, 482, 483, 577, 588; VI, 355, 358. A letter from Agar to Sir George Lane from the Crown Office, 9 December 1662, will be found in the Marquise of Ormonde's collection (HMC, *Fourth Report,* Part I, Vol. IV, 552). A message to Sir George Williamson, 12 May 1664, also from the Crown Office, asks for references to Serjeant Charlton concerning some unnamed matter (PRO, SP Dom, Car. II, 440, No. 94). *The Calendar of Treasury Books,* Vol. 3, Part I, 385 (in the Minute Book, DXCCIV, p. 72), has a memorandum from Sir George Downing, Secretary to the Treasury, dated 12 March 1669/70, concerning a "Petition of the nobility, &c., innocent [Papists] in Ireland, with four other papers annexed, delivered to Sir John Belew [Commissioner

for Quit-Rents in Ireland] for a letter to be drawn by them. . . . Mr. Agar: against to-morrow to send it to Mr. Hall. . . ." This is followed up on 26 April 1671 (Vol. 3, Part II, 818) with a letter to Thomas Agar from Sir George, saying, "Send my Lords a list of the names of all the clerks of the peace within the respective counties of England and Wales that have been of any of them within that time, so as to show for how much of the said five years each has served."

161. British Library, MS Egerton 2534, ff. 99–100r.

162. Masson, VI, 162–95.

163. *CSPD*, Charles II, III, 639, 646.

164. *A Catalogue of Books (Coventry)* lists *Defensio prima, Literæ Pseudo-Senatûs Anglicani,* and *Paradise Lost,* and an unsigned letter to Henry Coventry on Daniel Skinner's deal-ings to publish Milton's papers after his death is found in the manuscript collection of the Marquis of Bath (see HMC, *Fourth Report.* Part I, Series 3, Part I, 227).

Chapter 3

1. He uses the wrong but frequent misspelling of the surname.

2. There are also an unpublished thesis at Oxford University (1950) by Frederick L. Beaty, "The Life and Works of John Phillips," and an unpublished dis-sertation by Melvin Hill at Columbia University.

3. Rajan's emphasis is on Godwin, and thus Miltonists have not appreciated the significance of her examination for a better understanding of Milton and his relationships with his nephews.

4. "Poem on the Coronation of his most sacred Majesty K. *Jam.* II. and his Royal Consort our gracious Que. *Mary.* Lond. 1685. in 2 sh. fol.," as Wood gives it in *Athenæ Oxonienses* (II, 1118), was by John Phillips of Lincoln's Inn. I cite the 1721 (augmented) edition of Wood. Edward is alluded to or discussed in I, Fasti, 263; II, 72–73, 1116–18, Fasti 60; John is alluded to or discussed in I, Fasti, 263; II, 337, 820, 1118–19. The first edition of 1691 and 1692 cites both under Milton, II, (Fasti) 880–84; Edward under Richard Baker II, 33–34 (and reference, 741); John under James Heath, II, 226, and Samuel Parker, II, 621.

5. He was born in the Strand near Charing Cross, Westminster, in the parish of St. Martin in the Fields. As noted in the previous chapter, the Crown Office, where his father and stepfather worked, was near at hand in Westminster, accounting for the place of residence. The father Edward was buried there on 25 August 1631; his will is dated 12 August 1631 and was proved on 12 September (see Prerogative Court of Canterbury, London, 99 St. John). The will leaves his "worldly estate" to his mother Katherine, and upon her death is to be divided among brothers and sisters then living (currently there had been four). If this did not come to the sum of £80, his wife Anne was to make up the difference; if it came to more, the remainder was to pass to Anne. It was attested in the presence of John Milton, Sr.

Edward Jones has discovered four documents in the Rate Books for St. Martin in the Fields parish, F350–53, which record payments by Edward Phillips for Poor Relief in April 1624–1627; he paid —/2/2 in 1624 and —/4/4 in 1625–27. His resi-dence is listed as "the High Street Ward Waterside" with the last entry adding "in Greene's Lane." This location is in agreement with the Wood's placement of the family in the Strand (which would have been called the High Street seventy years earlier) near Charing Cross. I assume that the Phillipses moved here right after their marriage in November 1623. The first residence would thus be between the Strand and the river, with a move to the "landside" second residence in St. Martin in the Fields parish around 1625. Phillips is not listed in the records for 1627–28 or 1629–30.

In reciting the reading that took place at Milton's "school," Phillips remarks "the many Authors both of the Latin and Greek, which . . . were run over within no greater compass of time, then from Ten to Fifteen or Sixteen Years of Age." Parker (304, 930 n40) and others read that to mean: "he was ten in August 1640, and soon after went to live with his uncle. It seems reasonable to infer, therefore, that his education by Milton ended in June or July 1646." Needless to say, I would hope, is the insubstantiality of that conclusion. Phillips had written to Aubrey, however, that he was ten and John nine when they joined Milton.

6. Edward Phillips's and Anne Milton's marriage settlement cites nine separate properties in Shrewsbury and one in Caersws. The marriage settlement, 27 November 1623, was signed by Edward, and witnessed by Sara Milton and John Milton, Jr., and others. Property was transferred to John Milton, Sr., and James Hodgkinson, in trust for Katherine Prowde Phillips (Milton's brother-in-law's mother), then for Edward and Anne Phillips, and then for their male heirs. Exactly how much property (perhaps all) was transferred then or later is unclear. Deed No. 1226, 18 January 1626/7, between "Edward Phillips of the Strand, Middlesex, gentleman, and Anne, his wife, and Katherine Phillips of Shrewsbury, his mother, and Richard Burde of Shrewsbury, a tanner," concerning Burde's tenancy, was signed by Edward and Anne, and marked by Katherine. The property had been owned by Edward's father, also Edward, of Atcham, Salop, gentleman, who is undoubtedly the Edward Phillips buried at St. Julian's, Shrewsbury, on 20 October 1618. Property came into his possession through his marriage settlement with the Prowdes (Deed No. 1189, 30 January 1596/7); he and Katherine were married on 7 February 1596/7. His widow, who had been baptized at St. Julian's on 31 July 1569, was buried there on 3 August 1650. Since there were no surviving siblings, her death transferred ownership of the property to her grandsons Edward and John Phillips, apparently precipitating Edward's removal to Shrewsbury in 1651. We should also register Phillips's comment placed between the time of the answer to Salmasius (February 1651) and John Phillips's *Responsio* (December 1651?) in rebuttal of the arguments that *Defensio prima* elicited: "And now I presume our Author had some breathing space; but it was not long" ("Life of John Milton," xxxii). That uncertainty seems to iterate that he was not in London in 1651, being at Oxford and then in Shrewsbury.

The previous chapter here indicated that the Clerkship of the Crown Office in Chancery had been held by Milton's brother-in-law and that it passed to his new brother-in-law, Thomas Agar, and then to his nephew Thomas Milton. But it also should be remarked that John Benbow(e), husband of a Dorothy Prowde (a second cousin of Edward's mother), held that office for forty years (from 1585) until his death on 7 October 1625, and that Edward, Milton's brother-in-law, assumed that position and witnessed his relative's will on 14 June. Benbow lived in the parish of St. Martin in the Fields, Westminster, as did the Phillipses. Such transferral of this politically important office would cause us to cry "nepotism." We should note also that Lewis Prowde, the brother of Edward's mother, was a lawyer and very important in the annals of Lincoln's Inn. See George Grazebrook and John Paul Rylands, 39.

7. "The British town [of Shrewsbury] occupied only the high ground, bounded by what are now Pride Hill, High Street, and Dogpole, but there is little doubt that it contained within its narrow circuit two ecclesiastical foundations now represented by the churches of St. Mary and St. Julian. St. Mary's occupies an open space in the very middle of what was then the town. . . . St. Julian's occupied a site which was equally striking. It stood on the very borders of the town, and overlooked whatever wall or other defence bounded it on that side." St. Mary's Church will be cited later, perhaps significantly. See Auden, 53–54.

Andrew Vyvers, a shoemaker and son of Daniel of Banbury, mercer, became a burgess in 1624. Richard Burde, a tanner and son of William of Haston, yeoman, became one in 1618; and Michael Ball, draper, son of Richard of Willston, deceased, became one in 1666. These may be the same people (or relatives) who will be cited later. See *Shrewsbury Burgess Roll,* rolls B105, B100, B139 respectively.

8. See Hobbs for some inferences. Sheldon was ousted from All Souls, Oxford, by the Parliamentarians in 1648 and is reported to have been in Staffordshire and Nottinghamshire during the Interregnum.

9. Commendatory poems by Edward and by John appeared in Henry Lawes's *Ayres* (1653), A1v and A2v respectively. One assumes that Milton's friendship with Lawes is the key to having these poems written and published in this volume. It likewise suggests Edward's contact with things going on in London around 1652 or 1653 and also that John was not out of touch with his uncle after 1652.

10. Maurice Kelley says eleven, apparently not counting the two separate ones on p. 12, whereas William B. Hunter correctly gives twelve; see *CPW,* VI, 16, and *Visitation Unimplor'd,* 2.

11. I discuss this fact elsewhere; it demands that the "Theological Index" was still in use and significant in 1651/52.

12. The implied continued connection with the Countess of Derby's family for Milton's nephew into the Interregnum period is surely significant. We also remember that Lawes had been music-teacher to the Countess's grandchildren (who appeared in *A Masque* in 1634), suggesting a network of interrelationships for the Phillipses as well as Milton. Anne, the Countess of Stratford, was married to Sir William Wentworth, the son of Sir Thomas Wentworth, Earl of Strafford, who was executed on 12 May 1641 by action of the Long Parliament. Milton became anathema to some like John Egerton, Viscount Brackley and Earl of Bridgewater, who wrote on the title page of a copy of *Defensio prima* that the book was fit to be burned and the author the gallows, but such political attitude was not extended to his nephew.

To be particularly remarked is Scott Nixon's "Milton's royalist friend: The peculiar pamphlets of Henry Lawes" in *TLS,* which presents a picture of Lawes during the Civil Wars period in his *Choice Psalms* (1648), "a volume dedicated to 'his Most Sacred Majestie, Charles's and memorializing Henry's brother William as a royalist martyr," and in *Ayres and Dialogues* (1653, 1655) where he "asserted that his art was fundamentally royalist and that, despite the defeats of the 1640s, he would continue to be an active supporter of the Crown." The implications for Milton's collaboration in "Arcades" and "A Maske" are thus equivocal. The explanation of the alleged discrepancy in Milton's attitude, I would argue, lies in the difference between acceptance of monarchy and the evaluation of this particular monarch and monarchy for Milton in the 1630s and 1640s; see chapters 4 and 5.

We might note that *Ayres and Dialogues,* which printed the two commendatory poems by Edward and John Phillips, was published by John Playford, who also published Matthew Locke's *Observations* in 1672 (on a book by Thomas Salmon) with a commendatory poem by John, and Locke's surrebuttal to Salmon's *Vindication,* entitled *The Present Practice of Music* in 1673 with John's poem reprinted and his attack on Salmon, *Duellum Musicum.* (See chapter 4.) Peter Lindenbaum discusses Playford's Royalist connections in "John Playford: Music and Politics in the Interregnum." Interesting too is the fact that William Faithorne's portrait of Henry Lawes appears in all three volumes of *Ayres and Dialogues;* he was, of course, the noted artist of Milton's most famous portrait in *A History of Britain* (1670).

13. The fourth issue, *The Most Elegant, and Elaborate Poems Of that Great Court-Wit, Mr William Drummond. Whose Labours, both in Verse and Prose, being heretofore so precious to Prince Henry, and to K. Charles, Shall live and flourish in all Ages whiles there are men to read them, or Art & Judgment to Approve them* (1659), continues the impression of the translations as to Edward's social and political relationships.

14. There were six states to this edition. Wood's copy with his holograph notes is owned by the Bodleian Library; alongside the entry for John Phillips, which cites but does not name Milton, he wrote "a rogue" and indicated that Edward and John were brothers.

15. Varley, 12.

16. See Burrows under "Index of Names: Members of Colleges and Halls," p. 513. This Edward Phillipps was a chorister in 1640, a clerk in 1648; he entered at age 17 from Worcester, matriculated in 1645, and his parentage is listed as "Pleb." (that is, a commoner). He was "non exp[elled]" when the visitation began in 1647. The editor specifically indicates that this is not Milton's nephew who was at Magdalen Hall in 1648–51, probably repeating information in Masson. Since this was a visitation of the Board appointed in 1647, Milton's nephew was not listed under Magdalen Hall.

17. See von Maltzahn's statement in *Milton Studies* 31 (1994): 172 n15.

18. See *The Diary of John Evelyn:* "Mr. Edw: *Philips,* came to be my sonns præceptor: This Gent: was Nephew to *Milton* who writ against *Salmasius's Defensio,* but not at all infected with his principles, & though brought up by him, yet no way tainted" (III, 364–65, dated 24 October 1663). Deptford is now part of Greater London, today not terribly far from Phillips's possible residence in Westminster. Sayes Court, named after the family of William de Saye (as was David Moore's residence in Chertsey, Surrey), was in West Greenwich, Deptford. (Parker unexplainably places Evelyn's home in Essex.)

A letter from Aletheia [Alathea], Countess of Arundel, to her [eldest] son Lord Andover (Charles Howard, Viscount Andover, who died in 1679), dated 14 September 1648, has this comment: "Next, you say that Mr Tailler, Junius, and Philipps, are like vermine, that engender in the destruction of the noblest creatures. As . . . for Mr Philipps he was likewise entrusted by my lord in following what concerned my lord of Oxford; so that your Lo[rdship] sees how carefull I have been to imploy those that were so much trusted by my lord, as you see they all three were" (*The Life Correspondence & Collections of Thomas Howard, Earl of Arundel,* ed. Mary F.S. Hervey, 470–71).

Mark Aloysius Tierney in *The History and Antiquities of the Castle and Town of Arundel,* 506, citing the two entries in Evelyn's diary, mistakenly writes: "Phillips was the nephew of Milton . . . and . . . was engaged in the service of the countess, in opposition to her son"; he apparently was unaware that Edward became 18 in August 1648, hardly being in a position to be a tutor sometime before that date.

19. His transcriptions of materials for Ashmole will be found in Bodleian MSS Ashmole 826 (f. 200a), 842 (f. 183a-b), 857 (pp.233–41), 865 (pp. 389-[442], 442-b, 443–65), 1109 (f. 217b), 1110 (ff. 51a-66b), 1111 (ff. 6b, 19a-24a, 82a-85a), 1115 (ff. 15a-b, 109a-12b, 125b-26b, 135a-38b, 174a), 1119 (ff. 1a-72), 1123 (ff. 160a-66b, leaf [166d], 167a-73b), 1125 (ff. 162a-202a), 1127 (ff. 1a-25b, [26 blank], 27a-46b, [47– 49 blank], corrections on 50a-57a, 82a-91b, 131a-35b, 139a-75b, 179a-214a), 1128 (some of the marginal corrections on ff. 17a-24a), 1139 (ff. 53a-68b), and 1149 (ff.1a-2b). A note on f. 17a of MS 1128 records in a different hand: "The Emendacons bye^th [?] Edw: Phillipps hand were by an old MS: Coppy of belonging to Sr: Seymer Shirley of Stanton Harold in Cout Leic: Bar^t:". Dates appearing on the copied letters in MS 857 range from 23 September 1662 through 18 January 1663. Phillips's work was used by Ashmole in *The Institution, Laws & Ceremonies of the Most Noble Order of the Garter* (1672). Compare, for example, Ashmole's discussion of "*The Order of Knights of the* Holy Ghost *in France*," chapter III, section 1, pp. 121–23, with MS Ashmole 1127, ff. 179 following. The printer was John Macock, Milton's printer for various items during the years 1670–1678, and the publisher was Nathanael Brooke who oversaw (and perhaps commissioned) books by Edward and by John Phillips. The second edition (1693) was printed by Thomas Dring, who produced the second edition of Milton's shorter poems in 1673. Phillips commends Ashmole in the 1665 edition of Baker's *Chronicle* on p. 806. There is also an inscription to the Bishop of London in a copy of this edition; see Sotheby, Plate XXIV, facing 190.

20. "Mr. *Philips* præceptor to my sonn, went to be with the E: of Penbroch sonn my L. *Herbert*" (Evelyn, III, 401, dated 27 February 1665).

21. "I preferred Mr. Philips to the service of my L. Chamb: who wanted a scholar to reade to & entertaine him some times: my Lord has a library at Euston full of excellent bookes" (Evelyn, IV, 120–21, dated 16 September 1677). Of this employment Parker says "About 1678" (655) and remarks, "This job did not last long," although Hone suggests it continued into 1679. According to Wood he was instructor to Isabella, Duchess of Grafton, the Earl's daughter, and to Henry Bennet, the Earl's nephew (II, 1117), suggesting more than just a short while. Further evidence of interconnections is a license in Ashmole's possession, dated 31 March 1670 and dedicated to Charles II, and signed "Arlington." Incidentally, Euston is close to Bury St. Edmunds, Suffolk, not far from Christopher Milton's home in Ipswich.

The Earl had a seesawing political career of his own making and revocations, but he was an adherent of Roman Catholicism and a promoter of popery. His daughter was married on 1 August 1672 at the age of 5 to Henry Fitzroy, Earl of Euston (1672) and Duke of Grafton (1675), who was nine, the illegitimate son of Charles II and Barbara Villiers, the Duchess of Cleveland as well as Lady Castlemaine, wife of the ardent Catholic Roger Palmer, Earl of Castlemaine, whose, *A Reply to the Answer of the Catholique Apology* (1668), [143], and *The Catholique Apology with a Reply to the Answer . . . The Third Edition Much Augmented* (1674), 305–06, 313, take Milton's anti-Catholic position to task. Arlington was one of the courtiers who had the management of Charles II's various mistresses. Isabella and Grafton were remarried on 6 November 1679 when she was twelve; the marriage was not consummated (apparently) until April 1681. In other words Phillips was Isabella's tutor around the time she was ten through twelve.

22. See *Edmund Ludlow. A Voyce from the Watch Tower,* ed. A.B. Worden, 19n.

23. Jonathan Richardson wrote that Sir William Morrice and Clarges "were his [Milton's] Friends, and manag'd Matters Artfully in his Favour" in 1660; see *Explanatory Notes and Remarks on Milton's Paradise Lost* (1734), 271 in Darbishire.

24. Phillips, xxxvi.

25. See also Shawcross, "Orthography."

26. *The History of Thomas Ellwood,* 233.

27. Where Edward stayed in his visits to London—for example, in late 1651 or early 1652—is not addressed in any of the biographical statements. Milton was living in Scotland Yard, Whitehall, in November 1649 through December 1651, and in Petty France, Westminster, in December 1651 through September(?) 1660. It was a full house at those times (and is assumed to have included John Phillips until at least around October 1651) and Mary Milton's pregnancy with Deborah, and her mother's attendance on her, all suggest that Edward would not have stayed with his uncle.

28. Did Wood really read Aubrey's notes? The sentence preceding Wood's gives the date and time of Milton's birth but not the place, though perhaps it should have; however, Sheet A, f. 1r, makes quite clear where he was born.

29. A number of establishments were located at or near the May-Pole in the Strand: those owned by Robert Chambers, apparently a grocer; Nathaniel Child, a grocer possibly licensed to sell wine; Phillip Complin, a distiller; John Dollen, a poulterer; and John Dutton; and one called "The Lobster." The first hackney coach stands were located at the May-Pole. See Jacob Henry Burn, 226–27.

30. Darbishire (xii) notes the problem but assumes that Edward is intended: "When Aubrey began his notes he did not know Edward Phillips, was ignorant even of his Christian name; but he made his acquaintance, evidently at a suggestion from Mrs. Milton." As pointed out, *on this same page* he makes reference to asking Edward for a catalogue of works; Darbishire's reading of the situation is untenable.

31. See *Shropshire Parish Registers, Lichfield Diocese,* 214. The HMC Thirteenth Report (1893), 147–48, records that in Shrewsbury, Country of Salop, Michael Ball who was examined before "Edward Phillips Eqre. mayor of the said towne, this 15th day of March 1678 [1679], deposeth as followeth . . . standing att his house doore being in Mardell in the said towne of Shrewsbury about May, June, or August, next comeing will be two years," in a report on carriages with arms for Lord Powis. Charles I had approved a charter constituting a new corporation of a mayor, twenty-four aldermen, forty-eight assistants, a coroner, a recorder, etc., for Shrewsbury on 16 June 1638; and Charles II, a charter nominating a mayor, aldermen, common councilmen, etc., on 6 July 1664. See HMC *Fifteenth Report, Appendix, Part X,* I, 407–09, 487. According to *The Victoria History of the Counties of England. A History of Shropshire,* ed. G.C. Baugh, "Shrewsbury was notably less loyalist than the rest of the county in 1660. . . . Despite the coporation's decision in July 1660 to restore those of its members who had been excluded in 1645, the Presbyterians remained strong . . ."; there were purges in the 1660s and it had a "predominantly Tory complexion after the beginning of parliamentary contests there in 1676," III, 264. There was an anti-Whig purge in 1681, riots as late as

May 1688, and resumption of quarter sessions only in 1689. It is likely that this Edward Phillips was a draper, whose wife was Elizabeth; they had a number of children. References to him suggest that he could have been elected mayor.

32. Toland (1699), 9, first published in *A Complete Collection of the Historical, Political, and Miscellaneous Works of John Milton, Both English and Latin* (London, 1698), I, 5–47.

33. Phillips wrote: "So that being now quiet from State-Adversaries and publick Contests, he had leisure again for his own Studies and private Designs; which were his foresaid *History* of England, and a New *Thesaurus Linguæ Latinæ*, according to the manner of Stephanus; a work he had been long since Collecting from his own Reading, and still went on with it at times, even very near to his dying day; but the Papers after his death were so discomposed and deficient, that it could not be made fit for the Press; However, what there was of it, was made use of for another Dictionary" (xxxiv).

Cyriack Skinner was a member of James Harrington's discussion group, The Rota, and this is apparently alluded to in Milton's sonnet to him beginning, "*Cyriack, whose Grandsire on the Royal Bench.*" It was proposed in *The Censure of the Rota*, probably correctly, that Milton owed much to Harrington's ideas in *The Ready and Easy Way*. A reference to Skinner that has not previously been noticed occurs in *Rump Songs*, Part II, in the poem "*The Rota:* Or / *News from the Common-wealths-Mens-*Club, / *Written by Mr.* Henry Stub: / *'Tis better than a Syllybub*" (p. 144):

> Last, *Skinner* of his Chair grown proud,
> Doth gravely weild the busie croud,
> And still to order cries aloud.
>   To tell you more of Mr. *Skinner,*
> He'd rather talk than eat his Dinner;
> 'Tis that which makes him look the thinner.

34. A letter from Aubrey to Wood (Bodleian MS Wood F.39, f. 372v), dated 25 May 1684, tells us that "Mr. J. Milton made two admirable Panegyricks (as to sublimitie of Witt) one on Ol: Cromwel, & the other on Th. Ld. Fairfax, both wch his nephew Mr. Philips hath; but he hath hung back these 2 yeares, as to imparting copies to me for ye Collect. of mine wth. you." Since Edward contributed to Aubrey's "minutes" around 1681 and since he published these sonnets (numbers 15 and 16) at the end of the "Life" of his uncle in 1694, it is reasonable to identify the reference here with Edward. I should point out, too, that a letter in this same manuscript, f. 387v, dated St. Peter's Day [29 June] 1689, informs Wood that Milton was at Cambridge and never at Oxford; the information comes from Edward Phillips. (The letter was not used by Parker, though it corroborates his argument about Milton's not being an Oxfordian despite inclusion in Wood's volume.) The sonnets are found in the Trinity MS, the first three in the basic quire of pages (and presumably, though now missing, in the quarto sheets) and the last in the quarto sheets. Does this mean that Phillips had access to the manuscript around 1694 (already in the Trinity College Library, it would seem) or that he had other copies which have disappeared (there is no evidence that copies were ever made)?

35. *Linguæ Romanæ Dictionarium Luculentum Novum. A New Dictionary . . . The Whole Completed and Improved from the Several Works of Stephens, Cooper, Gouldman, Holyoke, Dr. Littleton, a Large Manuscript, In Three Volumes, of Mr. John Milton, &c.* (1693) has a further citation of use in the Preface, A2v. Although this volume almost duplicates *Linguæ Latinæ Liber Dictionarius Quaripartitus. A Latine Dictionary, In Four Parts* (1678) by Adam Littleton, there is no indication of the use of the lost Latin thesaurus in it. But note Phillips's comment in n33 above, from which it appears that this Latin thesaurus by Milton had ceased to exist, although part(s) of it were used in some dictionary: Littleton's or is Phillips, in 1694, only repeating the tradition that the 1693 title page began? In turn this suggests (along with the lack of any publication corroboration) that neither of Phillips's two alleged volumes ever existed; his report says "another Dictionary" (indicating only one) and certainly does not suggest that he has used Milton's thesaurus in similar work of his own. Wood may again prove to be unreliable, despite the detail in his report.

36. Parker (655) may misrepresent Toland's statement by writing of these two prose works: "(which a 'worthy friend' had purchased from Milton's 'nephew')." Does "had" necessarily mean "bought"? However, Daniel Skinner in a document dated 18 October 1676 concerned with the publication of the State Papers attested that Moses Pitt told him that he had "bought some of Mr Miltons papers" (PRO, SP Dom 29/386/65).

37. For what little is known about the provenance of the manuscript, see French Fogle, Yale Prose, V, i (1971), 4–6. Toland is following Phillips: "Here it was also that he finisht and publisht his History of our Nation till the Conquest, all compleat so far as he went, some Passages only excepted, which being thought too sharp against the Clergy, could not pass the Hand of the Licencer, were in the Hands of the late Earl of *Anglesey* while he liv'd; where at present is uncertain. . . . The said Earl of *Anglesey* whom he presented with a Copy of the unlicens'd Papers of his History, came often here to visit him" (xxxix-xl).

38. In 1743 John Nickolls, Jr., a member of the Society of Antiquaries, published *Original Letters and Papers of State, Addressed to Oliver Cromwell; Concerning the Affairs of Great Britain. From the Year MDCXLIX to MDCLVIII. Found among the Political Collections of Mr. John Milton. Now first Published from the Originals.* None of the letters was written by Milton; they are still owned by the Society of Antiquaries, London. The Preface gives the provenance from Milton, who perhaps, it suggests, intended to use them "to illustrate either some particular or general history of his time," to the "possession of *Thomas Ellwood,* a person, who for several years was well acquainted with and esteemed by him," to Joseph Wyeth, "into whose hands, among the other papers of the said *Ellwood,* these letters fell; and through the hands of *J. Wyeth's* widow they came into the possession of the present editor" (iv).

39. Three other full or partial, translated or Latin, repeated or garbled collections derived from the 1676 editions appeared in the last quarter of the century (from 1682 through 1700); see *Milton: A Bibliography For The Years 1624–1700,* Nos. 333, 351, and 401.

40. See "A Survey of Milton's Prose Works," 354–57, in *Achievements of the Left Hand,* ed. Lieb and Shawcross, and Leo Miller, "Milton's State Letters: The Lünig Version," 95–96.

41. See William Riley Parker, "Milton and the News of Charles Diodati's Death," and Rose Clavering and John T. Shawcross, "Milton's European Itinerary."

42. Phillips's statement found with Aubrey's notes says, "immediately after his return he took a lodging at Mr Russell's a Taylour in St Brides churchyard" but Aubrey has: "when she [his first wife] came to live wth her husband at Mr Russells in St Brides ch: yd, she found it very solitary." The most notable "Mr. Russell" residing in St. Bride's at this time was Robert, apparently an Independent, elected by the vestry to be one of the ten Common Councilmen. St. Bride's was a large parochial community, peopled by a diverse group of poor (with hundreds of poor children) and tradesmen, only some of whom were financially well off. It seems to have been largely Presbyterian in the 1640s. In 1645–46 there was much religious agitation with some reorganization of the governmental structure of the parish, but Russell seems not to have been part of that Presbyterian action. He was, however, connected with the Army (who were Independents) and referred to as "Major." See Guildhall Library Manuscripts 6554/1, ff. 6–204 (especially 68 and 132b), 6554/2, 6552/1, and 9163; and Tai Liu, *Puritan London*. This identification for Milton's landlord is confirmed by a statement in *A Paire of Spectacles for the Citie* (Printed in the Yeare, MDCXLVIII), which George Thomason alters to "MDCXLVII" and gives the date 4 December: "Puny Captaine *Russell*. Surely this is one of the *Shakers* they talke of; a fellow that every *Step* he takes speakes him a *Tayler*" (p. 8 [recte 10]). Parker cites three other Russells in the area (Bartholomew, Joseph, Nicholas), 1230 in an added note for 838 n2, but Robert's occupation and position in the community make his identification certain. The connection between Robert Russell and Milton is also suggested by J.R. Woodhead in *The Rulers of London 1660–1689*, 142.

Woodhead indicates that Russell was a Common Councilman from Farringdon Without (that is, St. Bride) during the years 1649–1660 and Deputy during the years 1657–1660. He was "near Fleet Street" in 1644 (see the will of Edward Frank, a Common Councilman from Aldersgate Without, in the Prerogative Court of Canterbury #110, May 1644 and proved 19 July 1661). He is listed in the Vestry Books of St. Bride in 1649 and 1661; and of Bride Lane in 1663 according to the Hearth Tax Returns, f. 100. He had been apprenticed to Evan Gundey of Old Bailey in 1609/10 (Corporation of London Record Office, MS 40/3) and became Warden of the Merchant Taylors' Company in 1667 (Apprenticeship Bindings, VI, f. 56, which also indicates that his father was John Russell, a yeoman, of South Petherton, Somersetshire). Not cited by Woodhead are the following notations. Russell contributed £2. to the relief of Irish Protestants in 1642, from St. Bride's on 2 June 1642 (PRO SP 28/193; I thank Edward Jones for this reference); Milton also contributed £4. from St. Botolph's Street (PRO E179/252). Russell is recorded in the *Calendar of State Papers, Domestic*, three times probably and three definitely: [1], *CSPD* (1635), 555, 12 December 1635, "Affidavit of Robert Russell, citizen and weaver of London," concerning Robert Langdon and Roger Turtle; [2–3], *CSPD* (1645–47), 65 and 73, dated 14 and 16 August 1645, reports from Derby House in Canon Row, Westminster, where the Council of State met, "Sent by Russell," concerning the need for forces, which were apparently ready, to march against the King, sent to the counties of Norfolk, Suffolk, and Essex, and "Sent by Russell," concerning Captain Jordan, sent to the Association at Cambridge; [4], *CSPD* (1655–56), 239, 25 March 1656, listed as in attendance for the Proceedings of the Council of State, "Maj. Rob. Russell"; [5], *CSPD* (1658–59), 265,

25 January 1658/9, in the Proceedings of the Council of State: "The Nevis prisoners at Bristol sent up and referred, and Maj. Russell's commission recalled"; [6], *CSPD* (1662), 444, 20 July 1662: "Robert Russell, late a Parliamentary officer, was imprisoned at Salisbury for wearing his sword, probably in ignorance of the proclamation. Begs his release, as he has for some years past shown great affection to the King's service."

Robert Russell's house, therefore, was on Bride Lane, just off Fleet Street, in the area of St. Bride's Churchyard, where, from the west, Fleet Street runs into Ludgate Circle, and Ludgate Hill runs east. Christopher Milton's "Cross Keys" was on Ludgate Hill, "scituate in the lane or Alley commonly called or knowne by the name of Panyer Alley in the said parish of St. Martin." That is, it lay between Ludgate Circle (and St. Bride's) and St. Paul's Cathedral, the lesser messuage abutting Panyer Lane, which comes off Paternoster Row, the northern street around St. Paul's Churchyard. To say the least, Milton's lodging with Russell was in an area he knew well and close to family property; his connecting with Russell, a tailor, may have resulted, we can suppose, from familial knowledge of the man and his business. We should note that the move to Aldersgate Street in St. Botolph's parish was not far, being just north of St. Paul's near Little Britain, an area of many booksellers, later including his friend Edward Millington's establishment.

43. Important evidence, as Jones shows, is the *List of the Principal Inhabitants of the City of London, 1640.* Here are reported "the names of the Inhabitants of the better sort and conceaued to be of the best estate," drawn from the names who "were conceived able to lend the King (Charles I.) money upon security towards raising £200,000, according to order of the Privy Council, dated 10 May 1640." Milton's name does not appear in the report of Sir William Acton, Alderman, for Aldersgate Ward, St. Botolph's parish, implying that he was not resident there at that time. Parker, who refers to the "List" (845), did not apparently realize this significance. Milton does appear in the April 1641 subsidy tabulation.

44. Does this revision point to an explanation of the confusion that seems to exist in Milton's recital of his return from the Continent in the *Defensio Secunda* (87)? There he says he returned "at almost the same time as Charles broke the peace and renewed the war with the Scots, which is known as the second Bishops' War" (Yale Prose, IV, 620; "second," "alterum" in the Latin, should have been translated "other"). The Second Bishops' War was in August 1640, about a year after his return, but with the uncertainty of his residence, the changes in his life, and finally his move to Aldersgate Street after May 1640—June or July?—Charles's breaking of the peace may have all merged to become "at almost the same time."

45. See "New Light on the Milton-Phillips Family Relationship."

Chapter 4

1. An example of Wood's subjectivity in his biographical statements or of contamination by someone else (Thomas Tickell, the editor?) can be seen as well in Wood's animosity toward Bishop Crewe of Durham, who is called "an Olivarian and stuck in with the wicked Revolution." In Andrew Clark's edition of *Memoirs of Nathaniel, Lord Crewe,* is the comment, "It seems the Bp. is said in it *to have been first a Puritan, then a Papist, and at last an Orangian.* As I do not look upon this to have been written

by Ant. à Wood, so I suppose and believe that there are many such spurious Additions" in the 1721 edition of *Athenæ Oxonienses* (45). Godwin's attitude can be gleaned from chapter VII, where, mentioning Milton's death and burial, he posits the rupture between uncle and nephew: "John Philips on the contrary, who, we shall have reason to think, as long as he existed never relaxed in his unnatural animosity to Milton, did not, I trust, pollute the sad solemnity with his unhallowed presence."

2. In Stanza VII, p. 3, he writes: "They may talk what they will, but there ne're was a Satyr / Since *His* against *Hypocrites* writ, wou'd hold Water." The author is often given erroneously as Richard Ames, author of *A Search After Claret*, which the anonymous poem is lampooning. Milton is also referred to in Stanza XLVII, p. 11.

3. Dunton's full statement, p. 241 in the 1705 edition, is: "Mr *Philips*, a Gentleman of good Learning, and well born. He'll write you a *Design*, off in a very little Time, if the Gout (or Claret) don't stop him. He translates *The Present State of Europe; Or, the Monthly Mercury*, incomparably well, which is one of the finest *Journals* of the kind, the World has ever seen; I was once concern'd in it, but had the Misfortune to drop it." The editor of the 1818 edition, which includes "Selections from the Miscellaneous Works of John Dunton," cites vituperative discussions of "P——s" (II, 432, 450–52, 474) from "A Secret History of the Weekly Writers" and "The Living Elegy" under Phillips's name in the index. These are wrong: the references are to William Pittis; see Theodore F.M. Newton. (The editor also lists together as bookseller Mr. Philips of Boston, pp. 95–96, and Mr. Philips from London, p. 216; they are clearly different people, the first being married, the second being a bachelor. He further errs in listing Mr. Philips, the mayor-elect of Kilkenny, p. 595, as "Phillips, author.") But the editor, in his ignorance, improperly and reprehensibly altered Dunton's text on p. 474 to read: "Drunken *Philips* (my reeling Enemy) has interloped so long with my Whipping Project, that a London Jury have found him (and his Tacking Master) guilty of writing and printing scandalous libels; and, if he have justice done him, has whipped himself into the pillory." The original reads "P——s"! Dunton refers to his 1705 intention of producing *The Whipping Post*, which, however, did not appear until 1706 as *Dunton's Whipping Post*, and to Pittis's *The Whipping-Post, At a New Session of Oyer and Terminer* (1705). Dunton's reference to claret in connection with John Phillips (cited above) may have led the editor to these egregious errors, but perhaps Godwin's 1815 denunciations of John are also at fault.

4. Giles Jacob, *An Historical Account of the Lives and Writings of Our Most Considerable English Poets, Whether Epick, Lyrick, Elegiack, Epigrammatists, &c.*, 133.

5. See Sandelands's letter to John Thurloe, written from "Woodstreet compter" (that is, from the jail on Wood Street in Edinburgh), printed in *A Collection of the State Papers of John Thurloe* (1742), II, 226–27. He writes from jail as a result of "the abuse of a knavish attorney," one Knightsbridge who lived at Staple Inn, London. Milton had written to Sandelands on 3 January 1653 (the letter is lost), and he responded on 15 January from Edinburgh (PRO SP 18/23/6); he shows his abhorrence of Scotch Presbyterians. Another letter from Sandelands "ffor His much honnoured freind, John Milton Esquire" (PRO, SP Dom 18/34/105) is dated 29 March 1653 from Edinburgh.

Frederick L. Beaty has suggested that since John was in Scotland in 1654, his brother may have "sold" the copy of *A Satyr Against Hypocrites* to the bookseller Nathanael Brooke, which was written in 1654, because the Stationers' Register lists it on 14 March 1654/5 with Edward as author. See "Three Versions of John Phillips's *A Satyr Against Hypocrites*."

6. A letter from a John Phillips on 15 February 1653/4 to John Gunter at Clifford's Inn in London, apparently from Wales (which refers to a letter sent twelve months earlier on "articles of tyranny and oppression"), is probably from a different John Phillips. (Interestingly Gunter may have been at "his seat at the Six Clerks Office in London.") See Thurloe, II, 93. A John Phillips, probably the same one, signed a petition presented to Cromwell objecting to his usurpation of power; there are 321 signatures, among them Thomas Vaughan, Richard Baxter, Vavasor Powell, John Rowland, and Thomas Edwards (Thurloe, IV, 380–84). It is not dated but it lies between items from 3 January 1655/56? and 14 January 1656; it has, I think inaccurately, been dated 1655. One point of issue is the political/economic situation with Spain, and significantly it records the antipathy toward the Protectorate and the system of controls by the Major-Generals, which we will refer to later.

7. PRO SP 27/1; see Vol. 273, State Papers Domestic, Charles I to James II (SP16-SP31).

8. A "Mr. John Phillips at the Nag's Head tavern near Temple Bar" (HMC, Manuscripts of the Marquesse of Ormonde, New Series, Vol. I, p. 329) addressed a letter on the Spanish problems in the Lowlands: "These for Mr. George Bifield, recommended to Mr. John Shaw, English merchant in the Old Shoes Market at Antwerp." Perhaps this is the same "Mr. Phillips" who was in Breda with Lady Hyde, Sir John Mennes, and Mr. Heath (later joined by Mr. Chancellor) on 15/25 April 1656 (letter from Henry Coventry to James Butler, Marquis of Ormond, HMC, Manuscripts of the Marquesse of Ormonde, New Series, Vol. I, p. 323); and the "Mr. Phillip" in T. Cheverel's letter to M. de Selly, 3 November 1659 (ibid., pp. 330–31). Provocative is Milton's nephew's probable association with Mennes, Heath's association with Christopher, and Coventry's association with Thomas Agar (and see chapter 2, n164).

9. See *CSPD*, (Commonwealth), for 1654, 378–79, 417–18, dated 21 October 1654 and 28 December 1654.

10. This, however, conflicts with placing Phillips in Westminster in the deeds from 1651 to 1655, except that the deeds in 1654–55 may merely repeat (copy) what had been true earlier. These kinds of transactions frequently copied such material from an early one to a later one even though some such facts had changed. It also conflicts with the testimony in the case of *Sportive Wit* in 1656; see my next paragraph. If Wood's undated statement concerning Edward's being in the Strand near the May Pole, where he taught school, should be assigned to John, as considered before, it might refer to a period only in the early 1650s, whenever John left his uncle's home and before he may have moved to Aldersgate Street by November 1654.

11. Barkstead, who was a regicide, died in 1662, having been appointed governor of the Tower in 1652 and being knighted on 19 January 1656. His path crossed Milton's or his relatives at different times, it seems, although any significance is not determinable: he was governor of Reading in 1645, he represented Colchester and Reading in Parliament in 1654–56, he was one of the Major-Generals named in 1655, and he was an alderman in Cripplegate Ward from 22 February 1657/8 through 31 January 1659/60. He was excepted from amnesty, fled to Holland, but was apprehended and executed on 19 April 1662.

Brooks testified that the work (three "sections" printed in mid-February 1656) was a "collection of sundry papers, which he procured of several persons, and added together for that purpose," rather than the work of only Phillips. The "sparkling wits" of the Club who collected the poems are identified on the title page as "C.J.B.J.L.M.W.T."; they were not named and were not cited by Barkstead. Modern commentaries treat the book as totally the result of Phillips's editorial work, and there even seem to be implications that the poems are Phillips's. The poems are often coarse and witty, typical of what will be Restoration satire, but also many are typical of Cavalier "love" poetry. At least two poems that suggest Phillips as author, perhaps, when we think of Milton's influence upon him, are "A Speech," which refers to "*Burton, Prynne, and Bastwick*" (5) who, on 14 June 1637, were heavily fined and mutilated for their antiepiscopal writings; and "To his Friend; A Censure of the Poets," which has positive things to say about Joshua Sylvester's translation of Du Bartas's "La Semaine" (71). (See *Don Quixote* later for remarks on Du Bartas.) It should be noted that *Wit and Drollery* is cited in the volume. That collection consists of "Jovial Poems. Never before Printed. By Sir J.M. Ja: S. Sir W.D.J.D. and other admirable Wits" (1656); they are identified as Sir John Mennes, James Smith, Sir William Davenant, and John Dryden, who have not come in for opprobrium because of their connection with the collection. It is possible that unidentified poems by Phillips appear here as well as in *Sportive Wit*. Previous writers on Phillips have all included *Wit and Drollery* among his work, in this case, again, as editor. The edition, dated 18 January 1655/6 by George Thomason (and the 1661 printing, both for Nathaniel Brooks), included two acknowledged poems by John Suckling, poems by Ben Jonson, and a love elegy by J[ohn] D[onne], and a catalogue advertising books by both Edward and John, as does the quite different 1682 edition by Obadiah Blagrave (with an additional unassigned poem by Suckling). The "J. P." of the Preface to *Wit and Drollery* was identified as John Playford by Thomason. "J. P." also signed the address to the reader, but this is changed to "E. M." in the 1661 edition. Whether Phillips was the collector of either volume is not certain, but he was not the author of all the poems in them, if any. Those who were associated with either collection have not received the negative diatribe for licentious language that Phillips has—a sure sign of the prejudiced attitude toward Phillips. A third possible collection, which, however, may actually refer to either of these volumes or another, is inferred from PRO, SP Dom 25/77/108, dated 9 May 1656. Here "all the bookes, Entituled, Choice Drollery, Songs, and Sonnetts" are ordered seized. Apparently on the basis of Brooks's testimony about *Sportive Wit*, both *Wit and Drollery* and this further inferred collection have been assigned, I suggest erroneously, to John Phillips as editor. The naive discussions by Godwin and Hone indicate a naive lack of knowledge about the nature of the poetry of the period, which, if some of his poems are included, John's poetry exhibited as well.

12. *Marriage Licences Issued by the Dean and Faculty of Westminster 1558–1699* (London, 1886), 138 (Harleian Society Publications, XXIII). Perhaps also to be noted is the marriage of a Mr. John Phillips and Mrs. Lucey Essex on 24 November 1657 at St. Julian's in Shrewsbury. See *Transactions of the Shropshire Archælogical and Natural History Society*, Vol. 10 (1887), p. 289. There were other Phillipses in the area.

13. He writes (1–2), "a Serjeant or a Bayliff Shall dig him out of the Earth, with as much Diligence as if he were the Oar of Mexico; and never ceases till he has hid him again in some obscure place or other, never to be found"; he talks of the "Off-

spring of the Gentry" and the "Common shures of Povertie, *Fleet, Kings-Bench, Counters* or *Ludgate.*" Under December (remembering the birth of Christ) he laments, "But truly there are so many *Heresies* and *Sects* that care neither for *Christ,* nor his *Good time* neither, that the Trade of *Begging for Christ's sake* is hardly worth following now a dayes" (39).

14. "The Act for the better relief of the poor of this kingdom" (known as "The Act of Settlement"), Statutes, 14 Charles II, chapter 12 (1662), says, "Whereas the necessity, number and continual increase of the poor, not only within the Cities of London and Westminster with the liberties of each of them . . . is very great and exceeding burdensome, being occasioned by reason of some defects in the law concerning the settling of the poor and for want of a due provision of the regulations of relief and employment in such parishes or places where they are legally settled, which doth enforce many to turn incorrigible rogues and others to perish for want." Disorderly persons and "sturdy beggars" could be sentenced by Justices of the Peace to workhouses, not to exceed seven years (*English Economic History; Select Documents, Compiled and Edited by A.E. Bland, P.A. Brown, R.H. Tawney,* 647–49). The poor could also be transferred to a different county, but that made them liable to seizure as bad financial risks for the new locale. "An Act for the better regulating of Workhouses for setting the Poor on work" (Statutes, 22 and 23 Charles II, chapter 18 [1670–71]) was followed by "An Act for the Relief and Release of poor distressed Prisoners for Debt" (chapter 20): "For as much as many persons now detained in prison are miserably impoverished, either by reason of the late unhappy times, the sad and dreadful fire, their own misfortunes, or otherwise, so as they are totally disabled to give any satisfaction to their creditors, and so become without disadvantage to any, a charge and burthen to the kingdom" may have Justices of the Peace administer to the debtor an oath that "he hath no real or personal estate, in possession, reversion, or remainder, of the value of £10 in the whole, or sufficient to pay the debt." The creditor may thus discharge the said prisoner without fee or chamber-rent, and if not, he must "allow and pay weekly such reasonable maintenance to the said prisoner as the justices shall order, not exceeding eighteen pence a week; and upon non-payment of the same weekly, the said prisoner is to be set at liberty." (See Sir George Nicholls, *A History of the English Poor Law,* I, 304–06].) According to Christopher Harding, Bill Hines, Richard Ireland, and Philip Rawlings in *Imprisonment in England and Wales,* around 5000 convicts were sent to America in the last half of the century (65), a barrister, William Leach, estimated in 1651 that between 12,000 and 20,000 people were in prison, and "Criminals and debtors . . . made up the vast bulk of the prison population at any one time" (76–77).

15. Parker uses the probable date and issue of *The Present State of Europe,* perhaps still from Phillips (according to Dunton's remarks), and the advertisement in *The History of the Works of the Learned . . . For the Month of August, 1706* (Vol. VIII; London: Printed for H. Rhodes; A Bell, and D. Midwinter, 1706), 511[recte 510]-501[recte 511] (sigs. Sss3v-Sss4r), for *The Vision of Monsieur Chamillard* as proof that "He was still alive in 1706" (1168). The publication of the *Third Volume of the Works of Lucian* in 1711 included a "translation" that had been written earlier; see later.

16. See Leo Miller, *John Milton's Writings in the Anglo-Dutch Negotiations, 1651–1654,* 43–44 and ff.

17. See French, III, 388, and V, 443, for the probable circumstance being noted;

there is no date given, but Parker's comment on a pretended envoy named Jentilliot and such an order of 9 July 1652 is cogent.

18. See "Notes on Milton's Amanuenses." Among the items that seem certain (although others have not been convinced apparently because of the variations in all these hands) are "Ad Joannem Roüsiúm" (dated 23 January 1647; with correction in Milton's hand); the translations of two letters from Sophia, Princess of the Palatine, PRO, SP 18/1/55, ff. 142r, 143r (after 13 April 1649), one of which has a correction in Milton's hand; the inscription in Christopher Arnold's Album (19 November 1651, with signature by Milton); a note on the Oldenburgh Safeguard, Niedersächsische Staatsarchive, Oldenburg (as well as the note on the corresponding Latin version), dated 17 February 1652; the completion of an entry in Milton's Bible noting Deborah's birth (after 2 May 1652); Sonnet 16, Trinity MS (after May 1652); Sonnet 17, Trinity MS (after 3 July 1652); "New Forcers of Conscience," Trinity MS (after July 1652); note in the Trinity MS positioning "New Forcers" (after July 1652). On the basis of Phillips being eleven years old in 1642, I query whether he may not have been the probable student who entered Sonnet 8 ("Captaine, or Collonell") into the Trinity MS. Maurice Kelley has written that Hand 2 (Sonnet 16 and the Machiavelli notes on pp. 198 and 243 of the CPB) and Hand 3 (Sonnet 17, "New Forcers," the positioning note, and the Oldenburg Safeguard) are apparently the same. (For designation of Hands, see Maurice Kelley, "Milton's Later Sonnets and the Cambridge Manuscript.")

19. See Maurice Kelley, "Milton and Machiavelli's *Discorsi*," 123–28 (plus three pages of facsimiles).

20. It should be considered that Hand 9 may be John's, which would thus make him the writer of most of the Machiavelli entries and of the six letters to Mylius dated between 7 November 1651 and 21 February 1652. As noted in the previous chapter, Edward Phillips penned the letter to Mylius that refers to Bulstrode Whitelocke, dated 13 February 1652. There is also a letter to Whitelocke from Milton dated 12 February 1652 (owned by the Marquis of Bath) that has not been available for comparison of hands, but circumstantial evidence suggests it may have been written by Hand 9. Peter Beal confounds these two letters in his *Index of English Manuscripts*. All of this suggested work by Edward and John Phillips in 1651–1652 should be considered alongside the domestic facts that at this time Milton became totally blind and that shortly afterward Mary Powell Milton gave birth to Deborah and died (May 1652) and the son John, a little more than a year old, also died (June 1652). Catherine Gemelli Martin has suggested to me that the son, who would have been put under the care of a wet nurse, died from a problem of breast-feeding, apparently a fairly common cause of infant mortality at this time. Phillips writes of the son, "which through the ill usage, or bad Constitution of an ill chosen Nurse, died an Infant." Perhaps a similar problem resulted in the death of his daughter Katherine in March 1658.

21. See James Holly Hanford, "The Chronology of Milton's Private Studies," for designations of amanuenses in the CPB.

22. The well known musicologist Matthew Locke's critique *Observations upon a Late Book, Entituled, an Essay to the Advancement of Musick, &c. Written by Thomas Salmon, M.A.* (1672) included an epigram signed "J. Philips," A2r, which has the line referring to Salmon "*though he* Flea's *not his* Skin, *he* Tawes *his* Hide." In rebuttal, *A Vindi-*

cation of an Essay To the Advancement of Musick, From Mr. Matthew Lock's Observations (1672), Salmon quotes heavily from Locke but also takes out after Phillips: "a terrible fellow in Buff, an Epigrammatical Poetaster; This man, Sir, (one would think) dealt only with Pen, Ink, and Paper; but alas! he was arm'd with all the Instruments of Cruelty, and heated with such an implacable Malice, that he sentences me; first, to have my Hide taw'd etc. But 'twas well for us, his Pegasus was jaded; and so, farewel him" (4). On p. 77 he writes, "but at present I shall remit the *Observer* [Locke] to his Friend *J. Philips* for construction." In surrebuttal Locke reacted with *The Present Practice of Musick Vindicated against the Exceptions and New Way of Atttaining Musick Lately Publish'd by Thomas Salmon, M.A. &c. By Matthew Locke . . . To which is added Duellum Musicum by John Phillips, gent.* (1673). The epigram, "To my Friend Mr. *Matthew Locke,* On his ingenious Discovery of those Musical Innovations Held forth by the *Author* of *An Essay to the Advancement of Musick, &c.,*" π2v, is reprinted, and the prose "Musical Duel," 25–76, offers criticism of Salmon's logic, plays upon his being a "Man in Buff," refers to himself specifically on p. 39, and translates Martial's epigram, Book III, No. 43, which Salmon had cited but "deigned" not to translate. In a letter to Salmon dated 26 August 1672, John Playford, publisher of both Locke volumes, makes reference to "Mr. Philips," 77. Phillips's epigram and essay exhibit a ridiculing streak, but also a discussion of music theory and of logic. Locke's musical analyses have received approbation; Salmon's have not.

23. See Hone's dissertation and his entry on Phillips in *A Milton Encyclopedia,* VI, 137–39. Some sources of reference to works also lie in book catalogues of the period; for example, that of Dr. John Owen from the bookseller and friend of Milton Edward Millington in 1684: *Bibliotheca Oweniana, Sive Catalogus Librorum*; on p. 31 (second pagination) is "Jo. Phillip's Late Voyages to Constantinople, with Cuts 1683." Listings of Edward Phillips's work also appear in such catalogues here on p. 16 is "Phillips New World of Words (1671)." Narcissus Luttrell's copy of *A Continuation of the Compleat Catalogue of Stitch'd Books and Single Sheets, &c. Printed since the First Discovery of the Popish Plot, September 1678. From the 1st. of January 1679/80. to the 25th. of June 1680,* 18, lists "*Satyr against Hypocrites*; an old thing Reprinted. 1680," with the notation "Aprill 14" and the price paid, 4 pence. In his *A Second Continuation of the Complete Catalogue* is "Dr. *Oates* Narative of the Popish Plot vindicated, in answer to a Scurrilous Libel, called a Vindication of the English Catholicks &c. Printed for T. *Cocker'll,*" 4, which brought 1s, 6d. This catalogue also includes under "Poetry," 13, "*Jockies* downfal, a Poem on the late total defeat, given to the Scotish *Covenanters* near *Hamilton Park 22th. of June* 1679. by His Majesties Forces," which sold for one penny.

24. In *Speculum Crape-Gownorum: Or, A Looking-Glass for the Young Academicks, new Foyl'd. With Reflections On some of the late High-Flown Sermons, To which is added, An Essay towards a Sermon of the Newest Fashion. By a Guide to the Inferiour Clergie* Phillips includes a sermon, chapter 32, pp. 25–34, on a text from Rabelais, lampooning the homiletics of the clergy. It is not dissimilar to his travesty in *A Satyr Against Hypocrites.* Of them he writes, "But that they may see how ridiculous they are, when they stand fretting, and fuming, and heating themselves about *State Affairs* in their Pulpits, they are desired to read the short Sermon that follows, which if it be not altogether their own words, I am sure is altogether their own sense" (24). The work is satiric against Roger L'Estrange and the "Romish" clergy, talking of "Phylacteries" (p. 1), a word Milton used satirically in "New Forcers," and decidedly pro-Church of England. *The Second*

Edition Corrected and Enlarged advertises Phillips's *A Pleasant Conference upon the Observator and Heraclitus, &c. by the Author of this Speculum* (p. 34). *The Second Part. Or a Continuation of Observations and Reflections Upon the Late Sermons Of some that would be thought Goliah's for the Church of England By the same Author* interestingly spells the giant's name in the same variant and less frequent way as its single occasion in Milton's works in *Samson Agonistes,* 1249.

25. Published accounts of or references to *The Secret History* have been incomplete or erroneous. *The Secret History of the Reigns of K. Charles II, and K. James II.* (Printed in the Year 1690) appeared before *The Secret History of K. James I. and K. Charles I. Compleating the Reigns of the Four last Monarchs. By the Author of the Secret History of K. Charles II. and K. James II.* (Printed in the Year 1690). Thus we see that both volumes were written by the same person and that they were written and published in reverse regnal order. This later publication indicates the "Reigns of the Four last Monarchs," which points us immediately to *The Secret History of the Four Last Monarchs of Great Britain, Viz. James I, Charles I, Charles II, James II* (1691; Ed. 2, 1693), a volume (with an appendix updating James II's "history" after his abdication in 1688) ignored by those wishing to bring Phillips into authorship of the first published. The new edition alters verbally the beginning of the Preface and the life of James I, but is otherwise a reprint, and the life of Charles II, etc., is an unrevised reprint. This history of the four last monarchs is regularly assigned to Nathaniel Crouch, a frequent author (who at times used false initials or a pseudonym) and publisher.

26. *Wit and Drollery* was dedicated to Edward Pepes, but see n11 concerning Phillips's association with this publication. The only Edward Pepes (Pepis, Pepys) in Walter Courtenay Pepys's *Genealogy of the Pepys Family 1237–1887* is Edward of Broomsthorpe (part of the Second Norfolk Branch of the family), who was born in 1617 and died on 22 December 1663. He was a member of the Middle Temple, and perhaps this accounts for his connection with those who were responsible for the volume.

27. We might note that Robert Hooke bought "Philips Virgill" for one shilling on 31 May 1678; see *The Diary of Robert Hooke M.A., M.D., F.R.S. 1672–1680,* 361.

28. *Readings in English History,* ed. Edward P. Cheyney, 535–36. Fountainhall was Sir John Lauder of Fountainhall (1646–1722); on 23 April 1685 he was elected member of the Scottish Parliament for the County of Haddington. He was staunchly against the policy of James II concerning Covenanters and his attempt to establish Catholicism.

29. Hugh Wilson, in an unpublished study of the poem, argues that Milton's nephew was not the author because of certain lines and epithets that are certainly interpretable of Royalist sentiments and Tory language. Interesting is the basic similarity that John Dryden may offer in relation to Charles II and James II, although he and Phillips are politically and religiously opposed. Anne Barbeau Gardiner in "Dryden, Bower, Castlemaine, and the Imagery of Revolution, 1682–1687," writes: "even though the poet [in *Threnodia Augustalis,* 1685] and the medalist [George Bower's second medal in 1683] both concede the king's near-fatal negligence of his duty, they still see him as brave and as being under the special protection of divine Providence" (140), and further, "Like Dryden's poetry in 1687 and 1688, 'The King's Arms' [an illustration by James Michael Wright on Roger, Earl of Castlemaine's becoming ambassador to Rome, 1687] is deeply sympathetic to James II, but realistic

about the precarious state of his rule. Indeed, by 1687 . . . the Tory or church party eagerly awaited the coming of William's reign to take revenge on the supporters and co-religionists of James II" (145).

30. Austin Woolrych, Introduction, *Yale Prose* (1980), VII, Revised, 97. The full Introduction, pp. 1–176, should be consulted for a detailed examination of the confused years of 1658–1660.

Philips, "nephew of the author," presented to John Barker (according to the Latin manuscript notation on the title page) a copy of the second edition of *Eikonoklastes;* the volume is now owned by the Beinecke Library, Yale University. Barker became a member of the restored Rump Parliament in 1659, having been a captain in the Army in the early years of the Commonwealth and then a colonel. (See also *CSPD*, Commonwealth, 1651, 27 June 1651, 272; *CSPD*, Commonwealth, 1651–52, 29 January 1652, 123; *CSPD*, Commonwealth, 1652–53, March 1653, 248 [referring to 1 December 1652]; *CSPD*, Commonwealth, 1658–59, 16 June 1659, 376, and 25 June 1659, 387; *CSPD*, Commonwealth, 1659–60, 9 July 1659, 15, and 17 August 1659 from Whitehall, 119, and 4 October 1659, 4 October 1659, 238–39.) The 9 July 1659 record in the "Index entries of proceedings in the Council of State" includes the order for Colonel Barker to have lodgings in Whitehall; on 7 May, the Rump was restored and reestablished the Commonwealth on the twenty-fifth. He is called "the radical Barker" by David Underdown, *Somerset in the Civil War and Interregnum*, 176. Barker is said to have been in Lord Falkland's regiment at Dunkirk (in battle with Spain and where England lost many ships); they were ordered "to repair to their charge within ten days, on pain of dismissal" (*CSPD*, Charles II, 1661–62, 194). But by 21 July 1662 he and others were "in custody at Taunton, and shall be kept till further orders" (444). An enclosure of 18 July repeats information from John Heathfield that in connection with the plot at Bristol Fair, there was "a meeting at Taunton of 20 old commissioned officers. . . . They have 2,000 arms and 2,00*l.* at command. They expect the Londoners to begin; they are to be headed by Ludlow, who is said to be in the country." Reference is to what ensued after disorders in Bristol following the housing of Parliamentary regiments in mid-October 1659, the threatening antagonisms of the soldiers in December and the Common Councillors' raising arms as a precaution against them, the imprisonment of some for loyalty to Parliament and the disbanding of the city militia on 27 December, which led to the troops' being out of control and rioting. The Army terrorized adherents of the Rump and were ready to declare for a free Parliament with a major riot on 3 February 1660. But the Royalists took over the militia by mid-April 1660. A scare, called "a plot" in a letter from Thomas Jeynes to William Neast in November 1661, concerned the possible spread to Bristol of Army action in Worcester. By October 1663, there was "discovery of the Northern Rising which supposedly targeted Bristol and Gloucester among cities to be secured by the plotters' (probably non-existent) southern allies." See A.R. Warmington, *Civil War, Interregnum and Restoration in Gloucestershire 1640–1672*, 162–66, 184. On the order for billeting soldiers in 1659 and problems, see three letters from the Committee on Safety and the Mayor and Aldermen of Gloucester in HMC, *Manuscripts of the Duke of Beaufort, K.G., and Others* (Twelfth Report, Appendix, Part IX), pp. 517–18 (19, 24, and 26 November 1659). On continuing problems at Bristol, see *CSPD* (Charles II, 1663–64), 287, 289, 297, 300, 381–82. On 6 October 1663 (p. 289): "Account of a rising intended for the 12th; 7,000 or

8,000 are to surprise Bristol; they do not rely much on those within the walls of London, but those about the City are to join, and the soldiers to have ammunition and money for 10 or 12 days, in which time they hope to be masters of the country. There are designs against the King's person by some about Court. Endorsed 'Information concerning the plot, see from the Duke of Buckingham to His Majesty'"; and on 12 October, forces were sent to Bristol to do the "utmost to execute the King's pleasure against the sectarists of the city and their seditious meetings" (297).

There is no indication as to when Phillips presented the book to Barker, but it might have been in this 1659 period (4 October) when *CSPD*, Commonwealth, 1659–60, 239, records that "Barker argued for a Commonwealth against a single person, and Gough the contrary" (that is, William Goffe, a Cromwellian, who sat in the Second Parliament and was one of the Major-Generals). Milton's tract is clearly pertinent to the debate, and the presentation by Phillips indicates his awareness of what was going on in Parliament, his (and Milton's) agreement with Barker on a Commonwealth, and his position that we discern in *Montelion's Predictions* and a few years later in *Don Lamberto*. The presented book reminds us that Milton's 1660 *Ready and Easy Way* had not appeared, offering some corroboration that the gift should be dated around Autumn 1659 and underscoring the thesis of this chapter: Phillips's agreement and close connection with his uncle. Further testimony to the Committee of Safety in his article against Captain Goffe records that "Gough says he asked Barker to sit for Ilchester, as there would be a Commonwealth party in the House, and he might strengthen it. Barker remembers Gough's advising him to be chosen, which he was accordingly, but not his saying anything about Government" (239).

31. The group of army officers (including Charles Fleetwood, John Desborough, William Goffe, Sir John Barkstead) that formed when Richard Cromwell became Protector to create a kind of military parliament in support. They met at Wallingford House, Fleetwood's residence near Whitehall Palace.

32. David Quint, *Epic and Empire*, 338–40. "This fear of central state authority . . . is linked with . . . Milton's religious politics: his opposition to Presbyterianism, to tithes and a stipendiary clergy, to censorship, and to a state religion, even one constituted by the Independents themselves" (338).

33. Leon Howard, ed., *A Satyr Against Hypocrites* (1655), No. 38, The Augustan Reprint Society, ii.

34. Compare Milton's remarks on satire: "a Satyr as it was borne out of a *Tragedy*, so ought to resemble his parentage, to strike high, and adventure dangerously at the most eminent vices among the greatest persons, and not to creepe into every blinde Taphouse that fears a Constable more then a Satyr" (*Apology against a Pamphlet*, 33).

35. See my "Verse Satire: Its Form, Genre, and Mode."

36. See my discussions in "Stasis, and John Milton and the Myths of Time," and "Confusion: The Apocalypse, The Millennium."

37. E. g., "So that we who by Gods speciall grace have shak'n off the servitude of a great male Tyrant, our pretended Father the Pope, should now, if we be not betimes aware of these wily teachers, sink under the slavery of a Female notion, the cloudy conception of a demy-Iland mother, and while we think to be obedient sonnes, should make ourselves rather the Bastards, or the Centaurs of their spirituall fornications" (*Animadversions*, 63); or see Kester Svendsen's remarks in *Milton and Science*, chapter VI: "The Structure and Surgery of the Human Body," 186–90. In *Defensio pro populo*

Anglicano the pun on the male bird and the only way in which Salmasius resembles "a true cock" might specifically be noted for an understanding of Phillips's lines.

38. See Michael Lieb's *The Dialectics of Creation,* passim. I agree thoroughly with Parker's view of Milton's "fondness for satire—and for rough, coarse language too" as "gifts [to Phillips] from his mentor, actually cultivated in him by Milton" (1168 n95).

39. On A5v Phillips notes "the loud Cry of so many bloudy Massacres, far surpassing the Popish Cruelties in *Ireland.*" On A7v-A8r he remarks "*The blood* of Ireland, *spilt by the same Faction, in comparison of these Massacres, was but as a Drop to the Ocean.*"

40. I discuss this briefly in "'Depth' Bibliography: John Milton's Bibliographic Presence in 1740, As Example," 217–18.

41. Wood (II, 1118–19), an avowed Royalist and Church of England adherent, talks of Phillips as "having early imbib'd in a most plentiful manner the rankest Antimonarchical Principles, from that villanous leading Incendiary *Joh. Milton* his Uncle, but not in any University, proved in a short time so notable a Proficient in his bloody School of King-killing, that he judged himself sufficiently qualifyed publicly to engage in and espouse his Master's quarrel." We again note Wood's snobbish attitude toward those who had not gone to University.

42. As Blair Worden details in *The English Civil Wars and the Passions of Posterity,* Cromwell was hated by Royalists as a king-killer but also by the Parliamentarians for his tyranny and enslavement of the country through the enactment of the Protectorate. However, Worden writes in his edition of what becomes "Ludlow"'s *Truth Brought to Light* (1693) that Phillips collaborated with Slingsby Bethel in the Ludlow pamphlets, specifically referring to a note on the flyleaf of Bodleian Wood Pamphlets 363, and of Phillips's "flexible politics." Real evidence is lacking. In his latest book he sees John Toland as the forger of Ludlow's record as a Puritan fundamentalist.

43. Wood (II, 1118), referring to *A Satyr* and the almanacs, says, "Some time after this having seemingly removed his former Principles, he appeared against the Fanatics in some small Pieces," and Godwin (chapter IX) sees Phillips as "a strenuous royalist and courtier" from 1655 to 1675, but then turning with the tide and following the herd to become a Whig: "Like Shaftesbury, however, he probably thought the succession of the Duke of York was by any means to be prevented, and that the sacrifice of the lives of a few obscure individuals, through the medium of a little resolute and audacious perjury, was a cheap price for the accomplishment of such an end" (208).

44. For comparison, George McFadden argues persuasively that John Dryden's dedications are not fulsome flattery of Royal personages but a means to present advice, praise of meritorious achievements (as figurehead at least), and forecast of hoped-for further success. See *Dryden the Public Writer 1660–1685:* "the dedications show, not opportunism, but a constant regard for his own integrity and for a certain type of public man whom he genuinely admired: one who was a careful administrator, not too much a timeserver or a self-seeker, and above all a preserver of continuity in government . . . In these portraits genuine good qualities are made resplendent, not merely to give praise for performance in the past, but to keep the subject up to this mark in the future" (10).

45. It should be clear that Wood's statement (II, 1119) is specious: "When the Popish Plot broke out, this *Jo. Phillips* became for interest sake (being ready to turn

to any point of the compass for his own Ends) very great with *Tit. Oates* the pretended Discoverer of the Pop. Plot, who oftentimes satisfyed him for writing in his behalf, *for writing many lies and villanies, that even yet remain under his Name on every fanatical Bookseller's Stall,* &c." The quotation comes from William Smith's *Contrivances of the Fanatical Conspirators* (London, 1685), p. 34; it is also called *Intrigues of the Popish Plot Laid Open* (London, 1685). He was a schoolmaster in Islington, which the *Intrigues* volume calls "the Late." Smith's comment, in an added "Postscript" on an extra added page, attempts to exonerate himself from bad association with Oates and from payment for his work on Jesuit books allegedly for Oates, and finds a scapegoat in Phillips:

 One Slander more they cast upon me, was, that I writ Seditious Pamphlets for he promis'd me 20*l. per annum,* and Dyet, to Translate certain Books in Latine concerning the Institutions, Rules and Orders of the Jesuits; Some of which I put into *English,* and have part of them yet by me; all which, if Printed, would no ways prejudice jesuits, or other persons, but be useful to many curious men. Now for all my pains Oates never paid me one Peny, though he punctually satisfy'd *John Philips* for writing the many Lies and Villanies that even yet remain under his Name on every Fanatical Booksellers Stall. Many other wrongs I have long labour'd under, which I believe, if known, would drawe compassion from my greatest Enemies; But those having no relation to the Publick, shall be now conceal'd.

He doesn't name Phillips's books, but aside from *Dr. Oates Narrative* no Phillips book has been, nor seems capable of being, associated with Oates. Wood continues, "But by the way, I must let the Reader know, that when the said *Pop. Plot* broke out, *Joh. Phillips* fell back to his old road, struck in with the disaffected Party, and tho' accounted by those that knew him very well to have little or no Religion, yet many times he would squirt out little lying Pamphlets against the Church."

   In point of fact the "Narrative" was put together by Oates and Ezreel Tonge, a well known king-hater, and Oates worked with Shaftesbury's men, who coached him carefully in these matters, for which he was promised a bishopric. Further, one wonders about personal motives: it should be remembered that he had been ejected from a Catholic seminary for his inability to learn Latin and, so the rumor goes, his sodomy. See also John Warner, *The History of English Persecution of Catholics and the Presbyterian Plot.* It does not mention Phillips.

   46. The philosopher Heraclitus was called "The Obscure," which meaning Phillips uses to advantage, although Flatman would seem to mean Heraclitus's contention of the perpetual change of all things with only the Logos abiding. Flatman's periodical in 1681–82 frequently took Milton to task for his writings and opinions; see Nos. 10, 64, 67, 80. L'Estrange refers to Milton in 1682–83 in Nos. 133, 157, 190, 208, 274–77, 283, 292, 317, 382, 457 of *The Observator.*

   47. Phillips's antagonism toward "Figure-Casters" should be noted and compared with my previous remarks arguing his lampooning of such people and those who believe in astrological predictions, in contradiction of what has generally been said of him. His word "Enormity" is a particularly nasty gibe: it means a *monstrous* and overwhelming wickedness, *well beyond* an *un*acceptable morality. Likewise there is

punning involved in the mounting, riding, and full gallop to Rome upon the implied horse ("whores").

Incidentally, John Gadbury's horoscope of Milton is found in Bodleian Ashmole MS 436, Part I, f. 119. One wonders whether there is any connection between the astrologer (1627–1704) and the person to whom Milton rented part of his Wheatley property (acquired from his father-in-law Richard Powell), along with Graland Page, for six years at £20 per year to each on 25 March 1648. He was a witness in the Ashworth-Milton suit (11 January 1656), being "of Whately in ye County of Oxon' gent' aged five & forty yeares or thereabouts" (French, IV, 63). And is he related to the John Gadbury to whom Richard Powell lent money in 1624? (Parker, 998 n168, ignoring the given age, wonders whether these last two are the same person.) Powell had property in Oxfordshire made over to him by an Elmer Gadbury in 1628.

48. Milton had used the term long before. In the Preface to *Animadversions Upon the Remonstrants Defence, against Smectymnuus* (1641) we find, "Although it be a certaine truth that they who undertake a Religious Cause need not care to be Men-pleasers; yet because the satisfaction of tender and mild consciences is far different from that which is call'ed Men-pleasing, to satisfie such, I shall adresse my selfe in few words to give notice before hand of something in this booke, which to some men perhaps may seeme offensive" (1). In *Eikonoklastes* (1649), speaking of Charles I, "He never reck'ns those violent and merciless obtrusions which for almost twenty years he had bin forcing upon tender consciences by all sorts of Persecution" (98); "If this be a violation to his conscience, that it was hinderd by the Parlament from violating the more tender consciences of so many thousand good Christians, let the usurping conscience of all Tyrants be ever so violated" (130). In *A Treatise of Civil Power* (1659), "Lastly as a preface to force, it is the usual pretence, That although tender consciences shall be tolerated, yet scandals thereby given shall not be unpunishd, prophane and licentious men shall not be encourag'd to neglect the performance of religious and holy duties by color of any law giving libertie to tender consciences" (68).

49. Phillips's attitude toward the Test Act is not in disagreement with his uncle's, it would seem: for Milton it "not only turned aside toleration of one protestant group by another, . . . but forced profession and worked through prohibition, neither being a wise way to inhibit the growth of popery . . ."; "What the Test Act did was *compel* and that Milton could not condone; likewise compelling will not bring inner reformation, which is, he believed, the only avenue by which heretics might be renovated and saved." See my discussion in "'Connivers and the Worst of Superstitions': Milton on Popery and Toleration," 61. Phillips, again like his uncle, would be totally unaccepting of Parker's Erastian principles.

50. See *John Milton: The Self and the World* (1993), 247–59; quotation, 255.

Chapter 5

1. Keeble, *The Literary Culture of Nonconformity in Later Seventeenth-Century England*, 283.

2. Dryden, *The Satires of Decimus Junius Juvenalis*, Dedication, iii.

3. Owen Barfield, "Two Kinds of Forgetting," 1–11.

4. Graham Parry remarks that it destroyed "the tolerant compromise of the Restoration settlement" and dispossessed "many conscientious clergy who would not

conform." As he tells us, it "began to close the doors of the Church of England against Dissenters." See *The Seventeenth Century: The Intellectual and Cultural Context of English Literature, 1603–1700*, 112.

5. "The Christ-like imagery that had accompanied Charles I in his sufferings," Parry reminds us, "now glowed briefly around his son, until his emerging character effectively extinguished it" (107).

6. Cheyney, 459; from *Statutes of the Realm*, V, 23–24.

7. See my "Connivers and the Worst of Superstitions," 61, as well as Milton's *A Treatise of Civil Power*.

8. Compare n14 in chapter 4 here.

9. Cheyney, 495–97; from *Parliamentary History*, XX, 248.

10. His extensive argument against "compelling" in *A Treatise of Civil Power* (1659) should also be reviewed. Compare William Walwyn's: "To compell me against my conscience, is to compell me against what I beleive is not of faith is sin; To compell me therefore against my conscience is to compell me to doe that which is sinfull: for though the thing may be in it selfe good, yet if it doe not appeare to be so to my conscience, the practice thereof in me is sinfull, which therefore I ought not to be compelled unto," *The Compassionate Samaritane*, 43; see *The Writings of William Walwyn*, ed. Jack R. McMichael and Barbara Taft, 114. See also comments on "tender conscience" in chapter 4.

11. For a full discussion of this important issue in tolerant concerns, see Elizabeth Sauer, "Religious Toleration and Imperial Intolerance," *Milton and the Imperial Vision*, 214–30, and her forthcoming essay "Milton's Peculiar Nation." See also the study by Mary Fenton, "Milton's View of Ireland in the 1649 Tracts: When All Liberty is Not Created Equal," forthcoming.

12. Fredric Jameson, "Religion and Ideology," 335–36.

13. Compare my reading of the political dimension of Milton's brief epic in *Paradise Regain'd: 'Worthy Have Not Remain'd so Long Unsung,'* 116–30. The poem "is devoted to establishing the means to . . . individual liberty; its political dimension lies in its need and employment in public service"; "for Milton [public service] was a moral characteristic, engendered by such virtues as honesty (particularly to the self) and godliness (particularly the prevenient grace which a person has accepted from God). These concepts can be found throughout Milton's writing, whether poetry or prose, whether early or late" (126).

14. Pp. 53 and 77, pp. 116 and 123 in McMichael and Taft.

15. *The Works of Gerrard Winstanley*, ed. George H. Sabine, 251.

16. "The Curse and Blessing That is in Mankinde," *A New Years Gift for the Parliament and Armie*, 44; p. 390 in Sabine.

17. Hayes, *Winstanley the Digger: A Literary Analysis of Radical Ideas in the English Revolution*.

18. Wilding, *Dragons Teeth*, 247, 243.

19. Glanvill, *Essays on Several Important Subjects in Philosophy and Religion*, Essay V: "The Agreement of Reason, and Religion," 7–10.

20. Cumberland, *A Treatise of the Laws of Nature*, translated by John Maxwell, Essay I, "Concerning the City, or Kingdom, of GOD in the Rational World, and the Defects of HEATHEN DEISM," vi.

21. Ibid., Essay II, "Concerning the Imperfectness of the Heathen Morality," clxiv, clxvii.

22. John, Lord Hervey, *Ancient and Modern Liberty Stated and Compar'd*, 2–3.

23. We should constantly heed David Norbrook's perception that "Like Cromwell, Milton was far less a constitutional republican than a Protestant nationalist" (*Writing the English Republic*, 390).

24. *Oliver Cromwell.*

25. Parry, 105

26. *Reading Revolutions*, 245.

27. See "Milton's republicanism and the tyranny of heaven," *Machiavelli and Republicanism*, 226.

28. *Correspondence of the Family of Hatton Being Chiefly Letters Addressed to Christopher First Viscount Hatton A.D. 1601–1704*, 7.

29. See David Norbrook, *Writing the English Republic*, chapter 7: "King Oliver? Protectoral Augustanism and its critics, 1653–1658," 299–325.

30. Laura Lunger Knoppers, *Constructing Cromwell*, 107. She speaks of Cromwell in the complex and troubled period of April 1653 as "the military man chafing under delay and restraint and concerned to protect liberty" (66). See also David Armitage's statements in "The Cromwellian Protectorate and the Language of Empire," 532, that in 1654–56 talk of Cromwell as emperor gave him "a status above the law and sole legislative power." Most indicative of contemporary attitudes is Anna Trapnel's depiction of Gideon in "The Cry of a Stone or a relation of something spoken in Whitehall . . . Relating to the Governors, Army, Churches, Ministry, Universities, and the whole Nation . . . in the eleventh month, called January 1653 [1654]," in whom we see "someone who was seduced by luxury and flattery, who had taken on the trappings of monarchy." See Hilary Hinds's edition, xxxiv. Gideon had been chosen by God to free Israel from the Midianites (Judges vi–viii).

31. See the second edition of *Eikonoklastes* ("many yeares before not wishing only but with much industrie complotting, to do som eminent service for the Church of Rome . . . he agrees & concludes that so soon as both Armies in England were disbanded, the Irish should appear in Arms, maister all the Protestants, and help the King against his Parlament," 115; Yale Prose, III, 475) and the second edition of *The Ready and Easy Way* ("his endeavoring to bring in upon our consciencs a Popish religion, upon our liberties thraldom, upon our lives destruction, by his occasioning, if not complotting, as was after discoverd, the *Irish* massacre, his fomenting and arming the rebellion, his covert leaguing with the rebels against us," 6; Yale Prose, VII, 409–10).

32. See the essays in *Milton and the Imperial Vision*. Complex "motives" undoubtedly existed for Cromwell, the religious first off, the political, the nationalistic and internationalistic, but as well the personal advancement for self and posterity and family.

33. See "'Connivers and the Worst of Superstitions'," 67 n14.

34. See "Cultures of Intolerance: Re-reading Milton's 'On the Late Massacre in Piemont," forthcoming; compare also her "Milton's Peculiar Nation."

35. See *Memoirs of the Life of Colonel Hutchinson with the fragment of an autobiography of Mrs. Hutchinson*, 209.

36. Norbrook, *Poetry & Politics in the English Renaissance,* 238.

37. Fallon, "*A Second Defence:* Milton's Critique of Cromwell?" 175.

38. Milton, who is reported to have carried a sword, is not the "dove" in the 1640s and 1650s that many, apparently, would have wanted him to be. He recognized that action might have to be taken, including military action, to achieve a needed and desired end. Telling here is Fallon's *Captain or Colonel: The Soldier in Milton's Life and Art* and Lieb's *Milton and the Culture of Violence.*

39. I avoid using the term "Puritan" most of the time because of its imprecision of meaning. On the specific statement here one should compare Kristen Poole's discussion in *Radical Religion from Shakespeare to Milton: Figures of Nonconformity in Early Modern England.* Her near equation of the term with "separatist" is demonstrated by her examination of Milton's antiprelatical tracts, and with "sectarian" by the discussion of nudity in *Paradise Lost.* Of course there were many other sectarians who would not be classified as "Puritan."

40. See also Austin Woolrych's discussion of the address to Cromwell and the men who are celebrated alongside him in *Defensio secunda*—"Milton & Cromwell: 'A Short but Scandalous Night of Interruption'?" 192–95.

41. *Brief Notes Upon a late Sermon, Titl'd, The Fear of God and the King,* 10; Yale Prose, VII, 481–82. In *Milton and the Kingdoms of God* Michael Fixler has written about the discord in the Parliament of 1653 just after Milton's had translated these psalms: "the first psalm's phrase, 'th'assembly of just men', could have summed up Milton's view of the Nominated Parliament. For their programme was concerned with the enactment of righteousness in the kind of reforms long demanded by the sects and which the Rump had failed to provide, that is to say, the simplification of the laws and the administration of justice, and the abolition of tithes" (182). Michael J. Schwartz points out that "the 'extra' words and phrases [added to the translation of these Hebrew texts] serve either to add strength to the persecuted speaker or heap condemnation on the wicked" (88). He sees the publication of them in 1673 (the only source for the translations) as showing "Milton's desire to speak forcefully to his reader and demand change," relating them and the 1648 Psalms 80–88 to the publication of *Samson Agonistes* two years before as teaching "his fellow Englishmen not to fall into the same slavery and end" (90). See "The Political Inaccuracy of Milton's Psalms 1–8 and 80–88."

42. See the essays in Cummins, noted in chapter 4, n36.

43. Edward Chamberlayne, *Angliæ Notitia,* Twelfth Ed. (London, 1679), 320.

44. "Milton and Puritanism," in *A Companion to Milton,* 134.

45. Milton's "short but scandalous night of interruption" (*Hirelings,* sig. A5r-v, published in August 1659) has been much discussed and variously identified: the period of the Protectorate, the days just before his death when Cromwell's successor was decided upon, the anarchic times of Richard's rule, or the two-week period between the dissolution of the Protectorate Parliament and the return of the Rump in 22 April–6 May 1659. The phrase occurs in the preface to the tract, "To the Parlament of the Commonwealth of England With the Dominions Therof," and thus the last reading is most meaningful. See also Laura Lunger Knoppers, "Late Political Prose," *A Companion to Milton,* 309–25.

46. On the other hand, Hong-Han Song in "Milton's Republicanism in *Paradise Lost*" argues that Milton does not support human kingship although he in no way

resists God's monarchy. "Satan's republicanism (though disguised) discourse against God's monarchism seems to reflect the poet's republican resistance against earthly monarchism"; but this, he says, is a "spurious parallelism" (89–90).

47. In his Commonplace Book, he quoted from the *Art of War* twice, pp. 177 and 182, both dated 1640–42, and from the *Discorsi* fifteen times, pp. 148, 185, 195 (twice), 197 (twice), 198 (twice), 242 (three times), 243 (twice), 245, and 246, all dated 1651–52.

48. Thomas N. Corns, "Milton and the Characteristics of a Free Commonwealth," 26.

49. Quentin Skinner, "Machiavelli's *Discorsi* and the Pre-Humanist Origins of Republican Ideas," 125, 132.

50. Spehar, "Milton, Republicans, and the Buckinghamshire Anti-Stuart Initiatives, 1637–42."

51. Martin Dzelsainis, "Milton and the Protectorate in 1658," 181–205. The work was reissued as *Aphorisms of State, Grounded On Authority and Experience* in 1661 but without Milton's "To the Reader," probably because of the anathema his name and work would bring in this year; as *The Arts of Empire* (1692) with the preface; and as *The Secrets of Government and Misteries of State* (1697), a first issue with the preface, a second without it.

52. Paul Stevens, "Milton's 'Renunciation' of Cromwell: the Problem of Ralegh's *Cabinet-Council.*"

53. Dzelzainis, "Republicanism," in *A Companion to Milton*, 296.

54. See *A Voyce from the Watch Tower*, 112. According to Clarendon, "Ingoldsby, Whaley, and Goffe, three colonels of the army, and, the two former, men of signal courage, offered to stand by him [Richard Cromwell]; and one of them offered to kill Lambert (whom they looked upon as the author of this conspiracy,) if he would give him a warrant to that purpose"—*The History of the Rebellion and Civil Wars in England*, II, 917.

55. The Protestant emphasis on the decisive role to be played in the defeat of the Roman Antichrist by the Christian Emperor and his Church is examined by Robert Wilcher, *The Writing of Royalism 1628–1660*, 4ff.

56. See *A Letter to a Friend*, 22 (Yale Prose, VII, 329–30) and "Proposalls," Yale Prose, VII, 336.

57. David Loewenstein, "Milton among the Religious Radicals and Sects," 238, 241.

58. See Robert W. Ayers's editions of the three tracts in the Yale Prose, VII.

59. He quotes Proverbs 6:6–8 on the ant, who, without "prince, ruler, or lord," still carries on its sustenance of life. In *Paradise Lost* VII, 484–89, he calls the ant the "Pattern of just equalitie," and Annabel Patterson has explicated the wide-ranging significance of the reference. It points Milton toward economic and social changes that transform "the many-headed multitude into a large, industrious, self-determining working class." Here in *The Ready and Easy Way* it can be read as the first necessary step to setting up economic and social improvements for the populace through their rejection of the alleged "right" of a king to make them "his servants and his vassals, and so renounce thir own freedom" (5–6). See Patterson, "Imaging New Worlds: Milton, Galileo, and 'the Good Old Cause'," *The Witness of Times*.

60. Hong Won Suh, "'Ignoble Ease and Peaceful Sloth' in *The Readie and Easie Way* and *Paradise Lost*," 410.

61. Blair Hoxby, *Mammon's Music,* 77–78.

62. "Emphasis is on the two adjectives since time was essential in March/April 1660; he is not saying ideal or even *preferable* way to establish a *free Commonwealth*" (*Self and the World,* 315–16 n28).

63. See also Samuel Beer, *To Make a Nation: The Rediscovery of American Federalism,* 66–83, 125–28. Beer's analysis discusses the "less democratic and more decentralized version of *Oceana,* . . . a scheme of constitutional decentralization on the lines of national federalism" (126). Hereby "the federal division of power would make local and central self-government more effective; its bias in favor of the periphery would also presumably protect individual liberties against abuse by the central government" (127).

64. For discussion of the work as an anti-utopian Jeremiad, see James Holstun, *A Rational Millennium: Puritan Utopias of Seventeenth-Century England and America,* 247–65, and Laura Lunger Knoppers, "Milton's *The Readie and Easie Way* and the English Jeremiad," in Loewenstein and Turner, 213–25.

65. The assessment remains the same in 25 March 1652–23 June 2652, 24 June 1652–28 September 1652, 29 September 1652–24 December 1652, but is raised in 25 December 1652–24 June 1653 to 0/13/9 and 0/6/0; the next assessment (E1600, 25 March 1653–24 June 1653) duplicates part of the time of the previous one and reduces the assessment to 0/6/10 1/2 and 0/3/4. For 24 June 1653–29 September 1653 it is 0/6/11 and 0/3/4, but in the next two records that still exist it becomes 0/5/0 and 0/4/0 and 0/5/0 and 0/5/0. The shifting assessments play out against the political activity and the Army demands of those particular dates.

66. See Joshua Sprigge, *Anglia Rediviva,* 257 (Commissioners for Treaty with Oxford), 277 (at the Council of War held at Marston as Commissioner of Parliament), and 326, and St. Margaret's Rate Books, E166-E167, E172-E173, for 1652–53, 1658–59, and Army Assessments, E1595-E1603, for 25 December 1651–24 June 1654. Apparently during the years 1654–1657 his property was rented by Thomas Bulmer, a messenger to the Council of State (E168 for 1654 lists "Mrs. Mary Bulmer"). Appointed groom of the bedchamber by the king, Herbert wrote *Memoirs of the Last Two Years of the Reign of King Charles I.* He was created a baronet by Charles II on 3 July 1660; he retired to his native York and died there in 1682.

67. Even the word "royalty" is not used in the sense that "royalist" connotes until 1649; it appears in *Of Reformation* (I, 581) in denouncing the bishops and the Pope, and in *Doctrine and Discipline of Divorce* (II, 323) in referring to Justice and "her scepter'd royalty."

68. George F. Sensabaugh, *That Grand Whig Milton.*

Chapter 6

1. A rather amazing error occurs in the last line of "At a Solemn Music," which in four holograph writings in the Trinity MS is given as "To live & sing with him in endlesse morne of light." Allusion is to Revelation 7:9 and 14:3, the palmers before the throne of the Lamb and the harpers who "sung as it were a new song before the throne." Obviously and logically the Lamb, God, does not sing and would not be singing as this error purports. The printed version in 1645 corrects: "To live with him, and sing in endles morn of light." Perhaps the error in *Areopagitica* in reference to Sir Guyon and his Palmer (p. 13), which critics have been trying to explain with-

out impugning Milton's memorial ability and reading of Book II of *The Faerie Queene,* is just that: an error.

2. In this poem, written apparently soon after his rejection of a ministerial career and decision in favor of a poetical one, Milton remarks,

> . . . you did not bid me go
> where the way lies broad, where the field of wealth is easier
> and the golden hope of amassing money glitters sure;
> neither do you force me to the laws and the courts of the people,
> so poorly overseen, nor do you doom my ears to insipid noises.
>   (68–72)

Shortly before this he indicates that there was some negative reaction to his decision but argues the affinity between father and son:

> You should not despise the poet's task, divine song . . .
> Do not continue, I beg, to contemn the sacred Muses,
> and do not deem them fruitless and contemptible, by whose favor
> you yourself, skillful, compose a thousand sounds to apt numbers,
> and are trained to vary the melodious voice with countless modulations,
> so that you are deservedly the heir of Arion's name.
> Now since it has fallen to me to have been born a poet,
> why is it strange to you that we, so closely joined by dear blood,
> should follow related arts and kindred endeavor?
> Apollo, wishing to disperse himself between the two,
> gave to me certain gifts, to my father others,
> and father and son, we possess the divided god.
>   (17, 56–66)

3. Collinson, *Godly People: Essays on English Protestantism and Puritanism,* 535.

4. N.H. Keeble writes, "Puritans were distinguishable by their dissatisfaction with the rites and ceremonies of the Elizabethan church and by their desire to continue the process of Protestant reformation, halted in mid-career in England, they believed, in the compromise of an established church which retained government by bishops and a liturgy still modelled on that of Rome. They never, however, belonged to a single sect or constituted a clearly defined group within or without the episcopal Church of England." See "Milton and Puritanism," 124, in *A Companion to Milton.*

5. Susan Doran and Christopher Durston, *Princes, Pastors and People: The Church and Religion in England 1529–1689,* 28.

6. Eleanor Trotter, *Seventeenth Century Life in the Country Parish with Special Reference to Local Government,* 230.

7. See also the discussion of Norman Sykes in *From Sheldon to Secker.*

8. A report cited by Trotter, 121, announces "The King is nothing to us, the Queen is; the King is a Protestant in outward show and a Catholicke in his heart." The report suggests that Roman Catholics were well organized as a subversive and secret group during the Interregnum.

9. Horton Davies, *Worship and Theology in England from Andrewes to Baxter and Fox,* 125.

10. Warner cites Milton's name in referring to the 1683 Oxford University censorship of books (¶745), does not mention Crashaw, and apparently means Dryden as the Catholic layman who answered Edward Stillingfleet's 1686 denunciation of some documents reputedly written by Charles, *An Answer to Some Papers Lately Printed* (¶766).

11. Note also, speaking of Catholics, "tho' they are not openly and directly tolerated, they enjoy thro' the Gentleness of the *English* Government, greater Fredom than is allow'd to any Protestants, in any *Roman Catholick* Countries in *Europe,* tho' those Protestants have never been Convicted of Practices, tending to overthrow the Constitutions under which they have lived, which has been but too often experienc'd of the *Papists* among our selves" (145).

12. Parry, *The Seventeenth Century,* 83.

13. See Parry, 83, and compare remarks in chapter 3, n12, here.

14. David Loewenstein, *Representing Revolution,* 175.

15. John Walker, ed., *Letters Written By Eminent Persons,* Vol. II, Part I, Letter LXXXV, pp. 224–25, and Letter LXXXVI, pp. 225–27. The argument revolved around William of Wykeham (1324–1404), Bishop of Winchester and Chancellor of England under Henry IV; he was a Roman Catholic.

16. See Michael Lieb's magisterial discussion in *Religion and Literature* 32 (2000): 197–220.

17. *A Humble Advice Of the Assembly of Divines,* chapter II, section III, p. 6, declares the standard view: "In the Unity of the God-head there be Three Persons, of one substance, power and eternity; God the Father, God the Son, and God the Holy Ghost [footnote: 1 John 5, 7; Matt. 28, 29; 2 Cor. 13, 14]. The Father is of none, neither begotten, nor proceeding: The Son is eternally begotten of the Father [footnote: John 1, 14, 18]: the Holy Ghost eternally proceeding from the Father and the Son" [footnote: John 1, 15, 16; Gal. 4, 6].

18. See also Kristin Pruitt, "'United as one individual Soul': Hierarchy, Gender, and the Power of Relationship in *Paradise Lost,*" chapter I of *Pattern Divine: Milton's Triune God,* forthcoming, for a discussion of the separateness and unity of the triune being.

19. The tone of Carey's translation may be misleading; the translation in the Columbia Edition (XIV, 403) is: "and yet it is on the authority of this text, almost exclusively, that the whole doctrine of the Trinity has been hastily adopted." The Latin is: "et tamen hoc loco pene solo fundata TRIADIS doctrina tota, atque arrepta hinc esse potissimum videtur"; neither translation is exacting.

20. See Peter Berek's "'Plain' and 'Ornate' Styles and the Structure of *Paradise Lost*" for discussion of the Father's rhetoric and the Son's parodying of false heroism and employment of language that is appropriate to faithful self-sacrifice. Compare also my examination of the style of the epic in *With Mortal Voice,* 100–09.

21. A biblical source of the concept lies in Psalm 85, which Milton translated in April 1648:

Mercy and Truth *that long were miss'd*
    Now *joyfully* are met;
Sweet Peace and Righteousness have kiss'd
    And hand in hand are set. (41–44)

These "four daughters of God" are depicted in a medieval débat between Mercy and Justice (Righteousness), where the treatment to be meted to disobedient human-kind is argued. Only the unity of Truth, Mercy, and Justice (that is, the Trinity of the godhead) will yield Peace; it is a metaphoric statement of "three persons indivisible." The concept is repeated in "On the Morning of *Christs* Nativity" (1629).

> Yea Truth, and Justice then
> Will down return to men,
>   Orb'd in a Rain-bow; and like glories wearing
> Mercy will sit between,
> Thron'd in Celestiall sheen (141–44)—

The "then" is the "raign of peace upon the earth" (63), which begins with the nativ-ity of Jesus, when the "Maker" sends down "the meek-ey'd Peace" and "a universall Peace [is struck] through Sea and Land" (46, 52). Interestingly the earlier "On the Death of a Fair Infant Dying of a Cough" (1628) talks of the "just Maid" (Astræa), who may have returned to earth, or was it "Mercy that sweet smiling Youth? / Or that crown'd Matron sage white-robed truth?"

22. The Satan of *Paradise Regain'd* deludes himself:

> Thenceforth . . . I might learn
> In what degree or meaning thou art call'd
> The Son of God, which bears no single sence;
> The Son of God I also am, or was,
> And if I was, I am; relation stands;
> All men are Sons of God. (IV, 514–20)

23. For a full discussion of the Jungian material referred to here, see James P. Driscoll's examination of *The Unfolding God of Jung and Milton*. Driscoll points out a number of accounts that Milton might have been familiar with which explicitly cite Satan and the Son as brothers; see pp. 73, 215–26 nn. 98–99.

24. Lewalski (178) quotes this statement but does not comment upon it or cite its specific reference to the mother. Her sentence "Milton the translator can de-mand equal status with his author since he is a teacher and prophet instructed not by Bucer but by God," in fact, tends to obscure the point that he is making although the demand for equal status is certainly valid.

25. See *Paradise Regain'd: 'Worthy T'Have Not Remain'd So Long Unsung'*, especially chapter 5, 59–69.

26. Compare the concept of exodus and of the birth of the child from the mother's womb to begin to be part of the world lying before it. I discuss the meta-phoric relevance of the concept in *With Mortal Voice*, 119–38, where James Joyce's employment of it is also noted.

27. In "Milton's Theanthropos: the Body of Christ in *Paradise Regained*," by John P. Rumrich, an essay in *Milton Studies* 42 (2003), remarks the insertion of Mary into the temptation narrative. She is not part of that narrative in Matthew or Luke, and is not cited in Mark or John. As Rumrich shows: "Her seamless fit into Jesus's most consequential meditations indicates that she has intimately influenced his develop-

ing sense of identity. There is no gap separating them. She is evidently the single most influential person in his psyche" (62).

28. Probably the variations in characterization result from the poem's having been written over a period of time, these first sections of the council in Hell followed by the council in Heaven, and echoing the structure of *Paradise Lost,* having been composed after later parts of the brief epic were.

29. Making the literary comparison with Jesus even more interesting, Samson tells the Chorus: "I was his nursling once and choice delight, / His destin'd from the womb" (633–34). Samson seems to ignore the mother and has transferred motherly reference to God.

30. Jackie Di Salvo has looked at "Samson's Struggle with the Woman Within" from an angle involving Dalila: "This power of women, associated as it is with love, stems from a projection in which male desires are disowned by their attribution to female emotional and erotic manipulations, Dalila's 'venereal train' (l. 533)." She views its source as "Samson's hypermasculinity" and in turn "its infantile source in its identification with a Father who appears, as always to a child, all-mighty" (220).

31. Even renovation is rejected by Joseph Wittreich as being reached by the end of the poem when the "rouzing motions" rear up in Samson and he would seem to become a champion again through "inward eyes." See *Interpreting Samson Agonistes* and *Shifting Contexts* (note particularly the rejection of these two passages on p. 123). Compare my *The Uncertain World of Samson Agonistes.*

32. The word in the seventeenth century meant "making humble," "humility," not the eighteenth-century meaning of making one ashamed or foolish.

33. See Michael Lieb, *The Sinews of Ulysses,* 124.

34. See Lewalski, "The Ship-Tempest Imagery in *Samson Agonistes,*" as well as Knoppers, "'Sung and Proverb'd For a Fool': *Samson Agonistes* and Solomon's Harlot."

Works Cited

Adams, John. *Index Villaris: or, an Alphabetical Table of all the Cities, Market-Towns, Parishes, Villages, and Private Seats, in England and Wales.* London: A. Godhead and J. Playford, 1680.

"The Agreements of the People." 1647–49.

    An Agreement of the People for a Firme Peace. 1647.

    To the Commons. The Petition of Many Free-Born People. 1647.

    To the Commons of England. The Petition of Well Affected Persons Inhabiting London, Westminster, Southewark Hamblets and Places Adjacent. 1648.

    To the right Honourable and supreme Authority of This Nation the Commons in Parliament Assembled. The Petition of Many Thousands Earnestly Desiring the Glory of God. 1648

    An Agreement of the Free People of England. [London: G. Calvert, 1649.]

    The Remonstrance of Many Thousands of the Free-People of England. Together with the Resolves of the Young-men and Apprentices of the City of London, in Behalf of Themselves and Those Called Levelers, for the Attainment of Their Just Requests in Their Petition of 20 May 1647: also Their Petition of 19 Jan. 1647, and of 11 Sept. 1648. Together with the Agreement of the Free People of England, 1 May. 1649.

Aleman, Mateo. *The Rogue; or, the Life of Guzman de Alfarache.* London: G.E. for Edward Blount, 1622. Reprint, London: J.C., for the Author; and are to be sold by Tho. Johnson, and Stephen Chatfield, 1655.

All Souls College, Oxford. Library. Luttrell MS.

Ames, Richard. *A Search After Claret; or, A Vindication of the Vintners.* London: 1691.

Annual Register, or a View of the History, Politics, and Literature, for the Year 1769, The. London, 1770. 120 (first pagination).

Aristotle. *Poetics. Translated with an Introduction and Notes by Gerald F. Else.* Ann Arbor: University of Michigan Press, 1969.

Armitage, David. "The Cromwellian Protectorate and the Language of Empire." *The Historical Journal* 35 (1992): 531–55.

———, Armand Himy, and Quentin Skinner, eds. *Milton and Republicanism.* Cambridge: Cambridge University Press, 1995.

Armytage, George J., ed. *Allegations for Marriage Licences Issued from the Faculty Office of the Archbishop of Canterbury, London, 1654–1869.* Publications of the Harleian Society. London: 1886. Vol. XXIV.

Ashmole, Elias. Manuscripts. Bodleian Library. MSS Ashmole 240, 436 (Part I), 826, 842, 857, 865, 1109, 1110, 1111, 1115, 1119, 1123, 1125, 1127, 1128, 1136, 1139, 1149.

———. *The Constitution, Laws, & Ceremonies of the Most Noble Order of the Garter.* London: John Macock for Nathanael Brooke, 1672. Ed. 2, London: Thomas Dring, 1693.

———. *The Diary and Will of Elias Ashmole,* ed. R.T. Gunther. Oxford: Oxford University Press, 1927. From Bodleian Library, MS Ashmole 1135.

Aubrey, John. "Minutes of the Life of John Milton." Bodleian Library, Aubrey MS 8. Printed in Darbishire, 1–15.

———. *The Natural History and Antiquities of the County of Surrey, Begun in the year 1673.* London: E. Curll, 1719. 4 vols.

Auden, Thomas. *Shrewbury: a Historical and Topographical Account of the Town.* London: Methuen, 1905.

B., R.W. "The Family of Sir Christopher Milton." *Notes & Queries.* Series XI, No. 7 (1913): 113.

Baker, Sir Richard. *A Chronicle of the Kings of England . . . Whereunto is now added in this third edition, The Reign of King Charles II.* London: E. Cotes, and sold by G. Saubridg & T. Williams, 1660. Ed. 4, 1665; Ed. 5, 1670, etc.

Bannerman, W. Bruce, ed. *The Registers of All Hallows, Bread Street.* Harleian Society Publications. London: 1913. Vol. XLIII.

———, ed. *The Register of Marriages of St. Mary le Bone, Middlesex.* Harleian Society Publications. London: 1917. Vol. XLVII.

Barfield, Owen. "Two Kinds of Forgetting." *History, Guilt, and Habit.* Middletown: Wesleyan University Press, 1981.

Baugh, G.C., ed. *The Victoria History of the Counties of England. A History of Shropshire.* Oxford: Oxford University Press, 1979.

Baxter, Richard. *A Holy Commonwealth.* London: Thomas Underhill and Francis Tyton, 1659.

Beal, Peter. *Index of English Literary Manuscripts.* London: Mansell, 1980. Vol. 1, Part 2.

Beaty, Frederick L. "Three Versions of John Phillips' *Satyr Against Hypocrites.*" *Harvard Library Bulletin* 6 (1952): 380–87.

———. "The Works of John Phillips." Thesis, Oxford University, 1950.

Beer, Samuel. *To Make a Nation: The Rediscovery of American Federalism.* Cambridge: Belknap Press of Harvard University Press, 1993.

Berek, Peter. "'Plain' and 'Ornate' Styles and the Structure of *Paradise Lost.*" *PMLA* 85 (1970): 237–46.

Berkshire Records Office. Protestation Oath, 1641/42.

Bethel, Slingsby. *The Worlds Mistake in Oliver Cromwell.* London: 1668. Reprinted in *Harleian Miscellany,* Vol. VII. London: T. Osborne, 1746.

Bibliotheca Oweniana, Sive Catalogus Librorum. [London]: Edward Millington, 1684.

Biographia Britannica: or, The Lives of the Most Eminent Persons. London: 1747–66.

Birch, Thomas, ed. *A Complete Collection of the Historical, Political, and Miscellaneous Works of John Milton.* London: A. Millar, 1738. 2 vols. Revised by Richard Baron:

The Works of John Milton, Historical, Political, and Miscellaneous. London: A. Millar, 1753.

Blackburne, Francis. *Memoirs of Thomas Hollis.* London: 1780.

Blagg, Thomas M. and F. Arthur Wadsworth, eds. *Abstracts of Nottinghamshire Marriage Licences.* British Record Society Index Library. London: 1930. Vol. LVIII.

Blow, John. *Amphion Anglicus.* London: W. Pearson, for the Author, 1700.

Bock, Gisela, Quentin Skinner, Maurizio Viroli, eds. *Machiavelli and Republicanism.* Cambridge: Cambridge University Press, 1990.

Bodleian Library, Oxford University.

    MS Ashmole 240

    MS Ashmole 436, Part I

    MS Ashmole 1136

    MS Rawlinson A.181

    MS Rawlinson D.864

    MS Wood F.39

    Wood Pamphlets 363

Box, Alfred Ridley. *Allegations for Marriage Licences Issued by the Commissary Court of Surrey.* Norwich: 1907.

Boyd, W., ed. "The Final Concords, or Pedes Finium of Staffordshire . . . 1539 to 1603." *Collections for a History of Staffordshire.* London: 1895. Vol. XVI.

———, ed. "Final Concords, Staffordshire, 13 James I to 16 James I." *Collections for a History of Staffordshire.* London: 1903. N.S., Vol. VI, Part 1.

Boyse, Samuel. *An Historical Review of the Transactions of Europe, From the Commencement of the War with Spain in 1739, to the Insurrection in Scotland in 1745.* Reading: D. Henry, 1747–48. 2 vols.

Brennecke, Ernest. *John Milton the Elder and His Music.* New York: Columbia University Press, 1938.

British Library.

    MS Additional 5756

    MS Additional 18861

    MS Additional 19142

    MS Additional 24501

    MS Additional 35397

    MS Egerton 2387

    MS Egerton 2429A

    MS Egerton 2534

    MS Egerton 2539

    MS Harleian 5801

    MS Harleian 5802

    MS Harleian 6802

    MS Harleian 7003

    MS Lansdowne 238

    MS Lansdowne 821

    MS Sloane 254

    MS Sloane 3310

    MS Sloane 4078

MS Stowe 498

MS Stowe 745

Burke, Sir Bernard. *The General Armory of England, Scotland, Ireland, and Wales.* London: Harrison & Sons, 1884.

Burke, John and John Bernard. *A Genealogical and Heraldic Dictionary of the Landed Gentry of Great Britain and Ireland.* London: Scott, Webster, Geary, 1847.

Burn, Jacob Henry. *A Descriptive Catalogue of the London Traders, Taverns, and Coffee-House Tokens Current in the Seventeenth Century.* Ed. 2. London: 1855.

Burne, S.A.H. "The Staffordshire Quarter Sessions Rolls, 1590–1593." *Collections for a History of Staffordshire. William Salt Archaelogical Society.* London: 1932.

Burrows, Montagu, ed. *The Register of the Visitors of the University of Oxford, From A.D. 1647 to A.D. 1658.* Camden Society, N.S. Vol. XXIX, 1881.

Burton, Robert. *The Anatomy of Melancholy.* Ed. 3. Oxford: J. Lichfield and J. Short for H. Cripps, 1628.

Calendar of Marriage Licences Issued by the Faculty Office. London: British Record Society, 1905.

Calendar of State Papers, Domestic.

James I, 1603–10, Vol. 1: 1857

Charles I, 1627, Vol. 2: 1858

Charles I, 1629–31, Vol. 4: 1860

Charles I, 1635, Vol. 8: 1865

Charles I, 1645–47, Vol. 21: 1891

Commonwealth, 1649–50, Vol. 1: 1875

Commonwealth, 1651, Vol. 3: 1877

Commonwealth, 1651–52, Vol. 4: 1877

Commonwealth, 1652–53, Vol. 5: 1878

Commonwealth, 1653–54, Vol. 6: 1879

Commonwealth, 1654, Vol. 7: 1880

Commonwealth, 1655, Vol. 8: 1881

Commonwealth, 1655–56. Vol. 9: 1882

Commonwealth, 1656–57. Vol. 10: 1883

Commonwealth, 1658–59, Vol. 12: 1885

Commonwealth, 1659–60, Vol. 13: 1886

Charles II, 1660–61, Vol. 1: 1860

Charles II, 1661–62, Vol. 2: 1861

Charles II, 1663–64, Vol. 3: 1862

Charles II, 1664–65, Vol. 4: 1863

Charles II, 1666–67, Vol. 6: 1864

Charles II, 1667, Vol. 7: 1866

Charles II, 1667–68, Vol. 8: 1893

Charles II, 1668–69, Vol. 9: 1894

Charles II, 1670, Vol. 10: 1895

Charles II, 1677–78, Vol. 19: 1911

Charles II, 1682, Vol. 23: 1932

Charles II, 1683–84, Vol. 26: 1938

William III, July-December 1695; Addenda, 1689–95: 1908

William III, 1697: 1927

William III, 1699–1700: 1937

Calendar of the Proceedings of the Committee for Compounding, etc., 1643–1660, ed. Mary Anne Everett Green. London: Eyre and Spottiswoode, 1889–92. 5 vols.

Calendar of Treasury Books, ed. William A. Shaw.

I, 1660–67 (London: 1904)

III, Part I, 1669–72 (London: 1908)

III, Part II, 1669–72 (London: 1908)

IV, 1672–75 (London: 1909)

V , Part I, 1676–79 (London: 1911)

V, Part II, 1676–79 (London: 1911)

VI, 1679–80 (London: 1913)

VII, Part I, 1681–85 (London: 1916)

VII, Part II, 1681–85 (London: 1916)

VII, Part III, 1681–85 (London: 1916)

VIII, Part I, 1685–89 (London: 1923)

VIII, Part II, 1685–89 (London: 1923)

VIII, Part III, 1685–89 (London: 1923)

VIII, Part IV, 1685–89 (London: 1923)

IX, Part I, 1689–92 (London: 1931)

IX, Part II, 1689–92 (London: 1931)

IX, Part IV, 1689–92 (London: 1931)

X, Part I, 1693–96 (London: 1935)

X, Part III, 1693–96 (London: 1935)

XI, April 1696-March 97 (London: 1933)

Cambridge University. *Catalogus Graduatorum. The Book of Matriculations and Degrees, Compiled by John Venn and J.A. Venn.* Cambridge: Cambridge University Press, 1913.

Campbell, Gordon. *A Milton Chronology.* Basingstoke: Macmillan Press, 1997.

Canning, Richard. *The Principal Charters . . . of Ipswich in Suffolk.* London: 1754.

Carter, W. Fowler. "Notes on Staffordshire Families." *Collections for a History of Staffordshire.* William Salt Archæological Society. London: 1910.

Casa, Giovanni della. *Rime e Prose.* Venice: 1563. Copy owned by New York Public Library.

Cases Argued and Decreed in the High Court of Chancery, From the 12th Year of King Charles II. To the 31st. London: Assigns of Rich. and Edw. Atkins for John Walthoe, 1697.

Castlemaine, Roger Palmer, Earl of. *The Catholique Apology with a Reply to the Answer . . . The Third Edition Much Augmented.* [London?]: 1674.

———. *A Reply to the Answer of the Catholique Apology.* [London?]: 1668.

Catalogue of Books, of the Several Libraries of the Honourable Sir William Coventry, and the Honourable Mr. Henry Coventry, Sometime Secretary of State of King Charles II. [London]: William Cooper, et al., 1687.

Catalogue of Theological, Philosophical, Historical, Philological, Medicinal & Chymical Books. London: John Bullord, 1697(?).

Censure of the Rota Upon Mr Miltons Book, Entituled, The Ready and Easie way to Establish A Free Common-wealth. London: Paul Giddy, 1660.

Chamberlayne, Edward. *The Second Part of the Present State of England.* In the Savoy: T.N. for John Martyn, 1671. Reprinted, Ed. 6, London: 1676; Ed. 11, London: 1682. Reprinted in *Angliæ Notitia: or, The Present State of England Compleat.* Ed. 12, London: T.N. for J. Martyn, 1679; Ed. 13, London: Thomas Hodgkin, 1687; Ed. 16, London: R. Chiswell et al., 1687; Ed. 17, London: T. Hodgkin for R. Scot et al., 1692.

Chancery, Court of London. *Index of Chancery Proceedings (Series II) Preserved in the Public Record Office.* Public Record Office Lists and Indexes. London: 1896. No. 7.

Chancery Proceedings, Series II, Vol. II (1579–1621). New York: Kraus Reprint, 1963.

Chancery Proceedings, Series II, Vol. III (1621–60). New York: Kraus Reprint, 1963.

Chester, Joseph Lemuel. *The Marriage, Baptismal and Burial Registers of the Collegiate Church or Abbey of St. Peter, Westminster.* Harleian Society Publications. London: 1876. Vol. X.

Chetham Society Historical Remains. XXIV (1851): 18.

Cheyney, Edward P. *Readings in English History Drawn from the Original Sources. New Edition.* Boston: Ginn and Co., 1935.

Parliamentary History, XX

Statutes of the Realm, V

Clarendon, Earl of. *The Correspondence of Henry Hyde, Earl of Clarendon,* ed. Samuel Weller Singer. London: Henry Colburn, 1828. 2 vols.

———. *The History of the Rebellion and Civil Wars in England. By Edward Earl of Clarendon, A New Edition.* Oxford: University Press, 1840.

Clarke, A.W. Hughes, ed. *The Register of St. Dunstan in the East, London, 1558–1654.* Harleian Society Publications. London: 1939. Vol. LXIX.

Clarke, G.R. *The History and Description of the Town and Borough of Ipswich.* Ipswich: S. Piper, 1830.

Clarke, Hyde. "Milton Notes: Cousin Blackborough." *Athenæum.* No. 2739 (24 April 1880): 536–37, 566.

Clavering, Rose and John T. Shawcross. "Milton's European Itinerary." *Studies in English Literature.* 5 (1965): 49–59.

Collectanea Genealogica, ed. Joseph Foster. London: 1881–85. Twenty parts.

Collectanea Topographia & Genealogica. London: 1842. Vol. VII.

Collection of Several Relations & Treatises Singular and Curious, of John Baptista Tavernier, Baron of Aubonne, A. London: A. Godhead and J. Playford, for Moses Pitt, 1680.

Collections for a History of Staffordshire. Staffordshire Record Society. "The Staffordshire Sheriffs (1086–1912), Escheators (1247–1619), and Keepers or Justices of the Peace (1263–1702)." London: 1912.

Collinson, Patrick. *Godly People: Essays on English Protestantism and Puritanism.* London: Hambledon Press, 1983.

Columbia University, New York. Library. MS X823 M64/S52

Colville, Frederick Leigh. *The Worthies of Warwickshire.* Warwick: 1879.

Colyer-Fergusson, T.C., ed. *The Registers of the French Church, Threadneedle Street.* Aberdeen: Huguenot Society, 1906.

Cookson, Edward, ed. *The Registers of St. Nicholas, Ipswich.* London: 1897. Parish Register Society, Publications, VII.

Copinger, W.A. *The Manors of Suffolk.* London: T.F. Unwin, 1911. Vol. VII.

Corder, Joan. *A Dictionary of Suffolk Arms.* Ipswich: Suffolk Records Society, 1965.

Corns, Thomas N., ed. *A Companion to Milton.* Oxford: Blackwell, 2001.

———. "Milton and the Characteristics of a Free Commonwealth." See Armitage, Himy, Skinner. 25–42.

Corporation of London Record Office.
    MS 40/3
    Apprenticeship Bindings, VI

Coward, William. *Licentia Poetica Discuss'd.* London: William Carter, 1709.

Cox, J. Charles. *Notes on the Churches of Derbyshire.* Chesterfield: 1875–79. 3 vols.

Crewe, Nathaniel, Lord. *Memoirs of Nathaniel, Lord Crewe,* ed. Andrew Clark. Camden Society. The Camden Miscellany. Vol. 9, 1895.

Cumberland, Richard. *A Treatise of the Laws of Nature,* trans. John Maxwell. London: R. Phillips, 1727.

Cummins, Juliet, ed. *Milton and the Ends of Time: Essays on the Apocalypse and the Millennium.* Cambridge: Cambridge University Press, 2003.

Dale, T.C. *The Inhabitants of London in 1638. Edited from MS 272 in the Lambeth Palace Library.* London: Society of Genealogists, 1931.

Darbishire, Helen, ed. *The Early Lives of Milton.* London: Constable, 1932.

Davies, Horton. *Worship and Theology in England from Andrewes to Baxter and Fox, 1603–1690.* Princeton: Princeton University Press, 1975.

Davis, J.C. *Oliver Cromwell.* London: Arnold, 2001.

Declaration of the Nobility, Knights & Gentry of the County of Oxon Which have adhered to the King. For Tho. Bassett, 1660.

The Dictionary of National Biography, ed. Sir Leslie Stephen and Sir Sidney Lee. Oxford: Oxford University Press, 1921–22. 22 vols.

Di Salvo, Jackie. "Intestine Thorn: Samson's Struggle with the Woman Within." *Milton and the Idea of Woman,* ed. Julia Walker. Urbana: University of Illinois Press, 1988. 211–29.

Doran, Susan and Christopher Durston. *Princes, Pastors and People: The Church and Religion in England 1529–1689.* London: Routledge, 1991.

Driscoll, James P. *The Unfolding God of Jung and Milton.* Lexington: University Press of Kentucky, 1993.

Dryden, John. *The Satires of Decimus Junius Juvenalis.* London: Jacob Tonson, 1693.

———. *The State of Innocence, and Fall of Man.* London: T.N. for Henry Herrington, 1677.

Du Bartas, Guillaume Salluste, Sieur. *La Sepmaine, ou Création du Monde.* Paris: 1582.

Dugdale, William. *The Visitation of Derbyshire, Taken in 1662 and Reviewed in 1663.* London: Golding and Lawrence, 1879.

———. *The Visitation of the County of Yorke . . . 1665 . . . 1666 by Sir William Dugdale.* Durham: Surtees Society Publications, 1859. Vol. 36.

Dunton, John. *Dunton's Whipping Post: or, a Satyr upon Every Body.* London: B. Bragg, 1706.

———. *The Life and Errors of John Dunton Late Citizen of London; Written by Himself in Solitude.* London: S. Malthus, 1705.

Dzelsainis, Martin. "Milton and the Protectorate in 1658." See Armitage, Himy, and Skinner. 181–205.

———. "Republicanism." See Corns, 294–308.

Echard, Laurence. *The History of England.* London: Jacob Tonson, 1718.

Eikon Basilike. [London]: 1648[1649]. [Charles I, alleged author.]

Eliot, John. *The Christian Commonwealth.* London: Livewell Chapman, [1659].

Ellwood, Thomas. *The History of the Life of Thomas Ellwood.* London: Assigns of J. Sowle. 1714.

Empson, William. *Milton's God.* London: Chatto and Windus, 1961.

English Economic History; Select Documents, Compiled and Edited by A.E. Bland, P.A. Brown, R.H. Tawney. Ed. 2. London: G. Bell and Sons, 1915.

English Fortune-Tellers. See *New Almanacke and Prognostication.* London: Printed for A.R. and C.A., 1642; reprint, 1643. See also London: for W. Thackerary, T. Passenger, and W. Whitwood, [1686–88]; and *The Book of Fortune,* London: J. Heptinstall, for Brabazon Aylmer, 1698.

Erdeswick, Sampson. *A Survey of Staffordshire,* ed. Thomas Harwood. London: J.B. Nichols, 1844.

Evelyn, John. *The Diary of John Evelyn,* ed. E.S. de Beer. Oxford: Oxford University Press, 1955. 5 vols.

Fallon, Robert T. *Captain or Colonel: The Soldier in Milton's Life and Art.* Columbia: University of Missouri Press, 1984.

————. *"A Second Defence:* Milton's Critique of Cromwell?" *Milton Studies* 39 (2000): 167–83.

Fenton, Mary. "Hope, Land Ownership, and Milton's 'Paradise Within'." *Studies in English Literature 1500–1900* 43 (2003):151–80.

————. "Milton's View of Ireland in the 1649 Tracts: When All Liberty is Not Created Equal." Forthcoming.

Fisher, Payne. *Catalogue of the Tombs in the Churches of the City of London, A.D. 1666.* London: 1668.

Fixler, Michael. *Milton and the Kingdoms of God.* Evanston: Northwestern University Press, 1964.

Flatman, Thomas. *Heraclitus Ridens: or, a Discourse Between Jest and Earnest.* Nos. 10, 64, 67, 80. 1681–82.

Fletcher, Harris Francis. *The Intellectual Development of John Milton.* Urbana: University of Illinois Press, 1956. 2 vols.

Forde, Emanuel. *The Famous History of Montelyon, the Knight of the Oracle.* London: B. Alsop & T. Fawcet, 1633.

Forrest, H.E., ed. *Shrewsbury Burgess Roll.* Shrewsbury: W.B. Walker, 1924.

Foss[e], Edward. *Biographia Juridica. A Biographical Dictionary of the Judges of England.* London: 1870.

Foster, Joseph, ed. *Alumni Oxonienses: The Members of the University of Oxford, 1500–1714.* Oxford: Oxford University Press, 1891–92. 2 vols.

————, ed. *London Marriage Licences, 1521–1859.* London: Bernard Quaritch, 1887.

French, J. Milton. *The Life Records of John Milton.* New Brunswick: Rutgers University Press, 1949–58. 5 vols.

————. *Milton in Chancery: New Chapters in the Lives of the Poet and His Father.* New York: Modern Language Association, 1939.

Frye, Northrop. *The Great Code: The Bible and Literature.* New York: Harcourt Brace Jovanovich, 1982.

Frye, Roland Mushat. "Milton's First Marriage." *Notes and Queries* N.S. 3 (1956): 200–02.

Gardiner, Anne Barbeau. "Dryden, Bower, Castlemaine, and the Imagery of Revolution, 1682–1687." *Eighteenth-Century Life* 25 (2001): 135–46.

Gentleman's Journal, The, ed. Peter Motteux. London: Vol. III, 1694. See John Phillips and Thomas Power.

Gentleman's Magazine 39 (1769): 367.

Gibbons, Alfred. *Notes on the Visitation of Lincolnshire, 1634*. London: 1898.

Glanville, Joseph. *Essays on Several Important Subjects in Philosophy and Religion*. London: J.D. for John Baker and Henry Mortlock, 1676. Including, "The Agreement of Reason and Religion. 1676."

Glover, Stephen. *The History, Gazetteer, and Directory of the County of Derby*, ed. Thomas Noble. Derby: M. Mozley & Sons, 1829–33. 2 vols.

Godwin, William. *The Lives of Edward and John Philips, Nephews and Pupils of Milton*. London: Longman, Hurst, Rees, Orme, and Brown, by J. Hamilton, 1815.

Gott, Samuel. *Nova Solyma, Libri Sex*. Typis Joannis Legati, 1648.

Grazebrook, George and John Paul Rylands, eds. *The Visitation of Shropshire, Taken in the year 1623 . . . Part I*. Harleian Society Publications. 1889. Vol. XXVIII.

Grazebrook, H. Sydney, ed. "The Heraldic Visitations of Staffordshire made by Sir Richard St. George in 1614, and by Sir William Dugdale in the Years 1663 and 1664." *Collections for a History of Staffordshire*. Staffordshire Record Society. London: 1885. Vol. V, Part II.

———, ed. "The Visitation of Staffordshire Made by Robert Glover . . . 1583." *Collections for a History of Staffordshire*. William Salt Archæological Society. London: 1882. Vol. III.

Greenberg, Lynne A. "Paradise Enclosed and the *Feme Covert*," 150–73, 303–10. In *Milton and the Grounds of Contention*, ed. Mark R. Kelley, Michael Lieb, and John T. Shawcross. Pittsburgh: Duquesne University Press, 2003.

Großes Vollständiges Universal-Lexicon aller Wissenschaften und Künste. Leipzig und Halle: Johann Heinrich Zedler, 1739. Vol. XXI.

Guildhall Library. London.

MS 6554/1

MS 6554/2

MS 6552/1

MS 9163

Guillim, John. *A Display of Heraldry by John Guillim, Pursuivant at Arms. The Sixth Edition*. London: T.W. for R. and J. Bonwicke, R. Wilkin, J. Walthoe, and Tho. Ward, 1724.

Hallen, A.W. Cornelius, ed. *The Registers of St. Botolph, Bishopsgate, London*. Edinburgh: 1889–95. 2 vols.

Hanford, James Holly. "The Chronology of Milton's Private Studies." *PMLA* 36 (1921): 251–314.

Harding, Christopher and Bill Hines, Richard Ireland, and Philip Rawlings. *Imprisonment in England and Wales: A Concise History*. London: Croom Helm, 1985.

Harrington, James. *The Common-wealth of Oceana*. London: J. Streater, for Livewell Chapman, 1656.

Hatton, Christopher, First Viscount. *Correspondence of the Family of Hatton Being Chiefly Letters Addressed to Christopher First Viscount Hatton A.D. 1601–1704*, ed. Edward Maunde Thompson. Printed for the Camden Society, N.S. XXII, 1878.

Hatton, Edward. *A New View of London*. London: J. Nicholson, 1709.

Hayes, T. Wilson. *Winstanley the Digger: A Literary Analysis of Radical Ideas in the English Revolution.* Cambridge: Harvard University Press, 1979.

Heath, James. *A Chronicle of the Late Intestine War in the Three Kingdoms of England, Scotland and Ireland . . . To which is added a Continuation to this present year 1675 . . . by J.P.* London: Printed by J.C., for Thomas Basset, 1676.

Herbert, Thomas. *The Memoirs of the Last Two Years of the Reign of King Charles I.* London: Robert Clavell, 1702.

Hervey, John, Lord. *Ancient and Modern Liberty Stated and Compar'd.* London: J. Roberts, 1734.

Hervey, Mary F.S., ed. *The Life, Correspondence & Collections of Thomas Howard, Earl of Arundel.* Cambridge: Cambridge University Press, 1921.

Historical Manuscripts Commission. *Reports.* London: Eyre and Spottiswoode.

First Report (The Hatton Collections. Correspondence): 1870.

Third Report (with appendix): 1872.

Fourth Report and Appendix, Part I, Series 3. Part I: 1874.

Fourth Report (Calendar of the House of Lords), Part I: 1874.

Fourth Report, Part I (MSS of the Earl of Denbigh; MSS of the Marquise of Ormonde): 1874.

Seventh Report, Part I: 1879.

Eighth Report and Appendix, Part I: 1881.

Eighth Report and Appendix, Part II (MSS of the Duke of Manchester): 1881.

Eleventh Report, Appendix, Part VII (MSS of the Duke of Leeds, the Bridgewater Trust, Reading Corporation, the Inner Temple, &c.): 1888. Includes Reading Corporation, MS XXXIX.

Twelfth Report, Appendix, Part IX (MSS of the Duke of Beaufort, K.G., The Earl of Donoughmore, and Others): 1891.

Thirteenth Report, Appendix, Part V (MSS of the House of Lords, 1690–91): 1892.

Thirteenth Report, Appendix, Part I (MSS of His Grace the Duke of Portland, Preserved at Welbeck Abbey, Vol. 1): 1891.

Thirteenth Report, Appendix, Part II (MSS of His Grace the Duke of Portland, Preserved at Welbeck Abbey, Vol. 2): 1893.

Thirteenth Report, Part VI (Calendar of the MSS of the House of Lords): 1894.

Fourteenth Report, Appendix, Part III (MSS of His Grace the Duke of Portland, Preserved at Welbeck Abbey, Vol. III): 1894.

Fourteenth Report, Appendix, Part I (MSS of His Grace the Duke of Rutland, K.G., Preserved at Belvoir Castle, Vol. 4): 1905.

Fourteenth Report, Appendix, Part VI (MSS of the House of Lords, 1692–93): 1894.

Fourteenth Report, Appendix, Part VII (MSS of the Marquis of Ormonde, Preserved at the Castle, Kilkenny): 1895. Vol. I.

Fourteenth Report, New Series, Vol. 1, continuation of Appendix, Part VI (MSS of the House of Lords, 1693–95): 1900.

Fifteenth Report, Appendix, Part VIII (MSS of the Duke of Buccleuch and Queensbury): [Series 44] 1897. [Vol. I].

Fifteenth Report, Appendix, Part X (MSS of Shrewsbury and Coventry Corporations): 1899.

Calendar of the Manuscripts of the Marquess of Ormonde. New Series, Vol. I: 1902.

Calendar of the Manuscripts of the Marquess of Ormonde. New Series, Vol. III: 1904.

Calendar of the Manuscripts of the Marquess of Ormonde. New Series, Vol. IV: 1906.

Calendar of the Manuscripts of the Marquess of Ormonde. New Series, Vol. VIII: 1920.

The Manuscripts of the House of Lords. New Series, Vol. II (1695–97): 1903.

Report on the Manuscripts of Reginald Rawdon Hastings. Vol. II: 1930.

Report on the Manuscripts of the Most Honourable the Marquess of Bath Preserved at Longleat. Vol. IV: Seymour Papers 1532–1686. 1968.

History of the Works of the Learned . . . for the Month of August, 1706, The. London: H. Rhodes, A. Bell, and D. Midwinter, 1706. Vol. 8.

Hobbes, Thomas. "The Answer of Mr Hobbes to Sr Will. D'Avenant's Preface before Gondibert." Sir William Davenant, *Gondibert, An Heroick Poem.* London: Tho. Newcomb for John Holden, 1651. 71–88.

Hobbs, John L. "John Milton's Shrewsbury Connections." *Transactions of the Shropshire Archaelogical Society* 57 (1961): 26–30.

Hog, William, trans. *Paraphrasis Poetica in Tria Johannis Miltoni, Viri Clarissimi, Poemata, Viz. Paradisum Amissum, Paradisum Recuperatum, et Samsonem Agonisten.* Londini: Typis Johannis Darby, 1690.

Holstun, James. *A Rational Millennium: Puritan Utopias of Seventeenth-Century England and America.* Oxford: Oxford University Press, 1987.

Hone, Ralph. "Edward and John Phillips, Nephews and Pupils of John Milton." Dissertation, New York University, 1954. 3 vols.

———. "John Phillips." *A Milton Encyclopedia,* gen. ed. William B. Hunter. Lewisburg: Bucknell University Press, 1979. VI, 13739.

———. "New Light on the Milton-Phillips Family Relationship." *Huntington Library Quarterly* 22 (1958): 63–75.

Hooke, Robert. *The Diary of Robert Hooke M.A., M.D., F.R.S. 1672–1680,* ed. Henry W. Robinson and Walter Adams. London: Taylor & Francis, 1935.

Hopwood, Charles Henry, ed. *A Calendar of Middle Temple Records.* London: Butterworth & Co., 1903–05. 3 vols.

House of Lords. *Journal of the House of Lords.* London: Her Majesty's Stationery Office. Vol. VI.

Howard, Joseph Jackson, ed. *The Visitation of London, Anno Domini 1633, 1634, and 1635, Made by Sir Henry St. George.* Harleian Society Publications. London: 1883. Vol. XVII.

Hoxby, Blair. *Mammon's Music: Literature and Economics in the Age of Milton.* New Haven: Yale University Press, 2002.

Humble Advice Of the Assembly of Divines Now by Authority of Parliament Sitting at Westminster, A. Edinburgh: Evan Tyler, 1647.

Hunter, Joseph. *Hunter's Pedigrees,* ed. J.W. Walker. Harleian Society Publications. London: 1936. Vol. LXXXVIII.

Hunter, William B. *Visitation Unimplor'd.* Pittsburgh: Duquesne University Press, 1998.

Hutchinson, Lucy. *The Memoirs of the Life of Colonel Hutchinson with the fragment of an autobiography of Mrs. Hutchinson,* ed. James Sutherland. London: Oxford University Press, 1973.

Illingworth, Cayley. *A Topographical Account of the Parish of Scampton . . . Together with Anecdotes of the Family of Bolle* [*sic*]. London: T. Cadell and W. Davies, 1810.

Inderwick, F.A., ed. *Calendar of the Inner Temple Records.* London: Henry Sotheran, 1901. Vol. III.

Ipswich and East Suffolk Record Office. Beccles Register, 1723–27.
    Ref. No. XI/5/4.1
    Ref. No. XI/5/4.2
    Ref. No. XI/5/4.3

Jacob, Giles. *An Historical Account of the Lives and Writings of Our Most Considerable English Poets, Whether Epick, Lyrick, Elegiack, Epigrammatists, &c.* London: E. Curll, 1720.

Jameson, Frederic. "Religion and Ideology." 1642: *Literature and Power in the Seventeenth Century,* Proceedings of the Essex Conferences on the Sociology of Literature, July 1980, ed. Francis Barker et al. Colchester: University of Essex, 1981. 315–36.

Jane, Joseph. *ΕΙΚΩΝ ΑΚΛΑΣΤΟΣ. The Image Unbroaken.* [London]: 1651.

Jeayes, Isaac Herbert, ed. "Calendar of the Longdon, Lichfield and Other Staffordshire Charters, Etc. . . . of the Marquess of Anglesey." Staffordshire Record Society. *Collections for a History of Staffordshire.* London: 1939.

———. *Descriptive Catalogue of Derbyshire Charters in Public and Private Libraries and Muniment Rooms.* London: 1906.

Jockey's Farewell to Jenny, The. For R. Burton, [1670?]. Broadside.

Jones, Edward. "The Loyalty and Subsidy Returns of 1641 and 1542: What They Can Tell Us About the Milton Family." Forthcoming.

Keeble, N.H. *The Literary Culture of Nonconformity in Later Seventeenth-Century England.* Athens: University of Georgia Press, 1987.

———. "Milton and Puritanism," See Corns, 124–40.

Kelley, Maurice. "Milton and Machiavelli's *Discorsi.*" *Studies in Bibliography* 4 (1951–52): 123–28.

———. "Milton's Later Sonnets and the Cambridge Manuscript." *Modern Philology* 54 (1956): 20–25.

Kerrigan, William. *The Sacred Complex: On the Psychogenesis of* Paradise Lost. Cambridge: Harvard University Press, 1983.

Knoppers, Laura Lunger. *Constructing Cromwell: Ceremony, Portrait, and Print 1645–1661.* Cambridge: Cambridge University Press, 1999.

———. "Late Political Prose." See Corns, 309–25.

———. "Milton's *The Readie and Easie Way* and the English Jeremiad." *Politics, Poetics, and Hermeneutics in Milton's Prose,* ed. David Loewenstein and James Grantham Turner. Cambridge: Cambridge University Press, 1990. 213–25.

———. "'Sung and Proverb'd For a Fool': *Samson Agonistes* and Solomon's Harlot." *Milton Studies* 26 (1990): 239–51.

Lane, Jane (pseudonym of Elaine Kidner Dakers). *The Reign of King Covenant.* Fairlawn, N.J.: 1956.

Lawes, Henry. *Ayres and Dialogues.* London: T.H. for J. Playford, 1653–58. 3 vols.

———, and William Lawes. *Choice Psalmes Put into Musick.* London: James Young for Humphrey Moseley, 1648.

Le Neve, John. "Pedigrees of the Knights Made by King Charles II, King James II, King William III and Queen Mary, King William Alone, and Queen Anne." British Library, MS Harleian 5801. See *Publications of the Harleian Society,* VIII (1873).

L'Estrange, Sir Roger. *Considerations and Proposals in Order to the Regulation of the Press.* London: A.C., 1663.

———. *L'Estrange His Apology.* London: Henry Brome, 1660.

———. *L'Estrange No Papist.* London: T.B. for H. Brome, 1681.

———. *No Blind Guides.* London: Henry Brome, 1660.

———. *The Observator.* Nos. 133, 157, 190, 208, 274–77, 283, 292, 317, 382, 457. 1682–83.

———. *A Reply to the Second Part of the Character of a Popish Successor.* London: For Joanna Brome, 1681.

———. *Treason Arraign'd.* London: Printed in the Year 1660.

Leti, Gregorio. *Historia, e Memorie recondite sopra alla vita di Oliviero Cromvele.* Amsterdam: Pietro et Giovanni Blaev, 1692. 2 vols.

Lewalski, Barbara K. *The Life of John Milton.* Oxford: Blackwell, 2000.

———. "The Ship-Tempest Imagery in Samson Agonistes." *Notes & Queries,* N.S. 6 (1959): 372–73.

Lieb, Michael. *The Dialectics of Creation: Patterns of Birth and Regeneration in* Paradise Lost. Amherst: University of Massachusetts, 1974.

———. "Milton and 'Arianism'." *Religion and Literature* 32 (2000): 197–220.

———. *Milton and the Culture of Violence.* Ithaca: Cornell University Press, 1994.

———. *The Sinews of Ulysses: Form and Convention in Milton's Works.* Pittsburgh: Duquesne University Press, 1989.

Lilburne, John. *An Outcry of the Young Men and Apprentices of London.* [London: 1649].

Lindenbaum, Peter. "John Playford: Music and Politics in the Interregnum." *Huntington Library Quarterly* 64 (2001): 125–38.

Linguæ Romanæ Dictionarium Luculentum Novum. A New Dictionary. Cambridge: W. Rawlins, et al., 1693.

List of the Principal Inhabitants of the City of London, 1640, From Returns Made by the Aldermen of the Several Wards, ed. W.J. Harvey. London: Mitchell and Hughes, 1886.

Littleton, Adam. *Linguæ Latinæ Liber Dictionarius Quadripartitus. A Latine Dictionary, in Four Parts.* London: 1678.

Liu, Tai. *Puritan London: A Study of Religion and Society in the City Parishes.* Newark: University of Delaware Press, 1986.

Lloyd's Evening Post, and Chronicle. No. 1097. 15 (20–23 July 1764): 78–79.

———. No. 1881. 25 (24–26 July 1769): 86.

Locke, Matthew. *Observations upon a Late Book, Entituled, an Essay to the Advancement of Musick, &c. Written by Thomas Salmon, M.A.* London: W.G. and are to be sold by John Playford, 1972.

———. *The Present Practice of Musick Vindicated against the Exceptions and New Way of Attaining Musick Lately Publish'd by Thomas Salmon, M.A. &c. . . . To which is added Duellum Musicum by John Phillips, gent.* London: N. Brooke and J. Playford, 1673.

Loewenstein, David. "Milton among the Religious Radicals and Sects: Polemical Engagements and Silences." *Milton Studies* 40 (2001): 222–47.

———. *Representing Revolution: Milton and His Contemporaries. Religion, Politics, and Polemics in Radical Puritanism.* Cambridge: Cambridge University Press, 2001.

London Gazette. 5–9 June 1688.

Lucas, Perceval. "The Family of Sir Christopher Milton." *Notes & Queries,* Series 11, Vol. 7 (1913): 21–22.

Lucian. *The Third Volume of the Works of Lucian.* (London: Samuel Briscoe, and Sold by J. Woodward, 1711. "Tragopodagra, or Gout-Farce," 187–206.

Ludlow, Edmund [alleged author]. *Truth Brought to Light: or, the Gross Forgeries of Dr. Hollingworth.* London: 1693.

———. *A Voyce from the Watch Tower. Part Five: 1660–1662,* ed. A.B. Worden. Camden Society, Fourth Series, Vol. 21. London: Royal Historical Society, 1978.

Lünig, Johan Christian. *Literæ Procerum Europæ, ab Imperatoribus, Electoribus, Principibus, Statibusque Sacri Imperii Romano-Germanici.* Lipsiæ: Apud Jo. Frider. Gleditsch & Filium, 1712. 3 vols.

Luttrell, Narcissus. *Brief Historical Relation of State Affairs from September 1678 to April 1714.* Oxford: At the University Press, 1857. 6 vols.

———. *A Continuation of the Compleat Catalogue of Stitch'd Books and Single Sheets, &c. Printed since the First Discovery of the Popish Plot,* September 1678. London: 1680.

———. *A Second Continuation of the Complete Catalogue.* London: J.R., 1680.

Machiavelli, Niccolò. *The Arte of Warre.* New York: Da Capo Press, 1969.

———. *Discorsi sopra la prima deca de Tito Livio,* trans. Leslie J. Walker. London: Routledge, 1991.

MacNamara, F.N. and A. Story-Maskelyne, eds. *The Parish Register of Kensington, co. Middlesex.* Harleian Society Publications. London: 1890. Vol. XVI.

Maddison, A.R., ed. *Lincolnshire Pedigrees.* Harleian Society Publications. London: 1902.

Malady and Remedy of Vexations and the Unjust Arrests and Actions, The. 1646.

Man, John. *The History and Antiquities, Ancient and Modern, of the Borough of Reading, in the County of Berks.* Reading: Snare & Man, 1816.

Manning, Owen. *The History and Antiquities of . . . Surrey.* London: 1804–14. 3 vols.

Marriage Licences Issued by the Dean and Faculty of Westminster 1558–1699. London: 1886. Harleian Society Publications, Vol. XXIII.

Mason, Thomas and J.V. Kitto, eds. *A Register of St. Martin in the Fields, 1550–1636.* Harleian Society Publications. London: 1898. Vol. XXV.

Masson, David. *The Life of John Milton: Narrated in Connexion with the Political, Ecclesiastical, and Literary History of His Time.* Cambridge: Macmillan, 1859–80. 6 vols. with index, Vol. VII (1894).

Matthews, Arthur D. "Christopher Milton v. Ipswich." *Notes & Queries* 196 (1951): 205.

McFadden, George. *Dryden The Public Writer 1660–1685.* Princeton: Princeton University Press, 1978.

McGoldrick, Monica and Randy Gerson. *Genograms in Family Assessment.* New York: W.W. Norton, 1985.

Metcalfe, Walter C. *A Book of Knights Banneret.* London: Mitchell and Hughes, 1885.

Miller, Leo. *John Milton & the Oldenburg Safeguard.* New York: Loewenthal Press, 1985.

———. *John Milton's Writings in the Anglo-Dutch Negotiations, 1651–1654.* Pittsburgh: Duquesne University Press, 1992.

———. "Milton's State Letters: The Lünig Version." *Notes & Queries* 16 (1969): 95–96.

Milton, John. *Accedence Commenc't Grammar.* London: S. Simmons, 1669.

———. *Animadversions upon the Remonstrants Defence, Against Smectymnuus.* London: Thomas Underhill, 1641.

————. *An Apology Against a Pamphlet Call'd A Modest Confutation.* London: E.G. for Iohn Rothwell, 1642.

————. *Areopagitica.* London: 1644.

————. *Articles of Peace, Made and Concluded with the Irish Rebels, and Papists, by James Earle of Ormond.* London: Matthew Simmons, 1649. Including "Observations upon the Articles of Peace with the Irish Rebels, on the Letter of Ormond to Col. Jones, and the Representation of the Presbytery at Belfast."

————. *Artis Logicæ Plenior Institutio.* London: Spencer Hickman, 1672.

————. *A Brief History of Moscovia.* London: M. Flesher, for Brabazon Aylmer, 1682.

————. *Brief Notes Upon a Late Sermon.* London: 1660.

————. *The Cabinet-Council.* London: Tho. Newcomb for Tho. Johnson, 1658. Reprinted as *Aphorisms of State* (1661); *The Arts of Empire* (1692); *The Secrets of Government and Misteries of State* (1697).

————. "A Commonplace Book." See *Complete Prose of John Milton*, I (1953), 362–513, ed. Ruth Mohl.

————. *A Complete Collection of the Historical, Political, and Miscellaneous Works of John Milton, Both English and Latin.* Amsterdam [i.e., London]: 1698. 3 vols.

————. *The Complete Poetry of John Milton*, ed. John T. Shawcross. Garden City, N.Y.: Doubleday, 1971.

————. *Complete Prose of John Milton.* New Haven: Yale University Press, 1953–82. 8 vols. in 10.

————. *Considerations Touching the Likeliest Means to Remove Hirelings Out of the Church.* London: T.N. for L. Chapman, 1659.

————. "De Doctrina Christiana." Public Record Office, London. SP 9/61.

————. "De Doctrina Christiana." See *Complete Prose of John Milton*, VI (1973), ed. Maurice Kelley, with translation by John Carey.

————. *A Declaration, or Letters Patents.* London: Brabazon Aylmer, 1674.

————. *The Doctrine and Discipline of Divorce.* London: T.P. and M.S., 1643.

————. *Eikonoklastes.* London: Matthew Simmons, 1649.

————. *Epistolarum Familiarium Liber Unus.* Londini: Brabazoni Aylmeri, 1674.

————. *The History of Britain.* London: J.M. for James Allestry, 1670. See *Complete Prose of John Milton*, V, Part 1, ed. French Fogle.

————. "A Letter to a Friend." See *Complete Prose of John Milton*, VII (1980), 324–33.

————. *Literæ Pseudo-Senatûs Anglicani, Cromwellii.* [Amsterdam: Peter and John Blaeu], 1676.

————. *Literæ Pseudo-Senatûs Anglicani, Cromwellii.* [Brussels: E. Fricx], 1676.

————. *Mr John Miltons Character of the Long Parliament.* London: Henry Brome, 1681.

————. *Of Education. To Master Samuel Hartlib.* [London: Thomas Johnson, 1644.]

————. *Of Reformation.* London: Thomas Underhill, 1641.

————. *Of True Religion, Hærsie, Schism, Toleration.* London: 1673.

————. *Paradise Lost. A Poem.* London: 1667[–1669, varying legends]. Ed. 2, London: S. Simmons, 1674.

————. *Paradise Regain'd. A Poem. In IV Books. To which is added Samson Agonistes.* London: J.M. for John Starkey, 1671.

————. "The Present Means, and Brief Delineation of a Free Commonwealth." See *Complete Prose of John Milton*, VII (1980), 392–95.

————. *Pro Populo Anglicano Defensio*. Londini: Typis Du-Gardianis, 1651.

————. *Pro Populo Anglicano Defensio*. Londini: Typis Neucombianis, 1658.

————. *Pro Populo Anglicano Defensio Secunda*. Londini: Typis Neucomianis, 1654.

————. *Pro Se Defensio Contra Alexandrum Morum Ecclesiasten*. Londini: Typis Neucomianis, 1655.

————. "Proposalls of Certaine Expedients for the Preventing of a Civill War Now Feard, & the Settling of a Firme Government." See *Complete Prose of John Milton,* VII (1980), 336–39.

————. *The Readie & Easie Way to Establish a Free Commonwealth*. London: T.N. [for] Livewell Chapman, 1660.

————. *The readie and easie way to establish a free Commonwealth*. London: Printed for the Author, 1660. [Ed. 2].

————. *Scriptum Dom. Protectoris Reipublicæ Angliæ, Scotiæ, Hiberniæ . . . contra Hispanos*. Londini: Henricus Hills & Iohannes Field, 1655.

————. *The Tenure of Kings and Magistrates*. London: Matthew Simmons, 1649.

————. *A Treatise of Civil Power in Ecclesiastical Causes*. London: Tho. Newcomb, 1659.

————. Trinity Manuscript (also called, Cambridge Manuscript). *John Milton. Poems. Reproduced in Facsimile from the Manuscript in Trinity College, Cambridge*. Menston Ilkley: Scolar Press, 1970.

————. *The Works of John Milton*, gen. ed. Frank Patterson. New York: Columbia University Press, 1931–38. 18 vols in 21.

Miscellanea Genealogica et Heraldica.
   Series 1. London: 1866. Vol. I.
   Series 4. London: 1906. Vol. I.
   Series 5. London: 1937. Vol. IX.

Mitford, John, ed. *The Works of John Milton in Verse and Prose*. London: William Pickering, 1851. 6 vols.

Montelion 1661. London: Sold by Henry Marsh, [1661]. [Possible author, Thomas Flatman.]

Montelion 1662. London: Sold by Henry Marsh, [1662].

Moore, Sir Thomas. *Mangora, King of the Timbusians, or, The Faithful Couple*. London: 1718.

Munk, William. *The Roll of the Royal College of Physicians of London*. London: 1878–1955. Vol. I.

Musgrave, William. *Obituary*. Harleian Society Publications. London: 1900. Vol. XLVII.

Newton, Theodore F.M. "William Pittis and Queen Anne Journalism." *Modern Philology* 33 (1935–36): 169–86, 279–302.

Newton, Thomas, ed. *Paradise Lost*. London: J. and R. Tonson, and S. Draper, 1749. 2 vols. Seventh ed., London: J. Beecroft et al., 1770.

Nicholls, Sir George. *A History of the English Poor Law. New Edition*, by H.G. Willink. London: P.S. King and Son, 1898. 2 vols.

Nickolls, John, Jr. *Original Letters and Papers of State, Addressed to Oliver Cromwell*. London: William Bowyer, and sold by John Whiston, 1743.

Nixon, Scott. "Milton's royalist friend: The peculiar pamphlets of Henry Lawes." *TLS* (November 23, 2001): 14–15.

Norbrook, David. *Poetry & Politics in the English Renaissance*. London: Routledge & Kegan Paul, 1984.

————. *Writing the English Republic: Poetry, Rhetoric, and Politics, 1627–1660.* Cambridge: Cambridge University Press, 1999.

Nottinghamshire Parish Records, Marriages, ed. W.P.W. Phillimore and Thomas M. Blagg. London: 1898–1938. Vol. XII.

Nottinghamshire Visitation 1662–1664. Printed for the Thoroton Society, 1949. Record Series, Vol. XIII.

Oates, Titus. *True Narrative of the Horrid Plot and Conspiracy of the Popish Party, A.* London: Thomas Parkhurst and Thomas Cockerill, 1679.

Ode, on the Death of Mr. Henry Purcell, An. London: J. Heptinstall, for Henry Playford, 1696. Words by John Dryden; music by John Blow. Reprint, *Orpheus Britannicus.* London: J. Heptinstall, for Henry Playford, 1698.

Oldenburgh. Niedersächsische Staatsarchive.

Oldenburgh Safeguard. See Miller.

Owen, John [and others]. *Humble Proposals of Mr. Owen and Other Ministers Who Presented the Petition to Parliament.* London: Robert Ibbitson, 1652.

P., L.B. *ΠΛΑΝΗΣ ΑΠΟΚΑΛΥΨΙΣ. Popery Manifested, Or, the Papist Incognito made known.* London: R.C., 1673.

Pack, Richardson. *The Whole Works of Major Richardson Pack.* London: E. Curll, 1729.

A Paire of Spectacles for the Citie. 1648.

Parish Registers of Abinger, Wotton, and Oakwood Chapel, Co. Surrey. Surrey Record Society Publications. London: 1927.

Parker, Samuel. *A Defence and Continuation of Ecclesiastical Politie.* London: 1671.

————. *A Discourse of Ecclesiastical Politie.* London: 1670.

————. *Reasons for Abrogating the Test.* London: 1688.

————. *A Reproof to The Rehearsal Transprosed, in a Discourse to Its Author.* London: James Collins, 1673.

Parker, William Riley. *Milton: A Biography.* Oxford: Clarendon Press, 1968. Revised version edited by Gordon Campbell, 1996.

————. "Milton and the News of Charles Diodati's Death." *Modern Language Notes* 72 (1957): 486–88.

Parry, Graham. *The Seventeenth Century: The Intellectual and Cultural Context of English Literature, 1603–1700.* London: Longman, 1989.

Patterson, Annabel. "Imaging New Worlds: Milton, Galileo, and 'the Good Old Cause'." *The Witness of Times: Manifestations of Ideology in Seventeenth Century England,* ed. Katherine Z. Keller and Gerald J. Schiffhorst. Pittsburgh: Duquesne University Press, 1993. 238–60.

Peacock, Edward, ed. *The Army Lists of the Roundheads and Cavaliers.* London: John Camden Hotten, 1863.

Peile, John. *Biographical Register of Christ's College, 1515–1905.* Cambridge: Cambridge University Press, 1910.

Pepys, Walter Courtenay. *Genealogy of the Pepys Family 1237–1887.* London: Faber and Faber, 1951.

Philipps, John (of Norwich). *Mercurius Pædanus.* Norwich: By James Flesher, for Richard Royston; to be sold by Edward Martin, 1650.

Phillips, Edward, trans. Juan Pérez de Montalván. *The Illustrious Sheperdess.* London: J.C. for Nath. Brook, 1656.

————, trans. Juan Pérez de Montalván. *The Imperious Brother.* London: J.C. for Nath. Brook, 1656.

————. "The Life of John Milton." *Letters of State, Written by Mr. John Milton,* ed. and trans. Edward Phillips. London: 1694. Reprinted in Darbishire, 49–82.

————. *The Minority of St. Lewis.* London: R. Bentley and S. Magnes, 1685.

————. *The New World of English Words.* London: E. Tyler, for Nath. Brooke, 1658. Ed. 2, London: 1662 and 1663; Ed. 3, London: For Nath. Brooke, 1671; Ed. 4, London: W.R. for Obadiah Blagrove, 1678.

————. *Poems by that Most Famous Wit, William Drummond of Hawthornden.* London: W.H., 1656. Four issues: Issue 3, London: Richard Tomlins; Issue 4, *The Most Elegant, and Elaborate Poems of that Great Court-Wit, Mr William Drummond.* London: William Rands, 1659.

————. *Theatrum Poetarum, or a Compleat Collection of the Poets.* London: Charles Smith, 1675.

————. *Tractatulus de Carmine Dramatico Poetarum Veterum.* Londini: Typis T. Newcomb, 1670. In Johann Buchler. *Sacrum Profanarumque Phrasium Poeticarum Thesaurus.* Londini: Impensis Georgium Sawbridge, 1669: ed. 17 in 1670; ed. 18 in 1679.

————. *Tractatulus de Modo & Ratione formandi Voces Derivativus Linguæ Latinæ.* Londini: 1682.

————. *A Treatise of the Way and Manner of Forming the Derivatives of the Latin Tongue.* London: George Croom, 1685.

————, ed. John Speed. *Theatre of the Empire of Great-Britain.* London: Thomas Basset and Richard Chiswel, 1676.

Phillips, John. *Advice to a Painter.* [London]: 1688. Broadside.

————, trans. Madeleine de Scudery. *Almahide; or, the Captive Queen.* London: I.M. for Thomas Dring, 1677.

————, trans. Nicolas Abraham de La Framboisière. *The Art of Physick Made Plain & Easie.* London: H.C. for Dorman Newman, 1684.

————. *Augustus Britannicus.* London: Printed; and Sold by B. Whitlock, 1697.

————. *The Character of a Popish Successor, and What England may expect from such a one. Part the Second.* London: Richard Janeway, 1681.

————. *The Dilucidation of the Late Commotions of Turkey.* London: Randal Taylor, 1689. [Part of *Modern History.*]

———— (suggested author). *The Dilucidator: or, Reflections upon Modern Transactions.* London: Printed for Randall Taylor, 1689. Seven nos.

————. *Dr. Oates's Narrative of the Popish Plot Vindicated.* London: Thomas Cockerill, 1680.

————. *Don Juan Lamberto.* London: Henry Marsh, 1661.

————. "Duellum Musicum." See Locke, *Present Practice.*

————, trans. Miguel de Cervantes Saavedra. *The History of the Most Renowned Don Quixote of Mancha.* London: Tho. Hodgkin, and are to be sold by John Newton, 1687. Another issue: London: Thomas Hodgkin, and sold by William Whitwood, 1687.

————. *Horse-Flesh for the Observator.* London: R. Read, 1682.

————. *An Humble Offering to the Sacred Memory of the Late Most Serene and Potent Monarch Charles II.* London: Randal Taylor, 1685.

————. *In Memory of Our Late Most Gracious Lady, Mary Queen of Great-Britain, France, and Ireland.* London: John Harris, 1695.

———. *Jockey's Downfall.* 1679.

———. *Maronides or Virgil Travestie. Fifth Book.* [Part 1]. London: for Nathaniel Brooks, 1672. Reprint, London: By S. and B.G., to be sold by Nathaniel Brooks, 1672.

———. *Maronides or Virgil Travestie. Sixth Book.* [Part 2]. London: By S.G. and B.G. for Nathaniel Brooks, 1673. Reprint, *Fifth and Sixth Books.* London: for O. Blagrave, 1678.

———. *Mercurius Verax: or the Prisoners Prognostications for the year 1675.* London: R. Cutter, 1675.

———. *Mr. L'Estrange Refuted With his own Arguments.* London: R. Baldwin, 1681.

———. *Modern History, or a Monethly Account.* London: 1687–89. 3 vols.

———. *Montelion 1660.* [London]: Sold by Henry Marsh, [1660].

———. *Montelion's Predictions, or the Hogen Mogen Fortune Teller.* London: By S. and B. Griffin, for Thomas Palmer, 1672.

———. *News from the Land of Chivalry.* London: I.P., 1681.

———. *New News from Tory-Land and Tantivy-Shire.* London: S. Norman, 1682.

———. *Pantagruel's Prognostications.* Printed at London: N.D. Reprint from translation of c. 1660, ed. F.P. Wilson. Luttrell Society: Oxford, 1997. Luttrell Reprints No. 3.

———, trans. Gaultier de Coste, Seigneur de La Calprenède. Pharamond. London: For T. Bassett, T. Dring, and W. Cademan, 1677.

———. *A Pleasant Conference upon the Observator and Heraclitus.* London: H. Jones, 1682. *The Second Part. Or Continuation of Observations and Reflections Upon the Late Sermons.* London: 1682.

———. [Poems]. *The Gentleman's Journal* III (1694): 57, 91–92, 125–26, 195–96.

———. *The Present State of Europe.* London: 1690. Also titled, *The General State of Europe.* Translation of *Mercure Historique et Politique.* The Hague.

———. *Responsio Ad Apologiam Anonymi cujusdam tenebrionis pro Rege & Populo Anglicano infantissimam.* Londini: Typis Du-gardianis, 1652.

———. *Sam., Ld. Bp. of Oxon, his celebrated Reasons for Abrogating the Test, and Notions of Idolatry Answered by Samuel, Arch-Deacon of Canterbury.* [London?: 1688?].

———. *A Satyr Against Hypocrites.* Bodleian Library, MS Rawlinson Poetical 30.

———. *A Satyr Against Hypocrites.* London: Printed for N.B., 1655. Reprint and editions, London: Printed for Nathaniel Brooks, 1661 [called *Religion of the Hypocritical Presbyterians*]; London: Printed for N.B., 1671; London: Printed for N.B., 1674; London: For O.B. and R.H., 1677; London: Printed for O.B. and R.H., 1680; London: For O.B. and R.H., 1689. Reprint with Introduction by Leon Howard. Los Angeles: William Andrews Clark Memorial Library, 1953.

———. *The Six Voyages of John Baptista Tavernier, Baron of Aubonne. . . . Published by Dr. Daniel Cox.* London: William Godbid, for Robert Littlebury and Moses Pitt, 1677, 1678.

———. *Speculum Crape-Gownorum: Or, A Looking-Glass for the Young Academicks, new Foyl'd.* London: E. Rydal, 1682. Ed. 2: *The Second Edition corrected and Enlarged.* London: E. Rydal, 1682.

———. *Speculum Crape-Gownorum: Or, A Looking-Glass for the Young Academicks, new Foyl'd. Second Part.* London: R. Baldwin, 1682.

———. *Sportive Wit.* London: For Nath: Brook, 1656.

———. *The Tears of the Indians.* London: J.C. for Nath. Brooke, 1656.

————. *A True and Exact Relation of the Most Dreadful Earthquake which happened in the City of Naples*. London: Printed, and are to be sold by Randal Taylor, 1688.

————, trans. Paul Scarron. *Typhon: or, The Gyants War with the Gods. A Mock Poem.* London: For Samuel Speed, 1665.

————. *The Vision of Mons. Chamillard.* London: Wm Turner, 1706.

Phœnix Britannicus: or, London Rebuilt. London: By T.J. for S. Speed, 1672.

Pittis, William. *The Whipping-Post, At a New Session of Oyer and Terminer.* London: 1705. No. 1–27.

Plutarch. *Plutarch's Morals.* London: For J. Gellibrand [legend changes], 1684–1691. 5 vols. Further editions through 1694.

Poole, Kristen. *Radical Religion from Shakespeare to Milton: Figures of Nonconformity in Early Modern England.* Cambridge: Cambridge University Press, 2000.

Power, Thomas, trans. [Excerpts from *Paradise Lost*]. *The Gentleman's Journal.* III (1694): 129–31, 166–68, 201–02.

Prerogative Court of Canterbury. London.

Administrative Act Books. 1713.

74 Buckingham.

126 Edmunds.

Index of Wills Proved in the Prerogative Court of Canterbury. British Record Society Index Library. London: 1912. Vol. XLIII.

Index of Wills Proved in the Prerogative Court of Canterbury. British Record Society Index Library. London: 1942. Vol. LXVII.

Noel 46.

99 St. John.

Wills, London: 1901. Vol. XXV.

Pruitt, Kristin. *Pattern Divine: Milton's Triune God.* Pittsburgh: Duquesne University Press, forthcoming.

Prynne, William. *Soveraigne Power of Parliaments and Kingdoms.* London: Michael Sparke, Senior, 1643.

Public Record Office, London. Manuscripts.

Bridges Division: Bundle 436, No. 121.

Bridges Division: Bundle 436, No. 159.

C6/427/42.

Chancery Town Depositions. C24/825/89.

Composition Papers, Series 2, Vol. XIV.

E179/75/355.

E179/252.

E179/252/32.

Lists and Indexes, No. IX ("List of Sheriffs for England and Wales, from the Earliest Times to AD 1831").

Lists and Indexes, No. XXXIII; Vol. IV.

Prob. 24/13/311–313.

Req 2/630.

SP 9/61 [De doctrina christiana].

SP 18/1/55.

SP 18/23/6.

SP 25/77/108.

SP 27/1.

SP 28/193.

SP Dom 9/194 [Milton's State Papers].

SP 16-SP 31 [Vol. 273, State Papers Domestic, Charles I to James II].

SP Dom 18/34/105.

SP Dom 23/187.

SP Dom 29/386/65.

SP Dom, Car. II, 408, No. 10.

SP Dom, Car. II, 414, No. 153.

SP Dom, Car. II, 438, No. 74.

SP Dom, Car. II, 440, No. 94.

SP Dom, Entry Book 335.

SP Dom, Petition Entry Book 2.

Supplementary Series, No. IV: Proceedings in the Court of Requests of the Star Chamber.

Quint, David. *Epic and Empire: Politics and Generic Form from Virgil to Milton*. Princeton: Princeton University Press, 1993.

Rajan, Balachandra and Elizabeth Sauer, eds. *Milton and the Imperial Vision*. Pittsburgh: Duquesne University Press, 1999.

Rajan, Tilottama. "Uncertain Futures: History and Genealogy in William Godwin's *The Lives of Edward and John Philips, Nephews and Pupils of Milton*." *Milton Quarterly* 32 (1998): 75–86.

Redstone, Lilian J. *Ipswich Through the Ages*. Ipswich: East Anglican Magazine, 1948.

Redstone, Vincent B. *The Ancient House or Sparrowe House, Ipswich*. Ipswich: W.E. Harrison, 1912.

Registers of St. Margaret's, Westminster Part III, The. Publications of the Harleian Society. London: 1977. Vol. LXXXIX.

Reports de Gulielme Benloes Serjeant del Ley, et Gulielme Dalison Un de Justices del Banke le Roy, Les. N.P., [1686?].

Reports in the Court of Kings Bench at Westminster from The XII to the XXX Year of the Reign of our Late Sovereign Lord King Charles II. . . . The First Part. London: W. Rawlins, S. Roycroft and M. Flesher Assigns of Richard and Edward Atkins. For Thomas Dring, Charles Harper, Samuel Keble, and William Freeman, 1685.

Reports in the Court of King's Bench at Westminster, From the XIIth to the XXXth Year of the Reign of our Late Sovereign Lord King Charles II. . . . The Second Part. London: W. Rawlins, S. Roycroft and M. Flesher, Assigns of Richard and Edward Atkins. For Thomas Dring, Charles Harper, Samuel Keble and William Freeman, 1685.

Reports in the Court of Kings Bench at Westminster, from The XII to the XXX year of the Reign of our late Soveraign Lord King Charles II. . . . The Third Part. London: W. Rawlins, S. Roycroft and M. Flesher Assigns of Richard and Edward Atkins. For Thomas Dring, Charles Harper, Samuel Keble, and William Freeman, 1685.

Reports of Edward Bulstrode Of the Inner Temple, Esquire. In Three Parts, The. London: Printed by W. Rawlins, S. Roycroft, and M. Flesher, Assigns of Rich. and Ed. Atkyns; For H. Twyford, T. Buffett, T. Dring, B. Griffin, C. Harper, M. Pitt, T. Sawbridge, S. Keble, D. Brown, J. Place, G. Collins, M. Wotton, 1688.

Richardson, Jonathan. *Explanatory Notes and Remarks on Milton's* Paradise Lost. London: James, John, and Paul Knapton, 1734.

Rowland, John. *Pro Rege et Populo Anglicano Apologia, Contra Johannis Polypragmatici, (alias Miltoni Angli) Defensionem Destructivam, Regis & Populi Anglicani.* Antwerp: Apud Hieronymum Verdussen, 1651.

Rump: or an Exact Collection Of the Choycest Poems and Songs Relating to the Late times. By the most Eminent Wits, from Anno 1639 to Anno 1661. Vol. II. London: Printed for Henry Brome and Henry Marsh, 1662.

Rumrich, John P. "Miltons Theanthropos: the Body of Christ in Paradise Regained," *Milton Studies* 42 (2003): 50–67.

Rylands, W. Harry, ed. *Grantees of Arms.* Harleian Society Publications. London: 1915. Vol. LXVI.

———, ed. *The Visitation of the County of Warwick,* 1682–1683. Harleian Society Publications. London: 1911. Vol. LXII.

Rymer, Thomas. *The Tragedies of the Last Age Consider'd and Examin'd.* London: Richard Tonson, 1678.

St. Bride, London. Hearth Tax Returns. Vestry Books.

St. Dunstan in the West, London. Parish Register.

St. James Church, Duke's Place, London. Parish Register.

St. Margaret's Church, Westminster, London.

St. Margaret's Overseer Rate Books, E166-E173: 1652–1659.

St. Margaret's Army Assessments, E1595–1603: 1651–1654.

St. Martin in the Fields, Westminster, London.

St. Martin's Rate Books, F350–353.

Salmon, Thomas. *A Vindication of an Essay To the Advancement of Musick, From Mr. Matthew Lock's Observations.* London: A. Maxwell, and are to be sold by John Car, 1672.

Sandelands, Andrew. *Letter.* See Thurloe.

Sauer, Elizabeth. "Cultures of Intolerance: Re-reading Milton's 'On the Late Massacre in Piemont'." Forthcoming.

———. "Milton's Peculiar Nation." Forthcoming.

———. "Religious Toleration and Imperial Intolerance." See Rajan and Sauer, 214–30.

Schwartz, Michael J. "The Political Inaccuracy of Milton's Psalms 1–8 and 80–88." *Reassembling Truth: Twenty-first-Century Milton,* ed. Charles W. Durham and Kristin A. Pruitt. Selinsgrove: Susquehanna University Press, 2003. 79–94.

Scott, Sir William. Letter to Thomas Warton, 29 June/1 July 1789. Bodleian Library, MS Dep. c. 638.

Search After Wit, The. London: 1691.

Secret History of K. James I. and K. Charles I. Compleating the Reigns of the Four Last Monarchs. By the author of the Secret History of K. Charles II. and K. James II. [London]: 1690.

Secret History of the Four Last Monarchs of Great Britain, Viz. James I, Charles I, Charles II, James II. [London]: 1691. Ed. 2, [London]: 1693.

Secret History of the Reigns of K. Charles II. and K. James II, The. [London]: 1690.

Sensabaugh, George F. *That Grand Whig Milton.* Stanford: Stanford University Press, 1952.

Settle, Elkanah. *The Character of a Popish Successor, and what England may expect From such a One.* London: For T. Davies, 1681.

————. *The Character of a Popish Successour Compleat*. London: J. Graves, 1681.

Seventeenth-Century News. 15 (Summer 1957): 23–24.

Sharpe, Kevin. *Reading Revolutions: The Politics of Reading in Early Modern England*. New Haven: Yale University Press, 2000.

Shaw, Stebbing. *The History and Antiquities of Staffordshire*. London: J. Robson, 1798–1801. 2 vols.

Shawcross, John T. "Confusion: The Apocalypse, The Millennium." See Cummins, 121–36.

————. "'Connivers and the Worst of Superstitions': Milton on Popery and Toleration." *Literature & History* 7 (1998): 51–69.

————. "'Depth' Bibliography: John Milton's Bibliographic Presence in 1740, an Example." *TEXT* 9 (1996): 216–33.

————. *John Milton: The Self and the World*. Lexington: University Press of Kentucky, 1993.

————. *Milton: A Bibliography for the Years 1624–1700*. Binghamton: Medieval & Renaissance Texts & Studies, 1984.

————. "Notes on Milton's Amanuenses." *Journal of English and Germanic Philology* 58 (1959): 29–38.

————. "Orthography and the Text of *Paradise Lost*." *Language and Style in Milton: A Symposium in Honor of the Tercentenary of* Paradise Lost, ed. Ronald David Emma and John T. Shawcross. New York: Frederick Ungar, 1967. 120–53.

————. *Paradise Regain'd: 'Worthy T'Have Not Remain'd So Long Unsung'*. Pittsburgh: Duquesne University Press, 1988.

————. "Stasis, and John Milton and the Myths of Time." *Cithara* 8 (1978): 3–17.

————. "A Survey of Milton's Prose Works." *Achievements of the Left Hand: Essays on the Prose of John Milton*, ed. Michael Lieb and John T. Shawcross. Amherst: University of Massachusetts Press, 1974.

————. *The Uncertain World of* Samson Agonistes. Woodbridge, Suffolk: D.S. Brewer, 2001.

————. "Verse Satire: Its Form, Genre, and Mode." *Connotations* 10 (2000/2001): 18–30.

————. *With Mortal Voice: The Creation of Paradise Lost*. Lexington: University Press of Kentucky, 1982.

Shipman, Thomas. *Henry the Third of France, Stabb'd by a Fryer*. London: B.G., for Sam. Heyrick, 1678.

Shrewsbury, Shropshire, County Record Office.
  Deed No. 994 (1651).
  Deed No. 1189 (1597).
  Deed No. 1226 (1627).
  Deed No. 1230 (1653).
  Deed No. 1457 (1639).
  Deed No. 1460 (1654).

Shropshire Parish Registers, Lichfield Diocese. Vol. XII. 1911.

Sidney, Algernon. *The Very Copy of a Paper Delivered to the Sheriffs*. London: R.H.J.B. and J.R. for Walter Davis, 1683.

"Sir Christopher Milton and Richard Milton." *Notes & Queries*. Series XI, No. 6 (1912): 100.

Skinner, Cyriack. "The Life of Mr John Milton." Bodleian Library, Wood MS D.4. Printed in Darbishire. 17–34.

Skinner, Quentin. "Machiavelli's *Discorsi* and the Pre-Humanist Origins of Republican Ideas." See Bock, Skinner, Viroli.121–41.

Smith, J. Challenor C. *The Parish Registers of Richmond, Surrey. Surrey Parish Register Society Publications.* London: 1903.

Smith, William. *Contrivances of the Fanatical Conspirators.* London: Printed for the Author, and sold by the Booksellers, 1685. Another issue, *Intrigues of the Popish Plot Laid Open.* London: 1685.

Smyth, Richard. *The Obituary,* ed. Henry Ellis. London: 1849.

Song, Hong-Han. "Milton's Republicanism in *Paradise Lost.*" *Milton Studies in Korea* 11 (2001): 59–90.

Sotheby, Samuel Leigh. *Ramblings in the Elucidation of the Autograph of Milton.* London: Thomas Richards, 1861.

Spehar, Warren E. "Milton, Republicans, and the Buckinghamshire Anti-Stuart Initiatives, 1637–42." *Seventeenth-Century News* 59 (2001): 321–55.

Sprigge, Joshua. *Anglia Rediviva; England Recovery.* London: R.W. for Iohn Partridge, 1647.

State of Church-Affairs in This Island of Great Britain Under the Government of the Romans, and British Kings, The. London: Nat. Thompson, for the Author, 1687.

Stevens, David H. "Mary Powell's Lost Dowry." *Milton Papers.* Chicago: University of Chicago Press, 1927.

Stevens, Paul. "Milton's 'Renunciation' of Cromwell: the Problem of Ralegh's *Cabinet-Council.*" *Modern Philology* 98 (2001): 363–92.

Students Admitted to the Inner Temple, 1547–1660. [London: W. Clowes and Sons, 1878.]

Sturgess, H.A.C., ed. *Register of Admissions to . . . The Middle Temple.* London: 1949.

Suffolk Green Books. Vol. 13 (1905). "Suffolk in 1674, being the Hearth Tax Returns," No. 11.

Suh, Hong Won. "'Ignoble Ease and Peaceful Sloth' in *The Readie and Easie Way* and *Paradise Lost.*" *Milton Studies in Korea* 10 (2000): 399–415.

Surrey Hearth Tax, 1664, ed. C.A.F. Meekings. Surrey Record Society Publications. London: 1940. Vols. XLI-XLII.

Surrey Musters. Surrey Record Society Publications. London: 1918. Vol. XI.

Surrey Quarter Sessions Records: Order Books and Sessions Rolls, 1659–1666, ed. Dorothy L. Powells and Hilary Jenkinson. Surrey Record Society Publications. London: 1934. Vol. XXXV; London: 1935. Vol. XXXVI; London: 1938. Vol. XXXIX.

Svendsen, Kester. *Milton and Science.* Cambridge: Harvard University Press, 1956.

Swinburne, Henry. *A Treatise of Testaments and Last Wills . . . The Sixth Edition, Corrected and Very Much Enlarged.* London: In the Savoy, 1743.

Sykes, Norman. *From Sheldon to Secker: Aspects of English Church History 1660–1768.* Cambridge: Cambridge University Press, 1959.

Thurloe, John. *A Collection of the State Papers of John Thurloe, Esq.,* ed. Thomas Birch. London: Printed for the Executors of the Late Mr. Fletcher Gyles, Thomas Woodward, and Charles Davis, 1742. 7 vols.

Tierney, Mark Aloysius. *The History and Antiquities of the Castle and Town of Arundel.* London: G. and W. Nichols, 1834.

Tilley, Joseph. *The Old Halls, Manors, and Families of Derbyshire.* London: Simpkin, Marshall & Co. 1892–1902. Vol. II.

Todd, Henry John, ed. *The Poetical Works of John Milton.* London: C. and J. Rivington, 1826. 6 vols.

Toland, John. *The Life of John Milton.* London: John Darby, 1699. Reprinted in Darbishire. 83–197.

Transactions of the Shropshire Archaelogical and Natural History Society 10 (1887): 289.

Trapnel, Anna. *The Cry of a Stone or a relation of something spoken in Whitehall,* ed. Hilary Hinds. Tempe: Arizona Center for Medieval and Renaissance Studies, 2000.

Trotter, Eleanor. *Seventeenth Century Life in the County Parish with Special Reference to Local Government.* Cambridge: Cambridge University Press, 1919.

Turner, Frederick. "Notes from an Old Diary: The Moores of Milton Place, Egham, Surrey." *Notes & Queries.* Series 12, V (1919): 284–86.

Tutchin, John. *The Search After Honesty: A Poem By Mr. Tutchin.* London: Printed for the Author, 1697.

Underdown, David. *Somerset in the Civil War and Interregnum.* Hamden, Conn.: Archon Books, 1793.

Varley, F.A., ed. *The Restoration Visitation of the University of Oxford and Its Colleges* (1660). *Camden Miscellany.* Vol. XVII. London: Offices of the Royal Historical Society, 1949. [Camden Third Series. Vol. LXXIX, Part 3.]

Venn, John and J.A. *Alumni Cantabrigienses.* Cambridge: Cambridge University Press, 1922–27. 4 vols.

von Maltzahn, Nicholas. "The Whig Milton, 1667–1700." See Armitage, Himy, and Skinner. 229–53.

———. "Wood, Allam, and the Oxford Milton." *Milton Studies* 31 (1994): 155–77.

Walker, J.W., ed. *Yorkshire Pedigrees.* Harleian Society Publications. London: 1942. Vol. XCIV.

Walker, John, ed. *Letters Written by Eminent Persons in the Seventeenth and Eighteenth Centuries.* London: 1813.

W[alkley], T[homas]. *Catalogue of the Names of the Dukes, Marquesses, Earles and Lords.* London: I.D. for Thomas Walkley, 1642.

Walsham, Alexandra. *Church Papists: Catholicism, Conformity and Confessional Polemic in Early Modern England.* Woodbridge, Suffolk: Boydell & Brewer, 1993.

Walwyn, William. *The Compassionate Samaritane.* N.P., 1644.

———. *The Writings of William Walwyn,* ed. Jack R. McMichael and Barbara Taft. Athens: University of Georgia Press, 1989.

Warmington, A.R. *Civil War, Interregnum and Restoration in Gloucestershire 1640–1672.* Woodbridge, Suffolk: Boydell, 1997.

Warner, John. *The History of English Persecution of Catholics and the Presbyterian Plots* [1683–86], ed. T.A. Birrell, trans. John Bligh. London: John Whitehead & Son, 1953. 2 vols. Catholic Record Society, Vol. 48 in two parts.

———. *A Vindication of the Inglish Catholiks from the Pretended Conspiracy against the Life and Government of His Sacred Majesty.* [Antwerp]: 1680.

———. *A Vindication of the English Catholiks . . . The 2. Edition with some Additions.* Permissu Superiorum, 1681.

Watney, John. "Some Account of Leigh Place, Surrey, and of Its Owners." *Surrey Archeological Collections.* Vol. X: 1893.

Whitaker, William. *Opera Theologica*. Geneva: Samuel Crispin, 1610.

Whitelocke, Bulstrode. *The Diary of Bulstrode Whitelocke 1605–1675,* ed. Ruth Spalding. Oxford: Oxford University Press, 1990.

———. "The History of Whitelockes Ambassy from English to Sweden," British Library, Additional MS 37, 346. 2 vols. Printed as *A Journal of the Swedish Embassy,* ed. Henry Reeve. London: Longman, Brown, Greene, and Longmans, 1855.

———. *Memorials of the English Affairs,* ed. Arthur Annesley, Earl of Anglesey. London: Nathaniel Ponder, 1682.

———. *Parliamenti Angliæ Declaratio*. Londoni: Apud Franciscum Tytonium, 1648 (1649).

Wilcher, Robert. *The Writing of Royalism 1628–1660*. Cambridge: Cambridge University Press, 2001.

Wilding, Michael. *Dragons Teeth: Literature in the English Revolution*. Oxford: Clarendon Press, 1987.

Williamson, George C., ed. *Portraits, Prints and Writings of John Milton Exhibited at Christ's College, Cambridge, 1908, with an Appendix and Index by C. Sayle*. Cambridge: Cambridge University Press, 1908.

Wilson, Hugh. Unpublished article on John Phillips.

Winstanley, Gerrard. *The Law of Freedom in a Platform*. London: Giles Calvert, 1652.

———. *The New Law of Righteousness*. London: Giles Calvert, 1649.

———. *A New-Yeers Gift for the Parliament and Armie*. London: Giles Calvert, 1650.

———. *The True Levellers Standard Advanced, A Declaration from the Poor Oppressed People of England*. London: 1649.

———. *The True Levellers Standard Advanced: or, the State of Community opened, and Presented to the Sons of Men*. London: 1649.

———. *The Works of Gerrard Winstanley,* ed. George H. Sabine. Ithaca: Cornell University Press, 1941.

Winstanley, William. *The Lives of the Most Famous English Poets*. London: H. Clark, for Samuel Manship, 1687.

Wit & Drollery. London: For Nath. Brook, 1655/56. Reprint, London: For Nath. Brook, 1661; London: For Obadiah Blagrave, 1682.

Wittreich, Joseph. *Interpreting Samson Agonistes*. Princeton: Princeton University Press, 1986.

———. *Shifting Contexts: Reinterpreting Samson Agonistes*. Pittsburgh: Duquesne University Press, 2002.

Wodderspoon, John. *Memorials of the Ancient Town of Ipswich*. London: 1850.

Wollaston, William. *The Design of Part of the Book of Ecclesiastes*. London: James Knapton, 1691.

Wood, Anthony. *Athenæ Oxonienses. An Exact History of All the Writers and Bishops Who have had Their Education in the Most Ancient and Famous University of Oxford*. 2 vols. London: Thomas Bennet, 1691–92. Reprinted, corrected, and expanded, ed. Thomas Tanner. London: R. Knaplock, D. Midwinter, and J. Tonson, 1721.

Woodhead, J.R. *The Rulers of London 1660–1689*. London: London & Middlesex Archaeological Society, 1965.

Woolrych, Austin. "Milton & Cromwell: 'A Short but Scandalous Night of Interruption'?." *Achievements of the Left Hand: Essays on the Prose of John Milton,* ed. Michael

Lieb and John T. Shawcross. Amherst: University of Massachusetts Press, 1974. 185–218.

———. See *Complete Prose of John Milton*. VII, 1–176.

Worden, Blair. *The English Civil Wars and the Passions of Posterity.* London: Allan Lane, 2001.

———. "Milton's Republicanism and the Tyranny of Heaven." See Bock, Skinner, Viroli. 225–45.

Worthington, Dr. John. *The Diary and Correspondence of Dr. John Worthington,* ed. James Crossley. See *Remains Historical & Literary Connected with the Palatine Counties of Lancaster and Chester Published by the Chetham Society.* Manchester: 1847. Vol. XIII.

Wrottesley, G., ed. "Extracts from Plea Rolls, Temp. Edward IV, Edward V, and Richard III." *Collections for a History of Staffordshire.* London: 1903. N.S., Vol. VI, Part I.

———, ed. "Lane of King's Bromley, Formerly of Bentley and Hyde." *Collections for a History of Staffordshire.* London: 1910.

——— and W. Boyd, eds. "Final Concords or Pedes Finium of Staffordshire." *Collections for a History of Staffordshire.* London: 1895. Vol. XVI.

Youngs, Frederic A., Jr. *Guide to the Local Administrative Units of England. Volume I: Southern England.* London: Offices of the Royal Historical Society, 1979.

Index